George Whitefield

A Biography With Special Reference To His Labors In America

by

Joseph Belcher

Double9 BOOKS

George Whitefield
A Biography With Special Reference To His Labors In America

by Joseph Belcher

ISBN: 978-93-61425-23-3

Published by

DOUBLE 9 BOOKS

2/13-B, Ansari Road
Daryaganj, New Delhi – 110002
info@double9books.com
www.double9books.com
Tel. 011-40042856

ABOUT THE AUTHOR

Joseph Belcher became a distinguished nineteenth-century American author and minister recognized for his enormous contributions to religious literature. His masterpiece, "George Whitefield: A Biography with unique reference to His Labors in the us," stands as a complete account of the existence and impact of the famend evangelist George Whitefield. In this biography, Belcher meticulously chronicles the lifestyles and ministry of George Whitefield, focusing specially on his massive paintings in the usa for the duration of the super Awakening. Belcher delves into Whitefield's upbringing, conversion revel in, and his extraordinary journey as an influential preacher and evangelist. Via distinctive studies and brilliant storytelling, Belcher presents insights into Whitefield's charismatic preaching fashion, his tireless efforts to unfold the Gospel, and his profound influence on religious revival actions in each Britain and the usa. Belcher explores Whitefield's vast role in shaping the religious landscape of his time and examines the lasting legacy of his ministry on next generations of Christians. "George Whitefield: A Biography with unique connection with His Labors in america" stands as a testomony to Belcher's dedication to keeping and disseminating the history of evangelical Christianity, imparting readers a compelling portrait of one of the maximum influential figures in religious records.

CONTENTS

PREFACE

The excellent Matthew Henry has very truly said, "There are remains of great and good men, which, like Elijah's mantle, ought to be gathered up and preserved by the survivors—their sayings, their writings, their examples; that as their works follow them in the reward of them, they may stay behind in the benefit of them."

Influenced by this and kindred sentiments, the compiler of this volume has devoted no small labor to gather from every source to which he could gain access, whatever appeared to him important to be known respecting the most distinguished uninspired preacher perhaps of any age or country. Whatever may be the faults of the work, to use the language of the Rev. Dr. Campbell, one of the present pastors of Whitefield's churches in London, in reference to a short sketch he had himself prepared of our great evangelist, "It will serve to bring him and his apostolic labors before the minds of vast multitudes of the rising generation, to whom both are all but unknown; and this is far from unimportant. Whatever tends to fix the minds of men afresh upon the character of Whitefield is, and it always will be, something gained to the cause of true religion. The contemplation of that character is one of the most healthful exercises that can occupy a Christian heart, or a Christian understanding. It is an admirable theme for ministerial meditation. It tends equally to humble, to instruct, and to encourage; to excite love to Christ, zeal for his glory, and compassion for the souls of men. What Alexander and Cæsar, Charles XII. of Sweden and Napoleon the first, are to those of the sons of men who have not yet ceased to 'learn war,' that Whitefield and Wesley are to those who aspire to eminent usefulness as ministers and missionaries of the cross."

In the preparation of this memoir, the compiler has sought to collect together incidents which might interest and instruct, especially in connection with Whitefield's labors in America; to present him as much as possible in his own dress; and to use the facts of his life to excite and cherish his own spirit, so far as he had the spirit of Christ. Facts reflecting on the reputation and feelings of others have been used only as the interests of truth seemed to demand.

It would have been easy to place on almost every page an array of authorities, and to give here a long list of friends to whom the writer has been indebted for aid; but the sole object of the volume is the honor of Christ in the salvation of men, and that this may be accomplished, we pray that the blessing of Heaven may rest upon it.

Philadelphia, 1857.

CHAPTER I
MORAL STATE OF GREAT BRITAIN IN THE EARLY PART OF THE EIGHTEENTH CENTURY—WHITEFIELD FROM HIS BIRTH TO HIS FIRST SERMON

That we may have a clear and comprehensive view of the labors and success of George Whitefield, it is important that we consider the moral condition of Great Britain and its dependencies when the Head of the church brought him on the field of action. The latter part of the seventeenth and the beginning of the eighteenth centuries presented in that country a scene of moral darkness, the more remarkable as it so soon succeeded the triumph of evangelical truth which distinguished the seventeenth century, and which is perpetuated in a religious literature that will bless the world. Causes had long been at work which produced such insensibility and decline as to all that is good, and such a bold and open activity in evil, as it is hoped the grace of God may avert from his churches in all future time. The doctrine of the divine right of kings to implicit obedience on the part of their subjects; the principle of priestly control of the minds of men in religious matters; and clerical influence, sustained by kingly authority, in favor of sports on the Lord's day, together with the evil examples of men high in rank and power, had produced their natural results on the masses of the people, and make it painful, even at this distant period, to survey the scene.

Nor were these all the evils of that day. The expulsion from their pulpits, by the "Act of Uniformity," of two thousand of the most able and useful of the clergy in England, had led to great ignorance and neglect of religion; and though men like Leighton and Owen, Flavel and Baxter, with Bunyan and a host of others, had continued, in spite of opposing laws, to preach when they were not shut up in prison, and to write their immortal practical works, by the time of which we are speaking they had been called to their eternal reward, leaving very few men of like spirit behind them. Thus infidelity, profligacy, and formalism almost universally prevailed.

The low state of religion in the established church at that time may be learned from the Rev. Augustus M. Toplady, himself one of its ministers, who died in 1778. In a sermon yet extant he says, "I believe no denomination of professing Christians, the church of Rome excepted, were so generally void of the light and life of godliness, so generally destitute of the doctrine and of the grace of the gospel, as was the church of England, considered as a body, about fifty years ago. At that period a *converted* minister in the establishment was as great a wonder as a comet; but now, blessed be God, since that precious, that great apostle of the English empire, the late dear Mr. Whitefield, was raised up in the spirit and power of Elias, the word of God has run and been glorified; many have believed and been added to the Lord all over the three kingdoms; and blessed be his name, the great Shepherd and Bishop of souls continues still to issue his word, and great is the company of preachers, greater and greater every year."

If it be said that Toplady, as he belonged to a different school of theology from that which then generally prevailed, could scarcely be expected to be impartial, we ask leave to transcribe a few lines from Bishop Butler, who within six months of Whitefield's ordination wrote thus: "It is come, I know not how, to be taken for granted by many persons, that Christianity is not so much as a subject of inquiry; but that it is now at length discovered to be fictitious. And accordingly they treat it as if in the present age this were an agreed point among all people of discernment; and nothing remained but to set it up as a principal subject of mirth and ridicule, as it were by way of reprisals for its having so long interrupted the pleasures of the world." Bishop Warburton, who commenced his ministry a few years before Whitefield, and who cannot be charged with enthusiasm, says, "I have lived to see that fatal crisis, when religion hath lost its hold on the minds of the people."

Many other witnesses might be brought to testify that error and worldly mindedness had made mournful havoc among the clergy, and that spiritual religion had been almost buried in forms and ceremonies. A recent writer has well described the state of religion in the established church at that time, as only to be compared to a frozen or palsied carcass. "There," says this Episcopal clergyman, "were the time-honored formularies which the wisdom of the reformers had provided. There were the services and lessons from Scripture, just in the same order as we have them now. But as to preaching the gospel, in the established church there was almost none. The distinguishing doctrines of Christianity—the atonement, the work and office of Christ and the Spirit—were comparatively lost sight of. The vast majority of sermons were miserable moral essays, utterly devoid of any thing calculated to awaken, convert, save, or sanctify souls." Southey, a biographer of Wesley, who assuredly will not be accused of too strong a tendency to evangelical truth, is compelled to say, "A laxity of opinions as well as morals obtained, and infidelity, a plague which had lately found its way into the country, was becoming so prevalent, that the vice-chancellor of the university at Oxford, in a *programma*, exhorted the tutors to discharge their duties by double diligence, and had forbidden the under-graduates to read such books as might tend to the weakening of their faith."

There were undoubtedly some learned and conscientious bishops at this era. Such men were Secker and Gibson, Lowth and Horne, Butler, and others. But even the best of them seem sadly to have misunderstood the requirements of the day they lived in. They spent their strength in writing apologies for Christianity, and contending against infidels. They could not see that without the direct preaching of the essential doctrines of the gospel, their labors must be sadly defective. The man who dared to preach the doctrines of the Bible, and in harmony with the Articles and Homilies of his church, was set down as an enthusiast or fanatic.

Among those who had dissented from the established hierarchy, and who were untrammelled by the impositions of secular authority, the state of vital godliness was also unhappily very low. The noble spirits of early non-conformity had passed from earth, or crossed the Atlantic to the frozen shores of New England, and a race of men had sprung up, some of whom retained the tenets of orthodoxy, but had lost its power; while others reposed on comfortable endowments, and lulled themselves, or were drawn by favorable breezes, into the cold elements of Arianism and Socinianism. As persons in the frozen regions are said to sleep longer and more soundly than others, so did they; and a more terrific blast of the trumpet of the gospel was required to rouse and awake them from their spiritual slumbers. Happily indeed for the world, and for the church in it, there were some exceptions. Watts and Guyse and Doddridge, and their pious associates in different parts of the land, were laborers together in "God's husbandry," and ceased not to cultivate it with affectionate faithfulness and care; and wherever their labors extended, the plants of grace grew and flourished. Darracott, "the star of the west," threw his mild rays over the vales of Somerset; and in the north also a few faithful men were found.

Nor have we even now said all that should be written as to the character of those times. The highest personages in the land then openly lived in ways contrary to the law of God, and no man rebuked them. Profligacy and irreligion were reputable and respectable. Judging from the description we have of men and manners in those days, a gentleman might have been defined as a creature who got drunk, gambled, swore, fought duels, and violated the seventh commandment, and for all this very few thought the worse of him.

Those too were the days when the men whom even kings delighted to honor were such as Bolingbroke, Chesterfield, Walpole, and Newcastle. To be an infidel, to obtain power by intrigue, and to retain it by the grossest and most notorious bribery, were considered no disqualifications even for the highest offices. Such men indeed were not only tolerated, but praised. In those days too, Hume, an avowed infidel, put forth his History, and obtained a pension. Sterne and Swift then wrote their talented, but obscene books; both of them were clergymen, but the public saw little inconsistency in their conduct. Fielding and Smollett were the popular authors, and the literary taste of high and low was suited by Roderick Random, Peregrine Pickle, Joseph Andrews, and Tom Jones. These authors were ingenious heathen philosophers, assuming the name of Christians, and forcibly paganizing Christianity for the sake of pleasing the world.

Turning to *Scotland,* we find that the bold proclamation of the discriminating truths of the gospel which characterize the preaching of Knox, Welsh, and others, was being rapidly laid aside, and cold formal addresses, verging towards a kind of Socinianism were becoming fashionable. Old Mr. Hutchinson, minister of Kilellan, in Renfrewshire, who saw but the beginning of this sad change, used to say to Wodrow the historian, "When I compare the times before the restoration with those since the revolution, I must own that the young ministers preach accurately, and methodically; but there was far more of the power and efficacy of the Spirit and of the grace of God went along with sermons in those days than now. For my own part—all the glory be to God—I seldom set my foot in a pulpit in those days, but I had notice of the blessed effects of the word." It is true, that even then there were a few faithful witnesses for God in Scotland, such as the brothers Erskine, in the Secession church; but for the most part, coldness, barrenness, and death prevailed. The people knew not God, and were strangers to the life-giving influence and power of the gospel.

The Arianism of England had been carried to the north of *Ireland,* and finding a state of feeling suitable to its reception, it took root and grew up, so as to characterize a distinct section of the Presbyterian church, then and still distinguished by the name of the Remonstrant Synod. The south and west of Ireland were subjected to a blight not less withering, though of a different kind, and which continued much longer—continued, to a great extent, throughout the whole of the last century. The clergy were usually sons of the gentry, and accustomed to their sporting, drinking, and riotous habits.

They had no preparation for ministerial duties but a college degree; and no education, either literary or moral, which had not been obtained among wild young men at the university. According to the interest which they happened to have, they passed at once from college to ministerial charges, and again mixed in all the dissipations of the districts where these lay. Ignorant of the truth, they and their congregations were satisfied with some short moral discourse. Many of the people were almost as ignorant of the Scriptures and scripture truth as the inhabitants of Hindostan. The Catholic priests meanwhile were at work among the people, and they had many to help them. The sick and the dying were watched; their fears were wrought upon; they were told of the power which the priests had, of the influence possessed by the Virgin, and much about the *old church*; and as soon as any seemed to give way, on whatever point, the priest was sent for, who plied them anew, and seldom failed in succeeding with the poor ignorant people. They were now ready to receive absolution; but he had farther conditions to propose. The whole family must submit to be rebaptized, or at least promise to attend mass—and this also was not unfrequently gained; the Protestant clergyman being all the while at a distance, neither knowing nor much caring what was going on. In this way great numbers of the lower and middle classes of the Protestants went over to the church of Rome. Throughout whole districts the Protestant churches were almost emptied, and many of those in rural districts were allowed to fall into ruins.

Of *Wales* it is not important at present to say much. From the middle ages downwards, great darkness and superstition had prevailed among its mountains. It is true that in the days of James I., a clergyman named Wroth, whose conversion to the truth had been remarkable, had labored with eminent zeal and success, but at the period of which we are now writing declension had succeeded. Within the establishment all was cold and dead; nearly every minister was ignorant of the Welsh language, a fact which also applied to several successive bishops, while the state of morals, among even the leaders of the hierarchy, was truly deplorable. An old Methodist simply but truly described the country at this period, and of his correct narrative we will here give a free translation.

The land, he tells us, was dark indeed. Scarcely any of the lower ranks could read at all. The morals of the country were very corrupt; and in this respect there was no difference between high and low, layman and clergyman. Gluttony, drunkenness, and licentiousness prevailed through the whole country. Nor were the operations of the church at all adapted to repress these evils. From the pulpit the name of the Redeemer was scarcely heard; nor was much mention made of the natural sinfulness of man, or of the influence of the Holy Spirit. On Sunday mornings, the poor were more constant in their attendance at church than the gentry; but the Sunday evenings were spent by all in idle amusements. Every Sabbath there was practised a kind of sport, called in Welsh *Achwaren-gamp*, in which all the young men of the neighborhood had a trial of strength, and the people assembled from the surrounding country to witness their feats. On a Saturday night, particularly in the summer, the young men and women held what they called *Nosweithian cann*, or singing eves; that is, they met together and amused themselves by singing in turns to the harp, till the dawn of the Sabbath. These things, with the performance of rustic dramas, would occupy sometimes the whole of the sacred day itself; while a set of vagabonds, called the *Bobl gerdded*, or walking people, used to traverse the villages, begging with impunity, to the disgrace alike of the law and the country. With all this social sprightliness, the Welsh were then a superstitious, and even a gloomy people. They still retained many habits apparently derived from paganism, and not a few of the practices of popery. Their funerals, like those of the Irish, were scenes of riot and drunkenness, followed by prayers for the release of the deceased from the pains of purgatory. Such was the superstition of the people, that when Methodism was first introduced among them, many of the peasantry expressed their horror of the new opinions by the truly Popish gesture of crossing the forehead; and when Wesley first visited them, he pronounced them "as little versed in the principles of Christianity as a Creek or Cherokee Indian." To this declaration he added the striking remark, that, "notwithstanding their superstition and ignorance, the people 'were ripe for the gospel,' and most enthusiastically anxious to avail themselves of every opportunity of instruction."

As an illustration of the truth of the remark we have just introduced from the discerning Wesley, we may mention an incident which occurred in 1736. At this period dissent itself was reduced so low in the country, that there were only six dissenting houses of worship in all North Wales. One Sunday, Mr. Lewis Rees, a dissenting minister from South Wales, and the father of Dr. Rees, the author of the celebrated Cyclopedia which bears his name, visited Pwllheli, a town on the promontory of Slëyn, in Caernarvonshire, and one of the few places in which the Independents still had a chapel. After the service, the congregation, collecting around him, complained very sorely that their numbers were rapidly diminishing, that the few who yet remained were for the most part poor, and that every thing connected with their cause looked gloomy. To which the minister replied, "The dawn of religion is again breaking out in South Wales," referring them to the fact, that already a distinguished man—Howel Harris—had risen up, going about instructing the people in the truths of the gospel. Such was the character of the times when God was raising up agents to revive and extend his cause. We shall before long return to Wales with lively interest.

"Such," says the eloquent Robert Hall, "was the situation of things when Whitefield and Wesley made their appearance, who, whatever failings the severest criticism can discover in their character, will be hailed by posterity as the second reformers of England. Nothing was farther from the views of these excellent men than to innovate on the established religion of their country; their sole aim was to recall the people to the good old way, and to imprint the doctrines of the Articles and Homilies on the spirits of men. But this doctrine had been so long a dead letter, and so completely obliterated from the mind by contrary instructions, that the attempt to revive it met with all the opposition that innovation is sure to encounter, in addition to what naturally results from the nature of the doctrine itself, which has to contend with the whole force of human corruption. The revival of the *old*, appeared like the introduction of a *new* religion; and the hostility it excited was less sanguinary, but scarcely less virulent, than that which signalized the first publication of Christianity. The gospel of Christ, or that system of truth which was laid at the foundation of the Reformation, has since made rapid advances, and in every step of its progress has sustained the most furious assaults."

It ought here to be stated, as illustrating the providence of God in preparing the British empire for the reception of the gospel, that the revolution of 1688 introduced the spirit of toleration, and in 1714, the very year of Whitefield's birth, Anne, the last English sovereign of a persecuting spirit, died, and the throne was assumed by George I., the first prince of the house of Hanover. The way of the Lord was thus prepared for bright illustrations of his mercy.

Rising from the beautiful valley of the Severn, and on the borders of that noble stream, reposes in antique glory the affluent city of Gloucester, with its regular streets, and its majestic cathedral and other relics of bygone days. In that city the traveller may examine three spots which will long be interesting to the student of ecclesiastical curiosities. The first of these is the ancient church of Mary de Crypt, where reposes the dust of Robert Raikes, the founder of Sunday-schools; the second, is the little stone which, in a pensive-looking inclosure, marks the site on which the truly noble-minded and Protestant Bishop Hooper was burnt, an early martyr of bloody Mary's reign. There wicked men stood around to light up the flames, and to mock his sorrows; but as we stand and look, we exult in the subsequent triumphs of truth.

The third spot, and the one to us at the present moment the most interesting, is the Bell inn or hotel, yet standing, though enlarged and beautified since the period of which we write. There Whitefield—the saint, the seraph, the "angel flying in the midst of heaven, having the everlasting gospel to preach to them that dwell on the earth"—first breathed the vital air. Venerable city, we will rejoice that though within thy walls one glorious luminary of salvation was extinguished, another "burning and shining light" was raised up to diffuse joy and happiness over the two most influential quarters of the globe, and a third has since been given to suggest the simple plan by which millions of the young have already acquired the knowledge of salvation.

George Whitefield, the sixth son of Thomas and Elizabeth Whitefield, was born December 16, 1714, old style. Concerning his father and mother he writes, "The former died when I was two years old; the latter died in December, 1751, in the seventy-first year of her age, and has often told me how she endured fourteen weeks' sickness after she brought me into the world; but was used to say, even when I was an infant, that she expected more comfort from me than from any other of her children. This, with the circumstance of my being born in an inn, has often been of service to me, in exciting my endeavors to make good my mother's expectations, and so follow the example of my dear Saviour, who was laid in a manger belonging to an inn."

In one of his journals, which he commenced at a very early part of his ministry, Whitefield details with great simplicity many incidents of his childhood and youth; from which it appears, that though at times he had many serious thoughts and impressions, the general course of his life, till the age of sixteen, was irreligious. He tells us that in early youth he was "so brutish as to hate instruction, and used purposely to shun all opportunities of receiving it," and that he spent much money, improperly obtained from his mother, in cards, plays, and romances, "which," says he, "were my heart's delight. Often have I joined with others in playing roguish tricks; but was generally, if not always, happily detected: for this I have often since, and do now bless and praise God." His full confessions of this character are very affecting, and should be a caution to young persons to repel all such temptations.

When George was about ten years of age, his mother married a second time, thus forming a connection which led to much unhappiness. He was, however, continued at school; and when twelve years old, was transferred to the grammar-school of St. Mary de Crypt, where he remained about three years. Having a graceful elocution and a good memory, he gained much credit for delivering speeches before the city corporation at the annual visitation of the school, and received pecuniary rewards for his performances on those occasions. How deeply he afterwards deplored these celebrations, especially the performance of plays in connection with his school-fellows, may be learned from his own words: "I cannot but observe here, with much concern of mind, how this way of training up youth has a natural tendency to debauch the mind, to raise ill passions, and to stuff the memory with things as contrary to the gospel of Christ, as darkness to light, hell to heaven." This sad tendency was but too clearly evinced in the case of Whitefield himself. "I got acquainted," he says, "with such a set of debauched, abandoned, atheistical youths, that if God, by his free, unmerited, and special grace, had not delivered me out of their hands, I should have sat in the scorner's chair, and made a mock at sin. By keeping company with them, my thoughts of religion grew more and more like theirs. I went to public service only to make sport, and walk about. I took pleasure in their lewd conversation. I began to reason as they did, and to ask why God had given me passions, and not permitted me to gratify them. In short, I soon made great proficiency in the school of the devil. I affected to look rakish, and was in a fair way of being as infamous as the worst of them." These were the things, and not oratory, as has sometimes been said, which Whitefield learned from plays and acting.

In the midst of all this, his conscience often made him unhappy; and he wished, if possible, to combine religion with his pleasures. He purchased and carefully read "Ken's Manual for Winchester Scholars," a book which commended itself as having comforted his mother in her afflictions, and which he afterwards considered to have been "of great benefit to his soul."

At the age of fifteen, he thought he had acquired learning enough for any ordinary occupation in life, and as his mother's business was declining, he persuaded her to allow him to leave school and assist in labor. "I began," says he, "to assist her occasionally in the public-house, till at length I put on my blue apron and my snuffers, washed mops, cleaned rooms, and in one word, became professed and common *drawer* for nearly a year and a half." In the midst of the activity called for in such a situation, it pleased God to renew his religious impressions, which induced him, at least at intervals, to attend with much earnestness to the concerns of his soul.

From his childhood, Whitefield tells us, he "was always fond of being a clergyman, and used frequently to imitate the ministers' reading prayers." Nor did this tendency towards clerical engagements cease as he became older. "Notwithstanding," he says, "I was thus employed in a large inn, and had sometimes the care of the whole house upon my hands, yet I composed two or three sermons, and dedicated one of them to my elder brother. One day, I remember, I was very much pressed to self-examination, and found myself very unwilling to look into my heart. Frequently I read the Bible when sitting up at night. And a dear youth, now with God, would often entreat me, when serving at the bar, to go to Oxford. My general answer was, 'I wish I could.'"

His mother's difficulties increasing, it became necessary for her to leave the inn; in which she was succeeded by one of her married sons, with whom George for some time remained to continue his assistance in the business. Some disagreement, however, arising between them, he after a time took his departure from the inn, and went to spend a month with his eldest brother at Bristol. Returning from that city to Gloucester, he resided for a short season with his mother. While thus living unemployed, without any definite object before him, and waiting the openings of providence, his mother was visited by an Oxford student, a servitor of Pembroke college in that university. In the course of their conversation, he told her, that after all his expenses at college for the quarter were discharged, he had one penny remaining. She immediately exclaimed, "This will do for my son!" and turning to him, said, "Will you go to Oxford, George?" He replied, "With all my heart." Application was immediately made to several friends who had influence at the college, and they pledged themselves to serve her. In this confidence, her favorite son returned to the grammar-school, where he not only resumed his studies with greater diligence, but endeavored, and not altogether in vain, to promote religion and virtue among his associates.

Having fully secured his literary preparation for the university, Whitefield removed to Oxford in his eighteenth year, and was immediately admitted, as a servitor, into Pembroke college. He soon found that the seat of learning was also a scene of danger. From the period of 1662, when the two thousand Non-conformists had been expelled from the church, the universities had been sinking into a moral lethargy, preferring uniformity to vital religion. Our young servitor was shocked with the impiety of the students in general, and dreading their influence on himself, he as much as possible abstained from their society, and shut himself up in his study.

Before he went to Oxford, Whitefield had heard of a class of young men in the university who "lived by rule and method," and were therefore called *Methodists*. They were much talked of, and generally despised. Of this party, John Wesley, a Fellow of Lincoln college, and already in holy orders, was the leader, his brother Charles being also as warmly attached to it. They avowed that the great object of their lives was to save their souls, and to live wholly to the glory of God; and rarely have men subjected themselves to greater self-denials and austerities. Drawn towards them by kindred feelings, Whitefield strenuously defended them whenever he heard them reviled, and when he saw them going, through a crowd manifesting their ridicule, every Sunday to receive the sacrament at St. Mary's or Christ church, he was strongly inclined to follow their example.

For more than a year he intensely desired to be acquainted with them, but a sense of his pecuniary inferiority to them prevented his advances. At length, learning that a pauper had attempted suicide, Whitefield sent a poor woman to inform Charles Wesley, that so he might visit her, and administer religious instruction. He charged the woman not to tell Mr. Wesley who sent her, but, contrary to this injunction, she told his name; and Charles Wesley, who had frequently seen Whitefield walking by himself, on the next morning invited him to breakfast. An introduction to the little brotherhood soon followed, and he also, like them, "began to live by rule, and pick up the very fragments of his time, that not a moment might be lost."

It is painful to read Whitefield's own account of the mortifications of body to which he now submitted; and we are not surprised that, as the result, his health was so reduced as to place even his life in danger. All this time he had no clear view of the way of salvation, and was "seeking to work out a righteousness of his own." In this state he lay on his bed, his tongue parched with fever, and the words of the dying Saviour, "I thirst," were impressed on his mind. Remembering that this thirst occurred near the end of the Saviour's sufferings, the thought arose in his mind, "Why may it not be so with me? Why may I not now receive deliverance and comfort? Why may I not now dare to trust and rejoice in the pardoning mercy of God?" There was, as Tracy has said, no reason why he might not—why he ought not. He saw nothing to forbid him. He prayed in hope, borrowing language from the fact which suggested the train of thought—"I thirst, I thirst for faith in pardoning love. Lord, I believe; help thou mine unbelief." His prayer was heard. He dared to trust in the mercy of God, as revealed in the death of Jesus Christ for sinners. Conscience and his Bible bore witness that he did right. The load that had so heavily oppressed him, the load of guilt and terror and anxiety, that weighed down his spirit while he sinfully and ungratefully hesitated to trust in divine mercy, was gone. He saw the trustworthiness of the mercy of God in Christ, and his heart rejoiced.

"Though," as Tracy has well said, "the English universities were established mainly for the purpose of educating men for the ministry, Whitefield was not likely to gain a good knowledge of theology there. He took another, and a characteristic course. Some time after his conversion, when he was at Gloucester, he says, 'I began to read the holy Scriptures upon my knees; laying aside all other books, and praying over, if possible, every line and word. This proved meat indeed and drink indeed to my soul. I daily received fresh life, light, and power from above. I thus got more true knowledge in reading the book of God in one month, than I could ever have acquired from all the writings of men.'"

Every hour of Whitefield's time, especially after he had been "filled with peace and joy in believing," was sacredly devoted to preparation for the great work to which he had now solemnly devoted himself. He visited the prisoners in the jail, and the poor in their cottages, and gave as much time as he could to communion with God in his closet. His friends now earnestly importuned him to apply for ordination; but from this his deep sense of unworthiness made him shrink. Besides, he intended to have a hundred and fifty sermons carefully written before he began to preach. He had as yet but one, and he lent that to a neighboring clergyman, to convince him that he was not yet fit to be ordained. The clergyman kept it for two weeks, divided it into two, preached it to his own people, and then returned it to Whitefield, with a guinea for the use of it.

Still, however, the work of preparation for the ministry was rapidly going on. The state of his health compelled him to retire for a season from Oxford, and he returned home to increase the depth of his piety, and to be led, little as he thought of it, at once to the pulpit. He writes, "O what sweet communion had I daily vouchsafed with God in prayer, after my coming to Gloucester. How often have I been carried out beyond myself, when meditating in the fields. How assuredly I felt that Christ dwelt in me, and I in him; and how daily did I walk in the comforts of the Holy Ghost, and was edified and refreshed in the multitude of peace. I always observed that as my inward strength increased, so my outward sphere of action increased proportionably."

Thus, happy in himself, and thankful to the gracious God who made him so, the affectionate soul of George Whitefield ardently desired that others might participate in his sacred joys. In order to advance this object, he mixed in the society of young people, and endeavored to awaken them to a just sense of the nature of true religion. Some were convinced of the truth, and united with him in religious exercises; and these were some of the first-fruits of his pious labors. His discovery of the necessity of regeneration, like Melancthon's great discovery of the truth, led him to imagine that no one could resist the evidence which convinced his own mind. He writes, "Upon this, like the woman of Samaria, when Christ revealed himself to her at the well, I had no rest in my soul till I wrote letters to my relations, telling them there was such a thing as the *new birth*. I imagined they would have gladly received it; but, alas, my words seemed to them as idle tales. They thought I was going beside myself." He visited the jail every day, and read and prayed with the prisoners; attended public worship very frequently, and read twice or three times a week to some poor people in the city. In addition to all this, he tells us, "During my stay here, God enabled me to give a public testimony of my repentance as to seeing and acting plays; for hearing the strollers had come to town, and knowing what an egregious offender I had been, I was stirred up to extract Mr. Law's excellent treatise, entitled, "The absolute Unlawfulness of the Stage Entertainment." The printer, at my request, put a little of it in the newspaper for six weeks successively; and God was pleased to give it his blessing."

In this manner Whitefield employed himself during nine months; and one effect of so doing was, that the partition wall of bigotry was soon broken down in his heart. He says, "I loved all, of whatever denomination, who loved the Lord Jesus Christ in sincerity." This statement in his diary is connected with an account of the benefit he derived from studying the works of the Non-conformists. "Baxter's Call," and "Alleine's Alarm," so accorded with his own ideas of fidelity and unction, that wherever he recognized their spirit he acknowledged "a brother beloved." On this portion of his history we dwell with unspeakable delight; the only drawback is an undue importance he appears to have attached to *dreams*; and even those, considered as an *index* to his waking hours, are interesting, revealing as they do his deep solicitude on the behalf of souls.

Here then, before he had completed his twenty-first year, we see Whitefield returned to Gloucester, and such was already the fame of his piety and talents, that Dr. Benson, the bishop of the diocese, offered to dispense, in his favor, with the rule which forbids the ordination of deacons at so unripe an age. Thus graphically did he afterwards describe his acceptance of this proposal.

"I never prayed against any corruption I had in my life so much as I did against going into holy orders so soon as my friends were for having me go. Bishop Benson was pleased to honor me with peculiar friendship, so as to offer me preferment, or to do any thing for me. My friends wanted me to mount the church betimes. They wanted me to knock my head against the pulpit too young; but how some young men stand up here and there and preach, I do not know. However it be to them, God knows how deep a concern entering into the ministry and preaching was to me. I prayed a thousand times, till the sweat has dropped from my face like rain, that God of his infinite mercy would not let me enter the church till he called me and thrust me forth in his work. I remember once in Gloucester—I know the room; I look up to the window when I am there and walk along the street—I said, 'Lord, I cannot go; I shall be puffed up with pride, and fall into the condemnation of the devil. Lord, do not let me go yet.' I pleaded to be at Oxford two or three years more. I intended to make one hundred and fifty sermons, and thought that I would set up with a good stock in trade. I remember praying, wrestling, and striving with God. I said, 'I am undone, I am unfit to preach in thy great name. Send me not. Lord, send me not yet.' I wrote to all my friends in town and country to pray against the bishop's solicitation; but they insisted I should go into orders before I was twenty-two. After all their solicitations these words came into my mind: 'Nothing shall pluck you out of my hands;' they came warm to my heart. Then, and not till then, I said, 'Lord, *I will go*; send me when thou wilt.'"

Sunday, June 20, 1736, was the day appointed for his ordination in the cathedral at Gloucester. On the preceding evening he spent two hours in prayer for himself and the others who were to be set apart to the sacred office with him; and on the day itself he rose early, and passed the morning in prayer and meditation on the qualifications and duties of the office he was about to undertake. On a review of the solemn services of the day, he says, "I trust I answered every question from the bottom of my heart, and heartily prayed that God might say, Amen. And when the bishop laid his hands upon my head, if my vile heart do not deceive me, I offered my whole spirit, soul, and body to the service of God's sanctuary. Let come what will, life or death, depth or height, I shall henceforward live like one who this day, in the presence of men and angels, took the holy sacrament, on the profession of being inwardly moved by the Holy Ghost to take upon me that ministration in the church. I call heaven and earth to witness, that when the bishop laid his hands upon me, I gave myself up to be a martyr for Him who hung upon the cross for me. Known unto him are all future events and contingencies; I have thrown myself blindfold, and I trust without reserve, into his almighty hands. When I went up to the altar, I could think of nothing but Samuel's standing before the Lord with a linen ephod."

Having thus received ordination as a deacon of the church of England, he delayed not to enter upon the work to which he was appointed; and accordingly, on the next Sabbath he preached his first sermon in his native city of Gloucester, selecting for his subject, "The necessity and benefit of religious society." At the appointed time he ascended the pulpit, in the church of St. Mary de Crypt. We have his own record of the service: "Last Sunday, in the afternoon, I preached my first sermon in the church where I first received the Lord's supper. Curiosity drew a large congregation together. The sight, at first, a little awed me; but I was comforted with a heartfelt sense of the divine presence, and soon found the advantage of having been accustomed to public speaking when a boy at school, and of exhorting and teaching the prisoners and the poor people at their private houses, while at the university. By these means I was kept from being daunted overmuch. As I proceeded, I perceived the fire kindled, till at last, though so young, and amidst a crowd of those who knew me in my childish days, I trust I was enabled to speak with some degree of gospel authority. Some few mocked, but most, for the present, seemed struck; and I have since heard that a complaint was made to the bishop, that I drove fifteen people mad the first sermon. The worthy prelate, as I am informed, wished that the madness might not be forgotten before the next Sunday. Before then, I hope that my sermon upon, 'He that is in Christ is a new creature,' will be completed. Blessed be God, I now find freedom in writing. Glorious Jesus,

> "'Unloose my stammering tongue to tell
> Thy love immense, unsearchable.'"

It is remarkable, under all the circumstances of the case, that Bishop Benson, a man never distinguished for his evangelical views, always showed his friendship for Whitefield. Not only did he offer him ordination when others might have refused, and defend him against the persecutions to which he was exposed, but he more than once gave him pecuniary help when it was much needed, though the young clergyman had never complained.

Thus early apprized of the secret of his strength, his profound aspirations for the growth of Christianity, the delight of exercising his rare powers, and the popular admiration, operating with combined and ceaseless force upon a mind impatient of repose, urged him into exertions which, if not attested by irrefragable proofs, might appear incredible. It was the statement of one who knew him well, and who was incapable of wilful exaggeration, and it is confirmed by his letters, journals, and a "cloud of witnesses," that "in the compass of a single week, and that for years, he spoke in general forty hours, and in very many sixty, and that to thousands: and after his labors, instead of taking any rest, he was engaged in offering up prayers and intercessions, with hymns and spiritual songs, as his manner was, in every house to which he was invited." Never perhaps, since the apostolic age, has any man given himself so entirely to preaching the gospel of Christ for the salvation of souls, adopting as his motto the language of the apostle Paul, *"This one thing I do."*

CHAPTER II
WHITEFIELD'S SUCCESS AS A PREACHER IN ENGLAND—FIRST VISIT TO AMERICA. 1736-1738

Whitefield, though thus prepared for action, was not impatient, but willing to wait till his duty was fully ascertained. On the Wednesday after his first sermon he went to Oxford, where, he says, "I was received with great joy by my religious friends. For about a week I continued in my servitor's habit, and then took my degree of Bachelor of Arts, after having been at the university three years and three quarters, and going on towards the twenty-second year of my age. My dear and honored friends, the Rev. Messrs. John and Charles Wesley, being now embarked for Georgia, and one or two others having taken orders, the interest of Methodism, as it was then and is now termed, had visibly declined, and very few of this reputedly mad way were left at the university. This somewhat discouraged me at times, but the Lord Jesus supported my soul, and made me easy by giving me a strong conviction that I was where he would have me to be. My degree, I soon found, was of service to me, as it gave me access to those I could not be seen with when in an inferior station; and as opportunity offered, I was enabled to converse with them about the things which belonged to the kingdom of God. The subscriptions for the poor prisoners, which amounted to about forty pounds per annum, were soon put into my hands; two or three charity schools, maintained by the Methodists, were under my more immediate inspection; which, with the time I spent in following my studies, private retirement, and religious converse, sweetly filled up the whole of my day, and kept me from that unaccountable but too common complaint of having any time hang upon my hands."

The stay of Mr. Whitefield at Oxford, however, was very short. He says, "By a series of unforeseen, unexpected, and unsought-for providences, I was called in a short time from my beloved retirement to take a journey to the metropolis of England. While I was an under-graduate, among the religious friends, I was very intimate with one Mr. B——n, a professed Methodist, who had lately taken orders, and was curate at the Tower of London. With him, when absent, I frequently corresponded, and when present took sweet counsel, and walked to the house of God as friends. He mentioned me to that late good and great man, Sir John Phillips; and being called down for a while into Hampshire, he wrote to me to be of good courage, and in the strength of God bade me hasten to town to officiate in his absence, and to be refreshed with the sight and conversation of many who loved me for Christ's sake, and had for a long time desired to see me."

On his arrival in London, Whitefield delivered his first sermon there in Bishopsgate church, on the afternoon of Lord's day, August 8. On entering the pulpit, his juvenile aspect excited a general feeling of his unfitness for the station, but he had not proceeded far in his sermon before it gave place to universal expressions of wonder and pleasure. If however he was thus exposed to the danger of vanity, as he says, "God sent me something to ballast it. For as I passed along the streets, many came out of their shops, admiring to see so young a person in a gown and cassock. One I remember in particular, cried out, 'There's a boy parson;' which, as it served to mortify my pride, put me also upon turning that apostolical exhortation into prayer, 'Let no man despise thy youth.'" From his first sermon to his departure, at the end of two months, his popularity in London continued to increase, and the crowds were so vast that it was necessary to place constables both inside and outside of the churches to preserve the peace. He tells us himself, "Here I continued for the space of two months, reading prayers twice a week, catechizing and preaching once, visiting the soldiers in the infirmary and barracks daily. I also read prayers every evening at Wapping chapel, and preached at Ludgate prison every Tuesday. God was pleased to give me favor in the eyes of the inhabitants of the Tower; the chapel was crowded on Lord's days; religious friends from divers parts of the town attended the word, and several young men came on Lord's-day morning, under serious impressions, to hear me discourse about the *new birth*, and the necessity of renouncing all in affection in order to follow Jesus Christ."

The preaching of Mr. Whitefield now excited an unusual degree of attention among persons of all ranks. In many of the city churches he proclaimed the glad tidings of great joy to listening multitudes, who were powerfully affected by the fire which was displayed in the animated addresses of this man of God. Lord and Lady Huntingdon constantly attended wherever he preached, and Lady Anne Frankland became one of the first-fruits of his ministry among the nobility of the metropolis. Her ladyship spent much of her time with Lady Huntingdon, from whose society and conversation she derived great comfort. She was a daughter of Richard, the first Earl of Scarborough; was for many years lady of the bedchamber to the Princess Anne, and to the Princesses Amelia and Caroline; and finally became the second wife of Frederic Frankland, Esq., a member of Parliament, from whose cruelty she endured much.

We have already said, that some time before this Messrs. John and Charles Wesley had embarked for Georgia, and to their names we might have added that of Mr. Ingham, also a member of the Methodist fraternity at Oxford.

Georgia, which was explored by Sir Walter Raleigh in 1584, had been colonized by debtors from Europe, by multitudes who had fled from the grasp of persecution, and by others who were interested in constructing a barrier against Spanish aggression. It originally had trustees in England, concerned for its interests, including sons of the nobility. The chief agent in executing the benevolent designs in view was the truly excellent General Oglethorpe, who admirably carried out the motto he gave to his companions in the work, "*Non sibi sed aliis*" —"Not for themselves, but for others." The children of poverty, taken from the overgrown agricultural population, already a tax upon parish bounty at home, were to be transferred in large numbers to the silk and indigo plantations which were established on the savannahs and bottoms south and west of the river, which thence derived its name from the peculiar conformation of the adjoining plains. Combined with these leading purposes, it was a cherished principle with the early patrons of this colony, that it should become the centre for the diffusion of the gospel among the natives; while charitable foundations were also laid for the secular and religious education of all who would take advantage of such provisions. The first Christians who left Europe to advance the spiritual interests of Georgia were Moravians, and the next were the Wesleys and Ingham. The records of the colony, as quoted in White's Historical Collections of Georgia, show that, Sept. 14, 1735, Charles Wesley was appointed "Secretary for the Indian affairs in Georgia," and that, Oct. 10, 1735, John Wesley was appointed "missionary at Savannah."

Whitefield had left London, and was laboring among a poor and illiterate people in Hampshire, when his attention was directly drawn to Georgia. This was not, indeed, the first time his heart had been interested in the matter. He writes, "When I had been about a month in town, letters came from the Messrs. Wesley, and the Rev. Mr. Ingham their fellow-laborer, an Israelite indeed, from Georgia. Their accounts fired my soul, and made me long to go abroad for God too. But having no outward call, and being as I then thought too weak in body ever to undertake a voyage at sea, I endeavored to lay aside all thoughts of going abroad. But my endeavors were all in vain; for I felt at times such a strong attraction in my soul towards Georgia, that I thought it almost irresistible. I strove against it with all my power, begged again and again, with many cries and tears, that the Lord would not suffer me to be deluded, and at length opened my mind to several dear friends. All agreed that laborers were wanted at home, that I had as yet no visible call abroad, and that it was my duty not to be rash, but wait and see what Providence might point out to me. To this I consented with my whole heart."

The path of duty, however, soon opened before him. While fulfilling his duties at Dummer, in Hampshire, preaching for the Rev. Mr. Kinchin, who was now absent from home, to which labors we have already referred, he received an invitation to a lucrative curacy in London; but Georgia still rested like one of the prophetic "burdens" on his mind. At this juncture he received a letter from his clerical friend at the Tower, saying that Mr. Charles Wesley had arrived in London. Very soon Mr. Wesley himself wrote to Whitefield, saying, that he was come over to procure laborers, "but," added he, "I dare not prevent God's nomination." "In a few days after this," writes Mr. Whitefield, "came another letter from Mr. John Wesley, wherein were these words: 'Only Mr. Delamotte is with me, till God shall stir up the hearts of some of his servants, who putting their lives in their hands, shall come over and help us, where the harvest is so great, and the laborers so few. What if thou art the man, Mr. Whitefield?' In another letter were these words: 'Do you ask me what you shall have? Food to eat and raiment to put on, a house to lay your head in—such as our Lord had not—and a crown of glory that fadeth not away.' Upon reading this my heart leaped within me, and as it were echoed to the call."

After having consulted his bishop, Dr. Benson, as also the archbishop of Canterbury, and the trustees of Georgia including General James Oglethorpe who was then in London, he went to Bristol, Bath, and other places, to take leave of his personal friends. As he could not refrain from preaching, so every sermon increased his popularity. We give his account of his preaching at Bristol, as a specimen of the reception he met with.

"It was wonderful to see how the people hung upon the rails of the organ-loft, climbed upon the leads of the church, and made the church itself so hot with their breath, that the steam would fall from the pillars like drops of rain. Sometimes almost as many would go away for want of room as came in, and it was with great difficulty I got into the desk to read prayers or preach. Persons of all ranks not only publicly attended my ministry, but gave me private invitations to their houses. A private society or two were erected. I preached and collected for the poor prisoners in Newgate twice or thrice a week, and many made me large offers if I would not go abroad."

Having mentioned General James Edward Oglethorpe, the first governor, and indeed the founder of the colony of Georgia, and to the end of Whitefield's life his cordial friend, a few additional facts concerning him may here be stated. He was the son of Sir Theophilus Oglethorpe, and was born in London, December 21, 1688. At sixteen he was admitted a student at Oxford, but did not finish his studies, as the military profession had more charms for him than literary pursuits. He was first commissioned as an ensign. After the death of Queen Anne, he entered into the service of Prince Eugene. When he attained the age of twenty-four years, he entered Parliament, for Haslemere, where he continued thirty-two years. In November, 1732, Oglethorpe, with one hundred and sixteen settlers, embarked for Georgia, and landed at Charleston, S. C., January 13, 1733. They shortly afterwards proceeded to Georgia, where Oglethorpe laid out a town, and called it Savannah. He very happily secured the good will of the Indians. In 1743, he left Georgia for England, to answer charges brought against him by Lieutenant-colonel Cook. A court martial declared the charges groundless and malicious, and Cook was dismissed from the service. In 1744 he was appointed one of the field-officers under field-marshal the Earl of Stair, to oppose the expected invasion of France. He died in 1785. He was truly a noble man.

As the period approached when Whitefield was to leave England, the people showed their esteem for him in almost every possible way. They followed him so closely, and in such numbers, for holy counsels, that he could scarcely command a moment for retirement. They begged to receive from him religious books, and to have their names written therein with his own hand, as memorials of him, and very many followed him from place to place till his final embarkation.

It was indeed a surprising fact, that a young man, scarcely more than twenty-two years of age, and previously unknown to the world, should be able to collect such immense congregations, and rouse and command their attention; multitudes hanging upon and receiving instructions from his lips. But God had endowed him with a singular union of qualities, which most eminently fitted him for the work of an evangelist. He was faithful to his trust, and his divine Master abundantly blessed and honored him in the discharge of its momentous duties.

We have now traced the amazing effects of Whitefield's *first* sermons, and it may be interesting briefly to inquire into their general character, and to ascertain what truths thus aroused the public mind. Three of these sermons can, happily, be identified with these "times of refreshing;" and they may be depended on, as specimens of both the letter and the spirit of his preaching, because they were printed from his own manuscripts: they are those on "*Early Piety*," "*Regeneration*," and "*Intercession*." Whoever will read the appeals in these sermons, realizing the circumstances under which they were made, will scarcely wonder at the effect produced by them. The topics of the second and third, and the tone of all the three, are very different from the matter and manner of sermonizing then known to the masses of the people. They do not surprise *us*, because happily neither the topics nor the tone of them are "strange things to our ears." Both, however, were novelties in those days, even in London. When or where had an appeal been made like this?

"I beseech you, in love and compassion, to come to Jesus. Indeed, all I say is in love to your souls. And if I could be but an instrument of bringing you to Jesus, I should not envy, but rejoice in your happiness, however much you were exalted. If I was to make up the *last* of the train of the companions of the blessed Jesus, it would rejoice me to see you above me in glory. I could willingly go to prison or to death for you, so I could but bring one soul from the devil's strong-holds, into the salvation which is by Christ Jesus. Come then to Christ, every one that hears me this night. Come, come, my guilty brethren; I beseech you, for your immortal souls' sake, for Christ's sake, come to Christ. Methinks I could speak till midnight unto you. Would you have me go and tell my Master that you will not come, and that I have spent my strength in vain? I cannot bear to carry such a message to him. I would not, indeed, I would not be a swift witness against you at the great day of account; but if you will refuse these gracious invitations, I must do it."

In this spirit, not very prevalent even now, Whitefield began his ministry. There is a fascination as well as fervor, or rather a fascination arising from fervor, in some of his earliest as well as his later discourses. How bold and beautiful is the peroration of that on "*Intercession*." Referring to the holy impatience of "the souls under the altar," for the coming of the kingdom of God, he exclaims,

"And shall not we who are on earth be often exercised in this divine employ with the glorious company of the spirits of just men made perfect? Since our happiness is so much to consist in the communion of saints in the church triumphant above, shall we not frequently intercede for the church militant below, and earnestly beg that we may be all one? To provoke you to this work and labor of love, remember, that it is the never-ceasing employment of the holy and highly exalted Jesus himself; so that he who is constantly interceding for others, is doing that on earth which the eternal Son of God is always doing in heaven. Imagine, therefore, when you are lifting up holy hands for one another, that you see the heavens opened, and the Son of God in all his glory, as the great High-priest of your salvation, pleading for you the all-sufficient merit of his sacrifice before the throne. Join your intercession with his. The imagination will strengthen your faith, and excite a holy earnestness in your prayers."

The nearer the time approached for his leaving the country, the more affectionate the people grew towards him, and the more eagerly did they attend on his ministry. Many thousands of ardent petitions were presented to heaven on behalf of his person and his ministry; and multitudes would stop him in the aisles of the churches, or follow him with their tearful looks. Most of all was it difficult for him to part from his friends at St. Dunstan's, where he administered the sacrament, after spending the night before in prayer.

The man who had produced these extraordinary effects, says Dr. Gillies, had many natural advantages. He was something above the middle stature, well proportioned, though at that time slender, and remarkable for native gracefulness of manner. His complexion was very fair, his features regular, his eyes small and lively, of a dark blue color: in recovering from the measles, he had contracted a squint with one of them; but this peculiarity rather rendered the expression of his countenance more rememberable, than in any degree lessened the effect of its uncommon sweetness. His voice excelled both in melody and compass, and its fine modulations were happily accompanied by the grace of action which he possessed in an eminent degree, and which is said to be the chief requisite of an orator. An ignorant man described his eloquence oddly, but strikingly, when he said that Mr. Whitefield preached like a lion. So strange a comparison conveyed no unapt idea of the force, and vehemence, and passion—of the authority which awed the hearers, and made them tremble like Felix before the apostle. Believing himself to be the messenger of God, commissioned to call sinners to repentance, he spoke as one conscious of his high credentials, with authority and power; yet in all his discourses there was a fervor and melting charity, an earnestness of persuasion, an outpouring of redundant love, partaking of the virtue of the faith from which it flowed, insomuch that it seemed to enter the heart which it pierced, and to heal it as with a balm.

At length, having preached in a considerable number of the London churches, collected about a thousand pounds for the charity schools, and obtained upwards of three hundred pounds for the poor in Georgia, Whitefield left London, December 28, 1737, in the twenty-third of his age, and went in the strength of God, as a poor pilgrim, on board the Whitaker.

Scarcely had he entered on his voyage from London, when he discovered that but little comfort was to be expected in the ship on which he had embarked. There was no place for retirement, no disposition to receive him as an ambassador of Christ, and a decided dislike even to the forms of religion. They moved but slowly to the Downs, where they were detained for nearly a month, and where Whitefield went on shore to visit Deal, an ancient town, one of the Cinque-ports, so called, where "the common people," as in the case of his great Master, "heard him gladly." With him, through his whole ministry, it was of small importance whether he preached to the rich or the poor; for he viewed the gospel as a message of mercy to *sinners*, and wherever men were found, he was willing to persuade them to be reconciled to God.

The account given by Mr. Whitefield of his visit to Deal, and of the different treatment he received there from different persons, would be almost as correct a description of his labors and reception in a hundred other places. He spent his first evening very comfortably in religious conversation and family prayer, at which a poor woman was much affected. "Who knows," he says, "what a fire this little spark may kindle?" Next evening, eight or nine poor people came to him at the report of this poor woman; and when, after three or four days, the ship in which he had embarked was driven back to Deal, many met together to bewail their own sins and those of others. Soon the landlady who owned the house where he lodged, sent to her tenants, beseeching them not to let any more persons come in, for fear the floor should break under them; and they actually put a prop under it.

The minister of Upper Deal, a mile or two from the town, now invited Whitefield to preach in the church; it was much crowded, and many went away for want of room. Some stood on the leads of the building outside, and looked in at the top windows, and all around seemed eager to hear the word. "May the Lord," says the good man, "make them *doers* of it. In the evening I was obliged to divide my hearers into four companies, and was enabled to expound to them from six till ten. Lord, keep me from being weary of, or in well-doing."

The excitement at Deal became very great, in consequence of the conviction of the people that their own minister, the Rev. Dr. Carter, did not preach the gospel. The good man, to disprove the charge, published a volume of his sermons, which, however admired by gay formalists, furnished but too much evidence of the justice of the charge.

Just as he had left the church at Upper Deal, where he had been preaching to a vast congregation, Mr. Whitefield, in consequence of a sudden change of the wind, was summoned on board, and the Whitaker sailed for Georgia. A very few hours afterwards, the vessel which brought back John Wesley from that colony anchored in the Downs, when he learned that the ships had passed each other, but neither of these remarkable men then knew how dear a friend was on board the other. When Wesley landed, he found it was still possible to communicate with his friend, and Whitefield was surprised to receive a letter from him, saying, "When I saw God by the wind which was carrying you out brought me in, I asked counsel of God. His answer you have enclosed." The enclosure was a slip of paper with the words, "Let him return to London," which Wesley had obtained by lot, to which he had had recourse. Whitefield prayed for direction, and went on his voyage.

This first voyage of Whitefield to America was invested with scenes of far more than common interest. Perhaps, since the apostle Paul's memorable voyage to Rome, the ocean had never exhibited a more remarkable spectacle than that furnished by this ship. He was but a stripling in his twenty-third year, and a faint and hesitating homage once on a Sabbath-day, from a few of the less obdurate sinners among his hearers, would be all that such a clergyman could expect from an assemblage of gentlemen, of soldiers with their wives and families, and the ship's crew. Yet in the hands of this remarkable youth all became pliant as a willow. He converted the chief cabin into a cloister, the deck into a church, and the steerage into a school-room. He so bore down all opposition by love, reason, and Scripture, that we soon see him, at the request of the captain and officers, with the hearty concurrence of the gentlemen who were passengers, reading "full public prayers" to them twice a day in the great cabin, and expounding every night after the evening prayers, besides daily reading prayers, and preaching twice a day on deck to the soldiers and sailors, and increasing the services on Sundays. In addition to all this, he daily catechized a company of young soldiers, and engaged in the same exercise with the women apart by themselves.

Nor did even all this suffice to expend his zeal, for he commenced a course of expositions on the creed and ten commandments; and so convinced was he of the value of catechetical teaching, that on February 3d he writes, "I began to-night to turn the observations made on the lessons in the morning into catechetical questions, and was pleased to hear some of the soldiers make very apt answers."

Nor were the children forgotten; the Hon. Mr. Habersham, a personal friend who accompanied him, assumed their instruction as his department of holy labor. Mr. Whitefield wrote of him, that he was "pleased to see Mr. Habersham so active in teaching the children. He has now many scholars—may God bless him."

Friendship for Whitefield had influenced Mr. Habersham to accompany the young evangelist to Georgia. Mr. Habersham's friends, at Beverly, in Yorkshire, where he was born in 1712, were greatly opposed to his plans, but surely the hand of God directed them. He presided over the Orphan-house till 1744, when he entered into a commercial partnership. He occupied several important stations, till he became president of the colony in 1769. The proceedings connected with the revolutionary war more than once placed him in great difficulties; he did not live to see its happy results, for in 1775 the state of his health compelled him to visit the north, in hope of its renovation. The change, however, was of no benefit, and he died at New Brunswick, New Jersey, August 28, 1775. The "Gazette" of the day said of him, "In the first stations of the province he conducted himself with ability, honor, and integrity, which gained him the love and esteem of his fellow-citizens; nor was he less distinguished in private life by a conscientious discharge of the social duties, as a tender and affectionate parent, a sincere and warm friend, and a kind and indulgent master. Mr. Habersham was married by the Rev. Mr. Whitefield to Mary Bolton at Bethesda, on the 26th of December, 1740, by whom he had ten children, three of whom, sons, survived him, and were zealous in the cause of American liberty."

In harmony with the solemn duties which Mr. Whitefield had assumed, he watched over the conduct of all around him. He tells us that the ship's cook was awfully addicted to drinking, and when reproved for this and other sins, he boasted that he would be wicked till within two years of his death, and would then reform. Alas, he died on the voyage, after an illness of six hours, brought on by drinking.

One day on this voyage, finding on Captain Whiting's pillow "The Independent Whig," Whitefield exchanged it for a book entitled "The Self-Deceiver." The next morning, the captain came smiling and inquired who made the exchange. Mr. Whitefield confessed the fact, and begged his acceptance of the book, which he said he had read, and liked very well. From thenceforward a visible alteration took place in the conduct of the captain.

On their arrival at Gibraltar, where they had to continue some time, Mr. Whitefield found that Major Sinclair, without solicitation, had provided a lodging for him, and the governor and military invited him to their table. Being apprehensive that at a public military table he might be more than hospitably treated, to prevent any thing disagreeable, he reminded his excellency that, at the court of Ahasuerus, "none did compel." The governor took the hint, and pleasantly replied, "No compulsion of any kind shall be used at my table;" and every thing was conducted with the greatest propriety. Here he often preached, and was heard by many, including all in high offices. Unusual indeed were the scenes, both with respect to the place and the people. The adjacent promontories, and the vastness of the rock of Gibraltar, aided in the enlargement of the ideas of the preacher as to Him, who "in his strength setteth fast the mountains, and is girded about with power." And the place being a sort of public rendezvous of all nations, he thought, he says, "he saw the world in epitome."

The success of Whitefield's ministry at Gibraltar was truly remarkable. He quaintly says of it, "Samson's riddle was fulfilled there: 'out of the strong came forth sweetness.' Who more unlikely to be wrought upon than soldiers? And yet, among any set of people, I have not been where God has made his power more known. Many that were quite blind, have received their sight; many that had fallen back, have repented and turned to the Lord again; many that were ashamed to own Christ openly, have waxed bold; and many saints have had their hearts filled with joy unspeakable, and full of glory."

Among other religions societies to which Whitefield was introduced at Gibraltar, he one day attended the Jewish synagogue, and was agreeably surprised when one of the rulers handed him into the chief seat. The rabbi had the day before heard him preach against profane swearing, and now thanked him for his sermon. He remained in the synagogue during the whole service, engaged, he says, "in secret prayer that the veil might be taken from the heart of the Jews, and they grafted again into their own olive-tree."

Several facts occurred on the way to Savannah after their embarkation from Gibraltar, which are too interesting to pass without notice. On one occasion Captain Mackay, after Whitefield had preached against drunkenness, urged the men to attend to the things which had been spoken; telling them that he was a notorious swearer until he did so; and beseeching them for Christ's sake to give up their sins. On another occasion, while marrying a couple on deck, Whitefield suddenly shut the prayer-book in the midst of the ceremony, because the bridegroom had behaved with levity; and not until the laughter was turned into weeping, would he proceed. At the close of the service he gave the bride a Bible. When a shark was caught, with five pilot-fish clinging to its fins, he said, "Go to the pilot-fish, thou that forsakest a friend in adversity; consider his ways, and be abashed." When a dolphin was caught, the change of its hues from lovely to livid, reminded him to say, "Just so is man; he flourishes for a little while, but when death cometh, how quickly his beauty is gone! A Christian may learn instruction from every thing he meets with." While he was preaching on the death of Christ darkness came on, and he said, "It puts me in mind of that darkness which overwhelmed the world when the God of nature suffered."

In the latter part of the voyage, fever laid prostrate all in the ship except four persons, and at length it seized Whitefield, and confined him to his bed for a week. The attack, though short, must have been severe; for besides other remedies, he was bled three times. During his illness, the captain gave up his own bed to him, and Mr. Habersham watched him day and night; but that which gratified him most was, that the sick between decks, whom he had endangered his life to console, prayed for him with great fervor. He recovered, and repaid the kindness of all. At length, on May 5, they came in sight of Savannah river, and sent off for a pilot; and such was the joy of all, when they came to anchor at Tybee island, that he could not help exclaiming, "How infinitely more joyful will the children of God be, when, having passed through the waves of this troublesome world, they arrive at the haven of everlasting rest!" Though still weak, he preached a farewell sermon to his "red-coated and blue-jacketed parishioners," as he called his military and naval congregation. It was heard with floods of tears.

Upon this voyage, says Dr. Gillies, he made these reflections many years after: "Even at this distance of time, the remembrance of the happy hours I enjoyed in religious exercises on deck, is refreshing to my soul; and although nature sometimes relented at being taken from my friends, and I was little accustomed to the inconveniences of a sea-life, yet, a consciousness that I had the glory of God and the good of souls in view, afforded me, from time to time, unspeakable satisfaction."

Whitefield was cordially welcomed at Savannah by Delamotte and other friends of the Wesleys: the magistrates also offered to wait upon him to pay their respects; but this he declined, and waited upon them. They agreed to build him a tabernacle and a house at Frederica, and to accept his services at Savannah as long as he pleased. He was soon, however, again laid aside by the return of his fever, now accompanied with ague. This attack in a few days brought him so low, and made so great an alteration in his person, that he says, "Had my friends seen me at that hour, they might have learned not to have any man's person in admiration, and not to think more highly of me than they ought to think."

The first thing which Whitefield did after his recovery was to visit *Tomo-Chici*, the Indian king, then on his death-bed. This was the micoe, or king, whom Oglethorpe had taken to England, in 1734, and introduced to king George the Second. He was accompanied by his wife and son, and seven other Indians of the Creek nation. His eloquent speech to the king and queen was so well received at court, that he was loaded with presents, and when he had again to embark, was sent in one of the royal carriages to Gravesend. "He now lay," says Whitefield, "on a blanket, thin and meagre; little else but skin and bones. Senanki, his wife, sat by, fanning him with Indian feathers. There was no one could talk English, so I could only shake hands with him and leave him. A few days afterwards, Mr. Whitefield again went to visit Tomo-Chici, and found that his nephew, Tooanoowee, could speak English. Whitefield says, "I desired him to ask his uncle, whether he thought he should die; who answered, 'I cannot tell.' I then asked where he thought he should go after death. He replied, 'To heaven.' But alas, how can a drunkard enter there? I then exhorted Tooanoowee, who is a tall, proper youth, not to get drunk; telling him that he understood English, and therefore would be punished the more if he did not live better. I then asked him whether he believed in a heaven. He said, 'Yes.' I then asked whether he believed in a hell, and described it by pointing to the fire. He replied, 'No.' From whence we may easily gather, how natural it is to all mankind to believe there is a place of happiness, because they wish it to be so; and on the contrary, how averse they are to believe in a place of torment, because they wish it may not be so. But God is just and true; and as surely as the righteous shall go away into everlasting happiness, so the impenitently wicked shall go into everlasting punishment."

The records of Georgia say, under date of December 21, 1737, "Ordered, that a license be made out for the Rev. Mr. George Whitefield to perform ecclesiastical offices in Georgia, as a deacon in the church of England."

Before Whitefield had any thoughts of going abroad, Charles Wesley talked to him of an orphan-house in Georgia, which he and General Oglethorpe had contemplated. When he arrived in Savannah, and had sufficiently recovered from his illness to examine the state of the colony, the condition of the children deeply affected him; and he set his heart on founding the projected institution as soon as he should be able to collect the needful funds. In the mean time he opened schools in the villages of Highgate and Hampstead, and one also, for girls, in Savannah. He afterwards visited the Saltzburgher's orphan-school at Ebenezer; and if any thing had been wanted to settle his own determination, or to inflame his zeal, he found it there. The Saltzburghers were exiles for conscience' sake, and were eminent for piety and industry. Their ministers, the Rev. Messrs. Grenaw and Boltzius, were eminently evangelical, and their asylum, which they had been enabled to found by British benevolence, for widows and orphans, was flourishing. Whitefield was so delighted with the order and harmony of Ebenezer, that he gave a share of his own "poor's store" to Boltzius, for his orphans. Then came the scene which entirely completed his purpose: Boltzius "called all the children before him; catechized and exhorted them to give God thanks for his good providence towards them; then prayed with them, and made them pray after him; then sung a psalm. Afterwards, the little lambs came and shook me by the hand, one by one, and so we parted." Whitefield was now pledged to this cause for life.

Most of our readers probably know that the conductors of "The Gentleman's Magazine," a work which has now been regularly published in London for much more than a century, have never been favorable to evangelical truth, or its ministers; it is therefore the more gratifying to copy from that work for November, 1737, the following lines: it will be seen that they were published more than a month before Mr. Whitefield's departure to the American colonies.

"TO THE REV. MR. WHITEFIELD, ON HIS DESIGN FOR GEORGIA.

"How great, how just thy zeal, adventurous youth,
To spread in heathen climes the light of truth!
Go, loved of heaven, with every grace refined,
Inform, enrapture each dark Indian's mind;
Grateful, as when to realms long hid from day,
The cheerful dawn foreshows the solar ray.
How great thy charity, whose large embrace
Intends the eternal weal of all thy race;
Prompts thee the rage of waves and winds to scorn,
To effect the work for which thy soul was born.
What multitudes, whom Pagan dreams deceive,
Shall, when they hear thy heavenly voice, believe!
On Georgia's shore thy Wesley shall attend,
To hail the wished arrival of his friend;
With joy the promised harvest he surveys,
And to his Lord for faithful laborers prays;
Though crowded temples here would plead thy stay,
Yet haste, blest prophet, on thy destined way.
Be gentle, winds, and breathe an easy breeze,
Be clear, ye skies, and smooth, ye flowing seas!
From heaven, ye guardian angels, swift descend,
Delighted his blest mission to attend;
Which shall from Satan's power whole nations free,
While half the world to Jesus bow the knee.
Long as Savannah, peaceful stream, shall glide,
Your worth renowned shall be extended wide;
Children as yet unborn shall bless your lore,
Who thus to save them left your native shore;
The apostles thus, with ardent zeal inspired,
To gain *all nations* for their Lord desired.
They measured seas, a life laborious knew,
And numerous converts to their Master drew;
Whose hallelujahs, on the ethereal plains,
Rise scarce beneath the bright seraphic strains.

"Gloucester, Nov. 1, 1737."

After spending a few weeks at Savannah, laboring as much as his health would permit, Whitefield went to Frederica, where he was gladly received; the people "having had a famine of the word for a long season." They had no sanctuary, and therefore he had to preach under a tree, or in Mr. Habersham's house. This visit, although short, endeared him to all the people; and he had the satisfaction before he left, to see them "sawing timber for a commodious place of worship, until a church could be built." His return, however, to Savannah was hastened by a somewhat painful event. One of his friends was lost in the woods, and missing from Tuesday till Friday. The great guns had been fired to direct the wanderer, but in vain; and some of the people had searched for him day and night, without success. This report was sent to Whitefield, and it hurried him away from Frederica. He had the pleasure, however, on his arrival at Savannah, to find his "lost sheep."

During the stay of Whitefield in Georgia, the weather was intensely hot, sometimes almost burning his feet through his shoes. Seeing others do it, he determined to accustom himself to hardship by lying constantly on the floor; which by use he found to be so far from being uncomfortable, that afterwards it became so to lie on a bed. Nor was he more ready to deny himself than he was assiduous to do good; preaching often, catechizing the young, visiting the sick, and exhorting from house to house. Entirely independent and unrestrained, he knew no fear in the discharge of what he regarded as his duty. Knowing that some men of influence, to whom his voice could not be addressed from the pulpit, were living in open defiance of morality and shame, he went into the court and made an address to the grand jury, urging them to present all such offenders without partiality or fear, since the miserable state of the colony was doubtless owing to divine displeasure against their sins.

Reflection on the character, labors, and success of his predecessors, stimulated his zeal and encouraged his hope. It could not be denied that John Wesley had been misrepresented and unkindly treated, both in Savannah and Frederica, and Whitefield therefore rejoiced to bear honorable testimony of him and his colleagues. He says, "Surely I must labor most heartily, since I come after such worthy men. The good Mr. John Wesley has done in America is inexpressible. His name is very precious among the people, and he has laid such a foundation, that I hope neither men nor devils will be able to shake it. O that I may follow him as he has followed Christ."

Mr. Whitefield having as yet only received deacon's orders, and wishing to be ordained priest, for the more complete performance of his duty as a minister of the church of England, it became necessary for him to return to Europe for that purpose; and being also desirous of making collections for his Orphan-house, he left Mr. Habersham at Savannah, and went to Charleston, S. C., on his way to England.

At Charleston he became acquainted with the Rev. Alexander Garden, the ecclesiastical commissary of the Bishop of London, who with apparent cordiality twice invited him into his pulpit, and assured him that he would defend him with his life and property, should the same arbitrary proceedings ever be commenced against him which Mr. Wesley had met with in Georgia. Dr. Deems, in his recently published volume, "The Annals of Southern Methodism," tells us, when speaking of his first sermon, "The people at first despised his youth, but his engaging address soon gained their general esteem, and Mr. Garden thanked him most cordially." In an after-period, however, when Mr. Garden more fully understood the evangelical character of Mr. Whitefield's preaching, he frequently took occasion to point out what he called the pernicious tendency of his doctrines, and irregular manner of life. He represented him as a religious quack, who had an excellent way of setting off and rendering palatable his poisonous tenets. On one occasion Garden, to keep his flock from going after this strange pastor, preached from the text, "These that have turned the world upside down are come hither also." Whitefield, however, was not to be silenced in this way, and returned the compliment by preaching from the words, "Alexander the coppersmith did me much evil; the Lord reward him according to his works."

On September 6, 1738, Whitefield embarked for London. The voyage was perilous in the extreme. They were tossed about with bad weather, in a ship out of repair, and in sad want of provisions. When they were over about one-third of the Atlantic, a vessel from Jamaica would have gladly received him, but he chose to share the lot of his shipmates. They highly valued his services, and one of his fellow-passengers, Captain Gladman, became, as the result of this voyage, a truly pious man. The captain, in a subsequent period, at his own earnest request, became the fellow-traveller of his teacher.

After a passage of about nine weeks, they made the port of Limerick, in Ireland. "I wish," Whitefield says, "I could never forget what I felt when water and provisions were brought us from the shore. Mr. M'Mahon, a country gentleman, came from his seat at midnight on purpose to relieve us, and most kindly invited me, though unknown, to his house, to stay as long as I pleased." At Limerick he was cordially received by that worthy prelate, Bishop Birscough, who engaged him to preach at the cathedral. From thence he went to Dublin, where he preached, and was hospitably entertained by Archbishop Bolton, Bishop Rundel, and Dr. Delany.

Remaining but a short time in Ireland, he proceeded to London, where he arrived December 8. Here he had the pleasure of conversing with some of the Moravian brethren, whose faith and love refreshed his spirit, though he did not entirely approve some of their views. He soon discovered somewhat of a change of feeling towards him on the part of many of the London clergy. Within two days, he found five of the churches were closed against him. He called on the Archbishop of Canterbury and the Bishop of London, who received him with cold civility. The bishop asked him if his journals were not tinctured with enthusiasm; and he replied, with his usual meekness and candor, that they were written only for his own use, and that of his private friends, and that they were published without his knowledge. So anxious was he to avoid giving offence, that he took the earliest opportunity to expunge from his journals whatever he discovered to be erroneous, and whatever he had said without imperative necessity, or which was likely to injure the character and feelings of any one.

The trustees of Georgia, at a meeting in London, received Whitefield with great cordiality, and in compliance with the wishes of the colonists, they presented him with the living of Savannah, the salary of which he declined to receive; but he thankfully accepted five hundred acres of land, on which he proposed to erect his orphan-house.

On Sunday, January 14, 1739, being then in his twenty-fifth year, Whitefield was ordained priest at Oxford, by his worthy friend Bishop Benson. Having preached twice to very crowded congregations, and administered the Lord's supper at the castle, he returned to London the next day. As Dr. Benson once expressed regret that he had ordained Mr. Whitefield, it may be proper here to explain the circumstances. Shortly after the late Countess of Huntingdon first became acquainted with the truth as it is in Jesus, Bishop Benson, who had been lord Huntingdon's tutor, was sent for to remonstrate with her ladyship, and to induce her to relinquish what were then considered her erroneous views; but she pressed him so hard with the Articles and Homilies of his own church, and so plainly and faithfully urged upon him the awful responsibility of his station, that for the moment his mind was hurt, and he rose up to depart, lamenting that he had ever laid his hands upon George Whitefield, to whom he imputed the change which had been wrought in her ladyship. "My lord," said she, "mark my words; when you come upon your dying bed, that will be one of the few ordinations you will reflect upon with pleasure." It would seem that it was so; for, on his death-bed, the Bishop sent ten guineas to Mr. Whitefield as a token of his favor and approbation, and begged to be remembered by him in his prayers.

The interval between his taking priests' orders, and embarking a second time for Georgia, was employed by Whitefield, with his usual energy and success, in preaching the gospel of the kingdom of God, and in making collections for his Orphan-house. Having, before his visit to America, collected large sums for the charity schools in the metropolis, he naturally expected that the pulpits would not be denied him now, in which to plead the interests of his own poor. But he was scarcely yet aware that the tide of clerical opinion had turned so extensively and strongly against him. The doctrines he had preached, and the manner in which he had preached them, had produced a sensation so strong, that he found himself excluded from most of the churches in London. A few, however, were yet open to him for his benevolent design. The Rev. Mr. Broughton conducted himself, among others, very nobly. Having been urged to refuse his pulpit, as some of his neighbors had done, he boldly replied, that "having obtained the lectureship of St. Helen's by Whitefield's influence, he should have the pulpit if he desired it." Mr. Whitefield preached, but Mr. Broughton thus losing the lectureship, Whitefield blamed himself for having done so. Whatever he might himself be willing to suffer, he was not willing to inflict inconvenience on others.

Only a few days before his being ordained as priest, Whitefield offered his first public *extempore* prayer, in a large meeting in Red Cross-street, London. He mentions this fact in a note of his diary as "the first time I ever prayed extempore before such a number." He did not even then suppose that his preaching, as well as his prayers in this manner, were to develop his mighty power. The crowding of the churches now suggested the idea of preaching in the open air. He says, "When I was informed that nearly a thousand people stood out in the church-yard, and that hundreds returned home, this put me first upon thinking of preaching without doors. I mentioned it to some friends, who looked upon it as a *mad* motion. However, we kneeled down and prayed that nothing might be done rashly. Hear and answer, O Lord, for thy name's sake."

We shall soon see how his extempore expositions and prayers were fitting him for this new enterprise. He would have commenced in London now, but he lacked a fair opportunity.

CHAPTER III
OPEN-AIR PREACHING IN ENGLAND AND WALES—ERECTION OF THE TABERNACLE IN LONDON. 1738-1739

Under the circumstances we have related in our last chapter, Whitefield paid another visit to Bristol, and soon found that he had to meet with new and very unexpected opposition. When he arrived in the city, the chancellor of the diocese, while he did not approve of what he considered his irregular conduct, told him that he would not prohibit any clergyman from lending him his church; but in a few days afterwards he sent for the evangelist, and announced his entire opposition to his movements. Strangely enough, he now asked Whitefield by what authority he preached in the diocese of Bristol without a license. The reply of the intrepid minister was, that he supposed such a custom had become obsolete, and asked the chancellor in his turn, "And pray, sir, why did you not ask the clergyman who preached for you last Thursday this question?" The chancellor then read to him the canons which forbid any clergyman from preaching in a private house; to which Whitefield replied, that he did not suppose these canons referred to professed ministers of the church of England; and when the chancellor told him he was mistaken, he reminded his superior, "There is also a canon, sir, forbidding all clergymen to frequent taverns and play at cards; why is not that put in execution?" And he then added, that notwithstanding any canons to the contrary, he could not but speak the things which he knew, and that he was resolved to proceed as usual. His answer was written down, and the chancellor closed the interview with the words, "I am resolved, sir, if you preach or expound anywhere in this diocese till you have a license, I will first suspend, and then excommunicate you." The crisis was now come; the Rubicon had been passed, and the inquiry might well be made, "What will Whitefield now do?"

Already have we seen that he had earnestly desired, in London, to preach in the open air, for want of room in the churches, and indeed also from the opposition of the clergy, which had begun so strongly to manifest itself; and during this journey to Bristol, he found it necessary to preach in the open air or not at all. As this event was of vast importance in its results, both in his own history and that of Mr. Wesley, who also began to preach on the same spot within two months after Whitefield had opened the way, we must stay a while to narrate the facts.

TABERNACLE.

HANHAM MOUNT

At that time, the colliers of Kingswood, near the city of Bristol, were a most depraved and reckless class of men. Inconceivably barbarous and ignorant, they trampled on all laws, human and divine, and hesitated not to set the magistrates at defiance. It was dangerous to pass near the scene of their labors, even in open day, for robberies and murders were of frequent occurrence; in a word, it was truly "a seat of Satan." When Whitefield was at Bristol, making collections for his projected orphan institution in Georgia, not a few persons had said to him, "Why go abroad; have we not Indians enough at home? If you have a mind to convert Indians, there are colliers enough in Kingswood." "I thought," says he, "it might be doing the service of my Creator, who had a mountain for his pulpit, and the heavens for his sounding-board, and who, when his gospel was refused by the Jews, sent his servants into the highways and hedges." After much prayer and many inward struggles, he went one day to a gentle elevation on the south side of Kingswood, called Hanham Mount, and there, under an old sycamore-tree, he preached his first sermon in the open air to about a hundred colliers. The scene must have been very impressive. Before him stretched the rich and beautiful valley of the Avon, through which the river was gently winding, bordered in the distance by the undulating hills; while on his right and left the cities of Bath and Bristol were within sight.

The fact of his preaching here soon and extensively spread, and at meeting after meeting his audience increased, till he found himself addressing *nearly twenty thousand persons*. His own account of the effects produced is very striking. He says, "The first discovery of their being affected, was in the white gutters made by their tears, which plentifully fell down their black cheeks, as they came out of their coal pits. Hundreds and hundreds of them were soon brought under deep convictions, which happily ended in sound and thorough conversion. As the scene was quite new, and I had just begun to be an extempore preacher, I had often many inward conflicts. Sometimes, when twenty thousand people were before me, I had not, as I thought, a word to say; but I was never deserted; and I was often so assisted as to understand what that meaneth, 'Out of his belly shall flow rivers of living water.' The open firmament above; the prospect of the adjacent fields; with the sight of thousands and thousands, some in coaches, some on horseback, and some in the trees, and all so affected as to be drenched in tears together, to which sometimes was added the solemnity of the approaching night, were almost too much for me; I was occasionally all but overcome." Writing to Mr. Wesley a few weeks afterwards, he says, "Yesterday I began to play the madman in Gloucestershire, by preaching on a table in Thornbury-street. To-day I have exhorted twice, and by and by I shall begin a third time; nothing like doing good by the way. I suppose you have heard of my proceedings in Kingswood."

We scarcely need to remark here, that Kingswood has ever since been regarded as a sacred spot in ecclesiastical history. Here houses for Wesleyan Methodists and Independents were soon erected, and in them thousands have been converted to God. Here was placed the first school for the sons of Methodist preachers, and on Hanham Mount, besides the voice of Whitefield, those of the Wesleys, Coke and Mather, Pawson and Benson, and Bradburn, accomplished some of the mightiest effects which attended their powerful preaching. There are yet some living in the neighborhood who were awakened under their ministry, and whose eyes glisten as they tell of the blessed days that are past.

Besides the colliers, and thousands from the neighboring villages, persons of all ranks daily flocked out of Bristol. And he was soon invited by many of the most respectable people to preach on a large bowling-green in the city itself. Many of the people indeed sneered to see a stripling with a gown mount a table on unconsecrated ground; this even excited once or twice the laugh of some of the higher ranks, who had admired him in the churches. But he was unmoved, and his preaching was so blessed, that many were awakened. Sometimes he was employed almost from morning till night answering those who, in distress of soul, cried out, "What shall I do to be saved?" He now sought the help of Mr. John Wesley, who, after much reasoning with himself on the subject, complied with the invitation, and followed Whitefield's example, who immediately committed the work to him. Before leaving the neighborhood, however, Whitefield had the satisfaction of laying the foundation of a school for Kingswood; for the support of which the colliers liberally and cheerfully subscribed.

Taking an affectionate leave of his Bristol friends, Whitefield made an excursion into Wales, where a revival of religion had commenced several years before, under the ministry of the Rev. Griffith Jones, and was now carried on by the ministry of Mr. Howel Harris, a man of strong mental powers, great Christian zeal, and considerable learning. They met at Cardiff. Whitefield's heart was then glowing with the fire he had himself kindled at Bristol and Kingswood. On his way from Bristol to Cardiff, he was delayed at the New Passage by contrary winds. He says, "At the inn there was an unhappy clergyman who would not go over in the passage-boat, because I was in it. Alas, thought I, this very temper would make heaven itself unpleasant to that man, if he saw me there. I was told that he charged me with being a dissenter. I saw him, soon after, shaking his elbows over a gaming-table. I heartily wish those who charge me causelessly with schism and being righteous overmuch, would consider that the canons of our church forbid the clergy to frequent taverns, or to play at cards or dice, or any other unlawful games. Their indulging themselves in these things is a stumbling-block to thousands."

We have said that Whitefield first met Howel Harris at Cardiff. After preaching in the town-hall, from the judges' seat, he says, "I was much refreshed with the sight of Mr. Howel Harris; whom, though I knew not in person, I have long loved, and have often felt my soul drawn out in prayer in his behalf.... When I first saw him, my heart was knit closely to him. I wanted to catch some of his fire, and gave him the right hand of fellowship with my whole heart. After I had saluted him, and given an exhortation to a great number of people, who followed me to the inn, we spent the remainder of the evening in taking sweet counsel together, and telling one another what God had done for our souls. A divine and strong sympathy seemed to be between us, and I was resolved to promote his interest with all my might. Accordingly we took an account of the several societies, and agreed on such measures as seemed most conducive to promote the common interest of our Lord. Blessed be God, there seems a noble spirit gone out into Wales; and I believe that, ere long, there will be more visible fruits of it. What inclines me strongly to think so is, that the partition wall of bigotry and party spirit is broken down, and ministers and teachers of different communions join, with one heart and one mind, to carry on the kingdom of Jesus Christ. The Lord make all the Christian world thus minded; for, until this is done, we must, I fear, despair of any great reformation in the church of God."

Before leaving Cardiff, Whitefield preached again in the town-hall, to a large assembly. He says, "My dear brother Harris sat close by me. I did not observe any scoffers within; but without, some were pleased to honor me so far as to trail a dead fox, and hunt it about the hall. But, blessed be God, my voice prevailed. This being done, I went, with many of my hearers, among whom were two worthy dissenting ministers, to public worship; and in the second lesson were these remarkable words: 'The high-priests, and the scribes, and the chief of the people sought to destroy him; but they could not find what they might do to him; for all the people were very attentive to hear him.'

"In the afternoon I preached again, without any disturbance or scoffing. In the evening, I talked for above an hour and a half with the religious society, and never did I see a congregation more melted down. The love of Jesus touched them to the quick. Most of them were dissolved in tears. They came to me after, weeping, bidding me farewell, and wishing I could continue with them longer. Thanks be to God, for such an entrance into Wales. I wrestled with God for them in prayer, and blessed be His holy name for sending me into Wales. I hope these are the first-fruits of a greater harvest, if ever it should please God to bring me back from Georgia. 'Father, thy will be done.'"

Whitefield returned from this short excursion, to Bristol, baptized with Welsh fire, and renewed his labors among the Kingswood colliers with more than his usual power and success. He could not, however, forget the tears which had entreated him to stay longer in Wales, and in three or four weeks he visited Usk and Pontypool, where he was again met by Howel Harris. At Usk, "the pulpit being denied, I preached upon a table, under a large tree, to some hundreds, and God was with us of a truth. On my way to Pontypool, I was informed by a man who heard it, that Counsellor H— — did me the honor to make a public motion to Judge P— — to stop me and brother Howel Harris from going about teaching the people. Poor man, he put me in mind of Tertullus, in the Acts; but my hour is not yet come. I have scarcely begun my testimony. For my finishing it, my enemies must have power over me from above. Lord, prepare me for that hour."

The report to which we have just referred did not prevent the curate of Pontypool from cordially inviting Whitefield into his pulpit. He also read prayers for him. After the sermon, it was found that so many had come to hear who could not find room in the church, that another sermon was loudly called for. He says, "I went and preached to all the people in the field. I always find I have most power when I preach in the open air; a proof to me that God is pleased with this way of preaching. I betook myself to rest, full of such unutterable peace as no one can conceive of but those who feel it."

In several other places did our evangelist, during this excursion, unfurl the banner of the cross; and at its close he writes, "Oh how swiftly this week has glided away. To me it has been but as one day. How do I pity those who complain that time hangs on their hands! Let them but love Christ, and spend their whole time in his service, and they will find but few melancholy hours." Nor will any wonder that he should thus speak, who consider the spirit which animated his soul. What he some time afterwards wrote to Howel Harris, from Philadelphia, indicated the spirit he himself cherished: "Intersperse prayers with your exhortations, and thereby call down fire from heaven, even the fire of the Holy Ghost,

"'To soften, sweeten, and refine,
And melt them into love.'

Speak every time, my dear brother, as if it were your last; *weep out*, if possible, every argument, and compel them to cry, 'Behold how he loveth us.'"

From Wales, Whitefield went to visit his native city, Gloucester; and after one or two sermons, he found himself here also excluded from the parochial pulpits. But notwithstanding his persecutions, and the infirm state of his health at that time, his labors in Gloucester and its vicinity were constant and eminently successful. Bowling-greens, market-crosses, highways, and other such places, bore witness to his faithful and tearful labors.

At Gloucester lived at that time the Rev. Mr. Cole, an old dissenting minister, who often heard Whitefield preach, and used to say, "These are the days of the Son of man indeed!" Whitefield, when a boy, had been taught to ridicule this Mr. Cole; and when he was once asked what profession he would engage in, replied, "I will be a minister, but I will take care never to tell stories in the pulpit like old Cole." Twelve years afterwards, the old minister heard the young one preach, and tell some story to illustrate his subject, when the venerable servant of Christ remarked, "I find young Whitefield can tell stories now as well as old Cole." The good man was much affected with the preaching of his young friend, and was so humble, that he used to subscribe himself his curate, and went about in the country preaching after him. One evening, while preaching, he was struck with death, and asked for a chair to lean on till he had finished his sermon. Having done this, he was carried up stairs and died. When the fact was told to Whitefield, he said, "O blessed God, if it be thy holy will, may my exit be like his!" How striking is this fact when looked at in connection with the circumstances of his own removal from earth.

Intent on the advancement of his orphan-house in Georgia, Whitefield soon went to London, passing on his way through Oxford. At both places he found opposition, and in London was shut out of the churches. He preached to thousands in Islington churchyard, and now resolved to give himself to the work in the open air.

From the conflict with the enemies who a few years before had threatened her existence, the polemics of the church of England now turned to resist the unwelcome ally who menaced her repose. Bishop Warburton led the van, and behind him many a mitred front scowled on the audacious innovator. Divested of the logomachies which chiefly engaged the attention of the disputants, the controversy between Whitefield and the bishops lay in a narrow compass. It being mutually conceded that the virtues of the Christian life can result only from certain divine impulses, and that to lay a claim to this holy inspiration when its legitimate fruits are wanting, is a fatal delusion, he maintained, and they denied, that the person who is the subject of this sacred influence has within his own bosom an independent attestation of its reality. So abstruse a debate required the zest of some more pungent ingredients, and the polemics with whom Whitefield had to do were not such sciolists in their calling as to be ignorant of the necessity of riveting upon him some epithet at once opprobrious and vague. While therefore milder spirits arraigned him as an *enthusiast*, Warburton, with constitutional energy of invective, denounced him as a *fanatic*. In vain Whitefield demanded a definition of these reproachful terms. To have fixed their meaning would have been to blunt their edge. They afforded a solution, at once compendious, obscure, and repulsive, of whatever was remarkable in his character, and have been associated with his name from that time to the present.

The spots on which Whitefield now began, in his own language, "to take the field," and publicly to erect the standard of the Redeemer's cross, are well known. Moorfields, then a place of general rendezvous and recreation from the crowded city, Kennington Common then about two, and Blackheath about five miles from London, were the favorite sites to which he loved to resort, and "open his mouth boldly" to listening thousands, in honor of his crucified and glorified Lord. Recording his first engagement of this kind in his diary of Sabbath evening, April 29, 1739, he writes, "Begun to be yet more vile this day, for I preached at Moorfields to an exceeding great multitude; and at five in the evening went and preached at Kennington Common, where upwards of twenty thousand were supposed to be present. The wind being for me, it carried my voice to the extreme part of my audience. All stood attentive, and joined in the psalm and the Lord's prayer so regularly, that I scarce ever preached with more quietness in a church. Many were much affected.

"'For this let men revile my name,
I'll shun no cross, I'll fear no shame;
All hail, reproach, and welcome pain,
Only thy terrors, Lord, restrain.'"

For several successive months, the places we have named were his chief scenes of action. At a moderate computation, the audience frequently consisted of twenty thousand. It is said that the singing could be heard two miles, and the voice of the preacher nearly one. Sometimes there were upwards of a hundred coaches, besides wagons, scaffolds, and other contrivances by which a sight of him could be obtained. The rising ground on Blackheath, from which Whitefield preached, is still known as "Whitefield's mount," and after his death, Lord Dartmouth planted it with fir-trees. It will ever be a grateful recollection to the author of this volume, that during the summer of 1839 he prevailed on some of the most eminent ministers of England to preach on every successive Monday evening on this hallowed spot; and that here many thousands then heard the way of salvation, and not a few were brought to the cross of Christ. In that immediate neighborhood too, now densely populated, he organized, and for some years preached to a Christian church. Memorable times! Many were the manifestations of the Redeemer's favor.

An anecdote which we heard many years ago from one of Whitefield's Blackheath hearers, may here be related. While one day preaching on "the heath," there passed along the road at some distance, an old man and "Mary" his wife, with their ass and his loaded panniers, returning from London to their home in Kent. Attracted alike by the crowd and the preacher's voice, the old man and his wife turned a little out of their way to hear "what the man was talking about." Whitefield spoke of somewhat which occurred eighteen hundred years ago, and the old man said, "Mary, come along, it is only something which happened a long while ago;" but Mary's attention had been arrested, and she wished to stay a minute or two longer. They were both soon in tears, and the inquiry was excited in their hearts, "What shall we do to be saved?" On their way home, while "talking of all these things," the old man recollected his neglected Bible, and asked, "Why, Mary, does not our old book at home say somewhat about these things?" They went home, and examined the old book with new light. "Why, Mary," asked the old man, "is this indeed our old book? why, every thing in it seems quite new." So true is it, that the teaching of the Spirit gives new discernment as to the truths of divine revelation.

A fact strikingly illustrating the children's love to our evangelist may be here mentioned. In his open-air preachings, especially in and about London, he was usually attended by many of them, who sat round him, in and about the pulpit, and handed to him the notes of those who desired his counsels and prayers. These children were exposed to the missiles with which he was often assailed, but however terrified they might be, or even hurt, they seldom shrunk; "but," says he, "on the contrary, every time I was struck, they turned up their little weeping eyes, and seemed to wish they could receive the blows for me."

Speaking of his open-air labors, the devoted preacher says, "Words cannot express the displays of divine grace which we saw, and heard of, and felt. Lord, not unto me, but unto thy name be all the glory." On a subsequent occasion he writes, "We have had a glorious season, a true Easter. Jesus Christ is risen indeed. I have been preaching in Moorfields, and our Saviour carries all before us. Nothing can resist his conquering blood. It would have delighted you to see poor sinners flock from the booths to see Jesus lifted up on the pole of the gospel." The climax of his success there, is one of the most remarkable letters that ever came from a mortal's pen. He records at its close, "We then retired to the Tabernacle, with my pockets full of notes from persons brought under concern, and read them amidst the praises and spiritual acclamations of thousands, who joined with the holy angels in rejoicing that so many sinners were snatched, in such an unexpected, unlikely place and manner, out of the very jaws of the devil. This was the beginning of the Tabernacle society. Three hundred and fifty awakened souls were received in one day; and I believe the number of notes exceeded a thousand. But I must have done, believing you want to retire, to join in mutual praise with me in thanksgiving to God and the Lamb."

Having thus introduced the name of the Tabernacle, it is important that the reader should be acquainted with the origin of the buildings which have borne that name. From the very first of what may be called his irregular labors, Whitefield always declared that he "would never be the founder of a sect." He kept his word; yet two London churches remain as his memorial—the Tabernacle, and Tottenham Court-road chapel, the one in the north, and the other in the western part of the metropolis. The Tabernacle, which was first erected, was his more especial and favorite field of labor, and he dwelt in the house adjoining it, which is still the pastoral residence.

Moorfields, just without the limits of the old north city wall of London, was, a few years before Whitefield first knew it, a marsh, and during the greater part of the year, was absolutely impassable. Having been partially drained, a brick kiln was erected, and the first bricks used in London are said to have been manufactured there. Afterwards it was a field for the practice of archery, when it was laid out in walks, and called the City Mall. Though improved in name and appearance, it became the rallying ground for the rabble of London; wrestlers, boxers, and mountebanks, the idle, the dissolute, and the profane, held here their daily and nightly revels. It appeared, in fact, to be one of the strong-holds of Satan, and therefore became a most tempting and important point of attack for the daring eloquence of Whitefield. All London rang one day with the announcement that Whitefield would preach the day following at Moorfields.

This was in January, 1739. Gillies says, "The thing being strange and new, he found, on coming out of the coach, an incredible number of people assembled. Many told him that he would never come out of that place alive. He went in, however, between two friends, who by the pressure of the crowd were soon parted from him entirely, and obliged to leave him to the mercy of the rabble. But these, instead of hurting him, formed a lane for him, and carried him along to the middle of the fields, where a table had been placed. This, however, having been broken by the crowd, he mounted a wall, and preached to an exceeding great multitude in tones so melting, that his words drew tears and groans from the most abandoned of his hearers. Moorfields became henceforth one of the principal scenes of his triumphs. Thirty thousand people sometimes gathered together to hear him, and generous contributions here poured in for his orphan-house at Bethesda. On one occasion twenty pounds—about one hundred dollars—were received in half-pennies, more than one person was able to carry away, and enough to put one out of conceit with a specie currency."

It was not till his fifth visit to London, in March, 1741, that Whitefield ventured to preach in Moorfields on *a week-day*; the day selected for this bold action being Good-Friday. His chief, if not his only friends on this occasion, he tells us, were a few "orthodox dissenters." These people perceiving the inconvenience to which he was subjected by the weather, during the morning and evening services in Moorfields, procured the loan of a piece of ground, and employed a carpenter to build a large temporary shed, to screen the auditory from the cold and rain. This building Whitefield called a "tabernacle," as it was only intended to be used a few months during his stay in his native country, previous to his return to America. Providence, however, had otherwise determined, and this proved the commencement of a permanent establishment of the means of grace. A great spiritual awakening took place; congregations became very large, acquiring at the same time considerable cohesion, and assuming a stationary character. This original fabric of wood was a place of large dimensions; and notwithstanding its rude aspect and temporary design, it sufficed for the accommodation of Whitefield and his flock, during the twelve succeeding years—a period the most brilliant and useful of his extraordinary career.

Some of Whitefield's friends, however, did not approve of the original wooden structure; and anticipating or desiring the formation of a Christian church, they called for the immediate erection of a substantial brick building, a point which was debated with a warmth approaching to violence, of which Whitefield makes pathetic mention seven years afterwards. Here then several important facts are established: that the original tabernacle sprang not from Whitefield, but from a voluntary movement among his adherents, composed chiefly, if not wholly, of Protestant dissenters; that the expense was borne not by him, but by them; that much debate and dissension attended the measure, proving the thoroughly free and popular character of the original movement; and that, as the edifice originated with the people alone, so did the institution of regular worship. It is certain that fears existed in the mind of Whitefield as to the success of such an organization; but the results most happily disappointed his expectations.

The subject of the erection of a more spacious edifice in the place of the tabernacle of wood, was first discussed at the mansion of Lady Huntingdon, in Leicestershire, when Drs. Doddridge and Stonehouse, and the Rev. Messrs. Hervey and Whitefield happened to meet together, in the summer of 1751. During the following winter, Whitefield began to make collections for the object, and on almost its first presentation in London, nine hundred pounds, or four thousand five hundred dollars, were subscribed. "But," he says, "on the principle that burned children dread the fire, I do not mean to begin until I get one thousand in hand, and then to contract at a certain sum for the whole." The fact was, that Whitefield had often been in great straits for the support of his orphan-house in Georgia, "for I forgot," he says, "that Professor Francke built in Glaucha, in a populous country, and that I was building at the very tail of the world." In March, 1753, he wrote to Mr. Charles Wesley, "On Tuesday morning the first brick of our new Tabernacle was laid with awful solemnity. I preached from Exodus 20:24, 'In all places where I record my name, I will come unto thee, and I will bless thee.' The wall is now about a yard high. The building is to be eighty feet square. It is on the old spot. We have bought the house, and if we finish what we have begun, shall be rent free for forty-six years." In June the dedicatory services took place, when the Tabernacle, though capable, with its capacious galleries, of holding *four thousand* people, was crowded almost to suffocation. Often have we seen this vast building crowded with worshippers, with delight have we occupied its pulpit, and with devout gratitude do we record, that never for a moment has the frown of heaven rested upon it. Thousands will ever bless God for its erection.

Not unfrequently has the question been discussed, to what denomination of Christians does the Tabernacle really belong? In answer to this question, we give a legal document which may also show what is done in reference to houses of worship in England, under the laws for the maintenance of religious toleration.

"These are to certifie whom it may Concern, that a Certificate bearing date the Eighteenth Day of June, in the year of Our Lord One Thousand Seven Hundred and Sixty-four, under the Hands of Starkey Myddleton Minister, Robert Keen, Thomas Cox, Samuel Grace, Robert Hodgson, James Smith, Thomas Robinson, Benjamin Coles, Thomas Brooks, and Samuel Lockhart, for appropriating and setting apart a Certain Building for that purpose erected, situate near the Barking Dogs in the Parish of Saint Luke in the County of Middlesex, and intended for the meeting place of a certain Congregation of Protestant Dissenters from the Church of England, calling themselves Independents, was Registered in the Registry of the Dean and Chapter of the Cathedral Church of Saint Paul, London, This Twenty-first Day of June in the year of Our Lord One Thousand Seven Hundred and Sixty-four.

"THOMAS COLLINS, Deputy Registrar."

While the new Tabernacle was in the course of erection, Whitefield visited Norwich, where his ministry was largely attended, and notwithstanding much opposition, was followed with considerable success. Writing to his friend Keen, he says, "How does God delight to exceed even the hopes, and to disappoint the fears of his weak, though honest-hearted people. In spite of all opposition, he hath caused us to triumph even in Norwich. Thousands attend twice every day, and hear with the greatest eagerness. I hope it will appear yet more and more that God hath much people here." Compelled by alarming illness, the result of his too much preaching, he suddenly returned to London, from whence he thus wrote to one of the converts at Norwich: "I shall little regard the weakness and indisposition of my body, if I can but have the pleasure of hearing, if not before, yet at the great day, that good was done to one precious soul at Norwich. Blessed be God for the seed sown there. I doubt not but it will be watered with the dew of his heavenly blessing, and bring forth a divine increase."

Truly the gospel did triumph, not only in the erection of the Tabernacle in that city, but in preparing sinners to be pillars in the temple of God, and to win others to his service.

Among other converts won at Norwich, was the afterwards popular and useful minister of Christ, the Rev. Robert Robinson, of Cambridge, England. When a young man, about eighteen, he resided in that city, and was engaged in the business of a barber. When he was walking one morning with several companions who had agreed that day to take their pleasure, the first object which attracted their attention was an old woman who pretended to tell fortunes. They immediately employed her to tell theirs, and that they might qualify her for the undertaking, first made her thoroughly intoxicated. Robinson was informed, among other things, that he would live to a very old age, and see his children, grandchildren, and great-grandchildren growing up around him. Though he had assisted in intoxicating the old woman, he had credulity enough to be struck with those parts of the prediction which related to himself. "And so," said he when alone, "I am to see children, grandchildren, and great-grandchildren. At that age I must be a burden to the young people. What shall I do? There is no way for an old man to render himself more agreeable to youth, than by sitting and telling them pleasant and profitable stories. I will then," thought he, "during my youth, endeavor to store my mind with all kinds of knowledge. I will see and hear, and note down every thing that is rare and wonderful, that I may sit, when incapable of other employments, and entertain my descendants. Thus shall my company be rendered pleasant, and I shall be respected, rather than neglected, in old age. Let me see, what can I acquire first? Oh, here is the famous Methodist preacher, Whitefield; he is to preach here, they say, to-night; I will go and hear him."

From these strange motives, as he told the celebrated Rev. Andrew Fuller, he went to hear Whitefield preach. That evening his text was, "But when he saw many of the Pharisees and Sadducees come to his baptism, he said unto them, O generation of vipers, who hath warned you to flee from the wrath to come?" Matt. 3:7. "Mr. Whitefield," said Robinson, "described the Sadducees' character; this did not touch me; I thought myself as good a Christian as any man in England. From this he went to that of the Pharisees. He described their exterior decency, but observed, that the poison of the viper rankled in their hearts. This rather shook me. At length, in the course of his sermon, he abruptly broke off; paused for a few moments; then burst into a flood of tears, lifted up his hands and eyes, and exclaimed, 'Oh, my hearers, *the wrath's to come! the wrath's to come!*' These words sunk into my heart like lead in the water; I wept, and when the sermon was ended retired alone. For days and weeks I could think of little else. Those awful words would follow me wherever I went: 'The wrath's to come! The wrath's to come!'"

Scarcely had Whitefield completed the Tabernacle in London, before he was earnestly solicited to hold public services at the west end of the city, and Long-Acre chapel, then under the charge of a dissenter, was offered for his use. An unruly rabble endeavored to drive the preacher from his post; but a running fire of brickbats, broken glass, bells, drums, and clappers, neither annoyed nor frightened the intrepid evangelist; nor did an interference on the part of the hierarchy, which followed soon after, prohibiting his preaching in an incorporated chapel. "I hope you will not look on it as contumacy," said Whitefield to the bishop, "if I persist in prosecuting my design until I am more particularly apprized wherein I have erred. I trust the irregularity I am charged with will appear justifiable to every lover of English liberty, and what is all to me, be approved at the awful and impartial tribunal of the great Bishop and Shepherd of souls." Writing to Lady Huntingdon, he says, "My greatest distress is so to act as to avoid rashness on the one hand and timidity on the other;" and this shows, what indeed was proved in his whole life, an entire absence of that malignant element of fanaticism which courts opposition and revels in it.

"Determined," as Mrs. Knight says, in her beautiful volume, "*Lady Huntingdon and her Friends*," "not to be beaten from his ground, yet hoping to escape some of its annoyances, Whitefield resolved to build a chapel of his own. Hence arose Tottenham Court-road chapel, which went by the name of 'Whitefield's soul-trap.'" Admirably does he say, "I pray the Friend of sinners to make it a soul-trap indeed to many wandering creatures. My constant work is preaching fifteen times a week. Conviction and conversion go on here, for God hath met us in our new building." It was completed and dedicated in November, 1756. Though not equal in its triumphs to the Tabernacle, the congregation has always been large, and its preachers—always the same as those at the Tabernacle—have not labored in vain. In 1829, '30, improvements were made in the building, which still, however, contains Whitefield's pulpit. A vast area in the centre was originally filled with plain seats, where the masses of the people were accommodated free of all pew rent.

Let not infidels tell us, that the religion of these men and of those times was mere enthusiasm, and that the temporal interests of men were neglected in professions of high regard for those of a spiritual character. Let such men know that within two years of the opening of Tottenham Court-road chapel, not only did the congregation build a parsonage-house for their minister, but twelve almshouses for as many poor widows. The Tabernacle has always acted with equal generosity. In proportion to their means, few congregations in the world have exceeded these two in works of benevolence.

Assuredly what has sometimes been charged on evangelical ministers—that they attend to the spiritual interests of mankind, but neglect their temporal sufferings—would never apply to Mr. Whitefield. No sooner had he completed these large edifices, where vast congregations assembled, than he was heard frequently to plead for those laboring under oppression or distress in foreign lands. He preached in both these houses in behalf of the poor French Protestants in Prussia, who had suffered much from the cruelty of the Russians, when great numbers of the nobility, and some of the highest officers of the crown went to hear him. The collections for this object amounted to upwards of fifteen hundred pounds, or seven thousand five hundred dollars; and for this disinterested act of benevolence Whitefield received the thanks of his Prussian Majesty.

Again, on the day recommended by the government for a general fast, Mr. Whitefield preached both at the Tabernacle and at Tottenham Court-road chapel, after which he collected five hundred and sixty pounds for the relief of the German Protestants, and the sufferers by fire at Boston, for which he received the unanimous thanks of the inhabitants of that town. Lady Huntingdon wrote to one of her friends, "It would delight you to have seen what crowds of the mighty and noble flocked to hear him. The collection was for the relief of the poor German Protestants. I invited several to come who probably would not attend his ministry on other occasions." Few places at that time could boast of such a constellation of transcendent genius and senatorial talent, such a brilliant assemblage of wisdom, magnanimity, and oratorical powers, as were then found within these houses of the living God.

One word may be allowed here on the plain architecture of these buildings. "We are," says the excellent Mr. James, "in many things improved, and I rejoice in the improvement; but the occasion of my joy is at the same time the occasion of my fear and my jealousy also. Our ecclesiastical architecture is just now a special object of our attention. Whitefield, it may be confessed, paid too little attention to this; we, perhaps, are paying too much. His only solicitude was to save souls, careless altogether of the tastefulness of the building within which that work, which has no relation to styles of architecture, was carried on. His only calculation in the construction of a building was, how many immortal souls could be crowded within four square walls, and under a roof, to hear 'the joyful sound.' Hence the somewhat uncouth buildings which he erected. Ah, but when I consider that every stone in those unsightly walls has echoed to the sound of salvation and the hymns of redeemed spirits, and that almost every spot on the floor has been moistened by the tears of penitence, then, in a feeling of sanctity I seem to lose the sense of deformity, and there comes over me an awe and solemnity which no modern gothic structure with its lofty arches and painted windows can inspire. But still, as religion is not only the most holy, but the most beautiful thing in God's universe, there is no reason why taste and devotion should not be united. It is the ministry of the word, however, upon which the church must be chiefly intent."

CHAPTER IV
WHITEFIELD'S SECOND VISIT TO AMERICA. 1739, 1740

As in the preceding chapter, for the sake of connecting the history of Whitefield's church edifices in London, we have anticipated the order of events, we go back to the period shortly before his second voyage to America.

About the time of which we are now writing, a circumstance occurred of deep interest, which Whitefield relates at considerable length. Joseph Periam, a young man in London, who had read his sermon on "regeneration," became deeply impressed by it; he sold all that he possessed, and prayed so loud and fasted so long, that his family supposed him deranged, and sent him to the Bedlam madhouse, where he was treated as "methodistically mad," and as "one of Whitefield's gang." The keepers threw him down, and forced a key into his mouth, while they drenched him with medicine. He was then placed in a cold room without windows, and with a damp cellar under it. Periam, however, found some means of conveying a letter to Whitefield, requesting both advice and a visit. These were promptly given. The preacher soon discovered that Periam was not mad; and taking a Mr. Seward and some other friends with him, he went before the committee of the hospital to explain the case. It must have been somewhat of a ludicrous scene. Seward so astounded the committee by quoting Scripture, that they pronounced him to be as mad as Periam. The doctors frankly told the deputation, that in their opinion, Whitefield and his followers were "really beside themselves." It was however agreed, that if Whitefield would take Periam out to Georgia, his release would be granted. Thus the conference ended, and the young man went out as a schoolmaster at the Orphan-house. There he was exemplary and useful, and when he died two of his sons were received into the institution.

Mr. Whitefield so successfully pleaded the cause of his American orphans, that during his journeys of twelve months he collected upwards of one thousand pounds towards the erection of his intended house for their accommodation. With this sum in his possession, he set sail for America the second time, August 14, 1739, accompanied by his friend Mr. Seward, eight men, one boy, and two children.

While all this was going on, the inhabitants of Georgia were making every possible preparation for his reception. The records of the trustees say, May 16, 1739, "Read a commission to the Rev. George Whitefield to perform all religious and ecclesiastical offices at Savannah, in Georgia." Again: "June 2, 1739. Sealed a grant of five hundred acres of land to the Rev. George Whitefield, in trust for the use of the house to be erected and maintained for the receiving such children as now are, and shall hereafter be left orphans in the colony of Georgia, in pursuance of the direction of the Common Council held the 30th of last month."

Not only was Whitefield anxious to establish the orphan-house for the benefit of the whole colony of Georgia, but having been ordained priest, for the purpose of instructing the inhabitants of the town of Savannah, he was desirous of making full proof of his ministry among them. After a passage of nine weeks he landed at Philadelphia, and was immediately invited to preach in the churches; to which people of all denominations thronged as in England. He was especially pleased to find that they preferred sermons when "not delivered within the church walls." And it was well they did, for his fame had arrived in the city before him, and crowds were collected to hear him which no church could contain.

A letter written on this voyage to America has recently come to light, which beautifully illustrates the spirit by which Whitefield was now animated. It was addressed to the Rev. John Cumming of Andover, Hampshire, England.

"Wrote at Sea, dated at Philadelphia, Nov. 9, 1739.

> "Reverend and dear Sir—You see by my writing this how willing I am to cultivate a correspondence with you. I wish Christians in general, and ministers of Christ in particular, were better acquainted. The cause of Christ thereby must be necessarily promoted. But bigotry and sectarian zeal have been the bane of our holy religion. Though we have one Lord, one faith, and one baptism, yet if we do not all worship God in one particular way, we behave to each other like Jews and Samaritans. Dear sir, I hope that neither of us have so learned Christ. Blessed be God for his free grace in Christ. The partition wall has for some time been broken down out of my heart, and I can truly say, whosoever loves the Lord Jesus, 'the same is my brother, and sister, and mother.' For this reason, dear sir, I love you. For this reason, though I decrease, yet I heartily wish you may increase, even with all the increase of God. I am persuaded you are like-minded. I

believe my friends have prayed for me. The Lord hath dealt most lovingly with me his servant. He has chastened and corrected, but hath not given me over into the hands of the enemy. A future journal will acquaint you with particulars. What I have sent over to be published will afford you abundant matter for thanksgiving in behalf of,

"Dear sir, your affectionate friend,

Brother, and servant,
"G. WHITEFIELD."

The old court-house of Philadelphia, then standing on Second and Market streets, had a balcony, which several years before the visit of Whitefield had been often used instead of a pulpit. In 1736, we find that Mr. Abel Noble had preached "from the court-house steps," on a Monday, to a large congregation standing in Market-street, on the subject of keeping the Sabbath. In the same year, Michael Welfare appeared there to give his "warning voice," and now, in 1739, it became one of the favorite preaching stands of the great evangelist. Here he stood, surrounded by many thousands, even down to the side of the Delaware river, not a few bathed in tears, and inquiring after the way of salvation.

OLD COURT-HOUSE, PHILADELPHIA.

TENNENT CHURCH, FREEHOLD, N. J.

Dr. Franklin says, "The multitudes of all sects and denominations that attended his sermons were enormous; and it was a matter of speculation with me to observe the influence of his oratory on his hearers, and how much they admired and respected him, notwithstanding his common abuse of them, by assuring them that they were, naturally, half beasts and half devils. It was wonderful to see the change soon made in the manners of our inhabitants. From being thoughtless and indifferent about religion, it seemed as if all the world was growing religious; so that one could not walk through the town in an evening without hearing psalms sung in different families in every street."

A constant attendant on his ministry at this time says, "His hearers were never weary; every eye was fixed on his expressive countenance; every ear was charmed with his melodious voice; every heart captivated with the beauty and propriety of his address. He was no contracted bigot; all denominations partook of his religious charity. Anxious in America for our civil privileges, he was alike solicitous for the spiritual and temporal happiness of mankind. No man since the apostolic age preached oftener or with better success. He was, moreover, a polite gentleman, a faithful friend, an engaging companion, and a sincere Christian. His sermons in the open air lasted about one and a half hours."

Watson, in his "Annals of Philadelphia," speaking of Whitefield's first visit to that city, tells us that he preached to a crowd of fifteen thousand persons on Society hill, and adds, "About the same time he so far succeeded to repress the usual public amusements, that the dancing-school was discontinued, and the ball and concert rooms were shut up, as inconsistent with the requisitions of the gospel. No less than fourteen sermons were preached on Society hill in the open air in one week, during the session of the Presbyterian church; and the gazette of the day, in noticing the fact, says, 'The change to religion here is altogether surprising, through the influence of Whitefield; no books sell but religious, and such is the general conversation.'"

It is said, that though some gentlemen broke open the assembly-rooms, no company could be induced to visit them. Such was the popularity of Whitefield, that when he left the city, about one hundred and fifty gentlemen accompanied him as far as Chester, fifteen miles from Philadelphia, where he preached to about seven thousand people. At White Clay creek, he preached to eight thousand people, three thousand of whom, it is said, were on horseback. Many complimentary effusions to him appeared in the newspapers, and James Pemberton, a very distinguished *Friend*, said of him, "In his conversation he is very agreeable, and has not much of the priest; he frequents no set company."

An old gentleman assured Watson, the annalist, that on one occasion the words, "And he taught them, saying," as pronounced by Whitefield on Society hill, were heard at Gloucester point, a distance by water of two miles.

Abundant reasons might be assigned for our introducing in this place an account of the institution called "the Log college." It has proved the parent of every collegiate and theological institution connected with the large and wealthy body of Presbyterians in this country; it was originated by a family which became especially endeared to Mr. Whitefield; and from his journal, recording his visit to it, we have, in some respects at least, the clearest statement of facts concerning it which history has preserved.

As we have already shown, about one hundred and forty years ago, the state of religion, both in Europe and America, was very low. Nor was the condition of the Presbyterian body an exception. As the late Dr. Alexander, in his interesting volume, called "The Log College," says, "The ministers composing the Presbyterian church in this country were sound in the faith, and strongly attached to the Westminster confession of faith and catechisms, as were also their people; and there were no diversities or contentions among them respecting the doctrines of the gospel; but as to the vital power of godliness, there is reason to believe that it was little known or spoken of. Revivals of religion were nowhere heard of, and an orthodox creed, and a decent external conduct were the only points on which inquiry was made, when persons were admitted to the communion of the church. Indeed, it was very much a matter of course, for all who had been baptized in infancy, to be received into communion at the proper age, without exhibiting or possessing any satisfactory evidence of a change of heart by the supernatural operations of the Holy Spirit. And the habit of their preachers was to address their people as though they were all pious, and only needed instruction and confirmation."

Such was the lamentable state of things when the Rev. William Tennent, sen., an Irish clergyman past the middle stage of life arrived in this country, about the year 1716. After laboring for a season in the state of New York, till about 1721, he received an invitation to settle at Bensalem, where he ministered to the small Presbyterian congregation till 1726, when he was called to Neshaminy, in the same county, where he labored for the rest of his life, living till 1746, when he died, aged seventy-three. In Neshaminy the good man felt that he was called not only to discharge the duties of a preacher and pastor, but to look over the whole country, and to devise means for the extension of the cause of Christ. He had himself four sons, the subjects of divine grace, and blessed with talents for usefulness in the kingdom of the Redeemer, and he felt that when other young men rose up in the church, favored with ministerial talents, they also would need mental cultivation. Hence his determination to erect the humble building of which we now write, which was the first Presbyterian literary and theological institution in this country, the immediate parent of the college at Princeton, and from which, indeed, all similar institutions emanated.

The site of the Log college is about a mile from Neshaminy creek, where the Presbyterian church has long stood. The ground near and around it lies handsomely to the eye, and the more distant prospect is very beautiful; for while there is a considerable extent of fertile, well-cultivated land, nearly level, the view is bounded to the north and west by a range of hills, which have a very pleasing appearance. Mr. Whitefield has left in his "Journal," the only description we have of the building. "The place," says he, "wherein the young men study now, is in contempt called 'the college.' It is a log-house about twenty feet long, and nearly as many broad; and to me it seemed to resemble the school of the old prophets, for their habitations were mean.

That they sought not great things for themselves is plain from these passages of Scripture, wherein we are told that each of them took a beam to build them a house; and that at the feast of the sons of the prophets, one of them put on the pot, while the others went to fetch some herbs out of the field. All that we can say of most of our universities is, they are glorious without. From this despised place, seven or eight worthy ministers of Jesus have lately been sent forth; more are almost ready to be sent, and the foundation is now laying for the instruction of many others."

Of the senior Tennent, the founder of the Log college, little more is known than what we have already given. He was a member of the synod of Philadelphia, who were satisfied with his reasons for leaving the Established church of Ireland, and for several years this body cordially coöperated with him in his zealous labors. Their unity of feeling, however, seems to have declined. This we learn from a passage in Whitefield's "Journal," which also gives us a beautiful view of the good old man. "At my return home, was much comforted by the coming of one Mr. Tennent, an old gray-headed disciple and soldier of Jesus Christ. He keeps an academy about twenty miles from Philadelphia, and has been blest with four gracious sons, three of which have been, and still continue to be eminently useful in the church of Christ. He brought three pious souls along with him, and rejoiced me by letting me know how they had been evil spoken of for their Master's sake. He is a great friend of Mr. Erskine, of Scotland; and as far as I can learn, both he and his sons are secretly despised by the generality of the synod, as Mr. Erskine and his friends are hated by the judicatories of Edinburgh, and as the Methodist preachers, as they are called, are by their brethren in England."

Not long after this, the Log college was visited by Whitefield, who wrote the account we have already given. He also says, under the date of Nov. 29, 1739, "Set out for Neshaminy, twenty miles distant from Trent Town, where old Mr. Tennent lives, and keeps an academy, and where I was to preach to-day, according to appointment. About twelve o'clock, we came thither, and found about three thousand people gathered together in the meeting-house yard. Mr. William Tennent, junior, an eminent servant of Jesus Christ, because we stayed beyond the time appointed, was preaching to them. When I came up, he soon stopped; sung a psalm, and then I began to speak as the Lord gave me utterance. At first, the people seemed unaffected, but in the midst of my discourse, the power of the Lord Jesus came upon me, and I felt such a struggling within myself for the people as I scarce ever felt before. The hearers began to be melted down immediately, and to cry much; and we had good reason to hope the Lord intended good for many. After I had finished, Mr. Gilbert Tennent gave a word of exhortation, to confirm what had been delivered. At the end of his discourse, we sung a psalm, and dismissed the people with a blessing; O that the people may say Amen to it. After our exercises were over, we went to old Mr. Tennent's, who entertained us like one of the ancient patriarchs. His wife, to me seemed like Elizabeth, and he like Zachary; both, as far as I can learn, walk in the commandments and ordinances of the Lord blameless. Though God was pleased to humble my soul, so that I was obliged to retire for a while, yet we had sweet communion with each other, and spent the evening in concerting what measures had best be taken for promoting our dear Lord's kingdom. It happened very providentially that Mr. Tennent and his brethren are appointed to be a presbytery by the synod, so that they intend bringing up gracious youths, and sending them out from time to time into the Lord's vineyard."

We may be permitted to add here, that among the ministers sent out by Mr. Tennent, from the Log college, to preach the gospel, were his four sons, Gilbert, William, John, and Charles, the Rev. Messrs. Samuel Blair, John Blair, Charles Beatty, and Rev. Dr. Samuel J. Finley, President of Princeton College; of some of these excellent men the reader will hear again in the course of this volume.

In reference to his first visit to Philadelphia, Whitefield thus writes: "I have scarcely preached among them, but I have seen a stirring among the dry bones. Go where I will, I find people with great gladness receive me into their houses. Sometimes I think I am speaking to stocks and stones; but before I have done, the power of the Lord comes over them, and I find I have been ploughing up some fallow ground, in a place where there has been a great famine of the word of God. But as God's word increases, so will the rage and opposition of the devil. Scoffers seem to be at a stand what to say. They mutter in coffee-houses, give a curse, drink a barrel of punch, and then cry out against me for not preaching more morality. Poor men, if God judges them, as he certainly will do, by *their* morality, out of their own mouths will he condemn them. Their morality, falsely so called, will prove their damnation. God has enlarged my heart to pray. Tears trickle down my face, and I am in great agony; but the Lord is pleased to set his seal to what he enables me to deliver. Amid cries and groans in the congregation, God gives me much freedom of speech. Many people and many ministers weep. My own soul is much carried out. I preached to a vast assembly of sinners; nearly twelve thousand were collected; and I had not spoken long, before I perceived numbers melting; as I proceeded, the power increased, and thousands cried out; never before did I see so glorious a sight. Oh, what strong crying and tears were poured forth after the dear Lord Jesus! Some fainted; and when they had gotten a little strength, they would hear and faint again. Never was my soul filled with greater power. Oh, what thoughts and words did God put into my heart. As great, if not greater commotion was in the hearts of the people. Look where I would, most were drowned in tears."

An aged man who was living in 1806, and who well remembered the scenes he witnessed, bore testimony that after this visit of the great evangelist, public worship was regularly celebrated in Philadelphia twice a day for a whole year; and that on the Lord's day it was celebrated three, and frequently four times in each church. He said there were not less than twenty-six societies regularly held for prayer and Christian conference.

Such was the influence of Whitefield, not only in Philadelphia, but throughout the colony of Pennsylvania, that in the city attention to commerce was suspended, and in the country the cultivation of the land for the time being was abandoned, that people might hear him proclaim the gospel of the Lord Jesus.

Among other very striking conversions in Philadelphia at this period, was that of a young lady, who had for several years made a public profession of Christianity, but who now became fully convinced that "she was totally unacquainted with vital piety." When Mr. Whitefield began his labors in that city, she was greatly affected by his preaching, on which she constantly attended, and often afterwards told her friends, that after the first sermon she heard him preach, she was ready to say with the woman of Samaria, "Come see a man who told me all things that ever I did." The preacher, she said, so exactly described all the secret workings of her heart, her wishes, and her actions, that she really believed he was either more than human, or else that he was supernaturally assisted to know her heart. She was not then aware that all depraved hearts are much alike, and that he who in lively colors can paint one, gives a description which will be recognized by many as their own. This young lady once walked twenty miles to hear a sermon from Whitefield; she became a most eminent Christian, and was one of the constituent members of the church organized by Mr. Tennent. She married Mr. Hugh Hodge, who was also one of the seals of Mr. Whitefield's ministry, and a deacon of the church, and for more than sixty years she eminently "adorned the gospel of God in all things."

During this first visit of Mr. Whitefield to Philadelphia, another interesting circumstance occurred. Whitefield preached one evening standing on the steps of the court-house, in Market-street, which became, as we have said, his favorite spot during that and subsequent visits. A youth some thirteen years of age stood near him, and held a lantern for his accommodation; but becoming deeply absorbed in the sermon, and strongly agitated, the lantern fell from his hands, and was dashed in pieces. Those near the boy, observing the cause of the accident, felt specially interested, and for a few moments the meeting was discomposed by the occurrence. Some fourteen years afterwards, Mr. Whitefield, on his fifth visit to this country, was visiting St. George's, in Delaware. He was one day riding out with the Rev. Dr. John Rodgers, then settled as the minister at St. George's, in the closed carriage in which Whitefield generally rode. Mr. Rodgers asked him whether he recollected the occurrence of the little boy who was so affected with his preaching as to let his lantern fall. Mr. Whitefield replied, "O yes, I remember it well; and have often thought I would give almost any thing in my power, to know who that little boy was, and what had become of him." Mr. Rodgers replied with a smile, "I am that little boy." Mr. Whitefield, with tears of joy, started from his seat, took him in his arms, and with strong emotion remarked, that he was the *fourteenth* person then in the ministry whom he had discovered in the course of that visit to America, in whose conversion he had, under God, been instrumental.

From Philadelphia, Whitefield was invited by Mr. Noble to New York; this gentleman being the only person with whom he then had an acquaintance in that city. Upon his arrival, he waited with his friend on the commissary, but he refused to Whitefield the use of the church. This commissary of the bishop, he says, "was full of anger and resentment, and denied me the use of his pulpit before I asked for it. He said they did not want my assistance. I replied, that if they preached the gospel, I wished them good luck: I will preach in the fields; for all places are alike to me." The undaunted evangelist therefore preached in the fields; and on the evening of the same day, to a very thronged and attentive audience, in the Rev. Mr. Pemberton's meeting-house, in Wall-street; and continued to do so twice or three times a day, with apparent success.

Of this visit to New York, and of Whitefield's labors there, we have a graphic account, furnished by one of his hearers, for "Prince's Christian History." Of the first sermon in the fields, the writer says, "I fear curiosity was the motive that led me and many others into that assembly. I had read two or three of Mr. Whitefield's sermons and part of his Journal, and from them had obtained a settled opinion, that he was a good man. Thus far was I prejudiced in his favor. But then having heard of so much opposition, and many clamors against him, I thought it possible he might have carried matters too far; that some enthusiasm might have mixed itself with his piety, and that his zeal might have exceeded his knowledge. With these prepossessions I went into the fields. When I came there, I saw a great number of people, consisting of Christians of all denominations, some Jews, and a few, I believe, of no religion at all. When Mr. Whitefield came to the place designated, which was a little eminence on the side of a hill, he stood still and beckoned with his hand, and disposed the multitude upon the descent, before, and on each side of him. He then prayed most excellently, in the same manner, I suppose, that the first ministers of the Christian church prayed. The assembly soon appeared to be divided into two companies, the one of which I considered as God's church, and the other the devil's chapel. The first were collected round the minister, and were very serious and attentive; the last had placed themselves in the skirts of the assembly, and spent most of their time in giggling, scoffing, talking, and laughing. I believe the minister saw them, for in his sermon, remarking on the cowardice and shamefacedness in Christ's cause, he pointed towards *this* assembly, and reproached the former, those who seemed to be Christians, with the boldness and zeal with which the devil's vassals serve him. Towards the last prayer the whole assembly appeared more united, and all became hushed and still; a solemn awe and reverence appeared in the faces of most, a mighty energy attending the word. I heard and felt something astonishing and surprising, but I confess I was not at that time fully rid of my scruples. But as I thought I saw a visible presence of God with Mr. Whitefield, I kept my doubts to myself.

"Under this frame of mind, I went to hear him in the evening at the Presbyterian church, where he expounded to above two thousand people within and without doors. I never in my life saw so attentive an audience. All he said was demonstration, life, and power. The people's eyes and ears hung on his lips. They greedily devoured every word. I came home astonished. Every scruple vanished; I never saw nor heard the like; and I said within myself, 'Surely God is with this man, of a truth.' He preached and expounded in this manner twice every day for four days, and his evening assemblies were continually increasing.

"On Sunday morning at eight o'clock, his congregation consisted of about fifteen hundred people; but at night several thousands came together to hear him; and the place being too strait for them, many were forced to go away, and some, it is said, with tears lamented their disappointment. After sermon he left New York at ten at night, to fulfil a promise that he had made to preach at Elizabethtown, at eleven A. M. the next day."

We give a few paragraphs from the same vigorous pen, relating to the personal manners and the doctrines of our evangelist. "He is a man of a middle stature, of a slender body, of a fair complexion, and of a comely appearance. He is of a sprightly, cheerful temper, and acts and moves with great agility and life. The endowments of his mind are very uncommon; his wit is quick and piercing; his imagination lively and florid; and as far as I can discern, both are under the direction of an exact and solid judgment. He has a most ready memory, and I think speaks entirely without notes. He has a clear and musical voice, and a wonderful command of it. He uses much gesture, but with great propriety. Every accent of his voice, every motion of his body *speaks*, and both are natural and unaffected. If his delivery is the product of art, it is certainly the perfection of it, for it is entirely concealed. He has a great mastery of words, but studies much plainness of speech.

"His doctrine is right *sterling*. I mean, perfectly agreeable to the Articles of the church of England, to which he frequently appeals for the truth of it. He loudly proclaims all men by nature to be under sin, and obnoxious to the wrath and curse of God. He maintains the absolute necessity of supernatural grace to bring men out of this state. He asserts the righteousness of Christ to be the only cause of the justification of the sinner; that this is received by faith; that this faith is the gift of God; that where faith is wrought, it brings the sinner under the deepest sense of his guilt and unworthiness to the footstool of sovereign grace, to accept of mercy as the free gift of God, only for Christ's sake. He denies that good works have any share in our justification: that indeed they do justify our faith, and necessarily flow from it, as streams from the fountain; but Christ's external righteousness imputed to us, and his inherent righteousness wrought in us, is the only cause of man's salvation. He asserts the absolute necessity of the new birth, where a principle of new life is ingenerated in the heart of man, and an entire change is produced in the temper and disposition of the soul; and that this new production is the work only of God's blessed Spirit. That wherever this change is wrought, it is permanent and abiding, and that the gates of hell shall never prevail against it. He asserts that the special influence and indwelling of the Spirit, was not peculiar to the first Christians, but that it is the common privilege of believers in all ages of the church; that the Holy Spirit is the author of the sanctification and comfort of all God's people; and that, even in these days, if any man have not the spirit of Christ, he is none of his. He said, that to many of his hearers, he feared he spoke in an unknown tongue; that he preached great mysteries; that true Christians knew what he meant, and that all his hearers, if they are saved, must be brought to understand them. These are some of the doctrines which have been attended with such mighty power in this city. This is the doctrine of the martyrs. This they sealed with their blood; notwithstanding that so many in our days have departed from it.

"Mr. Whitefield speaks much of the language of the New Testament; and has an admirable faculty in explaining the Scriptures. He strikes out of them such lights, and unveils those excellencies which surprise his hearers, when he expounds them. He expresses the highest love and concern for the souls of men; and speaks of Christ with the most affectionate appropriation—'*My*

Master! My Lord!' He is no enemy to the innocent freedoms and liberties of the gospel; nor does he affect singularity in indifferent things. He spends not his zeal in trifles, but says, 'The kingdom of God consists not in meats and drinks; but in righteousness, and peace, and joy in the Holy Ghost.' He breathes a most catholic spirit, and prays most earnestly that God would destroy all that bigotry and party zeal which has divided Christians. He supposes some of Christ's flock are to be found under every denomination, and upbraids the uncharitableness of those who confine the church to their own communion. He professes a most sincere love to all those who love our Lord Jesus Christ in sincerity, and declares that he has no design to make a party in religion. He professes that his whole design in preaching the gospel is to bring men to Christ, to deliver them from their false confidences, to raise them from their dead formalities, and to revive primitive Christianity among them; and if he can obtain this end, he will leave them to their liberty, and they may go to what church, and worship God in what form they like best."

While going from Philadelphia to New York, or on his return, Whitefield appears to have preached at Maidenhead, Abington, Neshaminy, Freehold, Burlington, Elizabethtown, and New Brunswick, to many thousands, gathered from various parts, among whom there had been a considerable awakening under the ministry of Mr. Frelinghuysen, a Reformed Dutch minister, and the Rev. Messrs. Tennent, Blair, and Rowland. It was no less pleasing to him than strange to see such congregations in a foreign land; ministers and people shedding tears, sinners struck with awe, and religious persons who had been much persecuted, filled with joy. The old *Tennent church* at Freehold, where preached Whitefield, Brainerd, Davies, and other "famous men" of that day, still echoes with the same gospel. In size the building is forty feet by sixty, with three entrances on the larger side. The pulpit is on the north side of the house, immediately opposite the central door, so that the minister faces the width of the church instead of its length. The pulpit is very narrow, and is surmounted with a sounding-board, according to the custom of our fathers. In the middle aisle lie buried the remains of the sainted William Tennent, whose death took place about seven years after that of Whitefield, at the age of seventy-two years. A handsome monumental tablet records the leading dates of his pilgrimage.

Some of our readers may inquire as to the localities honored by Whitefield's preaching in and about the city of New York. We find many records of his discoursing in the open fields of the surrounding country; the old City Exchange, which stood at the foot of Broad-street, near Water-street, and which was built on large arches, was a favorite spot for itinerant preachers, and for Whitefield among the rest. During his various visits to

New York, from 1745 to 1760, he generally preached in the Presbyterian church in Wall-street, which was then the only church of that denomination in the city, and of which the Rev. Dr. Pemberton, from Boston, was the minister. Afterwards, a few years before his death, he was accustomed to preach in the Brick church in Beekman-street; which was then familiarly called the "Brick meeting," and in common parlance, said to be "in the fields;" so little was the city extended at that period. So prosperous was his ministry in New York, that it was found necessary immediately to enlarge the Presbyterian church in Wall-street, by the erection of galleries; and a year or two afterwards it was again enlarged about one-third, in order to accommodate the stated worshippers.

When Whitefield was preaching before a very large number of the seamen of New York, he introduced the following bold apostrophe into his sermon: "Well, my boys, we have a cloudless sky, and are making fine headway over a smooth sea, before a light breeze, and we shall soon lose sight of land. But what means this sudden lowering of the heavens, and that dark cloud arising from beneath the western horizon? Hark! don't you hear the distant thunder? Don't you see those flashes of lightning? There is a storm gathering. Every man to his duty. How the waves rush and dash against the ship! The air is dark. The tempest rages. Our masts are gone! What next?" The unsuspecting tars, reminded of former perils on the deep, as if struck by the power of magic, arose, and with united voices exclaimed, "Take to the longboat, sir!" The reader may well imagine how this very natural answer would be used by the preacher.

While at New York, Whitefield wrote, "God willing, in about seven months I hope to see New England on my return to Europe. An effectual door is there opened, and no wonder there are many adversaries. Shortly I expect to suffer for my dear Master." And after his return to Philadelphia, he showed his piety and meekness by writing to the Rev. Dr. Pemberton, of New York, "I have been much concerned since I saw you, lest I behaved not with that humility towards you which is due from a babe to a father in Christ; but you know, reverend sir, how difficult it is to meet with success, and not be puffed up with it; and therefore, if any such thing was discernible in my conduct, O pity me, and pray to the Lord to heal my pride. All I can say is, that I desire to learn of Jesus Christ to be meek and lowly in heart; but my corruptions are so strong, and my employ so dangerous, that I am sometimes afraid."

One of the most important incidents of this journey to New York, was the meeting of Whitefield with Gilbert Tennent. Two powerful preachers could hardly resemble each other less; and the great strength of each lay in characteristics in which the other was deficient. In one point, especially,

Whitefield felt and recorded his new friend's superiority. He heard Tennent preach. "Never before heard I such a searching sermon. He went to the bottom indeed, and did not 'daub with untempered mortar.' He convinced me, more and more, that we can preach the gospel of Christ no further than we have experienced the power of it in our hearts. I found what a babe and novice I was in the things of God." These men, as Tracy says, having once met, could not but be friends and allies for life; and the effects of their alliance could not fail to be felt by thousands.

Both at Philadelphia and New York, printers applied to Whitefield for copies of his sermons for publication, and two were so issued, in the influence of which their author had cause to rejoice. In an after-period, the celebrated Benjamin Franklin printed Whitefield's "Journal in New England," still extant; a copy of which was sold at auction in Philadelphia in 1855, for about thirty times its original price. His journals, indeed, and his sermons became considerable articles in commerce, and did not a little, amid the comparatively sparse population of the country, to extend both his fame and his usefulness.

But the time was now come when it became important that Whitefield should pursue his course towards Savannah. He could not, however, regret his stay so long on the road. "It is unknown," he says, "what deep impressions have been made on the hearts of hundreds. Many poor sinners have, I trust, been called home, and great numbers are under strong convictions. An opposer told me I had unhinged many *good sort of people*. I believe it."

Nor was this the only good he had done. No small sympathy had been excited among Christian people in favor of his orphan family, and a spirit of liberality and of prayer was extensively cherished. "They sent me," says the grateful evangelist, "butter, sugar, chocolate, pickles, cheese, and flour, for my orphans; and indeed, I could almost say, they would pluck out their own eyes and give me. O that what God says of the church of Philadelphia may now be fulfilled in the city called after her name—'I know thy works.'"

The ready liberality which everywhere met Whitefield, determined him to pursue his journey by land. He therefore procured a vessel, in which he sent on his family and their supplies to Savannah. Of this sloop, Captain Gladman was master; and a young man who had recently been converted by the preaching of the great evangelist, willingly offered himself as mate. We have already seen that he was accompanied southward as far as Chester by a very large company of gentlemen of Philadelphia; and on his arrival at that place, a court was about to open, but the judges sent him word that they would not commence their business until the sermon, which they expected from him, was over. Nearly a thousand people had travelled from Philadelphia to hear it, and it was thought that those collected from places many miles around, composed an assembly of not less than seven thousand persons. A platform was erected, and it was believed that many of his hearers obtained something infinitely better than the mere gratification of their curiosity.

Among other places at which he preached on this journey, was White Clay creek, endeared to him not only as the place where he first met with his beloved friend William Tennent, but as the residence of a Welsh family who had heard him preach at Cardiff and Kingswood before they emigrated, and who bore, what was to him a fact of endearing interest, the name of *Howell*. But during this tour Whitefield had to endure considerable privations and peril in riding through the woods. On one occasion, he heard the wolves "howling like a kennel of hounds" near to the road; on another, he had a narrow escape in trying to cross the Potomac in a storm. Here also he had once to swim his horse, owing to the floods; for it was now the depth of winter. One night, Seward and he lost their way in the woods of South Carolina, and were much alarmed at seeing groups of negroes dancing around large fires. Notwithstanding all the hardships, however, of the journey, no real injury was sustained from it.

Our evangelist at length arrived at Charleston in good health and spirits. But he could not obtain admittance to St. Philip's church; Garden, the commissary, who had once promised to "defend him with life and fortune," was absent, and the curate would not open the doors without his leave. The people, however, had not forgotten him, and the Rev. Josiah Smith, the congregational minister, and the pastor of the French church, at once threw open their houses and pulpits, and rich indeed were the blessings they enjoyed.

The congregations during his present visit to Charleston were large and polite; but he says they presented "an affected finery and gayety of dress and deportment, which I question if the court-end of London could exceed." Before he left, however, there was what he called "a glorious alteration in the audience." Many of them wept; and the hitherto light and airy had visibly strong feelings, as shown in their countenances. Such was their extreme anxiety to hear more from him, that after he had gone to the shore to sail for Georgia, they prevailed on him to preach again.

On the next morning, Whitefield and his companions left Charleston in a canoe for Savannah; and on their way lay on the ground in the woods, surrounded by large fires to keep off the wild beasts. On this fact he makes the reflection, "An emblem, I thought, of the divine love and presence keeping off evils and corruptions from the soul." On his arrival at Savannah, January 11, 1740, he was very happy to meet his family, who had arrived there three weeks before him; and to find, by letters from England, New York, etc., that the work of the Lord prospered. One thing, however, greatly distressed him. The colony of Georgia was reduced even to a much lower state than when he left it, and was deserted by nearly all who could get away. He thought that to employ those who were left, would render them an important service, and that the money thus expended might be the means of keeping them in the colony.

During the absence of Mr. Whitefield from Georgia, Mr. Habersham had fixed on a plot of ground of five hundred acres, about ten miles from Savannah, on which the orphan-house should stand, and had already commenced to clear and stock it. The orphans, in the mean time, were accommodated in a hired house. Whitefield afterwards regretted the course pursued. He found the condition of the orphans so pitiable, and the inhabitants so poor, that he immediately opened an infirmary, hired a large house at a great rent, and took in, at different times, twenty-four orphans.

In the March following, Whitefield was again at Charleston, where he went to meet his brother, the captain of a ship, from England. Here he was requested by many of the inhabitants to give some account of his poor orphans, which he did in the house of worship occupied by his friend the Rev. Josiah Smith, the first native of South Carolina who received a literary degree. Such was the spirit excited, that the collection amounted to seventy pounds sterling. This was no small encouragement, especially as he had reason to believe that most of it came from those who had received spiritual benefit from his ministry.

But if Whitefield now had his joys in Charleston, so he had also his sorrows. We have seen that in a previous visit to this city, he had considered himself "set for the defence of the gospel." He had remarked, in reference to the twelfth article of the church of England, "Observe, my dear brethren, the words of the article, 'Good works are the fruit of faith, and follow after justification.' How can they then precede, or be in any way the cause of it? No, our persons must be justified, before our performances can be accepted." Commissary Garden, of whom we have already spoken, now seized the opportunity of Whitefield's visit to Charleston, to write him a letter, dated March 17, attacking his doctrine of justification, and challenging him to defend what he had said concerning the bishop of London and his clergy. In this letter, he urged in reply to what the evangelist had said, "If good works do necessarily spring out of a true and lively faith, and a true and lively faith necessarily precedes justification, the consequence is plain, that good works must not only follow after, but precede justification also." Whitefield replied the next day, "I perceive that you are angry overmuch. Was I never so much inclined to dispute, I would stay till the cool of the day. Your letter more and more confirms me, that my charge against the clergy is just and reasonable. It would be endless to enter into such a private debate as you, reverend sir, seem desirous of. You have read my sermon: be pleased to read it again; and if there be any thing contrary to sound doctrine, or the Articles of the church of England, be pleased to let the public know it from the press; and then let the world judge whether you or my brethren the clergy have been rashly slandered." This was but the commencement of a controversy, in which were concerned Garden of Charleston, and the Rev. Messrs. Croswell and Gee of Boston, portions of which are preserved in the Old South church library, in the latter city; and which was afterwards resumed between Garden and Smith, of Charleston, in the "South Carolina Gazette," as may be seen in the library of the American Antiquarian Society at Worcester, Massachusetts.

In the mean time, Whitefield had returned to Savannah, and on March 25, he laid the first brick of the main building of the orphan-house, which he called *Bethesda*, that is, a house of mercy. It was built of wood, and measured seventy feet by forty. By this time nearly forty children had been received, to be provided for with food and raiment; and counting the workmen with these, he had nearly one hundred persons to feed day by day. To do all this he had very little money in the bank; still he was not discouraged, being persuaded that his present duty was to advance the interests of the colony by carrying on his work. "As yet," says he, "I am kept from the least doubting. The more my family increases, the more enlargement and comfort I feel. Set thy almighty *fiat* to it, O gracious Father, and for thine own name's sake convince us more and more, that thou wilt never forsake those who put their trust in thee." On reviewing this passage fifteen years afterwards, he wrote, "Hitherto, blessed be God, I have not been disappointed of my hope."

We close our present chapter with a very short visit to Charleston. In this city Whitefield had assuredly produced a very extraordinary excitement, and very opposite opinions were entertained in reference to his character and doctrines. On the day after he had laid the first stone of Bethesda, Mr. Smith undertook at Charleston to defend the conduct and character of his beloved friend, in a sermon from Job 32:17: "I said, I will answer also my part; I also will show mine opinion." As this discourse was published during the following June, with a commendatory preface by the Rev. Drs. Colman and Cooper of Boston, and is still highly valued as a piece of contemporary history, we give an extract, particularly as to the *manner* of the preaching of the great evangelist.

"He is certainly a finished preacher. A noble negligence ran through his style. The passion and flame of his expressions will, I trust, be long felt by many. My pen cannot describe his action and gestures, in all their strength and decencies. He appeared to me, in all his discourses, to be very deeply affected and impressed in his own heart. How did that burn and boil within him, when he spake of the things which he had 'made touching the King.' How was his tongue like the pen of a ready writer, touched as with a coal from the altar. With what a flow of words, what a ready profusion of language, did he speak to us upon the great concerns of our souls. In what a flaming light did he set *our* eternity before us. How earnestly he pressed Christ upon us. How did he move our passions with the constraining love of *such* a Redeemer. The awe, the silence, the attention which sat upon the face of the great audience, was an argument how he could reign over all their powers. Many thought he spake as never man spake before him. So charmed were the people with his manner of address, that they shut up their shops, forgot their secular business, and laid aside their schemes for the world; and the oftener he preached, the keener edge he seemed to put upon their desires to hear him again.

"How awfully, with what thunder and sound, did he discharge the artillery of heaven upon us. And yet, how could he soften and melt even a soldier of Ulysses with the mercy of God. How close, strong, and pungent were his applications to the conscience; mingling light and heat; pointing the arrows of the Almighty at the hearts of sinners, while he poured in the balm upon the wounds of the contrite, and made broken bones rejoice. Eternal themes, the tremendous solemnities of our religion, were all *alive* upon his tongue. So, methinks—if you will forgive the figure—St. Paul would *look* and speak in a pulpit. In some such manner, I am tempted to conceive of a seraph, were he sent down to preach among us, and to tell us what things he had seen and heard above.

How bold and courageous did he look. He was no flatterer; he would not suffer men to settle on their lees; and did not prophesy smooth things, nor sew pillows under their arms. He taught the way of God in truth, and regarded not the persons of men. He struck at the politest and most modish of our vices, and at the most fashionable entertainments, regardless of every one's presence, but His in whose name he spoke with this authority. And I dare warrant, if none should go to these diversions until they have answered the solemn questions he put to their consciences, our theatre would soon sink and perish. I freely own he has taken my heart."

CHAPTER V
CONTINUATION OF WHITEFIELD'S SECOND VISIT TO AMERICA. 1740

At the period when Whitefield laid the cornerstone of his Bethesda, his health was much impaired, and his spirits depressed. But it was necessary that funds should be obtained, to meet the claims now daily made upon him. He had received handsome donations from Charleston, New York, and Philadelphia, yet the urgent demand was for more. He therefore embarked from Charleston for Newcastle, Delaware, in a sloop, and arrived there in about ten days. Passing on from thence to Philadelphia, he found the churches closed against him. The commissary told him that he would lend the church to him no more. The laconic answer of Whitefield was, "The fields are open;" and eight thousand people assembled to hear him the same evening, and ten thousand on the following day. On the following Lord's day morning, he collected one hundred and ten pounds sterling for his "poor orphans," and then went to the Episcopal church, where the commissary preached a sermon on justification by works. As Whitefield was recognized at church, it was naturally expected that in the evening he would answer the sermon; nor was the public expectation disappointed. After his sermon, he collected eighty pounds more for Bethesda.

But far higher success than this attended his labors. Societies for worship were commenced in different parts of the town; not a few began seriously to inquire after the way of salvation; many negroes came to the evangelist with the inquiry, "Have I a soul?" and a church was formed, of which the distinguished Gilbert Tennent was the eminently useful pastor. No less than one hundred and forty, who had undergone a previous strict examination as to their personal piety, were received as constituent members of the church, and large additions were from time to time made to their number.

Several events of special interest occurred during this visit to Philadelphia. Tennent had to tell a series of delightful facts as to the usefulness of Whitefield's former labors. He began to deliberate on a plan for a negro school in Pennsylvania, as he did afterwards also in Virginia, but unexpected difficulties intervened, and both in the end were abandoned.

Mr. Jones, the Baptist minister of the city, told Whitefield of the change produced by his former preaching on the minds of two ministers; one of whom stated to his congregation that he had hitherto been deceiving both himself and them, and added, that he could not preach to them at present, but requested them to unite in prayer with him; and the other resigned his charge, to itinerate among the unenlightened villages of New Jersey and elsewhere. Another fact was, that an Indian trader became so impressed with the preaching of Whitefield, that he had given up his business, and was gone to teach the Indians with whom he used to trade. Nor had his usefulness stopped here: he heard of a drinking club, which had attached to it a negro boy remarkable for his powers of mimicry. This boy was directed by the gentlemen who composed the club to exercise his powers on Mr. Whitefield: he did so, but very reluctantly; at length he stood up and said, "I speak the truth in Christ, I lie not; unless you repent, you will all be damned." This unexpected speech had such an effect as to break up the club, which met no more.

We add a few paragraphs from Seward's journal, who soon after sailed for England to promote the interests of Georgia, and who died in the parent country. They date from the 24th to the 26th of April. "Came to Christopher Wigner's plantation in Skippack, where many Dutch people are settled, and where the famous Mr. Spalemburg lately resided. It was surprising to see such a multitude of people gathered together in such a wilderness country, thirty miles distant from Philadelphia. Mr. Whitefield was exceedingly carried out, in his sermon, to press poor sinners to come to Christ by faith, and claim all their privileges; namely, not only righteousness and peace, but joy in the Holy Ghost; and after he had done, our dear friend Peter Bohler preached in Dutch, to those who could not understand Mr. Whitefield in English."

"Before Mr. Whitefield left Philadelphia, he was desired to visit one who was under a deep sense of sin, from hearing him preach. In praying with this person, he was so carried beyond himself, that the whole company, about twenty, seemed to be filled with the Holy Ghost, and magnified the God of heaven."

"Arose at three o'clock, and though Mr. Whitefield was very weak in body, yet the Lord enabled him to ride nearly fifty miles, and to preach to about five thousand people at Amwell, with the same power as usual. Mr. Gilbert Tennent, Mr. Rowland, Mr. Wales, and Mr. Campbell, four godly ministers, met us here."

"Came to New Brunswick. Met Mr. Noble from New York, a zealous promoter of our Lord's kingdom. He said their society at New York was enlarged from seventy to one hundred and seventy, and was daily increasing; and that Messrs. Gilbert and William Tennent, Mr. Rowland, and several others, were hard laborers in our Lord's vineyard."

It will be readily supposed that by this time Whitefield and his movements had become so much a matter of interest as to be frequently discussed in the newspapers of the day.

The "New England Weekly Journal" of April 29, 1740, copies from a Philadelphia paper of April 17: "The middle of last month the Rev. Mr. Whitefield was at Charleston, and preached five times, and collected at one time upwards of £70 sterling for the benefit of the orphan-house in Georgia; and on Sunday last, after ten days' passage from Georgia, he landed at Newcastle, where he preached morning and evening. On Monday morning he preached to about three thousand at Wilmington, and in the evening arrived in this city. On Tuesday evening he preached to about eight thousand on Society hill, and preached at the same place yesterday morning and evening." Then follows a list of his appointments daily to April 29, during which time he was to preach at Whitemarsh, Germantown, Philadelphia, Salem, N. J., Neshaminy, Skippack, Frederick township, Amwell, New Brunswick, Elizabethtown, and New York. On May 6th, the Journal copied a Philadelphia notice of April 24th, that he had preached on the previous Sabbath to fifteen thousand hearers, and on Monday at Greenwich and Gloucester, and that he would return to Georgia before visiting New England.

The Journal of May 20th, contains a letter from Whitefield to a friend in England, dated New Brunswick, N. J., April 27. Of his visit to Charleston he says, "A glorious work was begun in the hearts of the inhabitants, and many were brought to cry out, 'What shall we do to be saved?' A fortnight ago, after a short passage of ten days, I landed in Pennsylvania, and have had the pleasure of seeing and hearing that my poor endeavors for promoting Christ's kingdom, when here last, were not altogether in vain in the Lord. I cannot tell you how many have come to me laboring under the deepest convictions, and seemingly truly desirous of finding rest in Jesus Christ. Several have actually received him into their hearts by faith, and have not only righteousness and peace, but joy in the Holy Ghost. In short, the word has run and been much glorified, and many negroes also are in a fair way of being brought home to God. Young ones I intend to buy, and do not despair of seeing a room full of that despised generation, in a short time, singing and making melody with grace in their hearts to the Lord.

"An effectual door is opened for preaching the everlasting gospel, and I daily receive fresh and most importunate invitations to preach in all the counties round about. God is pleased to give a great blessing to my printed sermons. They are in the hands of thousands in these parts, and are a means of enlightening and building up many in their most holy faith. The clergy, I find, are most offended at me. The commissary of Philadelphia, having gotten a little stronger than when I was here last, has thrown off the mask, denied me the pulpit, and last Sunday preached up an historical faith, and justification by works. But the people only flock the more. The power of God is more visible than ever in our assemblies, and more and more are convinced that I preach the doctrine of Jesus Christ. Some of the bigoted, self-righteous Quakers now also begin to spit out a little of the venom of the serpent. They cannot bear the doctrine of original sin, and of an imputed righteousness as the cause of our acceptance with God. I have not yet met with much opposition from the dissenters; but when I come to tell many of them, ministers as well as people, that they hold the truth in unrighteousness, that they talk and preach of justifying faith, but never felt it in their hearts, as I am persuaded numbers of them have not, then they no doubt will shoot out their arrows, even bitter words."

While on his voyage from Charleston to Newcastle, Whitefield seems to have devoted the 4th of April, 1740, to correspondence on the subject of marriage. "I find," said he, "by experience, that a mistress is absolutely necessary for the due management of my increasing family, and to take off some of that care which at present lies upon me." His letters were addressed to a young lady and her parents, connected with a family much devoted to piety. Here, as everywhere else, his heart is transparent. He says to the parents of Miss E——, "I write only because I believe it is the will of God that I should alter my state; but your denial will fully convince me that your daughter is not the person appointed for me. He knows my heart; I would not marry but for him, and in him, for ten thousand worlds."

The next year, having returned to England, Whitefield, like his eminent friend John Wesley, was married, and, like him also, was unhappy in his domestic relation. In each case, the husband exacted a previous pledge that the wife should never prevent the delivery of a single sermon; and this was followed by separation from the wife for weeks, months, or even years, in the prosecution of their arduous labors. In the case of Whitefield, his marriage in Wales, with a widow lady, in 1741, was followed by the birth of a son; previous to which event he had said, in the joy of his heart, that his name should be John, and that he should be a preacher of the everlasting gospel. The first prediction was realized, and when his child was a week old, the good man told his people in the Tabernacle, London, that he would live to preach, and "be great in the sight of the Lord." But alas, at the end of four months John died, and his father very wisely wrote in his journal: "I hope what happened before his birth, and since at his death, has taught me such lessons as, if duly improved, may render his mistaken parent more sober-minded, more experienced in Satan's devices, and consequently more useful in his future labors in the church of God."

On the death of his wife somewhat suddenly, August 9, 1768, Mr. Whitefield himself preached her funeral sermon, from Romans 8:28: "And we know that all things work together for good to them that love God, to them that are the called according to his purpose." In describing her character, he particularly mentioned her fortitude and courage, and suddenly exclaimed, "Do you remember my preaching in those fields by the stump of the old tree? The multitude was great, and many were disposed to be riotous. At first I addressed them with firmness; but when a gang of desperate banditti drew near, with the most ferocious looks, and horrid imprecations and menaces, my courage began to fail. My wife was then standing behind me, as I stood on the table. I think I hear her now. She pulled my gown"—himself suiting the action to the word, by placing his hand behind him and touching his robe—"and looking up, said, 'George, play the man for your God.' My confidence returned. I again spoke to the multitude with boldness and affection; they became still; and many were deeply affected."

Before we leave Philadelphia, we may relate an instance or two as to the power of his eloquence. Dr. Franklin says, "He had a loud and clear voice, and articulated his words so perfectly that he might be heard and understood to a great distance; especially as his auditors observed the most profound silence. He preached one evening from the top of the court-house steps, which are in the middle of Market-street, and on the west side of Second-street, which crosses it at right angles. Both streets were filled with his hearers to a considerable distance. Being among the hindmost in Market-street, I had the curiosity to learn how far he might be heard by setting backwards down the street towards the river; and I found his voice distinct till I came near Front-street, where some noise in that street obstructed it. Imagine, then, a semicircle of which my distance should be a radius, and that it was filled with auditors, to each of whom I allowed two square feet, I computed that he might well be heard by more than thirty thousand people."

But not only does Franklin bear witness of Whitefield's eloquence as to his voice, but still more strongly as to its *persuasiveness,* of which, it seems, he was himself a striking illustration. He says, "I refused to contribute to his orphan-house in Georgia, thinking it injudiciously located. Soon after, I happened to attend one of his sermons, in the course of which I perceived he intended to finish with a collection, and I silently resolved he should get nothing from me. I had in my pocket a handful of copper money, three or four silver dollars, and five pistoles in gold. As he proceeded, I began to soften, and determined to give the copper. Another stroke of his oratory made me ashamed of that, and determined me to give the silver; and he finished so admirably, that I emptied my pocket wholly into the collector's dish, gold and all. At this sermon there was also one of our club; who being of my sentiments respecting the building at Georgia, and suspecting a collection might be intended, had, by precaution, emptied his pockets before he came from home. Towards the conclusion of the discourse, however, he felt a strong inclination to give, and applied to a neighbor, who stood near him, to lend him some money for the purpose. The request was made to, perhaps, the only man in the company who had the firmness not to be affected by the preacher. His answer was, 'At any other time, friend Hodgkinson, I would lend to thee freely; but not now, for thee seems to be out of thy right senses.'"

Whitefield, much as he loved Philadelphia, had now again to leave it. Thus writes the correspondent of the "New England Weekly Journal," at Newcastle, May 15: "This evening Mr. Whitefield went on board his sloop here, to sail for Georgia. On Sunday he preached twice In Philadelphia, and in the evening, when he preached his farewell sermon, it is supposed he had twenty thousand hearers. On Monday he preached at Darby and Chester; on Tuesday, at Wilmington and White Clay creek; on Wednesday, twice at Nottingham; on Thursday, at Fog's Manor and Newcastle. The congregations were much increased since his being here last. The presence of God was much seen in the assemblies, especially at Nottingham and Fog's Manor, where the people were under such deep soul distress, that their cries almost drowned his voice. He has collected in this and the neighboring provinces, about £450 sterling for his orphans in Georgia."

He arrived at Savannah June 5, and most interesting was the manner of his reception. He says, "O what a sweet meeting I had with my dear friends! What God has prepared for me, I know not; but surely I cannot well expect a greater happiness, till I embrace the saints in glory. When I parted, my heart was ready to break with sorrow; but now it almost bursts with joy. O how did each in turn hang upon my neck, kiss, and weep over me with tears of joy! And my own soul was so full of a sense of God's love when I embraced one friend in particular, that I thought I should have expired in the place. I felt my soul so full of a sense of the divine goodness, that I wanted words to express myself. Why me, Lord; why me? When we came to public worship, young and old were all dissolved in tears. After service, several of my parishioners, all my family, and the little children, returned home, crying along the streets, and some could not avoid praying very loud.

"Being very weak in body, I laid myself upon a bed; but finding so many weeping, I rose and betook myself to prayer again. But had I not lifted up my voice very high, the groans and cries of the children would have prevented my being heard. This continued for near an hour; till at last, finding their concern rather increase than abate, I desired all to retire. Then some or other might be heard praying earnestly, in every corner of the house. It happened at this time to thunder and lighten, which added very much to the solemnity of the night. Next day the concern still continued, especially among the girls. I mention the orphans in particular, that their benefactors may rejoice in what God is doing for their souls."

On the 7th of June, he wrote, "I have brought with me a Latin master, and on Monday laid the foundation, in the name of the Lord Jesus, for a university in Georgia." On the 28th of the same month, he wrote to a Mr. W. D— —, in a style admirably corresponding with the meek spirit we have already seen in his letter to the Rev. Dr. Pemberton, of New York. "I thank you for your kind letters and friendly cautions; and I trust I shall always reckon those my choicest friends, who, in simplicity and meekness, tell me the corruptions of my heart. It is that faithfulness which has endeared J. S— — to me. I think I never was obliged to any one so much before. O my dear brother, still continue faithful to my soul; do not hate me in your heart; in any wise reprove me. Exhort all my brethren to forgive my past, I fear, too imperious carriage; and let them pray that I may know myself to be, what I really am, less than the least of them all."

Whitefield's family at Bethesda had now increased to not less than one hundred and fifty persons, and to advance their interests, it was needful that he should again visit Charleston, where he arrived on the third of July, and immediately commenced preaching, as on former visits. On the following Sabbath, three days after his arrival, he attended the Episcopal church, where, he says, "I heard the commissary preach as virulent and unorthodox, inconsistent a discourse, as ever I heard in my life. His heart seemed full of choler and resentment. Out of the abundance thereof, he poured forth so many bitter words against the Methodists, as he called them, in general, and me in particular, that several who intended to receive the sacrament at his hands, withdrew. Never, I believe, was such a preparation sermon preached before. After sermon, he sent his clerk to desire me not to come to the sacrament till he had spoken with me. I immediately retired to my lodgings, rejoicing that I was accounted worthy to suffer this further degree of contempt for my dear Lord's sake."

The next day, the commissary of the bishop of London issued against Whitefield the following ecclesiastical writ:

"Alexander Garden, lawfully constituted Commissary of the Right Reverend Father in Christ, Edmund, by divine permission Lord Bishop of London, supported by the royal authority underwritten:

"Alexander Garden, To all and singular clerks, and literate persons whomsoever, in and throughout the whole province of South Carolina, wheresoever appointed, Greeting:

"To you, conjunctly and severally, we commit, and strictly enjoining, command, that you do cite, or cause to be cited, peremptorily, George Whitefield, clerk, and presbyter of the Church of England, that he lawfully appear before us, in the parish church of St. Philip, Charleston, and in the judicial place of the same, on Tuesday, the fifteenth day of this instant July, 'twixt the hours of nine and ten in the forenoon, then and there in justice to answer to certain articles, heads, or interrogatories, which will be objected and ministered unto him concerning the mere health of his soul, and the reformation and correction of his manners and excesses, and chiefly for omitting to use the form of prayers prescribed in the Communion-Book; and further to do and receive what shall be just in that behalf, on pain of law and contempt. And what you shall do in the premises, you shall duly certify us, together with these presents.

"Given under our hands and seals of our office, at Charleston, this seventh day of July, in the year of our Lord one thousand seven hundred and forty."

Justice to all parties requires it should be said, that the phrase as to the health of Whitefield's *soul* was used by Garden not of choice, but in conformity with the forms of English ecclesiastical law; the theory of which is, that ecclesiastical courts are only held to promote the spiritual health or welfare of those who are cited into them. The principal sin of Whitefield was "omitting to use the form of prayer prescribed in the Common Prayer Book." The undisputed matter of fact, as Tracy says, was, that he always used that form when he could obtain an Episcopal church to preach in; but when he was shut out of such pulpits, and was preaching to Baptists, Presbyterians, and Congregationalists, in their own houses of worship, where none of the congregations had prayer books, or knew how to use them, and where the introduction of unaccustomed forms would not have promoted the devotion of the worshippers, he prayed extempore.

On the day this writ was issued, Whitefield preached for Mr. Chanler, "a gracious Baptist minister, about fourteen miles from Charleston;" and twice on the next day "to a large audience in Mr. Osgood's meeting-house, a young Independent minister," at Dorchester; the next day at Dorchester again, and at Charleston in the evening; the next day preached and read prayers in Christ's church, and twice at Charleston the next day, with great success. And now, on July 11th, a citation was served upon him to appear on the fifteenth, as required in the writ.

On the 12th, he preached and read prayers twice on John's island; and on the 13th, which was the Sabbath, he again listened to a sermon from the commissary. Of this sermon Whitefield says, "Had some infernal spirit been sent to draw my picture, I think it scarcely possible that he could paint me in more horrid colors. I think, if ever, then was the time that all manner of evil was spoken against me falsely for Christ's sake. The commissary seemed to ransack church history for instances of enthusiasm and abused grace. He drew a parallel between me and all the Oliverians, Ranters, Quakers, French prophets, till he came down to a family of Dutartes, who lived not many years ago in South Carolina, and were guilty of the most notorious incests and murders."

The next day Whitefield again preached twice; and on Tuesday appeared before the commissary, according to his citation. This is said to have been the first court of the kind ever attempted to be held in any of the colonies. It consisted of the reverend commissary A. Garden, and the Rev. Messrs. Guy, Mellichamp, Roe, and Orr, who, as well as Whitefield himself, and his able advocate, Mr. Andrew Rutledge, respectively showed their want of familiarity with such business, and, after a series of blunders on both sides, the court adjourned to nine o'clock the next morning, to afford Whitefield time to ascertain the extent of the jurisdiction of the bishop and his commissary. How little, however, he studied the subject may be inferred from the fact, that he preached twice during the remainder of the day. The next day, a Mr. Graham appeared as a prosecuting attorney, and Mr. Rutledge as counsel for the respondent. Whitefield made some mistakes, but hints from his quick-sighted advocate and his own adroitness saved him from their consequences; though he contrived to give the court a lecture on the meanness of catching at a word as soon as it was out of his lips, without allowing him time to correct it. He now filed his objection against being judged by the commissary, who, he alleged, was prejudiced against him. This gave rise to new questions: the court adjourned; and the evangelist went to James' island, read prayers, and preached. The next day he again appeared in court, and found that his exceptions were repelled, and that the arbitrators he had asked for would not be appointed. He now appealed to the high Court of Chancery in London, declaring all further proceedings in this court to be null and void. He then retired and read letters which refreshed his spirit, by informing him how "mightily grew the word of God and prevailed" at Philadelphia; and that Mr. Bolton, in Georgia, had nearly fifty negroes learning to read. On the 18th he preached twice, and on the 19th again appeared before the commissary, and bound himself, in a penalty of ten pounds, to prosecute his appeal in London within twelve months. The appeal was never tried, as the ecclesiastical authorities allowed it to die of neglect.

"The court being ended," says Whitefield, in his journal, "the commissary desired to speak with me. I asked him to my lodgings. He chose to walk on a green near the church. His spirit was somewhat calmer than usual; but after an hour's conversation, we were as far from agreeing as before." "All his discourse was so inconsistent and contrary to the gospel of our Lord, that I was obliged to tell him that I believed him to be an unconverted man, an enemy to God, and of a like spirit with the persecutor Saul. At this he smiled; and, after we had talked a long while, we parted, and God gave me great satisfaction that I had delivered my soul in my private conversation with the commissary."

The next day, July 20, was the Sabbath. The commissary preached in his usual style, and Whitefield preached his farewell sermon to the people of Charleston. By his recommendation two or three of the dissenting ministers had instituted a weekly lecture; and the evangelist "advised the people, as the gospel was not preached in church, to go and hear it in the meeting-house." On leaving the city, he summed up, in his journal, the results of his labors in this manner:

"What makes the change more remarkable in the Charleston people is, that they seemed to me, at my first coming, to be a people wholly devoted to pleasure. One well acquainted with their manners and circumstances, told me more had been spent on polite entertainments, than the poor's-rate came to; but now the jewellers and dancing-masters begin to cry out that their craft is in danger. A vast alteration is discernible in the ladies' dresses. And some, while I have been speaking, have been so convinced of the sin of wearing jewels, that I have seen them with blushes put their hands to their ears, and cover them with their fans. But I hope the reformation has gone farther than externals. Many moral, good sort of men, who before were settled on their lees, have been gloriously awakened to seek after Jesus Christ; and many a Lydia's heart hath been opened to receive the things that were spoken. Indeed, the word came like a hammer and a fire. And a door, I believe, will be opened for teaching the poor negroes. Several of them have done their usual work in less time, that they might come to hear me. Many of their owners, who have been awakened, resolved to teach them Christianity. Had I time, and proper schoolmasters, I might immediately erect a negro school in South Carolina, as well as in Pennsylvania. Many would willingly contribute both money and land."

The Baptist church in Charleston at this time was nearly extinct, being reduced to five or six communicants, but Whitefield's success greatly increased their number, and it thus gained strength which it has never lost. It is also gratefully mentioned even now by the church of that denomination at Eutaw, that Whitefield during this visit to South Carolina preached the dedication-sermon of their house of worship.

Whitefield left Charleston on July 21, visiting and preaching on his way homeward, which he reached towards the close of the same week. He preached on the Sabbath in extreme weakness of body, but "with the Holy Ghost from above," and several were hopefully converted to God. On the 18th of August, he again left Savannah for Charleston, where he was able, for want of bodily strength, to preach but once a day, but he thought that his sermons were attended with more power and success than ever before. In a few days after, having preached a farewell sermon to four thousand hearers, he sailed for New England, where he had been very cordially invited by leading ministers and others in Boston and many other places.

CHAPTER VI
WHITEFIELD'S FIRST VISIT TO NEW ENGLAND. SEPTEMBER TO NOVEMBER, 1740

The religious state of New England in the early part of the eighteenth century, was little better than the description we have already given of the state of Great Britain and its other dependencies at that period. Dr. Prince tells us, that the first age of New England was one of an almost continual revival. Preaching was attended with so much power in some places, "that it was a common inquiry, by such members of a family as were detained at home on a Sabbath, whether any had been visibly awakened in the house of God that day." And he adds, "Few Sabbaths did pass without some being evidently converted, and some convincing proof of the power of God accompanying his word."

Dr. Increase Mather, writing towards the close of the seventeenth century, while he confirms the statements we have already given, bears farther testimony which is of a very painful character. He says, "Prayer is necessary on this account, that conversions have become rare in this age of the world. They that have their thoughts exercised in discerning things of this nature, have sad apprehensions that the work of conversion has come to a stand. During the last age scarcely a sermon was preached without some being apparently converted, and sometimes hundreds were converted by one sermon. Who of us now can say that we have seen any thing such as this? Clear, sound conversions are not frequent in our congregations; the great bulk of the present generation are apparently poor, perishing, and if the Lord prevent not, undone; many are profane, drunkards, lascivious, scoffers at the power of godliness, and disobedient; others are civil and outwardly conformed to good order, because so educated, but without knowing aught of a real change of heart." The same estimable writer says, in 1721, "I am now in my eighty-third year, and having had an opportunity of conversing with the first planters of this country, and having been for *sixty-five* years a preacher of the gospel, I feel as did the ancient men who had seen the former temple, and who wept aloud as they saw the latter. The children of New England are, or once were, for the most part, the children of godly parents. What did our fathers come into this wilderness for? Not to gain estates as men do now, but for religion, and that they might have their children in a hopeful way of being truly religious. There was a famous man who preached before one of the greatest assemblies that ever was addressed; it was about seventy years ago; and he said to them, 'I lived in a country seven years, and all that time I never heard a profane oath, or saw a man drunk.' And where was that country? It was New England. Ah, degenerate New England! What art thou come to at this day? How are those sins become common that were once not even heard of!"

Passing over, for the present, indications of a revival of religion, which had appeared in other parts of the country, we speak now only of New England. In 1734, a very extraordinary work of grace appeared at Northampton, Massachusetts, under the ministry of the distinguished Jonathan Edwards, the elder, the history of which is given in his admirable "Narrative of the surprising Work of God" at that period, in Northampton and the vicinity.

It is important to remark here, that the preaching which led to such delightful results was of the most faithful and pungent character. We will give one instance, as illustrative of many, as will be distinctly seen by those who have read Edwards' sermon, "*Sinners in the hands of an angry God,*" or his "*Justice of God in the damnation of Sinners.*" Perhaps, however, no sermon in New England has ever acquired greater celebrity, or accomplished more good, than the one preached by President Edwards at Enfield, July 8, 1741, from the words, "Their feet shall slide in due time." Deut. 32:35. "When they went into the meeting-house, the appearance of the assembly was thoughtless and vain; the people scarcely conducted themselves with common decency." But as the sermon proceeded, the audience became so overwhelmed with distress and weeping, that the preacher was "obliged to speak to the people and desire silence, that he might be heard." The excitement soon became intense; and it is said that a minister who sat in the pulpit with Mr. Edwards, in the agitation of his feelings, caught the preacher by the skirt of his dress, and said, "Mr. Edwards, Mr. Edwards, is not God a God of mercy?" Many of the hearers were seen unconsciously holding themselves up against the pillars, and the sides of the pews, as though they already felt themselves sliding into the pit. This fact has often been mentioned as a proof of the strong and scriptural character of President Edwards' peculiar eloquence—the eloquence of truth as attended by influence from heaven; for his sermons were read, without gestures.

But there was another element which must be taken into account when we look at the result of this sermon, as well as others delivered in like circumstances, and one which we fear has been often overlooked. "While the people of the neighboring towns were in great distress about their souls, the inhabitants of Enfield were very secure, loose, and vain. A lecture had been appointed there, and the neighboring people were so affected at the thoughtlessness of the inhabitants, and had so much fear that God would, in his righteous judgment, pass them by, that many of them were prostrate before him a considerable part of the previous evening, supplicating the mercy of heaven in their behalf. And when the time appointed for the lecture came, a number of the surrounding ministers were present, as well as some from a distance"—a proof of the prayerful interest felt on behalf of the town. In all this we see much of the secret of the powerful impression produced by that sermon, and are taught that in seasons when God seems about to pour out his Spirit on a community, Christians should be found "continuing instant in prayer."

In this more hopeful state of things than had long before existed in New England, Whitefield, who was now the second time in America, was most urgently entreated to visit the descendants of the Pilgrim fathers. He complied with the request, and arrived at Newport on the evening of the Sabbath, September 14, 1740. We furnish an account, written chiefly by himself, in his journal, published in London, 1741, a copy of which may be found in the library of Harvard University, to which we have had a kind access, and which is rich in what we may term *Whitefieldian lore*. He writes,

"Was sick part of the passage, but found afterwards the sea-air, under God, much improved my health. Arrived at Newport, in Rhode Island, just after the beginning of evening service. We came purposely thither first with our sloop. I think it the most pleasant entrance I ever yet saw. Almost all the morning the wind was contrary; but I found a very strong inclination to pray that we might arrive time enough to be present at public worship. Once I called the people; but something prevented their coming. At last, finding my impression increase upon me, I desired their attendance immediately. They came. With a strong assurance that we should be heard, we prayed that the Lord would turn the wind, that we might give him thanks in the great congregation; and also that he would send such to us as he would have us to converse with, and who might show us a lodging. Though the wind was ahead when we began, when we had done praying, and came up out of the cabin, it was quite fair.

"With a gentle gale we sailed most pleasantly into the harbor; got into public worship before they had finished the psalms; and sat, as I thought, undiscovered. After service was over, a gentleman asked me whether my name was not Whitefield. I told him 'yes;' he then desired me to go to his house, and he would take care to provide lodgings and necessaries for me and my friends. I went, silently admiring God's goodness in answering my prayer so minutely. Several gentlemen of the town soon came to pay their respects to me, among whom was one Mr. Clap, an aged dissenting minister, but the most venerable man I ever saw. He looked like a good old Puritan, and gave me an idea of what stamp those men were who first settled New England. His countenance was very heavenly; he rejoiced much in spirit at the sight of me, and prayed most affectionately for a blessing on my coming to Rhode Island."

In the evening, in company with Mr. Clap and other friends, Whitefield visited Mr. Honeyman, the minister of the church of England, and requested the use of his pulpit. "At first he seemed a little unwilling, being desirous to know 'what extraordinary call I had to preach on week-days,' which he said was disorderly. I answered, 'St. Paul exhorted Timothy to 'be instant in season and out of season;' that if the orders of the church were rightly complied with, our ministers should read public prayers twice every day, and then it would not be disorderly at such times to give them a sermon. As to an extraordinary call, I claimed none otherwise than upon the apostle's injunction, 'As we have opportunity, let us do good unto all men.' He still held out, and did not give any positive answer; but at last, after he had withdrawn and consulted with the gentlemen, he said, 'If my preaching would promote the glory of God, and the good of souls, I was welcome to his church as often as I would, during my stay in town.' We then agreed to make use of it at ten in the morning, and three in the afternoon. After this, I went to wait on the governor, who seemed to be a very plain man, and had a very plain house, which much pleased me. By profession, I think he is a Seventh-day Baptist; he is a man of good report as to his conduct and dealing with the world." As might have been expected, the evening was spent in exposition and prayer, with a crowded company, in the house of his friend Bowers, the gentleman who first addressed him when coming out of church.

On Monday morning, he breakfasted with "old Mr. Clap, and was much edified by his conversation." Of this venerable servant of Christ he says, "I could not but think, while at his table, that I was sitting with one of the patriarchs. He is full of days, a bachelor, and has been minister of a congregation in Rhode Island upwards of forty years. People of all denominations, I find, respect him. He abounds in good works; gives all away, and is wonderfully tender of little children; many of different persuasions come to be instructed by him. Whenever he dies, I am persuaded, with good old Simeon, he will be enabled to say, 'Lord, now lettest thou thy servant depart in peace.'" Whitefield preached, according to appointment, morning and afternoon, "in the church. It is very commodious, and I believe will contain three thousand people. It was more than filled in the afternoon. Persons of all denominations attended. God assisted me much. I observed numbers affected, and had great reason to believe the word of the Lord had been 'sharper than a twoedged sword,' in some of the hearers' souls."

On the evening of the same day he received the following note:

> Reverend Sir and beloved Brother—Although mine eyes never saw your face before this day, yet my heart and soul have been united to you in love, by the bond of the Spirit. I have longed and expected to see you for many months past. Blessed be God, mine eyes have seen the joyful day. I trust, through grace, I have some things to communicate to you that will make your heart glad. I shall omit writing any thing, and only hereby present my hearty love, and let you know that I am waiting now at the post of your door for admission. Though I am unworthy, my Lord is worthy, in whose name, I trust, I come. I am your unworthy brother,
>
> "JONATHAN BARBER."

"On reading it," says Whitefield, "I could not but think this was one of those young ministers whom God had lately made use of in such a remarkable manner, at the east end of Long Island. I sent for him, and found he was the man. My heart rejoiced. We walked out, and took sweet counsel together; and among other things, he told me that he came to Rhode Island under a full conviction that he should see me there, and had been waiting for me about a week.... What rendered this more remarkable was, I had no intention of sailing to Rhode Island till about three days before I left Carolina; and I had a great desire to put in, if I could, at the east end of Long Island, to see this very person, whom the great God now brought unto me. Lord, accept our thanks, sanctify our meeting, and teach us both what we shall do for thine own name's sake. In the evening I went to the venerable Mr. Clap's, and exhorted and prayed with a great multitude, who not only crowded into the house, but thronged every way about it. The dear old man rejoiced to see the things which he saw; and after my exhortation was over, dismissed me with his blessing."

Tuesday, we scarcely need remark, was spent by Whitefield in the work of his great Master. He preached to a vast congregation, including the members of the House of Assembly, who adjourned to attend the service; and he had very delightful evidence that his labors had already been useful. On Wednesday he left Newport, and about noon preached at Bristol, at the request of the court, which was then in session, and slept that night at a hotel on the road to Boston. On Thursday morning he set out early, and as he passed on with his friends, he says, "Found that the people were apprized of my coming, and were solicitous for my preaching; but being resolved under God, if possible, to reach Boston, we travelled on for near fifty miles, and came to Boston about eight in the evening. When we were within four miles of the city, the governor's son, several other gentlemen, and one or two ministers, waited at a gentleman's house to give me the meeting. They received me with great gladness, and told me many more would have come, had not a large funeral been in the town, or if there had been more certain notice of my arriving. This rejoiced me; for I think I can stand any thing better than this. It savors too much of human grandeur. But I must be tried every way; the Lord be my helper. After stopping a while, we went together to Boston, to the house of one Mr. Sandiford, brother-in-law to the Rev. Dr. Colman, who long since had sent me an invitation.... My heart was but low, and my body weak; but, at the request of one of the ministers, I gave thanks to our gracious God for bringing me in safety, and prayed that my coming might be in the fulness of the blessing of the gospel of peace."

He slept well that night, and the next morning, he says, "I perceived fresh emanations of divine light break in upon and refresh my soul." He was visited by several gentlemen, including Josiah Willard, Esq., the secretary of the province, a man who feared God, and with whom Whitefield had for some time been in correspondence. The governor, Belcher, received him with the utmost respect, and requested frequent visits. He attended public worship at the church of England, and waited on the commissary home, who received him very courteously. As it was a day on which the clergy of that body had a meeting, he came into the company of five of them assembled together. They soon attacked him "for calling *that Tennent* and his brethren faithful ministers of Christ." He answered, that he believed they were so. They questioned the validity of Presbyterian ordination, and quoted from his journal his own words against him. He replied, that perhaps his sentiments were altered. They then went into a doctrinal discussion, which continued till Whitefield, finding how inconsistent they were, took his leave, resolving that they should not have the opportunity of denying him their pulpits. However, they treated him, on the whole, with more courtesy than he had lately been accustomed to receive from the ministers of his own church.

In the afternoon of the same day, he preached to a vast congregation in the Rev. Dr. Colman's meeting-house, in Brattle-street, and in the evening exhorted and prayed with such as came to his lodgings. On Saturday, in the forenoon, he discoursed to a crowded audience at the Old South church, where Dr. Sewall was pastor, the only church edifice in Boston with which Whitefield was connected which is still standing as it then was. In the afternoon he preached on the Common to about eight thousand persons, and, at night to a thronged company at his own lodgings.

On the morning of the next day, which was the Sabbath, he heard Dr. Colman preach; in the afternoon, he preached at Mr. Foxcroft's meeting-house to a vast auditory. This gentleman was the senior pastor of the First church, meeting in Chauncy-place, and the Rev. Charles Chauncy was his colleague. The church edifice was in Cornhill-square, not far from the old state-house, and was usually called the "Old Brick meeting." As this house was by far too small to contain his auditory, he almost immediately afterwards preached on the Common, to about fifteen thousand hearers; and again at night at his lodgings. He says, "Some afterwards came into my room. I felt much of the divine presence in my own soul, and though hoarse was enabled to speak with much power, and could have spoke, I believe, till midnight."

On Monday morning, Whitefield preached at Mr. Webb's meeting-house, the "New North," on the corner of Clark and Hanover streets. "The presence of the Lord," he says, "was among us. Look where I would around me, visible impressions were made upon the auditory. Most wept for a considerable time." In the afternoon he meant to have preached at Mr. Cheekley's, in Summer-street, but was prevented by an accident. Just before the time for the commencement of the service, a person broke a board in one of the galleries, of which to make a seat; the noise alarmed some who heard it, and they imprudently cried out that the galleries were giving way. The house being much crowded, the whole congregation were thrown into the utmost alarm and disorder; some jumped from the gallery into the seats below, others fell from the windows, and those below pressing to get out of the porch, were many of them thrown over each other and trodden upon. Many, as might be expected, were seriously bruised; others had bones broken; and within two days five persons died from the injuries they had received. Mr. Whitefield's presence of mind did not fail him; he immediately led the anxious throng to the Common, and preached to them from the text, "Go ye out into the highways and hedges, and compel them to come in." He says, "The weather was wet, but above eight thousand followed into the fields."

On Tuesday morning, Whitefield visited Mr. Walter, at Roxbury. This gentleman had been the colleague, and was now the successor of John Eliot, "the apostle of the Indians." These two men had been pastors of that church one hundred and six years. Whitefield was much pleased with Walter, who, in return, was glad to hear that he, like old Bishop Beveridge, called man "half a devil and half a beast." He preached that forenoon at Mr. Gee's meeting-house, the "Old North," of which church the celebrated Dr. Cotton Mather had formerly been pastor. The house stood in the North square, and was taken down by the British army and burned for fuel at the siege of Boston, in 1776. The auditory Whitefield preached to that morning was not very crowded, as the people were in doubt where he would preach. After dining with the secretary of the province, he says, "I preached in the afternoon at Dr. Sewall's to a thronged congregation, and exhorted and prayed as usual at my own lodgings; at neither place without some manifestations of a divine power accompanying the word."

Wednesday was not lost. Whitefield himself shall describe its proceedings. "Went this morning to see and preach at Cambridge, the chief college for training up the sons of the prophets in all New England. It has one president, I think four tutors, and about a hundred students. It is scarce as big as one of our least colleges in Oxford, and as far as I could gather from some who well knew the state of it, not far superior to our universities in piety and true godliness. Tutors neglect to pray with, and examine the hearts of their pupils. Discipline is at too low an ebb. Bad books are become fashionable. Tillotson and Clarke are read instead of Sheppard, Stoddard, and such like evangelical writers; and therefore I chose to preach on these words: 'We are not as many, who corrupt the word of God;' and in the conclusion of my sermon I made a close application to tutors and students. A great number of neighboring ministers attended, as indeed they do at all other times, and God gave me great boldness and freedom of speech. The president of the college and minister of the parish treated me very civilly. In the afternoon I preached again in the court, without any particular application to the students. I believe there were about seven thousand hearers. The Holy Spirit melted many hearts. The word was attended with a manifest power; and a minister soon after wrote me word, that 'he believed one of his daughters was savingly wrought upon at that time.' Paid my respects to the lieutenant-governor, who lives at Cambridge, and returned in the evening to Boston, and prayed with and exhorted many people who were waiting round the door for a spiritual morsel. I believe our Lord did not send them empty away."

An elm under which Whitefield preached in Cambridge became distinguished; it being under its shade that Washington, thirty-one years after, first drew his sword in the cause of the Revolution, on taking the command of the American army. From this circumstance, it has been called the "Washington elm." The last time the late distinguished Dr. Holyoke, of Salem, Mass., was in Cambridge, then nearly a hundred years old, while passing this tree with a friend, he said that he heard Whitefield's sermon, being at the time a student in college.

On Thursday he preached the weekly lecture at Mr. Foxcroft's, the First church. But he says, "I was so oppressed with a sense of my base ingratitude to my dearest Saviour, that Satan would fain have tempted me to hold my tongue, and not invite poor sinners to Jesus Christ, because I was so great a sinner myself. But God enabled me to withstand the temptation, and since Jesus Christ had shown such mercy to, and had not withdrawn his Holy Spirit from me, the chief of sinners, I was enabled more feelingly to talk of his love; and afterwards found that one stranger, in particular, was in all probability effectually convinced by that morning's sermon. After public worship, I went, at his excellency's invitation, and dined with the governor. Most of the ministers of the town were invited with me. Before dinner, the governor sent for me up into his chamber. He wept, wished me 'good luck in the name of the Lord,' and recommended himself, ministers, and people to my prayers. Immediately after dinner, I prayed explicitly for them all, and went in his coach to the end of the town; but had such a sense of my vileness upon my soul, that I wondered people did not stone me. Crossed a ferry, and preached at Charlestown, a town lying on the north side of Boston. The meeting-house was very capacious, and quite filled. A gracious melting was discernible through the whole congregation, and I perceived much freedom and sweetness in my own soul, though the damp I felt in the morning was not quite gone off. In the evening I exhorted and prayed as usual at my lodgings; and blessed be God, I found a great alteration in my hearers. They now began to melt and weep under the word."

On Friday, the following day, he preached in the morning at Roxbury, from a little ascent, to many thousands of people, with much of the divine presence. Several came to him afterwards, telling him how they were struck with the word. Having dined with Judge Dudley, he preached to a still larger congregation from a scaffold erected outside Mr. Byles' meeting-house in Hollis-street. Wrote to several friends in England; gave a short exhortation to a large crowd of hearers; and then spent the evening with several ministers in edifying conversation, singing, and prayer.

Saturday, he preached in the morning at Mr. Welsteed's meeting-house, and in the afternoon to about fifteen thousand people on the Common. "But Oh, how did the word run! It rejoiced me to see such numbers greatly affected, so that some, I believe, could scarcely abstain from crying out. That place was no other than a Bethel, and a gate of heaven." After he had gone home to his lodgings he says, "The power and presence of the Lord accompanied and followed me. Many now wept bitterly, and cried out under the word like persons that were really hungering and thirsting after righteousness; and after I left them, God gave me to wrestle with him in my chamber, in behalf of some dear friends then present, and others that were absent from us. The Spirit of the Lord was upon them all. It made intercession with groanings that cannot be uttered."

On the day following, being the Sabbath, in the morning he preached at the Old South church, Dr. Sewall's, to a very crowded auditory, "with almost as much power and visible appearance of God as yesterday. Collected £555 currency for my little lambs; was taken very ill after dinner; vomited violently, but was enabled to preach at Dr. Colman's in the afternoon to as great, if not a greater congregation than in the morning. Here also £470 were collected for the orphan-house in Georgia. In both places all things were carried on with decency and order. People went slowly out, as though they had not a mind to escape giving; and Dr. Colman said 'it was the most pleasant time he ever enjoyed in that meeting-house through the whole course of his life.' Blessed be God, after sermon I perceived myself somewhat refreshed. Supped very early. Had the honor of a private visit from the governor, who came full of affection to take his leave of me for the present. Went, at their request, and preached to a great company of negroes, on the conversion of the Ethiopian, Acts the eighth; at which the poor creatures, as well as many white people, were much affected; and at my return, gave an exhortation to a crowd of people who were waiting at my lodgings. My animal spirits were almost exhausted, and my legs, through expense of sweating and vomiting, almost ready to sink under me; but the Lord visited my soul, and I went to bed greatly refreshed with divine consolations." Even at this early period such sufferings of his bodily system frequently followed his herculean labors.

Early on Monday morning, Sept. 29, Whitefield left Boston on an excursion to the eastward. At Marblehead, he "preached to some thousands in a broad place in the middle of the town, but not with much apparent effect." At Salem, he "preached to about seven thousand people. Here the Lord manifested forth his glory. One man was, I believe, struck down by the power of the word. In every part of the congregation, persons might be seen under great concern." He went on to Ipswich, where he was kindly "entertained at the house of Mr. Rogers, one of the ministers of the place." Of this family our evangelist was soon to know more than he had hitherto done. At about this period, John Rogers, aged 77, and Nathanael Rogers, were joint pastors of the First church at Ipswich; both of them were ardent promoters of the revival, as was also Daniel Rogers, of the same family. Whitefield learned with deep interest that his host was a descendant of the celebrated martyr, John Rogers. The next day he preached there to some thousands. "The Lord," says he, "gave me freedom, and there was a great melting in the congregation." At Newbury, in the afternoon, the Lord accompanied the word with power. The meeting-house was very large, many ministers were present, and the people were greatly affected. Blessed be God, his divine power attends us more and more." Wednesday, he preached at Hampton, in the open air, to some thousands. He was here very highly gratified with the conversation of Mr. Colton, the minister, and with the Christian simplicity of his excellent wife. The high wind prevented his being heard so well as he usually was, and he did not enjoy his accustomed freedom; still, "some, though not many, were affected." At Portsmouth, he "preached to a polite auditory, but so very unconcerned, that I began to question whether I had been speaking to rational or brute creatures. Seeing no immediate effects of the word preached, I was a little dejected; but God, to comfort my heart, sent one young man, crying out in great anguish of spirit, 'What shall I do to be saved?'"

From Portsmouth, our evangelist proceeded to York, in Maine, "to see one Mr. Moody, a worthy, plain, and powerful minister of Jesus Christ, though now much impaired by old age. He has lived by faith for many years, would have no settled salary, and has been much despised by bad men, and as much respected by the true lovers of the blessed Jesus." The next morning he was much comforted to hear, from Mr. Moody, that he would preach that morning to a hundred new creatures; "and indeed," says he, "I believe I did; for when I came to preach, I could speak little or no terror, but most consolation." He preached morning and evening. "The hearers looked plain and simple, and the tears trickled apace down most of their cheeks." He returned to Portsmouth that night, and the next morning preached to a far greater congregation, and with much better effect than before. "Instead of preaching to dead stocks, I now had reason to believe I was preaching to living men. People began to melt soon after I began to pray; and the power increased more and more during the whole sermon." This was still more clearly evinced after Mr. Whitefield's departure from the town.

Returning to Boston, through Salem, Marblehead, and Malden, in each of which places he preached, and being now in improved health, he preached, October 7, both morning and evening, "with much power," at Brattle-street. There had been for several days a report in circulation, that he had died suddenly, or was poisoned, and the people greatly rejoiced again to see him alive. At Mr. Webb's, the New North church, on the following Wednesday, he thought there was more of the presence of God through the whole ministration, than he had before, known at one time in the course of his life. He went there with the governor, in his coach, and preached morning and evening. "Jesus Christ manifested forth his glory; many hearts melted within them; and I think I was never drawn out to pray for and invite little children to Jesus Christ, as I was this morning. A little before, I had heard of a child who was taken sick just after it had heard me preach, and said he would go to Mr. Whitefield's God, and died in a short time. This encouraged me to speak to the little ones. But O, how were the old people affected when I said, 'Little children, if your parents will not come to Christ, do you come, and go to heaven without them.' There seemed to be but few dry eyes, look where I would. I have not seen a greater commotion since my preaching at Boston. Glory be to God, who has not forgotten to be gracious." He collected, after this sermon, £440 for his orphan-house, which was now more generally supported than ever before.

The interesting fact we have just related of the impression produced on the mind of a little child by the preaching of Mr. Whitefield, may afford the opportunity to introduce one or two other facts bearing on the same general topic, and suggesting some practical lessons.

Whitefield could indeed descend to talk with children. Here is a specimen which at once impresses us with a lively idea of his spirit, and of the adaptation of the religion of Jesus to the young as well as the old. A little girl seven years of age, when on her death-bed, desired an interview with him; he came, and thus they conversed:

Whitefield. For what purpose, my dear child, have you sent for me?

Girl. I think I am dying, and I wished very much to see you.

Whitefield. What can I do for you?

Girl. You can tell me about Christ, and pray for me.

Whitefield. My dear girl, what do you know about Christ?

Girl. I know he is the Saviour of the world.

Whitefield. My dear child, he is so.

Girl. I hope he will be *my* Saviour also.

Whitefield. I hope, my dear, that this is the language of faith out of the mouth of a babe; but tell me what ground you have for saying this?

Girl. Oh, sir, he bids little children, such as I, to come unto him, and says, "Of such is the kingdom of heaven;" and besides, I love Christ, and am always glad when I think of him.

Whitefield. My dear child, you make my very heart to rejoice; but are you not a sinner?

Girl. Yes, I am a sinner, but my blessed Redeemer takes away sin, and I long to be with him.

Whitefield. My dear girl, I trust that the desire of your heart will be granted; but where do you think you will find your Redeemer?

Girl. O, sir, I think I shall find him in heaven.

Whitefield. Do you think you will get to heaven?

Girl. Yes, I do.

Whitefield. But what if you do not find Christ there?

Girl. If I do not find Christ there, I am sure it is not heaven; for where he dwells must be heaven, for there also dwells God, and holy angels, and all that Christ saves.

Who can tell the results of a single sermon, or trace the consequences of one conversion? When Mr. Whitefield was preaching in New England, a lady became the subject of divine grace, and her spirit was peculiarly drawn out in prayer for others. But in her Christian exercises she was alone; she could persuade no one to pray with her but her little daughter, about ten years of age. She took this dear child into her closet from day to day, as a witness of her cries and tears. After a time, it pleased God to touch the heart of the child, and to give her the hope of salvation by the remission of sin. In a transport of holy joy she then exclaimed, "O, mother, if all the world knew this! I wish I could tell every body. Pray, mother, let me run to some of the neighbors and tell them, that they may be happy and love my Saviour too." "Ah, my dear child," said the mother, "that would be useless, for I suppose that were you to tell your experience, there is not one within many miles who would not laugh at you, and say it was all delusion." "Oh, mother," replied the dear girl, "I think they would believe me. I must go over to the shoemaker and tell him; he will believe me." She ran over, and found him at work in his shop. She began by telling him that he must die, and that he was a sinner, and that she was a sinner, but that her blessed Saviour had heard her mother's prayers, and had forgiven all her sins; and that now she was so happy that she did not know how to tell it. The shoemaker was struck with surprise, his tears flowed down like rain; he threw aside his work, and by prayer and supplication sought for mercy. The neighborhood were awakened, and within a few months more than fifty persons were brought to the knowledge of Jesus, and rejoiced in his power and grace.

But to return to our narrative of Whitefield's labors in Boston. On Thursday, October 9, he preached the public lecture at the Old South church. He had selected another text, but it was much impressed on his heart that he should preach from our Lord's conference with Nicodemus. A large number of ministers were present, and when he came to the words, "Art thou a master in Israel, and knowest not these things?" he says, "The Lord enabled me to open my mouth boldly against unconverted ministers, to caution tutors to take care of their pupils, and also to advise ministers particularly to examine into the experiences of candidates for ordination. For I am verily persuaded the generality of preachers talk of an unknown and unfelt Christ; and the reason why congregations have been so dead is, because they have had dead men preaching to them. O that the Lord may quicken and revive them, for his own name's sake. For how can dead men beget living children? It is true, indeed, God may convert men by the devil, if he pleases, and so he may by unconverted ministers; but I believe he seldom makes use of either of them for this purpose. No; the Lord will choose vessels made meet by the operations of the blessed Spirit for his sacred use: and as for my own part, I would not lay hands on an unconverted man for ten thousand worlds. Unspeakable freedom God gave me while treating on this head. After sermon, I dined with the governor, who seemed more kindly affected than ever, and particularly told me, of the minister who has lately begun to preach extempore, that 'he was glad he had found out a way to save his eyes.' In the afternoon I preached on the Common to about fifteen thousand people, and collected upwards of two hundred pounds for the orphan-house. Just as I had finished my sermon, a ticket was put up to me, wherein I was desired to pray for a person just entered upon the ministry, but under apprehension that he was not converted. God enabled me to pray for him with my whole heart; and I hope that ticket may teach many others not to run before they can give an account of their conversion. If they do, they offer to God strange fire." The same day and evening, Whitefield attended the funeral of one of the provincial council, preached at the almshouse, exhorted a great number of persons at the workhouse, who followed him there, and conversed with many who waited at his lodgings for spiritual advice. From the time of his return from the east, he had been thronged, morning and evening, with anxious inquirers. His friends cried, "Spare thyself;" but he says, "I went and ate bread very comfortably at a friend's house, where I was invited, and soon after retired to my rest. Oh, how comfortable is sleep after working for Jesus."

On Friday he preached at Charlestown and at Reading to many thousands, and on Saturday from the meeting-house door at Cambridge, on Noah as a preacher of righteousness; a great number of persons were present, who stood very attentively during a shower of rain, and were at the latter part of the sermon much affected. On the same afternoon he returned to Boston, and again preached, and was engaged till midnight, chiefly in conversation and prayer with persons anxious for their salvation.

Sunday, October 12, he rose with body and soul greatly refreshed, and spent its early hours in conversing with those who came for spiritual counsel. He then "preached with great power and affection" at the Old South church, which was so exceedingly thronged, that he was obliged to get in at one of the windows. He dined with the governor, who came to him after dinner weeping, and desired his prayers. He heard Dr. Sewall in the afternoon. Both during the exercises and after them he was sick, but went with the governor in his coach, and preached his farewell sermon on the Common, Gillies says, to twenty thousand, and Tracy to nearly thirty thousand people, though the whole population of Boston did not at that time exceed twenty thousand. Great multitudes were melted into tears when he spoke of leaving them. The governor then went with him to his lodgings. He stood in the passage and spoke to a great company, both within and without the doors; but they were so deeply affected, and cried out so loud, that he was compelled to leave off praying. The remaining part of the evening was chiefly spent in conversation with inquirers.

In closing his account of this day's work, he exclaims, "Blessed be God for what things he has done in Boston! I hope a glorious work is now begun, and that the Lord will stir up some faithful laborers to carry it on. Boston is a large, populous place, very wealthy. Has the form kept up, but has lost much of the power of religion. I have not heard of any remarkable stir for these many years. Ministers and people are obliged to confess, that the love of many is waxed cold. Both, for the generality, seem to be too much conformed to the world. There is much of the pride of life to be seen in their assemblies. Jewels, patches, and gay apparel are commonly worn by the female sex; and even the common people, I observed dressed up in the pride of life. There are nine meeting-houses of the Congregational persuasion, one Baptist, one French, and one belonging to the Scotch-Irish. One thing Boston is very remarkable for—the external observance of the Sabbath. Men in civil offices have a regard for religion. The governor encourages them, and the ministers and magistrates are more united than in any other place where I have been. Both were exceedingly civil to me during my stay. I never saw so little scoffing, never had so little opposition. But one might easily see much would hereafter arise, when I came to be more particular in my application to particular persons; for I fear many rest in a head-knowledge, are close pharisees, and have only a name to live. It must needs be so when the power of godliness is dwindled away, and where the form only of religion is become fashionable among people. Boston people are dear to my soul. They were greatly affected by the word, followed me night and day, and were very liberal to my dear orphans. I promised, God willing, to visit them again, and intend to fulfil my promise when it shall please God to bring me again from my native country. In the meanwhile, dear Boston, adieu. The Lord be with thy ministers and people, and grant that the remnant which is still left according to the election of grace, may take root downwards, and bear fruit upwards, and fill the land."

On the morning following these solemn services, Whitefield left Boston on his way to Northampton. To detail his four days' progress, would be almost to repeat what we have already written. At Concord, where he arrived on Monday about noon, he preached twice to some thousands in the open air, "and a comfortable preaching it was. The hearers were sweetly melted down." Mr. Bliss, the minister of the town, of whose subsequent labors it has been well said, more perfect accounts ought to have been preserved, wept abundantly. On Tuesday he "preached at Sudbury to some thousands with power, and observed a considerable commotion in the assembly;" as was also the case the same afternoon at Marlborough. At the latter place he was met by Governor Belcher, who went with him through the rain that night to Worcester. Here, on Wednesday, he "preached in the open air to some thousands. The word fell with weight indeed. It carried all before it. After sermon, the governor said to me, 'I pray God I may apply what has been said to my own heart. Pray, Mr. Whitefield, that I may hunger and thirst after righteousness.'" Passing on, he preached at Leicester, Brookfield, and Cold-Spring, on his way to Hadley, where he arrived on Friday, and preached about noon. In this place he says, "A great work was begun, and carried on some years ago; but lately the people of God have complained of deadness and losing their first love. However, as soon as I mentioned what God had done for their souls formerly, it was like putting fire to timber. The remembrance of it quickened them, and caused many to weep sorely." On the same afternoon he crossed the ferry to Northampton.

Of the great revival of religion in New England, which commenced at Northampton about 1734, and is the subject of President Edwards' "Narrative," we have already briefly spoken; its importance will justify a more extended notice. It began without any extraordinary circumstances to awaken the attention of the people, or any uncommon arrangements or efforts by the minister. The young people of the place had for two or three years shown an increased measure of thoughtfulness, and a growing disposition to receive religious instruction. There had been, from time to time, instances of strong religious impression and of hopeful conversion. But in the latter end of December, 1734, five or six persons, one after another, became very suddenly the subjects of the grace of God which newly creates the soul. Among these was a young woman distinguished for her gayety in youthful society, "one of the greatest company-keepers in the whole town," who came to the pastor with a broken heart and a contrite spirit, and with faith and hope in the Saviour of sinners, before any one had heard of her being at all impressed with serious things. The sudden, though, as time proved, the *real* conversion of this young woman, was the power of God striking the electric chain of religious sympathies which had imperceptibly, but effectually encircled all the families of Northampton. Mr. Edwards' "Narrative" says, "The news of it seemed to be almost like a flash of lightning upon the hearts of young people all over the town, and upon many others.... Presently a great and earnest concern about the great things of religion and the eternal world became universal in all parts of the town, and among persons of all degrees and all ages. All talk but about spiritual and eternal things was soon thrown by; all the conversation in all companies was upon these things only, except so much as was necessary for people carrying on their ordinary secular business. The minds of people were wonderfully taken off from the world; it was treated among us as a thing of very little consequence. All would eagerly lay hold of opportunities for their souls, and were wont very often to meet together in private houses for religious purposes. And such meetings, when appointed, were generally thronged. Those who were wont to be the vainest and loosest, and those who had been most disposed to think and speak lightly of vital and experimental religion, were now generally subject to great awakening. And the work of conversion was carried on in a most astonishing manner, and increased more and more. From day to day, for many months together, might be seen evident instances of sinners brought out of darkness into marvellous light. In the spring and summer following, the town seemed to be full of the presence of God; it was never so full of love, and yet so full of distress, as it was then. It was a time of joy in families, on account of salvation being brought to them; parents rejoicing over their children as new-born, and husbands over their wives, and wives over their husbands. The goings of God were then seen in his sanctuary, God's day was a delight, and his tabernacles were amiable. Our public assemblies were then beautiful; the congregation was alive in God's service, every one eagerly intent on the public worship, every hearer eager to drink in the words of the minister as they came from his mouth. The assembly were, from time to time, in tears, while the word was preached; some weeping with sorrow and distress, others with joy and love, others with pity and concern for their neighbors."

In December, 1743, nine years after this blessed work had begun, Edwards writes, "Ever since the great work of God that was wrought here about nine years ago, there has been a great, abiding alteration in this town, in many respects. There has been vastly more religion kept up in the town, among all sorts of persons, in religious exercises, and in common conversation, than used to be before. There has remained a more general seriousness and decency in attending the public worship. I suppose the town has been in no measure so free from vice, for any long time together, for these sixty years, as it has these nine years past. There has also been an evident alteration with respect to a charitable spirit to the poor. And though, after that great work of nine years ago, there has been a very lamentable decay of religious affections, and the engagedness of people's spirits in religion, yet many societies for prayer and social religion were all along kept up, and there were some few instances of awakening and deep concern about the things of another world, even in the most dead time. In the year 1740, in the spring, before Mr. Whitefield came to this town, there was a visible alteration. There was more seriousness and religious conversation, especially among young people. Those things that were of ill tendency among them were more forborne; and it was a more frequent thing for persons to visit their ministers upon soul accounts. In some particular persons, there appeared a great alteration about that time. And thus it continued till Mr. Whitefield came to town, which was about the middle of October following."

And what thought Whitefield himself on his arrival at Northampton? Let us hear him. "Their pastor's name is Edwards, successor and grandson to the great Stoddard, whose memory will be always precious to my soul, and whose books, entitled, *"A Guide to Christ,"* and *"Safety of appearing in Christ's righteousness,"* I would recommend to all. Mr. Edwards is a solid, excellent Christian, but at present weak in body. I think I may say I have not seen his fellow in all New England. When I came into his pulpit, I found my heart drawn out to talk of scarce any thing besides the consolations and privileges of saints, and the plentiful effusion of the Spirit upon the hearts of believers. And when I came to remind them of their former experiences, and how zealous and lively they were at that time, both minister and people wept much; and the Holy Ghost enabled me to speak with a great deal of power. In the evening, I gave a word of exhortation to several who came to Mr. Edwards' house."

On the following morning, "At Mr. Edwards' request, I spoke to his little children, who were much affected. Preached at Hatfield, five miles from Northampton, but found myself not much strengthened. Conversed profitably on the way about the things of God with dear Mr. Edwards, and preached about four in the afternoon to his congregation. I began with fear and trembling, feeling but little power in the morning, but God assisted me. Few dry eyes seemed to be in the assembly for a considerable time. I had an affecting prospect in my own heart of the glories of the upper world, and was enabled to speak of them feelingly to others. I believe many were filled, as it were, with new wine; and it seemed as if a time of refreshing was come from the presence of the Lord."

The day following this was the Sabbath. Whitefield tells us in his journal, that he "felt wonderful satisfaction in being at the house of Mr. Edwards. He is a son himself, and hath also a daughter of Abraham for his wife. A sweeter couple I have not yet seen. Their children were dressed, not in silks and satins, but plain, as becomes the children of those who in all things ought to be examples of Christian simplicity. She is a woman adorned with a meek and quiet spirit, talked feelingly and solidly of the things of God, and seemed to be such a help-mate for her husband, that she caused me to renew those prayers, which, for some months, I have put up to God, that he would be pleased to send me a daughter of Abraham to be my wife. I find, upon many accounts, it is my duty to marry. Lord, I desire to have no choice of my own. Thou knowest my circumstances; thou knowest I only desire to marry in and for thee."

Whitefield "preached this morning, and perceived the melting begin sooner and rise higher than before. Dear Mr. Edwards wept during the whole time of exercise. The people were equally, if not more affected; and my own soul was much lifted up towards God. In the afternoon the power increased yet more and more. Our Lord seemed to keep the good wine till the last. I have not seen four such gracious meetings together since my arrival. My soul was much knit to these dear people of God; and though I had not time to converse with them about their experiences, yet one might see they were for the most part, a gracious, tender people; and though their former fire might be greatly abated, yet it immediately appeared when stirred up."

Edwards had looked forward to Whitefield's visit to Northampton with interest, for he felt greatly concerned for his success. He wrote a week before his arrival to his friend Dr. Wheelock, then a young minister of twenty-nine, "I think that those that make mention of the Lord, should now be awakened and encouraged to call upon God, and not keep silence, nor give him any rest, till he establish and till he make Jerusalem a praise in the earth; and particularly should be earnest with God, that he would still uphold and succeed the Rev. Mr. Whitefield, the instrument that it has pleased him to improve to do such great things for the honor of his name, and at all times so to guide and direct him under his extraordinary circumstances, that Satan may not get any advantage of him."

After his visit, Edwards writes, "Mr. Whitefield's sermons were suitable to the circumstances of the town; containing just reproofs of our backslidings, and in a most moving and affecting manner, making use of our great profession and our great mercies as arguments with us to return to God, from whom we had departed. Immediately after this, the minds of the people in general appeared more engaged in religion, showing a greater forwardness to make it the subject of their conversation, and to meet frequently for religious purposes, and to embrace all opportunities to hear the word preached. The revival at first appeared chiefly among professors, and those who had entertained the hope that they were in a state of grace, to whom Mr. Whitefield chiefly addressed himself; but in a very short time, there appeared an awakening and deep concern among some young persons that looked upon themselves in a Christless state; and there were some hopeful appearances of conversion; and some professors were greatly revived. In about a month or six weeks, there was a great alteration in the town, both as to the revivals of professors, and awakenings of others."

During this visit of Whitefield to Edwards, some conversation was held between them, of which, several years afterwards, as it appears to us, far too much was said. Edwards took an opportunity, privately, to converse with his friend about *impulses*, and furnished him with some reasons for thinking that he gave too much attention to such things. Whitefield did not appear offended, neither did he seem inclined to converse much on the subject, or to yield to the reasonings of his friend Edwards. The latter says, "It is true, that I thought Mr. Whitefield liked me not so well for my opposing these things; and though he treated me with great kindness, yet he never made so much of an intimate of me, as of some others." It seems also, that they conversed on the strong language which the great evangelist was accustomed to employ as to those whom he considered to be unconverted, and the duty of the people to forsake the preaching of ministers whom he did not consider to be renewed in the spirit of their minds. Whitefield told Edwards also, of the design he had cherished of bringing over a number of young men from England, to be ordained by the Tennents, in New Jersey; an object, however, which he never accomplished.

It appears that after preaching at Northampton twice on the Sabbath, Whitefield, accompanied by his friend Edwards, rode to the house of the father of the last-named gentleman, the Rev. Timothy Edwards, in East Windsor, Connecticut. At this place, as also at Westfield, Springfield, Suffield, Hartford, Wethersfield, Middletown, and Wallingford, he preached to large assemblies, generally with his accustomed animation and power, and with the happy proofs of success which he so frequently witnessed. During this week also, he experienced a remarkable deliverance from great danger. He says, "A little after I left Springfield, my horse, coming over a broken bridge, threw me over his head, directly upon my nose. The fall stunned me for a while. My mouth was full of dust, I bled a little, but falling upon soft sand, got not much damage. After I had recovered myself, and mounted my horse, God so filled me with a sense of his sovereign, distinguishing love, and my own unworthiness, that my eyes gushed out with tears; but they were all tears of love. Oh, how did I want to sink before the high and lofty One who inhabiteth eternity!"

During this week also, on his way to Suffield, he met with a minister who said, "It was not absolutely necessary for a gospel minister, that he should be converted;" meaning, no doubt, that though conversion was necessary to his salvation, it was not indispensable to his ministerial character and usefulness. This gave Whitefield a subject. "I insisted much in my discourse upon the doctrine of the new birth, and also the necessity of a minister's being converted, before he could preach Christ aright. The word came with great power, and a great impression was made upon the people in all parts of the assembly. Many ministers were present. I did not spare them. Most of them thanked me for my plain dealing; but one was offended; and so would more of his stamp be, if I were to continue longer in New England. For unconverted ministers are the bane of the Christian church; and though I honor the memory of that great and good man Mr. Stoddard, yet I think he is much to be blamed for endeavoring to prove that unconverted men might be admitted into the ministry. How he has handled the controversy, I know not. I think no solid arguments can be brought to defend such a cause. A sermon lately published by Mr. Gilbert Tennent, entitled, '*The Danger of an Unconverted Ministry,*' I think unanswerable. Tracy truly says, that Stoddard, in his '*Appeal to the Learned,*' assumes that an unconverted minister is bound to continue in the performance of ministerial duties, and infers that unconverted men may therefore be admitted to the church. This opinion at one period extensively prevailed, though all held it desirable that a minister should be a converted man. By his attacks on this opinion, and especially by thus endorsing Tennent's Nottingham sermon, Whitefield gave great offence."

On Wednesday afternoon, he preached at East Windsor, and spent the night with Mr. Edwards, senior, "I believe," he says, "a true disciple and minister of the Lord Jesus Christ. After exercise, we supped at the house of old Mr. Edwards. His wife was as aged, I believe, as himself, and I fancied that I was sitting in the house of a Zacharias and Elisabeth." On the following day, he "preached to many thousands, and with much freedom and power," at Hartford in the morning, and at Wethersfield in the afternoon. Here he met Messrs. Wheelock and Pomeroy, "two young, faithful, and zealous ministers of Jesus Christ." From this place he had intended to go eastward as far as Plymouth, and return by another route to Providence, and notice had been given in the newspapers of about twenty sermons which he proposed to preach at the times and places specified. He was afterwards blamed for making these appointments without first consulting the pastors of the several churches; thus giving countenance, it was said, to the practice of itinerants intruding into other men's parishes without their consent. The proceeding was certainly somewhat irregular, but Whitefield was not much to be blamed for it. The details were settled, and the publication made, by men in whose judgment and knowledge of the customs of the country he had a right to confide; and the appointments were believed, in all cases, and doubtless known in some, to be agreeable to the parties concerned. At Wethersfield, however, the evangelist ascertained the necessity of his hastening on to New York, and immediately, therefore, published a note recalling these appointments.

On Friday, October 24, Whitefield arrived at New Haven, and was entertained at the house of Mr. James Pierpont, the brother-in-law of Mr. Edwards, and of Mr. Noyes, the minister of the First Congregational church. The Legislature of the colony being in session, he remained till after the Lord's day; and "had the pleasure of seeing numbers daily impressed," under his ministrations in the old polygonal meeting-house. Several ministers of the vicinity visited him, "with whose pious conversation he was much refreshed." Good old Governor Tallcott, on whom with due politeness he waited to pay his respects, said to him, "Thanks be to God for such refreshings in our way to heaven." Among others who heard his glowing appeals to the congregations that listened to him during this visit, was young Samuel Hopkins, still well known as an eminent divine. Hopkins was now nineteen, and was a student at college; his biographer tells us, that "he was much interested in the man, and much impressed by his solemn warnings."

The testimony of Hopkins himself may here be introduced. He says, speaking of Whitefield, "The attention of the people in general was greatly awakened upon hearing the fame of him, that there was a remarkable preacher from England travelling through the country. The people flocked to hear him when he came to New Haven. Some travelled twenty miles out of the country to hear him. The assemblies were crowded, and remarkably attentive; people appeared generally to approve, and their conversation turned chiefly upon him and his preaching. Some disapproved of several things, which occasioned considerable disputes. I heard him when he preached in public, and when he expounded in private in the evening, and highly approved of him, and was impressed by what he said in public and in private. He preached against mixed dancing and the frolicking of males and females together, which practice was then very common in New England. This offended some, especially young people. But I remember I justified him in this in my own mind, and in conversation with those who were disposed to condemn him. This was in October, 1740, when I had entered on my last year in college."

On this visit, Whitefield dined with the Rev. Mr. Clap, the rector of the college. Of the college he says, "It is about one-third part as big as Cambridge. It has one rector, three tutors, and about a hundred students. But I hear of no remarkable concern among them concerning religion." Mr. Clap, it is well known, afterwards became the public opponent of Whitefield; and it would seem that his dislike to him commenced with this first interview; for he "spoke very closely to the students, and showed the dreadful consequences of an unconverted ministry." In his journal of the day he says, "O that God may quicken ministers! O that the Lord may make them a flaming fire!" On the two days following, he preached at Milford, Stratford, and Fairfield, on his way to New York. On Wednesday, when at Stamford, he thus speaks of New England and his labors in it:

"I give God thanks for sending me to New England. I have now had an opportunity of seeing the greatest and most populous parts of it; and take it all together, it certainly on many accounts exceeds all other provinces of America, and for the establishment of religion, perhaps all other parts of the world. Never, surely, was so large a spot of ground settled in such a manner, in so short a space of one hundred years. The towns all through Connecticut and eastwards towards York in the province of Massachusetts, [Maine,] near the river-side, are large, well peopled, and exceedingly pleasant to travel through. Every five miles, or perhaps less, you have a meeting-house, and I believe there is no such a thing as a pluralist, or non-resident minister in both provinces. Many, nay, most that preach, I fear do not experimentally know Christ; yet I cannot see much worldly advantage to tempt them to take upon them the sacred function. Few country ministers, as I have been informed, have sufficient allowed them in money to maintain a family. God has remarkably, in sundry times and in divers manners, poured out his Spirit in several parts of both provinces; and it often refreshes my soul to hear of the faith of the good forefathers who first settled in these parts. Notwithstanding they had their foibles, surely they were a set of righteous men. They certainly followed our Lord's rule, sought first the kingdom of God and his righteousness; and behold, all other things God added unto them. Their seed are now blessed, in temporal things especially, and notwithstanding the rising generation seem to be settled on their lees, yet I believe the Lord hath more than seven thousand who have not bowed the knee to Baal. The ministers and people of Connecticut seem to be more simple than those that live near Boston, especially in those parts where I went. But I think the ministers' preaching almost universally by notes, is a certain mark they have in a great measure lost the old spirit of preaching. For though all are not to be condemned that use notes, yet it is a sad symptom of the decay of vital religion when reading sermons becomes fashionable, where extempore preaching did once almost universally prevail. As for the universities, I believe it may be said, their light is become darkness, darkness that may be felt, and is complained of by the most godly ministers. I pray God these fountains may be purified, and send forth pure streams to water the cities of our God.... As for the civil government of New England, it seems to be well regulated, and I think, at opening all their courts, either the judge or a minister begins with a prayer. Family worship, I believe, is generally kept up. The negroes I think better used, both in soul and body, than in any other province I have yet seen. In short, I like New England exceedingly well; and when a spirit of reformation revives, it certainly will prevail here more than in other places, because they are simple in their worship, less corrupt in their principles, and consequently easier to be brought over to the form of sound words, into which so many of their pious ancestors were delivered. Send forth, O Lord, thy light and thy truth, and for thine infinite mercy's sake, show thou hast a peculiar delight in these habitable parts of the earth. Amen, Lord Jesus, amen, and amen."

Among many who became the subjects of divine grace during this visit of Whitefield to New England, was Daniel Emerson, who was educated at Harvard college, where he received his first degree in 1739, and where he continued to reside for some time as a graduate. While at college, he is said to have been very fond of the gay pleasures of this life, until his attention was effectually called to religion by the preaching of Whitefield, whom he followed from place to place for several days. He was ordained at Hollis, New Hampshire, in 1743, where, in a ministry of fifty years, he was a worthy follower of his spiritual father. The chief excellences of his preaching were sound doctrine, deep feeling, and zeal at times almost overwhelming. He was truly a son of thunder, and a flaming light. He was almost incessantly engaged in labors, preaching, attending funerals, etc., far and near. His efforts were greatly blessed, especially among his own people, who under his ministry enjoyed extensive revivals of religion, and where also a large number of ministers have been called to their work. He died in 1801, aged eighty-five.

It may be appropriate to introduce here a sketch of Whitefield's doctrines and labors at this time, as given us by the eminent Dr. Thomas Prince, in his "Christian History," under date of January 26, 1744-5, but having reference to Whitefield's first visit to New England, which we have just described:

"He spoke with a mighty sense of God, eternity, the immortality and preciousness of the souls of his hearers, of their original corruption, and of the extreme danger the unregenerate are in; with the nature and absolute necessity of regeneration by the Holy Ghost; and of believing in Christ, in order to our pardon, justification, yielding an acceptable obedience, and obtaining salvation from hell and an entrance into heaven. His doctrine was plainly that of the reformers; declaring against our putting our good works or morality in the room of Christ's righteousness, or their having any hand in our justification, or being indeed pleasing to God while we are totally unsanctified, acting upon corrupt principles, and unreconciled enemies to him; which occasioned some to mistake him, as if he opposed morality. But he insisted on it, that the tree of the heart is by original sin exceedingly corrupted, and must be made good by regeneration, that so the fruits proceeding from it may be good likewise; that where the heart is renewed, it ought and will be careful to maintain good works, that if any be not habitually so careful who think themselves renewed, they deceive their own souls; and even the most improved in holiness, as well as others, must entirely depend on the righteousness of Christ for the acceptance of their persons and services. And though now and then he dropped some expressions that were not so accurate and guarded as we should expect from aged and long-studied ministers, yet I had the satisfaction to observe his readiness with great modesty and thankfulness to receive correction as soon as offered.

"In short, he was a most importunate wooer of souls to come to Christ for the enjoyment of him, and all his benefits. He distinctly applied his exhortations to the elderly people, the middle-aged, the young, the Indians, and negroes, and had a most winning way of addressing them. He affectionately prayed for our magistrates, ministers, colleges, candidates for the ministry, and churches, as well as people in general; and before he left us, in a public and moving manner, he observed to the people how sorry he was to hear that the religious assemblies, especially on lectures, had been so thin, exhorted them earnestly to a more general attendance on our public ministrations for the time to come, and told them how glad he should be to hear of the same.

"Multitudes were greatly affected, and many awakened with his lively ministry. Though he preached every day, the houses were crowded; but when he preached on the Common, a vaster number attended; and almost every evening the house where he lodged was thronged to hear his prayers and counsels.

"On Mr. Whitefield's leaving us, great numbers in this town [Boston] were so happily concerned about their souls, as we had never seen any thing like it before, except at the time of the general earthquake;[1] and their desires excited to hear their ministers more than ever. So that our assemblies, both on lectures and Sabbaths, were surprisingly increased, and now the people wanted to hear us oftener. In consequence of which a public lecture was proposed to be set up at Dr. Colman's church, near the midst of the town, on every Tuesday evening."

In reference to the work of grace which was connected with Whitefield's preaching in New England, the Rev. Dr. Baron Stow, in his "Centennial Discourse," says, "The result, by the blessing of God, was a powerful revival, such as New England had never witnessed. The work was opposed with great vehemence; and no impartial reader of the history of those extraordinary scenes can question that much of the hostility was provoked by improprieties of both speech and action, that would at any time be offensive to those who love good order and Christian decorum. But after making liberal allowance for all that was truly exceptionable, it is cheerfully admitted by the candid Christian, that the excitement was, in the main, the product of the Holy Spirit, and that its fruits were eminently favorable to the advancement of true religion. A torpid community was aroused, as by the trump of God, from its long and heavy slumber; ministers and people were converted; the style of preaching, and the tone of individual piety were improved; a cold, cadaverous formalism gave place to the living energy of experimental godliness; the doctrines of the gospel were brought out from their concealment, and made to reassert their claims to a cordial, practical credence, and all the interests of truth and holiness received new homage from regenerated thousands."

One or two other facts connected with Whitefield's usefulness in New England are too important to be omitted. During this visit he was much gratified by an interview with a colored man, who had been his chaise-driver when he first visited Cambridge. The negro had heard him preach in the college a sermon especially addressed "to those who labor and are heavy-laden." It took such a hold on the poor man, that he repeated it in the kitchen when he reached home. Mr. Cooper of Boston was so well satisfied, as was Whitefield also, with his account of his conversion, that he was admitted to the Lord's table.

Another "brand plucked from the burning" was a son of Mackintosh, an English rebel, who had been condemned to perpetual imprisonment, and had been allowed by George the First to settle in New England. One of his daughters, a lady of fortune, had heard Whitefield preach in Dr. Prince's church at Boston, and had been won by the word to Christ. She was soon after smitten by sickness, and ripened rapidly for heaven. On her death-bed she cried out for her "soul friend" Mr. Whitefield; but checking her own impatience, she asked, "Why should I do so? He is gone about his Master's work, and in a little time we shall meet to part no more." The distinguished evangelist had a very high opinion of her piety, and his interest in her was increased by the fact that she had a very remarkable escape from some ruffians who had been bribed to convey her and her sister to Scotland, that their uncle might seize on an estate worth a thousand pounds a year.

There were at this time not less than twenty ministers in the neighborhood of Boston who unhesitatingly spoke of Whitefield as their spiritual father, directly tracing their conversion to his ministry. Of one of these we have an account by Collins, the journalist of South Reading. Speaking of 1741, he says, "Mr. Whitefield preached upon our Common in the open air. Mr. Hobby the minister went with the multitude to hear him. It is said that Mr. Hobby afterwards remarked, he came to pick a hole in Mr. Whitefield's coat, but that Whitefield picked a hole in his heart. Mr. Hobby afterwards wrote and published a defence of Mr. Whitefield in a letter to Mr. Henchman, the minister of Lynn, who had written against him."

The letters of Whitefield, during his journeys of eleven hundred miles in New England, were few and brief; but they clearly indicated that at this time he was inclined "to return no more to his native country." New England, notwithstanding his trials there, had evidently won his heart, and for a time almost weaned him from Great Britain. When he left it, as he was now about to do, for the south, he wrote, "God only knows what a cross it was to me to leave dear New England so soon. I hope death will not be so bitter to me as was parting with my friends. Glad shall I be to be *prayed* thither again before I see my native land. I would just be where He would have me, although in the uttermost parts of the earth. I am now hunting for poor lost sinners in these *ungospelized* wilds."

Is there not an awfully retributive providence connected with the rejection of the gospel and its ministers? Do we not see this principle at work in the history and present state of the Jews; and has it not often appeared also in the history of Christianity? There was a beautiful village, now a city, in Massachusetts, from which Whitefield was driven with such rancorous abuse, that he shook off the dust of his feet, and proclaimed that the Spirit of God would not visit that spot till the last of those persecutors was dead. The good man's language had a fearful truth in it, though he was not divinely gifted with the prophet's inspiration. A consciousness of desertion paralyzed the energies of the church; for nearly a century it was nurtured on the unwholesome food of unscriptural doctrine. In the very garden of natural loveliness, it sat like a heath in the desert, upon which there could be no rain; and not till that whole generation had passed from the earth, did Zion appear there in her beauty and strength.

CHAPTER VII
LABORS IN NEW YORK AND THE MIDDLE AND SOUTHERN STATES. 1740, 1741

Whitefield was now again on his way to New York, preaching at Rye and King's Bridge on the road. At the latter place he was met by several friends from the city, with whom he pleasantly talked, "and found," he says, "an inexpressible satisfaction in my soul when I arrived at the house of my very dear friend Mr. Noble. After supper the Lord filled my heart, and gave me to wrestle with him for New York inhabitants and my own dear friends." He was also cheered by meeting Mr. Davenport from Long Island, whose labors as an evangelist were then exciting much interest. Here too he met with a violent pamphlet published against him. "Met also with two volumes of sermons published in London as delivered by me, though I never preached on most of the texts. But Satan must try all ways to bring the work of God into contempt."

On the morning after his arrival, Whitefield preached in Mr. Pemberton's meeting-house, and says concerning the service, "Never saw the word of God fall with such weight in New York before. Two or three cried out. Mr. Noble could scarce refrain himself. And look where I would, many seemed deeply wounded. At night the word was attended with great power. One cried out; and the Lord enabled me at the latter end of my sermon to speak with authority. Alas, how vain are the thoughts of men! As I came along yesterday, I found my heart somewhat dejected, and told Mr. Noble I expected but little moving in New York; but he bid me 'expect great things from God,' and likewise told me of several who were, as he hoped, savingly wrought upon by my ministry when I was there last."

On the following day he finished his answer to the pamphlet already referred to, and says, "God enabled me to write it in the spirit of meekness." He adds, "Preached twice as yesterday to very crowded auditories, and neither time without power. In the evening exercise some fainted, and the Lord seemed to show us more and more that a time for favoring New York was near at hand. Oh, wherefore did I doubt? Lord, increase my faith."

The following day, November 2, was the Sabbath. "Preached this morning with freedom and some power, but was much dejected before the evening sermon. For near half an hour before I left Mr. Noble's house, I could only lie before the Lord, and say I was a poor sinner, and wonder that Christ would be gracious to such a wretch. As I went to meeting I grew weaker and weaker, and when I came into the pulpit I could have chosen to be silent rather than speak. But after I had begun, the Spirit of the Lord gave me freedom, till at length it came down like a mighty rushing wind, and carried all before it. Immediately the whole congregation was alarmed. Shrieking, crying, weeping, and wailing were to be heard in every corner; men's hearts failing them for fear, and many falling into the arms of their friends. My soul was carried out till I could scarcely speak any more. A sense of God's goodness overwhelmed me."

After narrating two or three pleasing incidents as to the effect of his preaching even on the minds of children, and describing his feelings on his return home, he gives an account of the wedding of two young persons who were going as his assistants to Georgia. "Never," he says, "did I see a more solemn wedding. Jesus Christ was called, and he was present in a remarkable manner. After Mr. Pemberton had married them, I prayed. But my soul, how was it enabled to wrestle with and lay hold on God! I was in a very great agony, and the Holy Ghost was so remarkably present, that most, I believe, could say, 'Surely God is in this place.' After this, divine manifestations flowed in so fast, that my frail tabernacle was scarce able to sustain them. My dear friends sat round me on the bedsides. I prayed for each of them alternately with strong cries, and pierced by the eye of faith even within the veil. I continued in this condition for about half an hour, astonished at my own vileness and the excellency of Christ, then rose full of peace and love and joy."

On Monday, the 3d, he preached both morning and afternoon to increasing congregations, and says, "There was a great and gracious melting both times, but no crying out. Nearly £110 currency were collected for the orphans; and in the evening many came and took an affectionate leave. About seven we took boat; reached Staten Island about ten, greatly refreshed in my inner man. A dear Christian friend received us gladly, and we solaced ourselves by singing and praying. About midnight retired to sleep, still longing for that time when I shall sleep no more."

On Tuesday he preached on Staten Island from a wagon, to three or four hundred people. "The Lord came among them," and several inquired after the way of salvation. Here he met Gilbert Tennent and Mr. Cross. The former of these excellent ministers had recently lost his wife, and though he was ardently attached to her, he calmly preached her funeral sermon with the corpse lying before him. Tennent had lately been preaching in New Jersey and Maryland, and had a delightful account to give his friend of the progress of the good work. Nor was the account given by Mr. Cross of less interest. After sermon he rode to Newark, where he preached till dark, as he thought with but little good effect. "However, at night the Lord manifested forth his glory; for, coming down to family prayer where I lodged, and perceiving many young men around me, my soul was, as it were, melted down with concern for them. After singing, I gave a word of exhortation; with what power none can fully express but those that saw it. Oh, how did the word fall like a hammer and like a fire. What a weeping was there!"

We must stay a moment to give a fact or two in reference to the Rev. Aaron Burr, then quite a young man, who two or three years before had been ordained at Newark, and whose ministry had been attended with a delightful revival the year preceding Whitefield's visit. During the period of this revival, the neighboring village of Elizabethtown had been remarkable for its insensibility; even Whitefield had preached there, "and not a single known conversion," says Dr. Stearns, "followed his ministrations." Afterwards the pastor, the well-known Jonathan Dickinson, saw happy results from very plain preaching. Newark caught a new flame from its neighboring altar, and Mr. Burr, who had lately been to New England in quest of health, had heard the devoted evangelist again and again, and invited him to visit his flock, which he did about a month afterwards with happy results. The account given by Mr. Burr of Whitefield's preaching in New England was precisely what we should expect from the man who was afterwards the first president of Princeton college, and who, fourteen years after this, accompanied his eloquent friend to New England, "and saw at Boston, morning after morning, three or four thousand people hanging in breathless silence on the lips of the preacher, and weeping silent tears."

The Rev. Stephen Dodd of East Haven, Conn., relates that an old lady told him that when Mr. Whitefield came to preach in the old meeting-house at Newark, she was twelve years old, and as he entered the pulpit she looked at him with distrust, but before he got through his prayers herself and all the congregation were melted down, and the sermon filled the house with groans and tears. The next time he came, the congregation was so large that the pulpit window was taken out, and he preached through the opening to the people in the burying-ground.

On Wednesday, the 5th, he went to Baskinridge, Mr. Cross' parish, where he found Mr. Davenport, who, according to appointment, had been preaching to about three thousand people. He writes, "As I went along, I told a friend my soul wept for them, and I was persuaded within myself that the Lord would that day make his power to be known among them. In prayer, I perceived my soul drawn out, and a stirring of affections among the people. I had not discoursed long before the Holy Ghost displayed his power. In every part of the congregation somebody or other began to cry out, and almost all melted into tears. This abated for a few moments, till a little boy about seven or eight years of age cried out exceeding piteously indeed, and wept as though his little heart would break. Mr. Cross having compassion on him, took him up into the wagon, which so affected me, that I broke from my discourse, and told the people the little boy should preach to them, and that God, since old professors would not cry after Christ, had displayed his sovereignty, and out of an infant's mouth was perfecting praise. God so blessed this, that a universal concern fell on the congregation again. Fresh persons dropped down here and there, and the cry increased more and more."

In the evening, Gilbert Tennent preached excellently in Mr. Cross' barn, two miles off. His subject was the necessity and benefit of spiritual desertions, a remarkable subject, as has been said, at such a time, in a barn, and at night. "A great commotion," says Whitefield, "was soon observed among the hearers. I then gave a word of exhortation. The Lord's presence attended it in a surprising manner. One, in about six minutes, cried out, 'He is come, He is come!' and could scarcely sustain the discovery that Jesus Christ made of himself to his soul. Others were so earnest for a discovery of the Lord to their souls, that their eager crying obliged me to stop, and I prayed over them as I saw their agonies and distress increase. At length my own soul was so full that I retired, and was in a strong agony for some time, and wept before the Lord under a deep sense of my own vileness, and the sovereignty and greatness of God's everlasting love. Most of the people spent the remainder of the night in prayer and praise. Two or three young ministers spoke alternately, and others prayed as the Lord gave them utterance."

The next morning Whitefield exhorted, sung, and prayed with the people in the barn, and had some delightful conversation with a lad of thirteen, a poor negro woman, and several others. In company with several Christian friends, he then rode to the house of Gilbert Tennent in New Brunswick. Here he found letters from Savannah saying that great mortality existed in the neighborhood, but that the family at the orphan-house continued in health, and that a minister was about coming from England to take his church at Savannah. "This last," says he, "much rejoiced me, being resolved to give up the Savannah living as soon as I arrived in Georgia. A parish and the orphan-house together are too much for me; besides, God seems to show me it is my duty to evangelize, and not to fix in any particular place." Here he was met by William Tennent also, and after much conversation and prayer, it was settled that Gilbert Tennent should go to Boston to carry on the work so happily begun there. After preaching, exhortation, and prayer, Whitefield went with Davenport to Trenton, and so on to Philadelphia. On their way, they were twice remarkably preserved from drowning in creeks much swollen by the rains; and late on a very dark Saturday night arrived in the city, which had been already honored by his usefulness.

On the following day, he twice preached in the house which his friends were now building for him, and in which Gilbert Tennent labored for many years with great success. He says, "It is one hundred feet long and seventy feet broad. A large gallery is to be erected all around in it. Many footsteps of Providence have been visible in beginning and carrying it on. Both in the morning and evening God's glory filled the house, for there was great power in the congregation. The roof is not yet up, but the people raised a convenient pulpit and boarded the bottom. The joy of most of the hearers when they saw me was inexpressible. Between services, I received a packet of letters from England, dated in March last. May the Lord heal, and bring good out of the divisions which at present seem to be among the brethren there. God giving me freedom, and many friends being in the room, I kneeled down and prayed with and exhorted them all. But Oh, how did they melt under both; my soul was much rejoiced to look round on them."

A fact in connection with the building of this church edifice illustrates the practical philosophy of Dr. Franklin. Tennent waited on him for aid in the erection of the house, which was cheerfully afforded; the philosopher was asked by Tennent as to the best method of raising the necessary funds, who instantly recommended him to call at every house in the town to solicit help. He argued thus: "Many are really desirous to give, and will be glad to see you; others are inclined to be friendly, and will give if they are urged; a third will be sure, if they are omitted, to say they would have given had they been asked; and a fourth class will give you, rather than have it said they refused." Tennent acted on the doctor's counsel, and the funds were raised without difficulty.

Two instances of the happy influence of the truth in the conversion of sinners, in connection with this visit, must be given from Whitefield's own pen. The first related to a Mr. Brockden, a lawyer eminent in his profession, and the recorder of deeds for the city. For many years this gentleman had been distinguished for Deism. Whitefield writes, "In his younger days he had some religious impressions, but going into business, the cares of the world so choked the good seed, that he not only forgot his God in some degree, but at length began to doubt of and to dispute his very being. In this state he continued many years, and has been very zealous to propagate his deistical, I could almost say atheistical principles among moral men; but he told me he never endeavored to make proselytes of vicious, debauched people. When I came to Philadelphia, this time twelvemonth, he told me he had not so much as a curiosity to hear me. But a brother Deist, his choicest friend, pressed him to come and hear me. To satisfy his curiosity, he at length complied with the request. I preached at the court-house stairs, upon the conference which the Lord had with Nicodemus. I had not spoken much before the Lord struck his heart. 'For,' said he, 'I saw your doctrine tended to make people good.' His family knew not that he had been to hear me. After he came home, his wife, who had been at sermon, came in also, and wished heartily that he had heard me. He said nothing. After this, another of his family came in, repeating the same wish; and, if I mistake not, after that another; till at last, being unable to refrain any longer, with tears in his eyes, he said, 'Why, I have been hearing him;' and then expressed his approbation. Ever since he has followed on to know the Lord; and I verily believe Jesus Christ has made himself manifest to his soul. Though upwards of threescore years old, he is now, I believe, born again of God. He is as a little child, and often, as he told me, receives such communications from God, when he retires into the woods, that he thinks he could die a martyr for the truth."

The other instance was that of the captain of a ship, "as great a reprobate," says Whitefield, "as ever I heard of." This man used to go on board the transport ships, and offer a guinea for a new oath, that he might have the honor of making it. "To the honor of God's grace," says our evangelist, "let it be said, he is now, I believe, a Christian; not only reformed, but renewed. The effectual stroke, he told me, was given when I preached last spring at Pennepack. Ever since he has been zealous for the truth; stood like a lamb when he was beaten, and in danger of being murdered by some of my opposers, and, in short, shows his faith by his works."

The stay of Mr. Whitefield in Philadelphia at this time was about a week, during which he preached in the new house twice every day to large and deeply interested congregations. He says, "It would be almost endless to recount all the particular instances of God's grace which I have seen this week past. Many that before were only convicted, now plainly proved that they were converted, and had a clear evidence of it within themselves. My chief business was now to build up and to exhort them to continue in the grace of God. Notwithstanding, many were convicted almost every day, and came to me under the greatest distress and anguish of soul. Several societies are now in the town, not only of men and women, but of little boys and little girls. Being so engaged, I could not visit them as I would, but I hope the Lord will raise up some fellow-laborers, and that elders will be ordained in every place."

Perhaps no man was ever more free from sectarianism than George Whitefield. It is true, that he was ordained a clergyman of the church of England, and never manifested any degree of reluctance to officiate within its walls; but it is equally true, that the vast majority of his sermons were delivered in connection with other bodies of Christians. When he was once preaching from the balcony of the court-house, Market-street, Philadelphia, he delivered an impressive apostrophe: "Father Abraham, who have you in heaven? any Episcopalians?" "No." "Any Presbyterians?" "No." "Any Baptists?" "No." "Have you any Methodists, Seceders, or Independents there?" "No, no!" "Why, who have you there?" "We don't know those names here. All who are here are Christians, believers in Christ—men who have overcome by the blood of the Lamb, and the word of his testimony." "Oh, is that the case? then God help me, God help us all, to forget party names, and to become Christians, in deed and in truth." It might be well for the different bodies of Christians to think of the propriety of following this example of the holy man. The peculiarities of each Christian denomination may have their importance, but they ought not to keep good men in a state of separation, much less of alienation from each other.

On Monday, November 17, Whitefield left Philadelphia. He says, "Was much melted at parting from my dear friends. Had it much impressed upon my mind, that I should go to England, and undergo trials for the truth's sake. These words, 'The Jews sought to stone thee, and goest thou thither again?' with our Lord's answer, have been for some time lying upon me; and while my friends were weeping round me, St. Paul's words darted into my soul, 'What mean you to weep and break my heart? I am willing not only to be bound, but to die for the Lord Jesus.' After fervent prayer, I took my leave of some, but being to preach at Gloucester in the West Jerseys, others accompanied me in boats over the river. We sung as we sailed, but my heart was low. I preached at Gloucester, but found myself weighed down, and was not able to deliver my sermon with my usual vigor. However, there was an affecting melting, and several, as I heard afterwards, who had been in bondage before, at that time received joy in the Holy Ghost. I rode on in company with several to Greenwich, and preached to a few, with scarce any power. In the evening we travelled on a few miles, but my body was more and more out of order, and I thought God was preparing me for future blessings. It is good to be humbled. I am never better than when I am brought to lie at the foot of the cross. It is a certain sign God intends that soul a greater crown. Lord, let me always feel myself a poor sinner." On Tuesday he preached at Pilesgrove to about two thousand people, but saw only a few affected. "At night," he says, "God was pleased so abundantly to refresh my soul as to make me forget the weakness of my body; I prayed and exhorted with great power in the family where I lodged." On Wednesday, at Cohansey, where Gilbert Tennent had prepared the way for him, he says, "Preached to some thousands both morning and afternoon. The word gradually struck the hearers, till the whole congregation was greatly moved, and two cried out in the bitterness of their souls after a crucified Saviour, and were scarcely able to stand. My soul was replenished as with new wine, and life and power flew all around me." At Salem, on the 20th, he preached in the morning at the court-house, and in the afternoon in the open air before the prison, to about two thousand persons. "Both times God was with us." On Friday, November 21, he got with some difficulty to Newcastle, where he preached in the court-house, and "observed some few affected, and some few scoffing." Here he was joined by Mr. Charles Tennent, who had lately married a young lady awakened under Whitefield's ministry. They went on to White Clay creek, "and God," says he, "was pleased to appear for me in an extraordinary manner. There were many thousands waiting to hear the word. I have not seen a more lovely sight. I sang the twenty-third psalm, and these words gave my soul unspeakable comfort:

"'In presence of my spiteful foes,
He does my table spread.'

"The Lord Jesus assisted me in preaching. The melting soon began, and the power increased more and more, till the greatest part of the congregation was exceedingly moved. Several cried out in different parts, and others were to be seen wringing their hands and weeping bitterly. The stir was ten times greater than when I was here last." At Fagg's Manor, on Saturday afternoon, he preached "to many thousands, and God was pleased mightily to own his word. There was a wondrous powerful moving, but it did not rise to such a degree as when I preached here last spring. I was taken ill after preaching." After still farther labors, he retired to rest, and he says, "The Lord gave me sweet sleep, and in the morning I arose with my natural strength much renewed." This was the Sabbath, and he preached at Nottingham "to a large congregation, who seemed in no wise to regard the rain, so they might be watered with the dew of God's blessing."

On the following afternoon, at Bohemia, in Maryland, he says, "Preached to about two thousand, and have not seen a more solid melting, I think, since my arrival. Some scoffers stood on the outside, but the Holy Spirit enabled me to lay the terrors of the Lord before them, and they grew more serious. My soul much rejoiced in the Lord to see salvation brought to Maryland." On Tuesday, November 25, "came to Reedy Island, and had the wonderful presence of God in the assembly in the afternoon. Several of my dear Philadelphia friends came to take their last farewell." On Wednesday,

Saturday, and Sunday, he preached again. "The Lord was with us every time. I was greatly delighted to see the captains of the ships, and their respective crews, come constantly to hear the word of God on shore, and join with us in religious exercises on board."

On December 1, when they sailed from Reedy Island to Charleston, he wrote in his journal, "But before I go on, stop, O my soul, and look back a little on the great things the Lord hath done for thee during this excursion. I think it is now the seventy-fifth day since I arrived at Rhode Island. My body was then weak, but the Lord has much renewed its strength. I have been enabled to preach, I think, one hundred and seventy-five times in public, besides exhorting very frequently in private. I have travelled upwards of eight hundred miles, and gotten upwards of £700 sterling in goods, provisions, and money for my poor orphans. Never did God vouchsafe me such great assistances. Never did I perform my journeys with so little fatigue, or see such a continuance of the divine presence in the congregations to whom I have preached. All things concur to convince me that America is to be my chief scene for action."

In about eight days, he arrived at Charleston, where he found there had recently been a large fire, and to improve the sad event he preached a sermon, and passed on to his own home, where he found all well, and where he made arrangements for his voyage to England, leaving on the 29th of December. On that day he narrowly escaped death. A laborer was walking behind him with a gun under his arm, which went off unawares; happily its muzzle was towards the ground, "otherwise," says Whitefield, "I and one of my friends, in all probability, should have been killed; for we were directly before, and not above a yard or two distant from it. How ought we to live in such a state as we would not fear to die in; for in the midst of life we are in death!" In the evening he preached his farewell sermon as pastor of Savannah.

On Mr. Whitefield's arrival at Charleston, in company with two gentlemen named Bryan, who had been called to suffer persecution for Christ's sake, he had the happiness of meeting his brother, the captain of a vessel from England, who gave him much interesting intelligence of the Christians in that country. Commencing with the Sabbath, he preached twice every day, in addition to expounding the Scriptures almost every evening, and expresses his gratitude for divine assistance. But though he had much to rejoice in, he had also more than one source of sorrow. Some professors of religion, of whom he had hoped well, had fallen away, and not a few of his enemies were even more enraged than formerly. Hugh Bryan had written a letter, in which, among other matters, "it was hinted that the clergy break their canons." At the request of Jonathan Bryan, Whitefield had corrected it for the press, and it was published while he was now in the city. Hugh Bryan was apprehended, and on his examination, being asked, frankly confessed that Whitefield had corrected and made some alterations in it. Writing on January 10, he says, "This evening a constable came to me with the following warrant:

> "'South Carolina SS. By B— — W— —, etc. Whereas I have received information upon oath that George Whitefield, Clerk, hath made and composed a false, malicious, scandalous, and infamous Libel against the Clergy of this Province, in contempt of His Majesty and His Laws, and against the King's Peace: These are therefore, in His Majesty's Name, to charge and command you and each of you forthwith to apprehend the said George Whitefield, and to bring him before Me to answer the premises. Hereof fail not, at your peril. And for your so doing this shall be your and each of your sufficient Warrant. Given under my hand and seal this tenth day of January, in the fourteenth year of His Majesty's Reign, Anno Domini one thousand seven hundred and forty [one.]
>
> "'B— — W— —.'"

Whitefield gave security to appear by his attorney at the next quarter sessions, under penalty of one hundred pounds proclamation money. "Blessed be God," he says in his journal, "for this further honor. My soul rejoices in it. I think this may be called persecution. I think it is for righteousness' sake." The next morning he preached on Herod sending the wise men to find out Christ, professing a desire to worship him, but intending to kill him; *persecution under pretence of religion*, being his theme. The afternoon sermon was on the murder of Naboth, from which he discoursed on *the abuse of power by men in authority*. He says, "My hearers, as well as myself, made the application. It was pretty close." No doubt it was. In the evening he expounded the narrative of Orpah and Ruth, and exhorted his hearers to follow the Lord Jesus Christ, though his cause be never so much persecuted and spoken against.

On the following Thursday, he received several highly gratifying letters from his friends at Boston. Mr. Secretary Willard said to him, "Divers young men in this town, who are candidates for the ministry, have been brought under deep convictions by your preaching, and are carried off from the foundation of their false hopes to rest only upon Christ for salvation."

The Rev. Mr. Cooper wrote, "I can inform you that there are many abiding proofs that you did not run in vain, and labor in vain among us in this place. I can only say now in general, some have been awakened who were before quite secure, and I hope a good work begun in them. Others, who had been under religious impressions, are now more earnestly pressing into the kingdom of heaven, and many of the children of God are stirred up to give diligence for the full assurance of faith. There is a greater flocking to all the lectures in the town, and the people show such a disposition to the new Tuesday evening lecture, that our large capacious house cannot receive all that come. I am sure your visit to us has made a large addition to the prayers that are going up for you in one place and another, and I hope also unto the jewels that are to make up your crown in the day of the Lord."

In addition to these statements, Mr. Welch, a pious merchant, wrote, "I fear I am tedious, but I cannot break off till I just mention, to the glory of the grace of God, and for your comfort and encouragement, the success your ministry of late has had among us. Impressions made seem to be abiding on the minds of many. The doctrines of grace seem to be more the topic of conversation than ever I knew them. Nay, religious conversation seems to be almost *fashionable*, and almost every one seems disposed to hear or speak of the things of God. Multitudes flock to the evening lecture, though it has sometimes been the worst of weather. Ministers seem to preach with more life, and the great auditories seem to hear with solemn attention, and I hope our Lord Jesus is getting to himself the victory over the hearts of many sinners."

These, and other letters of a similar character, filled the heart of Whitefield with grateful pleasure; and he went on preaching and enjoying the society of his friends till Friday, January 16. He says, "I never received such generous tokens of love, I think, from any people before, as from some in Charleston. They so loaded me with sea-stores, that I sent many of them to Savannah." He now went on board, and was fully engaged in preparations for the voyage, which however was not entered on till the 24th. On that day the *Minerva* sailed over Charleston bar, and after a generally pleasant voyage, they landed at Falmouth, March 11. "This," says he, "was a profitable voyage to my soul, because of my having had many sweet opportunities for reading, meditation, and prayer."

The impartiality of history requires us, however reluctantly, here to notice the separation which to some extent now took place between Whitefield, and his old friends Messrs. John and Charles Wesley. Their mutual attachment in early life we have already seen, as also Whitefield's anxiety in Georgia to defend Mr. John Wesley's conduct against those who opposed him. Impartial observers, however, after a while began to remark, that on some doctrinal points, especially on that of predestination, a difference was springing up. On his passage to England, February 1, 1741,

Whitefield thus wrote to Mr. Charles Wesley: "My dear, dear brethren, why did you throw out the bone of contention? Why did you print that sermon against predestination? Why did you in particular, my dear brother Charles, affix your hymn, and join in putting out your late hymn-book? How can you say you will not dispute with me about election, and yet print such hymns? and your brother sent his sermon against election, to Mr. Garden and others in America. Do not you think, my dear brethren, I must be as much concerned for truth, or what I think truth, as you? God is my judge, I always was, and hope I always shall be desirous that you may be preferred before me. But I must preach the gospel of Christ, and that I cannot *now* do, without speaking of election." He then tells Mr. Charles Wesley, that in Christmas-week he had written an answer to his brother's sermon, "which," says he, "is now printing at Charleston; another copy I have sent to Boston, and another I now bring with me, to print in London. If it occasion a strangeness between us, it shall not be my fault. There is nothing in my answer exciting to it, that I know of. O, my dear brethren, my heart almost bleeds within me. Methinks I could be willing to tarry here on the waters for ever, rather than come to England to oppose you."

Dr. Whitehead, in his "Life of John Wesley," has very wisely said, "Controversy almost always injures the Christian temper, much more than it promotes the interests of speculative truth. On this question a separation took place between Mr. Wesley and Mr. Whitefield, so far as to have different places of worship; and some warm and tart expressions dropped from each. But their good opinion of each other's integrity and usefulness, founded on long and intimate acquaintance, could not be injured by such a difference of sentiment; and their mutual affection was only obscured by a cloud for a season."

The friendship between Mr. Whitefield and the Messrs. Wesley was very much increased and perpetuated by the wife of Mr. Charles Wesley. This very extraordinary lady, whose original name was Gwinne, was equally distinguished for her beauty, talents, and piety. She had a very cordial regard for Mr. Whitefield, who as cordially reciprocated it. She was married when the controversy among these eminent men was at its height, and stipulated that she should always be allowed to hear the preaching of Whitefield and his friends. In her latter years especially, and she lived till ninety-six, she expressed her pleasure in the belief that she promoted the continuance of that endearing intercourse which subsisted between Whitefield and her husband. She softened all parties, and was on all occasions a blessed peacemaker.

One fact relating to this eminently excellent woman may be mentioned. She was nearly twenty years younger than her husband, and four years after her marriage, and at the age of twenty-six, she was seized with small-pox, of which at that time her eldest child died. She lay twenty-two days in imminent danger of death, and when she recovered she was so much altered in features that no one could recognize her; but never did woman before lose her beauty with so little regret. She used sportively to say, that the change in her appearance "afforded great satisfaction to her dear husband, who was glad to see her look so much older, and better suited to be his companion."

On Whitefield's arrival at Falmouth, he immediately set off in a post-chaise to London, in order to preach on the following Sabbath. But he now found occasion for all the patience he had acquired. He had, he says, "written two well-meant, though ill-judged letters against England's two great favorites, '*The Whole Duty of Man*,' and Archbishop Tillotson, who, I said, knew no more about religion than Mohammed. The Moravians had made inroads on our societies;" besides which, the controversy with the Messrs. Wesley injured him. His congregations on the Sabbath were still large, but on week-days he had not more than two or three hundred hearers. He says, "Instead of having thousands to attend me, scarcely one of my spiritual children come to see me from morning to night. Once, on Kennington Common, I had not above a hundred to hear me."

Even this was not all. He says, "One that got some hundreds of pounds by my sermons, refused to print for me any more. And others wrote to me, that God would destroy me in a fortnight, and that my fall was as great as Peter's." Still other sorrows attended him. He writes, "I was much embarrassed in my outward circumstances. A thousand pounds I owed for the orphan-house. Two hundred and fifty pounds drawn on Mr. Seward, [who was now dead,] were returned upon me. I was also threatened to be arrested for two hundred pounds more." Besides all this, he had "a family of one hundred persons to be maintained, four thousand miles off, in the dearest part of his majesty's dominions." He now began to preach in Moorfields on week-days, under one of the trees; where he saw numbers of his spiritual children running by him without looking at him, and some of them putting their fingers in their ears, that they might not hear one word he said. "A like scene," he says, "opened at Bristol, where I was denied preaching in the house I had founded." It was the Kingswood school-house, built for the children of the colliers.

But Whitefield could not long be kept down. His friends built a new house and opened a new school at Kingswood. Some "free-grace dissenters," as Gillies calls them, procured the loan of a building lot in London, on which, as we have already seen, they built the Tabernacle. Here his congregations immediately increased, and he addressed them with his usual power and success. Invitations soon poured in from the country, and even from places where he had never been. At a common near Braintree, in Essex, he had more than ten thousand hearers, and at many other places congregations were large and much affected. "Sweet," says he, "was the conversation which I had with several ministers of Christ." Soon again did he triumph, even in England.

Among the men who were now invited to aid, and who rendered important assistance to Whitefield in his houses of worship in London and Bristol, as well as in his itinerant labors, was Howel Harris, a native of Wales, a gentleman, and a magistrate, to whom we have already referred. His name in Wales is yet "a household word," and his labors form a part of the history of Welsh Calvinistic Methodism. As soon as he had embraced the gospel for himself, he became intensely solicitous respecting the condition of his neighbors. The scenes of profligacy and vice which everywhere presented themselves burdened his heart, and he became anxious to be actively employed in removing evil and doing good. He determined on taking orders in the church of England, and accordingly entered St. Mary's Hall, in Oxford university; but shocked at the dissolute habits of the collegians, and finding what were called his methodistical views were in the way of his ordination, he returned to Wales, and began to evangelize its towns and villages. Wherever there was an opening, there he went, and preached Christ to the people; and although defamed and persecuted, he manfully prosecuted his work, and thousands were by his agency brought to repentance. He and Mr. Whitefield were kindred spirits, moved by the same impulses, and pursuing the same course. Mr. Whitefield spoke of him as "'a burning and shining light,' a barrier against profaneness and immorality, and an indefatigable promoter of the true gospel of Jesus Christ. For these years he has preached almost twice a day, for three or four hours together. He has been in seven counties, and has made it his business to go to wakes and fairs to turn people from their lying vanities. He has been made the subject of numbers of sermons, has been threatened with public prosecutions, and had constables sent to apprehend him. But God has blessed him with inflexible courage; strength has been communicated to him from above, and he still goes on from conquering to conquer. God has greatly blessed his pious endeavors; many call, and own him as their spiritual father, and would, I believe, lay down their lives for his sake."

In the year 1759, when England was threatened with a French invasion, Mr. Harris became a captain in the Brecknockshire militia, and into whatever place in England the regiment was ordered, he uniformly began to preach, and was the means of introducing the gospel into many ignorant and depraved districts. Thus an unusual act and an undesirable office were overruled to doing much good. When the regiment was disbanded, he again regularly entered on his ministerial duties with all his former zeal and activity. In a word, he may justly be regarded the evangelist of Wales.

As an illustration of the spirit of the energetic ministers of Christ in those days, we quote a fact or two from the life of Rowland Hill; the more readily as Howel Harris is the principal subject. In 1774, four years after the death of Whitefield, Mr. Hill travelled through Wales, preaching three or four times every day; many conversions took place, which greatly sustained him under an attack of illness; and led to the remark in his "Journal," "My body quite weak, but my soul was refreshed." "A like example," says Sidney, one of the biographers of Hill, "had been previously before his eyes in the case of Howel Harris, one of Mr. Whitefield's energetic followers, who was a man of extraordinary powers of body and mind. Harris used to relate of himself, that being once on a journey through Wales, he was subjected to great temptation to desert his Master's cause, when he said, 'Satan, I'll match thee for this;' and 'so I did,' he used to add; 'for I had not ridden many miles before I came to a revel, where there was a show of mountebanks, which I entered, and just as they were commencing, I jumped into the midst of them and cried out, 'Let us pray,' which so thunderstruck them that they listened to me quietly, while I preached to them a most tremendous sermon, that frightened many of them home.' Mr. Hill greatly delighted in this anecdote, and often said that amidst somewhat similar scenes, he had been enabled successfully to attack the kingdom of Satan."

CHAPTER VIII
FIRST AND SECOND VISITS TO SCOTLAND—LABORS IN ENGLAND AND WALES. 1740-1744

We have seen the spirit in which Mr. Whitefield returned to London, and the cool manner in which he was too generally received. It is painful to say that this coldness was not confined to enemies of the truth; it appeared in some degree in eminent dissenting ministers, as Watts and Bradbury, Barker, and even, to some extent, Doddridge. A plan had a few years before been agitated to restore the dissenters to the church, usually called the *Comprehension scheme*, and assuredly, under the circumstances, friendship with Whitefield was by no means favorable to such a plan being accomplished, though it was at this period greatly desired by many of both parties. Still, however, good was done; Whitefield preached, and God was glorified. More union between Christians in advancing the cause of Christ would have been exceedingly desirable, but even the want of this was not permitted to stay the progress of this man of God.

One of the most popular and useful ministers employed by Whitefield and his friends at this time was John Cennick, the author of two well-known hymns, beginning,

> "Jesus, thy blood and righteousness;"
> "Jesus, my all, to heaven is gone."

He was the preacher who, in Ireland, discoursed from the text, "Ye shall find the babe wrapped in swaddling clothes," which gave occasion for the Methodists in that country to be called "*Swaddlers*." The parents of this excellent man were Quakers, who had been imprisoned in Reading jail for the maintenance of their religious principles. This persecution reduced them from respectability to want, so that, like John Bunyan, they were forced to make shoe-laces in prison for their support.

The conversion of the son was very remarkable. His first deep and lasting religious convictions flashed upon his mind like lightning from heaven, while walking in the crowds of Cheapside, in London. The effects were soon manifested; he became a new man, pursuing a new course, and entering on a new work. His ministry was very efficient, his views of truth were evangelical, his public speaking popular, his zeal so great as sometimes to lead him to preach six times in one day—all which labors were followed with abundant success.

Mr. Cennick was rather below the middle stature, of a fair countenance, and though by no means robust in health, he knew little of timidity. The spirit in which he discharged his ministry may be seen in a letter he wrote to a friend: "We sang a hymn, and then the devil led on his servants; they began beating a drum, and then made fires of gunpowder: at first the poor flock was startled; but while God gave me power to speak encouragingly to them, they waxed bolder, and very few moved. The mob then fired guns over the people's heads, and began to play a water engine upon brother Harris and myself, till we were wet through. They also played an engine upon us with hog's-wash and grounds of beer-barrels, and covered us with muddy water from a ditch; they pelted us with eggs and stones, threw baskets of dust over us, and fired their guns so close to us that our faces were black with the powder; but, in nothing terrified, we remained praying. I think I never saw or felt so great a power of God as was there. In the midst of the confused multitude, I saw a man laboring above measure, earnest to fill the buckets with water to throw upon us. I asked him, 'What harm do we do? Why are you so furious against us? We only come to tell you that Christ loved you, and died for you.' He stepped back a little for room, and threw a bucket of water in my face. When I had recovered myself, I said, 'My dear man, if God should so pour his wrath upon you, what would become of you? Yet I tell you that Christ loves you.' He threw away the bucket, let fall his trembling hands, and looked as pale as death; he then shook hands with me, and parted from me, I believe under strong convictions."

Mr. Cennick had heretofore labored with Whitefield and Wesley, but now adhered to the former, and labored very successfully in the Tabernacle. After some years he united with the Moravian brethren, and died in triumph at thirty-five.

In the summer of 1741, some three or four months after his arrival from America, Whitefield paid his first visit to Scotland. The state of religion in that country at the commencement of the ministry of this distinguished evangelist, has been already glanced at. It is here important to remark, that in 1740 an indication of better things began to appear in several places, especially in Cambuslang, under the ministry of the Rev. Mr. M'Culloch. This excellent man, for nearly a year before the revival began, had been preaching to his people on those subjects which tend most directly to explain the nature and prove the necessity of regeneration, according to the different aspects in which it is represented in the holy Scriptures. The church edifice had become too small for the congregation, and the minister, in favorable weather, frequently conducted the public worship on a green brae on the east side of a deep ravine near the church, scooped out in the form of an amphitheatre. In this retired and romantic spot, the worthy pastor preached in the most impressive manner to the listening multitudes, and not unfrequently, after his sermons, detailed to them the astonishing effects of Whitefield's preaching in America, which did not a little to increase the interest of the people, as well as lead them to wish to see such an extraordinary preacher.

While on his voyage to Scotland, Whitefield gave evidence that he had not forgotten America. In his second visit to America, he had become intimately acquainted with the Rev. Daniel Rodgers of Exeter, New Hampshire, a direct descendant of the seventh generation of John Rogers, who was burnt at the stake for the testimony of Christ in the days of the bloody Mary. It is not surprising that Whitefield's original letter to him, now in the possession of the family of the grandson of Daniel Rodgers, is highly valued. It is dated on board the Mary and Ann, bound from London to Scotland, July 25, 1741.

> "My dear Brother Rodgers—How glad was I to receive a letter from your hands, having heard nothing from you or of you particularly since we parted. Oh, what great things has the Lord shown us since that time! methinks I hear you say; and yet I can tell of greater things. And I believe we shall see far greater yet before we die. The work is beginning afresh here. I sometimes think brother Gilbert [Tennent] must take a voyage to old England. Most of our London ministers too much shun the cross, and do not appear boldly for God. Now the Lord has worked so powerfully in your college, I have less to object against your joining Mr. Web. I am glad to hear that you speak *plain and close*. What comfort will this afford you in a dying hour. Go on, my dear brother, go on; venture daily upon Christ. Go out in his strength, and he will enable us to do wonders. He is with me more and more. I have sweetly been carried through the heat and burning of every day's labor. Jesus bears all my burdens. Jesus enables me to cast all my care upon him. Oh then, let us magnify his name together. I am now going to Scotland, knowing not what will befall me. What God does, you may expect to hear of shortly. In the meanwhile, let us pray for and write to each other. As iron sharpeneth iron, so do the letters of a man his friend. Your last I have printed. God's glory called me to it.

"My dear brother, adieu. Dear brother Sims sits by and salutes you. My kind love awaits Mr. Web, and all who love the Lord in sincerity. In hopes of receiving another letter from you shortly, I subscribe myself, dear Mr. Rodgers, your most affectionate, though very unworthy brother and servant in the sweetest Jesus,

"G. W."

Among those who were most anxious that Mr. Whitefield should visit Scotland, were the Rev. Messrs. Ebenezer and Ralph Erskine. These two excellent brothers had separated themselves from the established church, chiefly on the ground of its cold formalism, and with some other zealous ministers had formed what has since been known as the Associate Presbytery. Their wish was, that in coming to Scotland, Whitefield should preach only in connection with their body, and so help forward the work in which they were engaged. To this he objected, regarding himself as an evangelist at large. As he proceeded, they rather opposed him, as not sufficiently particular and discriminative in his zeal. They wished him not to labor in the church from which they had seceded, saying, "God had left it." "Then," said he, "it is the more necessary for me to preach in it, to endeavor to bring him back. I'll preach Christ wherever they'll let me." On the 30th of July he arrived in Edinburgh, where he was urged to preach, but declined till he had seen the Messrs. Erskine; and accordingly proceeded to Dunfermline. Writing on the 1st of August, he says, "I went yesterday to Dunfermline, where dear Mr. Ralph Erskine hath got a large and separate, or as it is commonly termed, seceding meeting-house. He received me very lovingly. I preached to his and the town's people—a very thronged assembly. After I had done prayers and named my text, the rustling made by opening the Bibles all at once quite surprised me—a scene I never was witness to before."

On the day following, Whitefield returned to Edinburgh, accompanied by Mr. Ralph Erskine, and preached in the Orphan-house park to a large and attentive audience. His text was, "The kingdom of God is not meat and drink, but righteousness, and peace, and joy in the Holy Ghost." Rom. 14:17. After the sermon, a large company, including some of the nobility, came to bid him God-speed; and among others a portly Quaker, a nephew of the Messrs. Erskine, who, taking him by the hand, said, "Friend George, I am as thou art; I am for bringing all to the life and power of the ever-living God; and therefore, if thou wilt not quarrel with me about my hat, I will not quarrel with thee about thy gown." On Sabbath evening, he preached in the same place, to upwards of fifteen thousand persons; and on the evenings of Monday, Wednesday, and Friday, to nearly as many; on Tuesday in the

Canongate church; on Wednesday and Thursday at Dunfermline; and on Friday morning at Queensferry. "Everywhere," says he, "the auditories were large and very attentive. Great power accompanied the word. Many have been brought under convictions, and I have already received invitations to different places, which, God willing, I intend to comply with." Writing a week later, he says, "It would make your heart leap for joy to be now in Edinburgh. I question if there be not upwards of three hundred in this city seeking after Jesus. Every morning I have a constant levee of wounded souls, many of whom are quite slain by the law. God's power attends the word continually, just as when I left London. At seven in the morning we have a lecture in the fields, attended not only by the common people, but also by persons of rank. I have reason to think that several of the latter sort are coming to Jesus. Little children also are much wrought upon. God much blesses my letters from the little orphans, [girls in the hospital.] He loves to work by contemptible means. Oh, my dear brother, I am quite amazed when I think what God has done here in a fortnight. My printed sermons and journals have been blessed in an uncommon manner. I am only afraid lest people should idolize the instrument, and not look enough to the glorious Jesus, in whom alone I desire to glory. Congregations consist of many thousands. Never did I see so many Bibles, nor people looking into them, while I am expounding, with so much attention. Plenty of tears flow from the hearers' eyes. Their emotions appear in various ways. I preach twice daily, and expound at private houses at night, and am employed in speaking to souls under distress great part of the day. I have just snatched a few moments to write to my dear brother. Oh, that God may enlarge your heart to pray for me. This afternoon I preach out of town, and also to-morrow. Next post, God willing, you shall have another letter. I walk continually in the comforts of the Holy Ghost. The love of Christ quite strikes me dumb. O grace, grace! let that be my song. Adieu."

In this manner Whitefield continued to preach very extensively over Scotland; and early in September he arrived at Glasgow. On the eleventh of that month he began his labors in the High Church-yard, and for five days in succession preached there twice a day—at an early hour in the morning, and again in the evening. The expectations of the people were high, not only in Glasgow, but all around, and crowds flocked to hear him preach. Morning after morning, and evening after evening, that vast church-yard, almost paved as it is with tombstones, was crowded with living worshippers, trembling under the word. But not satisfied with hearing, the pen of the ready writer was from day to day at work, and each sermon was printed by itself, and put immediately into circulation. His sermons were characterized by great simplicity, as if the language of the preacher merely expressed what he felt, and yet there was so much earnestness, and so much closeness of application, as to account for the effects they produced. He was in the pulpit very much what Baxter was in the press. He spoke as a man realizing all that he said, and laying open the feelings of his own heart in addressing the hearts of others.

Very few men better knew the human heart than Whitefield. He seemed to know all the thoughts and feelings of his hearers, and the best way in which to meet them. He once preached in Scotland from the text, "The door was shut." Matt. 25:10. A respectable lady who heard him sat near the door, a considerable distance from the pulpit, and observed two showy and trifling young men who appeared to turn the solemn appeals of the preacher into ridicule; she heard one of them say in a low tone to the other, "Well, what if the door be shut? another will open." In a very few minutes, to the great surprise of the lady, Mr. Whitefield said, "It is possible there may be some careless, trifling person here to-day, who may ward off the force of this impressive subject by lightly thinking, 'What matter if the door be shut? another will open.'" The two young men looked at each other as though they were paralyzed, as the preacher proceeded: "Yes, another door will open; and I will tell you what door it will be: it will be the door of the bottomless pit, the door of hell!—the door which conceals from the eyes of angels the horrors of damnation."

After Mr. Whitefield's return to England, at the close of October, among many letters which followed him, detailing the results of his labors, was one from Mr. M'Culloch, the excellent minister already referred to:

"As it is matter of joy and thankfulness to God, who sent you hither, and gave you so much countenance, and so remarkably crowned your labors with success here at Glasgow, so I doubt not but the following account of the many seals to your ministry in and about that city, will be very rejoicing to your heart, especially as the kingdom of our glorious Redeemer is so much advanced thereby, and as the everlasting happiness of souls is promoted. I am well informed by some ministers, and other judicious and experienced Christians, that there are to the amount of fifty persons already known, in and about Glasgow, who appear to be savingly converted, through the blessing and power of God on your ten sermons. And there are, besides these, several others apparently under conviction, but not reckoned, as being still doubtful. Several Christians also, of considerable standing, were much strengthened, revived, and comforted by what they heard. They were made to rejoice in hope of the glory of God, having attained to the full assurance of faith. Among those lately converted, there are several young people who were before openly wicked and flagitious, or at best but very negligent as to spiritual things; and yet they are now in the way of salvation. Some young converts are yet under doubts and fears, but a considerable number of them have attained to peace and joy in believing. Several of those who were lately wrought on in a gracious way, seem to outstrip Christians of considerable standing, in spiritual-mindedness, and in many other good qualifications; particularly in their zeal for the conversion of others, in their love to ordinances, and in their freedom from bigotry and party zeal. Those converted by your ministry have not been discovered at once, but only from time to time. A good many of them have been discovered only of late. Their convictions were at first less pungent, and through the discouragements they met with in the families where they resided, as well as from their own feelings, they endeavored for a time to conceal their state. These circumstances afford ground for hoping, that there are yet others who may afterwards become known. Besides such as have been awakened through the power of God accompanying your sermons, there have been others who have been since awakened, and who have been discovered in consequence of the change observable in their conduct. These, dear brother, are a few hints concerning some of the most remarkable things, as to the blessing which accompanied your labors at Glasgow."

At Edinburgh, when first visited by Whitefield, many persons of the highest rank constantly attended his ministry. Among them were the Marquis of Lothian, the Earl of Leven, Lord Ray, Lady Mary Hamilton, Lady Frances Gardiner, Lady Jane Nimms, and Lady Dirleton; and at some one of their houses he expounded almost every evening. Numbers of ministers and students crowded to hear him; and aged Christians told him they could set their seal to what he preached.

In connection with this first visit to Edinburgh, several incidents have been related which show the power that accompanied his preaching, and the skill with which he could seize upon passing circumstances, and apply them to the great purpose which he always had in view. A gentleman, on returning from one of his sermons, was met on his way home by an eminent minister whom he usually heard, and who expressed great surprise that he should go to hear such a man. The gentleman replied, "Sir, when I hear you, I am planting trees all the time; but during the whole of Mr. Whitefield's sermon, I could not find time to plant one." A similar instance is related of a ship-builder, who usually could "build a ship from stem to stern during the sermon; but under Mr. Whitefield, could not lay a single plank."

Another narrative has been thus given. An unhappy man who had forfeited his life to the offended laws of his country, was executed in that neighborhood. Mr. Whitefield mingled with the crowd collected on the occasion, and was much impressed with the decorum and solemnity which were observable in the awful scene. His appearance, however, drew the eyes of all upon him, and produced a variety of opinions as to the motives which led him to join the multitude.

The next day, being Sunday, he preached to a very large congregation in a field near the city; and in the course of his sermon, he adverted to the scenes of the preceding day. "I know," said he, "that many of you may find it difficult to reconcile my appearance yesterday with my clerical character. Many of you, I know, will say that my moments would have been better employed in praying for the unhappy man, than in attending him to the fatal tree; and that perhaps curiosity was the only cause that converted me into a spectator on that occasion; but those who ascribe that uncharitable motive to me, are under a mistake. I went as an observer of human nature, and to see the effect that such an occurrence would have on those who witnessed it. I watched the conduct of those who were present on that awful occasion, and I was highly pleased with their demeanor, which has given me a very favorable opinion of the Scottish nation. Your sympathy was visible on your countenances; particularly when the moment arrived that your unhappy fellow-creature was to close his eyes on this world for ever. Then you all, as if moved by one impulse, turned your heads aside, and wept. Those tears were precious, and will be held in remembrance. How different it was when the Saviour of mankind was extended on the cross! The Jews, instead of sympathizing in his sorrows, triumphed in them. They reviled him with bitter expressions, with words even more bitter than the gall and vinegar which they handed him to drink. Not one of all who witnessed his pains, turned his head aside, even in the last pang. Yes, my friends, there was *one*—that glorious luminary," pointing to the sun, "veiled his brightness, and travelled on his course in tenfold night."

On another occasion, near the same city, and probably in the field to which we have already referred, under the shade of a venerable tree, in a lovely meadow, a poor unhappy man, thinking to turn him into ridicule, placed himself on one of the overhanging boughs, immediately above the preacher's head, and with monkey-like dexterity mimicking his gestures, endeavored to raise a laugh in the audience. Guided by the looks of some of his hearers, Whitefield caught a glance of him, but without seeming to have noticed him, continued his discourse. With the skill of a wise orator, he reserved the incident for the proper place and time. While forcibly speaking on the power and sovereignty of divine grace, with increasing earnestness he spoke of the unlikely objects it had often chosen, and the unlooked for triumphs it had achieved. As he rose to the climax of his inspiring theme, and when in the full sweep of his eloquence, he suddenly paused, and turning round, and pointing slowly to the poor creature above him, he exclaimed, in a tone of deep and thrilling pathos, "Even *he* may yet be the subject of that free and resistless grace." It was a shaft from the Almighty. Winged by the divine Spirit, it struck the scoffer to the heart, and realized in his conversion the glorious truth it contained.

Yet another fact may be told connected with Whitefield and Edinburgh. When he was once there, a regiment of soldiers were stationed in the city, in which was a sergeant whose name was Forbes, a very abandoned man, who, everywhere he could do so, run in debt for liquor, with which he was almost at all times drunk. His wife washed for the regiment, and thus obtained a little money. She was a pious woman, but all her attempts to reclaim her husband were unsuccessful. During one of Mr. Whitefield's visits to the city, she offered her husband a sum of money, if he would for once go and hear the eloquent preacher. This was a strong inducement, and he engaged to go. The sermon was in a field, as no building could have contained the audience. The sergeant was rather early, and placed himself in the middle of the field, that he might file off when Mr. Whitefield ascended the pulpit; as he only wished to be able to say that he had seen him. The crowd, however, increased; and when the preacher appeared, they pressed forward, and the sergeant found it impossible to get away. The prayer produced some impression on his mind, but the sermon convinced him of his sinfulness and danger. He became a changed man, and showed the reality of his conversion by living for many years in a very penurious manner, till he had satisfied the claims of every one of his creditors.

One fact more should be stated in connection with this visit. Mr. James Ogilvie was one of the ministers of Aberdeen. This city was not in that day, nor indeed in any part of the eighteenth century, warmly attached to a fully-exhibited gospel. At this time, however, both Mr. Ogilvie and his colleague, Mr. Bisset, who, as Sir Henry Moncrieff says, was the highest of the High church, were evangelical, though otherwise very opposite men. "Though colleagues of the same congregation," says Whitefield, "they are very different in their natural temper. The one is, what they call in Scotland, a sweet-blooded man, the other of a choleric disposition. Mr. Bisset is neither a seceder nor quite a true kirkman, having great fault to find with both. Soon after my arrival, dear Mr. Ogilvie took me to pay my respects to him. He was prepared for it, and pulled out a paper containing a great number of insignificant queries, which I had neither time nor inclination to answer." For several years Mr. Ogilvie had been corresponding with Mr. Whitefield to induce him to visit Aberdeen, hoping that some good might be done; and as he was himself to preach on Sabbath forenoon in presence of the magistrates, he gave Mr. Whitefield his place. The congregation was large, and apparently much interested. Mr. Bisset, in the afternoon, preached against Mr. Whitefield by name. Mr. Ogilvie, without either consulting his friend, or noticing the conduct of his colleague, stood up, after the sermon, and intimated to the congregation that Mr. Whitefield would again preach in about half an hour. The magistrates remained in the session-house, and the people hastened back, expecting to bear a reply. Mr. Whitefield, waiving as much as possible all controversial matter, preached Christ. The audience was silent, solemn, and deeply impressed. Next day, the magistrates apologized for their minister; and as a mark of their own respect, presented to Mr. Whitefield the freedom of their city. The effect of this visit to Aberdeen was great and beneficial.

In 1742, Mr. Whitefield again visited Scotland. In the mean time he had heard that his dear friends the Erskines had become greatly offended, on account of what they considered his lax views of church government. But notwithstanding this difference with the seceders, he was received by great numbers, among whom were some persons of distinction, with cordiality and joy, and had the satisfaction of hearing more and more of the happy fruits of his ministry. At Edinburgh he again preached twice a day, as before, in the Hospital-park, where a number of seats and shades, in the form of an amphitheatre, were erected for the accommodation of his hearers. On the day of his arrival at Cambuslang, he preached three times to an immense body of people, although he had preached that same morning at Glasgow. The last service continued till eleven o'clock; and so much were the people interested, that Mr. M'Culloch, after preaching till past one in the morning, could scarcely persuade them to depart. Mr. Whitefield himself thus describes the scene: "Persons from all parts flocked to see, and many, from many parts, went home convinced and converted to God. A brae, or hill, near the manse at Cambuslang, seemed to be formed by Providence for containing a large congregation. People sat unwearied till two in the morning, to hear sermons, disregarding the weather. You could scarcely walk a yard, but you must tread upon some either rejoicing in God for mercies received, or crying out for more. Thousands and thousands have I seen, before it was possible to catch it by sympathy, melted down under the word and power of God. At the celebration of the holy communion, their joy was so great, that, at the desire of many, both ministers and people, in imitation of Hezekiah's passover, they had, a month or two afterwards, a second, which was a general rendezvous of the people of God. The communion was in the field; three tents, at proper distances, all surrounded with a multitude of hearers; above twenty ministers, among whom was good old Mr. Bonner, attending to preach and assist, all enlivening and enlivened by one another."

In addition to his labors at Glasgow and Cambuslang, it is surprising to observe the number of places in the west of Scotland which Whitefield visited in the course of a few weeks; preaching wherever he went, with his usual frequency, energy, and success. A gentleman of piety and intelligence thus refers to one of them several years afterwards: "When Mr. Whitefield was preaching at Kilmarnock, on the twenty-third of August, from the words, 'And of his fulness have all we received, and grace for grace,' I thought I never heard such a sermon; and from the era above mentioned, I have always looked upon him as my spiritual father, and frequently heard him afterwards in Edinburgh and Glasgow with much satisfaction. When Cape Breton was taken, I happened to be at Edinburgh, and being invited to breakfast with Mr. Whitefield, I never, in all my life, enjoyed such another breakfast. He gave the company a fine and lively descant upon that part of the world, made us all join in a hymn of praise and thanksgiving, and concluded with a most devout and fervent prayer." About the end of October, Whitefield returned to London.

Probably few are aware that Mr. Whitefield visited Scotland no less than *fourteen* times. These visits extended over a period of twenty-seven years, beginning in 1741, and ending in 1768. In none of his visits after 1742 were there the same extensive awakenings as in his first two visits, yet his coming was always refreshing to serious persons, infusing new life, and increasing their numbers. Young people, too, were much benefited by his ministry, and especially young students, who afterwards became zealous and evangelical preachers. His morning discourses, which were generally intended for sincere but disconsolate souls, were peculiarly fitted to direct and encourage such in the Christian life; and his addresses in the evening to the promiscuous multitudes who then attended him, were powerful and alarming. There was great solemnity in his evening congregations in the Orphan-house park at Edinburgh and the High Church-yard at Glasgow, especially towards the conclusion of his sermons—which were usually long, though they seemed short to his hearers—when the whole multitude stood fixed, and like one man, hung upon his lips with silent attention, and many were under deep religious impressions.

His conversation was no less useful and delightful than his sermons. Many in Glasgow, Edinburgh, and other parts of the land, bore witness of this fact. In Glasgow especially, when in company with his excellent friends M'Laurin, Scott, and others, one might challenge the professed sons of pleasure, with all their wit, humor, and gayety, to furnish entertainments so gratifying; nor was any part of it more agreeable than it was useful and edifying.

Mr. Whitefield's friends in Scotland, among whom were many of all ranks, from the highest to the lowest, were constant and steady in their great regard for him, and his opposers from year to year became less violent. Indeed, his whole behavior was so transparent to the eyes of the world, and his character, after it had stood many attacks from all quarters, became so thoroughly established, that some of his opposers in Scotland seemed to acquire esteem for him; at least, they ceased to speak evil of him.

In closing our sketch of Whitefield in Scotland, we select a few paragraphs from his letters, which are the more interesting as being among the very last words he wrote in that country. June 15, 1768, he says, "You would be delighted to see our Orphan-house park assemblies, as large, attentive, and affectionate as ever. Twenty-seven-year-old friends and spiritual children remember the days of old; they are seeking after their first love, and there seems to be a stirring among the dry bones." Writing on the second of July, he says, "Could I preach ten times a day, thousands and thousands would attend. I have been confined for a few days; but on Monday or Tuesday next, hope to mount my throne again. O, to die there! too great, too great an honor to be expected." Again, on the ninth of July, "Every thing goes on better and better here; but I am so worn down by preaching abroad and talking at home almost all the day long, that I have determined, God willing, to set off for London next Tuesday."

The respect with which Whitefield was treated in Scotland, not only by professing Christians, but in general society, was shown by the fact that he was presented with the freedom of some of the principal cities and towns which he visited. This privilege was given him in Stirling, Glasgow, Paisley, and Aberdeen, in 1741, and at Irvine and Edinburgh some years afterwards.

It is difficult, in such a world as this, so to live as that "our good" shall not "be evil spoken of." Mr. Whitefield has sometimes been charged with motives of a mercenary character, but his whole life showed the fallacy of such a charge. Dr. Gillies, his original biographer, received from unquestionable testimony the knowledge of a fact which ought not to be forgotten. During his stay in Scotland, in the year 1759, a young lady,

Miss Hunter, who possessed a considerable fortune, made a full offer to him of her estate in money and lands, worth several thousand pounds. He promptly refused the offer; and upon his declining it for himself, she offered it to him for the benefit of his orphan-house. This also he absolutely refused.

Never could Whitefield be accused of moral cowardice. When the old Scotch Marquis of Lothian professed that his heart was impressed with the importance of religion, but wished to be a Christian in the dark, Whitefield said to him, "As for praying in your family, I entreat you not to neglect it; you are bound to do it. Apply to Christ to overcome your present fears; they are the effects of pride or infidelity, or both."

On his return from Scotland to London in 1741, Whitefield passed through Wales, where at Abergavenny he was married to a Mrs. James, a widow, some ten years older than himself. Of this marriage, as also of the death of his only child, we have already spoken. After preaching at Bristol twice a day for several days in succession, he returned to London in the beginning of December, where he found letters from Georgia, which, on account of the temporal circumstances of his orphan family, somewhat discouraged him. But to trace his progress, and to report all his labors, would be to extend our volume beyond its due limits.

He was soon again in the west of England, and writing from Gloucester, his native place, December 23, 1741, he says, "Last Thursday evening the Lord brought me hither. I preached immediately to our friends in a large barn, and had my Master's presence. Both the power and the congregation increased. On Sunday, Providence opened a door for my preaching in St. John's, one of the parish churches. Great numbers came. On Sunday afternoon, after I had preached twice at Gloucester, I preached at the hill, six miles off, and again at night at Stroud. The people seemed to be more hungry than ever, and the Lord to be more among them. Yesterday morning I preached at Painswick, in the parish church, here in the afternoon, and again at night in the barn. God gives me unspeakable comfort and uninterrupted joy. Here seems to be a new awakening, and a revival of the work of God. I find several country people were awakened when I preached at Tewkesbury, and have heard of three or four that have died in the Lord. We shall never know what good field-preaching has done till we come to judgment. Many who were prejudiced against me begin to be of another mind; and God shows me more and more that 'when a man's ways please the Lord, he will make even his enemies to be at peace with him.'"

In the following February he was still further encouraged by receiving letters from America, informing him of the remarkable success of the gospel there, and that God had stirred up some wealthy friends to assist his orphans in their extremity. He writes, "The everlasting God reward all their benefactors. I find there has been a fresh awakening among them. I am informed that twelve negroes belonging to a planter lately converted at the orphan-house, are savingly brought home to Jesus Christ." Nor were these things all which afforded him joy. Writing to a friend, April 6, he says, "Our Saviour is doing great things in London daily. I rejoice to hear that you are helped in your work. Let this encourage you; go on, go on; the more we do, the more we may do for Jesus. I sleep and eat but little, and am constantly employed from morning till midnight, and yet my strength is daily renewed. Oh, free grace! it fires my soul, and makes me long to do something for Jesus. It is true, indeed, I want to go home; but here are so many souls ready to perish for lack of knowledge, that I am willing to tarry below as long as my Master has work for me." It was at this period that he first ventured to preach in the fair in Moorfields, to which we have already referred. In this year he made also his second journey to Scotland, the particulars of which have been already given.

On his arrival from Scotland in London, October, 1742, Whitefield found a new awakening at the Tabernacle, which in the mean time had been enlarged. He says, "I am employed, and, glory to rich grace, I am carried through the duties of each day with cheerfulness and almost uninterrupted tranquillity. Our society is large, but in good order. My Master gives us much of his gracious presence, both in our public and private ministrations."

In March, 1743, he went again into Gloucestershire, where the people appeared to be more eager to attend on his ministry than ever before. "Preaching," says he, "in Gloucestershire, is now like preaching at the Tabernacle in London." And in a letter, April 7, he says, "I preached, and took leave of the Gloucester people with mutual and great concern, on Sunday evening last. It was past one in the morning before I could lay my weary body down, At five I rose again, sick for want of rest; but I was enabled to get on horseback and ride to Mr. T——'s, where I preached to a large congregation, who came there at seven in the morning. At ten, I read prayers and preached, and afterwards administered the sacrament in Stonehouse church. Then I rode to Stroud, and preached to about twelve thousand in Mr. G——'s field; and about six in the evening, to a like number on Hampton common." Next morning he preached near Dursley to some thousands; at about seven o'clock he reached Bristol, and preached to a full congregation at Smith's hall; and on the following morning, after preaching, set out for Waterford, in South Wales, where he opened the association which he and his brethren had agreed upon, and was several days with them, settling the affairs of the societies. The work in Wales, during his absence, had very greatly extended itself, not a few of the clergy having become converted, as well as their people. He tells us, "The power of God at the sacrament, under the ministry of Mr. Rowland, was enough to make a person's heart burn within him. At seven in the morning have I seen perhaps ten thousand from different parts, in the midst of a sermon, crying, *Gugunniaut—bendyth*—[glory—blessed]—ready to leap for joy." He continued in Wales some weeks, preaching with great apparent success, and in the latter part of April returned to Gloucester, after having, in about three weeks, travelled about four hundred miles, spent three days in attending associations, and preached about forty times. Among the interesting events of this journey may be reckoned the fact, that when he was at Caermarthen the quarterly sessions were held. When he was about to preach, the magistrates sent him word, that if he would stay till the court rose, they would attend on the service. He acceded to their proposal, and they were present, with many thousands more, including several persons of high rank.

After a few weeks spent in London, preaching to vast congregations in Moorfields, and exulting in his accustomed success, collecting too for his beloved orphans, so as to be able to pay all his debts, and to make a remittance to Georgia, we again find him at Bristol, and in a few days afterwards at Exeter. Among the clergymen who met him there was Mr. Cennick. As this gentleman was preaching during this visit in the High-street of the city, he was eloquently discoursing on the doctrine of the atonement by the blood of Christ, when a profane butcher in the crowd exclaimed, "If you love blood, you shall presently have enough of it," and ran to obtain some to throw on him. A Mr. Saunders, who was employed in conveying persons from one place to another, though an entire stranger to religion, from a sense of justice, determined to defend the preacher; and when the butcher came with a pail nearly filled with blood, he quietly took it from him, and poured it over the man's own head. This Mr. Saunders afterwards became an eminent Christian. He was, till extreme old age, the body-coachman of George III., with whom he frequently held Christian conversation, and died happily in 1799, at the age of eighty-nine.

During this visit to Bristol, Whitefield's ministry was owned of God in the conversion of Thomas Olivers, a young profligate Welshman. It is said, he had so studied profanity and cursing, that he would exemplify the richness of the Welsh language by compounding twenty or thirty words into one long and horrid blasphemy. He had often sang profane songs about Whitefield, and was now induced by curiosity to go to hear him. Being too late on the first occasion, he went on the following evening nearly three hours before the time. The text was, "Is not this a brand plucked out of the fire?" Zech. 3:2. His heart became broken with a sense of his sins, and he was soon enabled to trust in the mercy of Christ. He became a zealous and successful minister of Christ among the followers of Mr. Wesley, and was the author of the well-known hymn,

"The God of Abram praise," etc.

In August, Whitefield returned to London, but not to make a long stay there. "I thank you," he writes to a correspondent, "for your kind caution to spare myself; but evangelizing is certainly my province. Everywhere effectual doors are opened. So far from thinking of settling in London, I am more and more convinced that I should go from place to place." Accordingly, during the three last months of 1743, we find him in a large number of places in the central and western parts of England. At Birmingham, he writes, "I have preached five times this day, and weak as I am, through Christ strengthening me, I could preach five times more." At Kidderminster he met with a distinguished Christian merchant, a Mr. Williams, whose published "Memoirs" have been eminently useful. Whitefield writes, "I was kindly received by Mr. Williams. Many friends were at his house. I was greatly refreshed to find what a sweet savor of good Baxter's doctrine, works, and discipline remains to this day." Nor did he, amidst all his labors, feel his health much impaired. He observes, indeed, that he had taken a cold, but adds, "The Lord warms my heart."

In the beginning of March, 1744, he was compelled to attend the assizes at Gloucester. During the preceding summer, the enemies of the Methodists had been very violent, especially at Hampton, in that county. Forbearance in the case had ceased to be a virtue, and Mr. Whitefield was strongly urged to appeal to law, which in England in such cases is severe. At the preceding sessions the rioters had been convicted, but appealed to the assizes, a higher court. After a full hearing, a verdict was given in favor of Whitefield and his friends, and all the prisoners were found guilty. This exposed each to a fine of forty pounds, or six months' imprisonment; the rioters were greatly alarmed, public feeling on the subject was corrected, and the Methodists readily extended forgiveness to the unhappy offenders.

Whitefield was now invited by Mr. Smith, an American merchant then in England, in the name of thousands, to revisit this country, and took passage with that gentleman in a vessel sailing from Portsmouth. But the captain refused to take him, "for fear," as he said, "he would spoil the sailors." On this account Mr. Whitefield was compelled to go to Plymouth, another seaport, to accomplish his purpose. On his way, he preached at Exeter and other places, with delightful results. "But," he says, "the chief scene was at Plymouth and the Dock, [now called Devonport,] where I expected least success."

While he was at Plymouth, four well-dressed men came to the house of one of his particular friends, in a kind manner inquiring after him, and desiring to know where he lodged. Soon after, Mr. Whitefield received a letter informing him that the writer was a nephew of Mr. S— —, an attorney in New York; that he had the pleasure of supping with Mr. Whitefield at his uncle's house, and requested his company to sup with him and a few friends at a tavern. Mr. Whitefield replied to him that he was not accustomed to sup abroad at such houses, but he should be glad of the gentleman's company to eat a morsel with him at his own lodging. The gentleman accordingly came and supped, but was observed frequently to look around him, and to be very absent. At length he took his leave, and returned to his companions in the tavern, and on being asked by them what he had done, he answered, that he had been treated with so much civility and kindness that he had not the heart to touch him. One of the company, a lieutenant of a man-of-war, laid a wager of ten guineas that he would do his business for him. His companions, however, had the precaution to take away his sword.

It was now about midnight, and Mr. Whitefield having that day preached to a large congregation, and visited the French prisoners, had retired to rest, when he was awoke and told that a well-dressed gentleman earnestly wished to speak with him. Supposing that it was some person under conviction of sin, many such having previously called upon him, he desired him to be brought to his room. The gentleman came, sat down by his bedside, congratulated him upon the success of his ministry, and expressed considerable regret that he had been prevented from hearing him. Soon after, however, he began to utter the most abusive language, and in a cruel and cowardly manner beat him in his bed. The landlady and her daughter, hearing the noise, rushed into the room and laid hold of the assailant; but disengaging himself from them, he renewed his attack on the unoffending preacher, who, supposing that he was about to be shot or stabbed, underwent all the feelings of a sudden and violent death. Soon after, a second person came into the house, and called from the bottom of the stairs, "Take courage, I am ready to help you." But by the repeated cries of murder the neighborhood had become so alarmed, that the villains were glad to make their escape. "The next morning," says Mr. Whitefield, "I was to expound at a private house, and then to set out for Biddeford. Some urged me to stay and prosecute, but being better employed, I went on my intended journey, was greatly blessed in preaching the everlasting gospel; and, upon my return, was well paid for what I had suffered, curiosity having led perhaps two thousand more than ordinary to see and hear a man that had like to have been murdered in his bed. And I trust, in the five weeks that I waited for the convoy, hundreds were awakened and turned unto the Lord."

As Whitefield was one day preaching in Plymouth, a Mr. Henry Tanner, who was at work as a ship-builder at a distance, heard his voice, and resolved, with five or six of his companions, to go and drive him from the place where he stood; and for this purpose they filled their pockets with stones. When, however, Mr. Tanner drew near, and heard Mr. Whitefield earnestly inviting sinners to Christ, he was filled with astonishment, his resolution failed him, and he went home with his mind deeply impressed. On the following evening, he again attended, and heard Mr. Whitefield on the sin of those who crucified the Redeemer. After he had forcibly illustrated their guilt, he appeared to look intently on Mr. Tanner, as he exclaimed, with great energy, "Thou art the man!" These words powerfully impressed Mr. Tanner; he felt his transgressions of the divine law to be awfully great, and in the agony of his soul he cried, "God be merciful to me a sinner!" The preacher then proceeded to proclaim the free and abundant grace of the Lord Jesus, which he commanded to be preached among the very people who had murdered him; a gleam of hope entered the heart of the penitent, and he surrendered himself to Christ. Mr. Tanner afterwards entered the ministry, and labored with great success, for many years, at Exeter.

We are not quite certain whether it was on this or a subsequent visit to Plymouth, that Whitefield had preached on the Sabbath for the Rev. Mr. Kinsman, and after breakfast on Monday morning, said to him, "Come, let us visit some of your poor people. It is not enough that we labor in the pulpit; we must endeavor to be useful out of it." On entering the dwellings of the afflicted poor, he administered to their temporal as well as their spiritual wants. Mr. Kinsman, knowing the low state of his finances, was surprised at his liberality, and suggested that he thought he had been too bountiful. Mr. Whitefield, with some degree of smartness, replied, "It is not enough, young man, to pray, and put on a serious face; true religion, and undefiled, is this, to visit the widow and the fatherless in their affliction, and to supply their wants. My stock, it is true, is nearly exhausted; but God, whom I serve, and whose saints we have assisted, will, I doubt not, soon give me a supply." His expectation was not disappointed. A stranger called on him the same evening, who said, "With great pleasure I have heard you preach; you are on a journey, as well as myself, and travelling is expensive. Do me the honor to accept of this;" handing him five guineas, or twenty-five dollars. Returning to the family, Mr. Whitefield, very pleasantly smiling, showed them the money, saying, "There, young man, God has very speedily repaid what I lent him this morning. Let this in future teach you not to withhold what it is in the power of your hand to give. The gentleman to whom I was called is a perfect stranger to me; his only business was to give me the sum you see." It was a singular fact, that this gentleman, though rich, was notorious for a penurious disposition.

During his stay in Plymouth, Whitefield's usefulness daily increased. The ferry-men, who obtained their living by carrying persons between Plymouth and Dock, refused to take money from his hearers, saying, "God forbid that we should sell his word!" The evangelist exclaimed, "Oh, the thousands that flock to the preaching of Christ's gospel!" In the midst of these scenes, the convoy arrived, and in delicate health he embarked for America.

CHAPTER IX
WHITEFIELD'S SECOND VISIT TO NEW ENGLAND. 1744, 1745

Mr. Whitefield commenced his third voyage to America in August, 1744. His health while crossing the Atlantic became worse, rather than better, the voyage lasting eleven weeks. He had set out in company with about one hundred and fifty ships, attended by several men-of-war as convoys, which, however, they lost by storms separating them on the way. It was more than six weeks, owing generally to want of wind, before they reached any of the western islands. When the wind again sprung up, one of the vessels, which missed stays, drove upon the ship in which Whitefield was, striking her mainsail into the bowsprit. The alarm was very great, but no lives were lost. He had been singing a hymn on deck when the concussion took place; this fact, together with that of the concussion itself, was communicated to the convoy, and led to the use of much violent and wicked language. But the good man was not intimidated. He says, "I called my friends together, and broke out into these words in prayer: 'God of the sea, and God of the dry land, this is a night of rebuke and blasphemy. Show thyself, O God, and take us under thine own immediate protection. Be thou our convoy, and make a difference between those who fear thee, and those that fear thee not.'" A difference was soon made. Next day a heavy storm arose, which "battered and sent away our convoy, so that we saw him no more all the voyage." Whitefield at first did not at all regret the loss, but when two strange sails appeared in the distance, and preparation was made for action by mounting guns, slinging hammocks on the sides of the ships, and encircling the masts with chains, he being, as he says, "naturally a coward," found it formidable to have no convoy. The vessels, however, proved to be only a part of their own fleet. This was a pleasant discovery to them, especially to Whitefield. "The captain, on clearing the cabin, said, 'After all, this is the best fighting.' You may be sure I concurred, praying that all our conflicts with spiritual enemies might at last terminate in a thorough cleansing and an eternal purification of the defiled *cabin* of our hearts."

The tediousness of this voyage, in the feeble state of his health, seems to have tried Whitefield's patience; so that when he arrived in sight of the port of York, in the then territory of Maine, in order to land a few hours sooner he went on board a fishing smack then in the bay; but darkness coming on, she missed her course, and was tossed about all night. Unfortunately, too, she had no provisions, and he was so hungry that he says he "could have gnawed the very boards." Besides he was suffering from "nervous colic." He was greatly discouraged, until a man who was lying at his elbow in the cabin began to talk of "one Mr. Whitefield, for whose arrival the 'New Lights' in New England" were watching and praying. "This," he says, "made me take courage. I continued undiscovered; and in a few hours, in answer, I trust, to *new-light* prayers, we arrived safe." This was on October 19, 1744. He was quite ill when he landed; but was received by Dr. Sherburne, an eminent physician at York, who was once a Deist, but had been converted under Whitefield's ministry. This gentleman took him to his own house, and after a few days he began to recover.

The Rev. Mr. Moody, of York, the aged and excellent, but eccentric minister of whom we have already spoken, took the earliest suitable opportunity of calling on the great evangelist, and said very characteristically, "Sir, you are, first, welcome to America; secondly, to New England; thirdly, to all faithful ministers in New England; fourthly, to all the good people of New England; fifthly, to all the good people of York; and sixthly and lastly, to me, dear sir, less than the least of all." Prince's "Christian History" had announced his arrival, and that his intention was "to pass on to Georgia; and as he goes on, to meddle with no controversies, but only to preach up the parts of vital piety and the pure truths of the gospel, to all who are willing to hear them."

After giving Whitefield this hearty welcome, Moody urged him for a sermon. The preacher hesitated, on account of his illness, but "good old Mr. Moody" did not give him the benefit of his own favorite maxim, "When you know not what to do, you must *not* do you know not what." Whitefield preached, and immediately went to Portsmouth, where he preached the same evening, November 6, for Mr. Fitch, and was to have preached again the next morning, but was too ill, and deferred it till the afternoon. In the mean time, as he wrote, "My pains returned; but what gave me most concern was, that notice had been given of my being engaged to preach. I felt a divine life, distinct from my animal life, which made me, as it were, laugh at my pains, though every one thought I was taken with death. My dear York physician was then about to administer a medicine. I on a sudden cried out, 'Doctor, my pains are suspended; by the help of God, I will go and preach, and then come home and die.' With some difficulty I reached the pulpit.

All looked quite surprised, as though they saw one risen from the dead. I indeed was as pale as death, and told them they must look upon me as a dying man, come to bear my dying testimony to the truths I had formerly preached to them. All seemed melted, and were drowned in tears. The cry after me, when I left the pulpit, was like the cry of sincere mourners when attending the funeral of a dear departed friend. Upon my coming home, I was laid upon a bed on the ground, near the fire, and I heard them say, 'He is gone.' But God was pleased to order it otherwise. I gradually recovered."

In another account he himself says, "In my own apprehension, and in all appearance to others, I was a dying man. I preached—the people heard me—as such. The invisible realities of another world lay open to my view. Expecting to launch into eternity, and to be with my Master before the morning, I spoke with peculiar energy. Such effects followed the word, I thought it was worth dying for a thousand times. Though wonderfully comforted within at my return home, I thought I was dying indeed.... Soon after, a poor negro woman would see me. She came, sat down upon the ground, and looked earnestly in my face, and then said, 'Massa, you just go to heaven's gate, but Jesus Christ said, Get you down, get you down; you must not come here yet; but go first, and call some more poor negroes.' I prayed to the Lord, that if I was to live, this might be the event."

It was nearly three weeks before he was sufficiently recovered to proceed to Boston. The day before he left Portsmouth Mr. Shurtleff wrote, "The prejudices of most that set themselves against him before his coming, seem to be in a great measure abated, and in some, to be wholly removed; and there is no open opposition made to him. I have frequent opportunities of being with him, and there always appears in him such a concern for the advancement of the Redeemer's kingdom and the good of souls, such a care to employ his whole time to these purposes, such sweetness of disposition, and so much of the temper of his great Lord and Master, that every time I see him, I find my heart further drawn out towards him."

"Prince's Christian History," of December 15, says, "The Rev. Mr. Whitefield was so far revived as to be able to take coach with his consort, and set out from Portsmouth to Boston, Nov. 24; whither he came in a very feeble state, the Monday evening after; since which he has been able to preach in several of our largest houses of public worship, particularly the Rev. Dr. Colman's, Dr. Sewall's, Mr. Webb's, and Mr. Gee's, to crowded assemblies of people, and to great and growing acceptance. At Dr. Colman's desire, and with the consent of the church, on the Lord's day after his arrival, he administered to them the holy communion. And last Lord's day he preached for the venerable Mr. Cheever, of Chelsea, and administered the holy supper there. The next day he preached for the Rev. Mr. Emerson, of Malden. Yesterday he set out to preach for some towns to the northward; proposes to return hither the next Wednesday evening, and after a few days to comply with the earnest invitations of several ministers to go and preach to their congregations, in the southern parts of the province.

"He comes with the same extraordinary spirit of meekness, sweetness, and universal benevolence as before. In opposition to the spirit of separation and bigotry, he is still for holding communion with all Protestant churches. In opposition to enthusiasm, he preaches a close adherence to the Scriptures, the necessity of trying all impressions by them, and of rejecting whatever is not agreeable to them, as delusions. In opposition to Antinomianism, he preaches up all kinds of relative and religious duties, though to be performed in the strength of Christ; and, in short, the doctrines of the church of England, and the first fathers of this country. As before, he first applies himself to the understandings of his hearers, and then to the affections; and the more he preaches, the more he convinces people of their mistakes about him, and increases their satisfaction."

The administration of the Lord's supper by a priest of the church of England in the Congregational church in Brattle-street, Boston, gave great offence. Some said, the consent of the church was neither given nor asked, and Dr. Colman was blamed for introducing Whitefield by his own authority; to which Dr. Colman replied, that, as it was customary for pastors to invite the assistance of other ministers on such occasions, he thought it unnecessary to call for a vote of the church; that he plainly intimated his intention in his prayer after sermon, and then, on coming to the table, said, "The Rev. Mr. Whitefield being providentially with us, I have asked him to administer the ordinance;" and that by the countenances of the people it seemed to be universally agreeable to them, which he supposed to be all the consent which the case required.

Since Mr. Whitefield's former visit to New England, a considerable change had taken place in not a few of the ministers and churches. In 1740, he had inveighed strongly against many of the ministers, some of them even by name, as, in his opinion, unconverted; and after his departure, some preachers, who professed themselves to be his followers, had created great confusion by carrying these charges much farther than he would have approved. His second visit was therefore anticipated by many with anxiety, lest it might cause a new outbreak of enthusiasm and disorder. The General Association of Connecticut, in June, 1745, advised that he be not invited to preach in any of the churches. When he visited New Haven, he found himself shut out of the pulpit of the First church by its minister Mr. Noyes. A great crowd, however, assembled to hear him, from the neighboring towns, as well as from New Haven, and he preached from a platform erected in the street, before Mr. Pierpont's house on the Green, to a congregation which neither of the meeting-houses could have contained.

From Professor Kingsley's "Sketch of the History of Yale College," we learn that "President Clap issued a declaration, signed by himself and three tutors, that is, Samuel Whittlesey, afterwards minister of the First church in New Haven, Thomas Darling, for many years chief justice of the Court of Common Pleas for the county of New Haven, and John Whiting, in which some of the proceedings of Mr. Whitefield were condemned. In consequence of the religious fervor which had been excited, a much greater diversity of theological opinions prevailed in Connecticut than at any previous period. Violent controversies arose, churches were divided, and the government, by interfering to prevent these evils, increased rather than checked them. The college became an object of jealousy; and the declaration of the rector and tutors, respecting the preaching of Whitefield, offended some, without effectually conciliating others."

The opposition to Mr. Whitefield of which we have spoken, was by no means all that he met with. Even before the Association in Connecticut had taken action, several similar bodies in Massachusetts had acted in a similar manner. The corporation of Harvard college published a testimony against him, while that of Yale represented that he intended to root out all the standing ministers in our land, and to introduce foreigners in their stead. The good man, notwithstanding all this opposition, and much more, went on laboring for the salvation of souls, and God still honored him with success.

While the impartiality to which we hold ourselves bound demanded the statement just made, and while we are compelled to admit the existence of evils attendant on these revivals, we also record some of the facts connected with a convention of ministers, who assembled in Boston in pursuance of a previous notice in the Boston Gazette of May 30, 1743. We copy the original invitation.

"It is desired and proposed by a number of ministers, both in town and country, that such of their brethren as are persuaded that there has been of late a happy revival of religion through an extraordinary divine influence, in many parts of this land, and are concerned for the honor and progress of this remarkable work of God, may have an interview at Boston, the day after the approaching commencement, to consider whether they are not called to give an open, conjunct testimony to an event so surprising and gracious; as well as against those errors in doctrine, and disorders in practice, which through the permitted agency of Satan have attended it, and in any measure blemished its glory and hindered its advancement; and also to consult as to the most likely method to be taken to guard people against such delusions and mistakes as in such a season they are in danger of falling into, and that this blessed work may continue and flourish among us." Those who could not be present were invited to send written attestations.

In accordance with this proposal, the convention met in Boston on Thursday, July 7. The Rev. Dr. Sewall of Boston officiated as Moderator, and the Rev. Messrs. Prince of Boston, and Hobby of Reading, as Scribes. Ninety persons thus assembled, and letters were read from twenty-eight who were absent. A committee was appointed, consisting of the Rev. Dr. Sewall, the Rev. Messrs. Wigglesworth, Prince, Adams, Cooper, Nathanael Rogers, Leonard, and Hobby, to prepare a report. On the next morning this committee presented a document, which, after full discussion, was signed by all present; and the meeting was dissolved.

Our limits will not allow us to give the whole of the report to which we have referred, but a few sentences will show its general character:

"We, whose names are undersigned, think it our indispensable duty—without judging or censuring such of our brethren as cannot at present see things in the same light with us—in this open and conjunct manner to declare, to the glory of sovereign grace, our full persuasion, either from what we have seen ourselves, or received upon credible testimony, that there has been a happy and remarkable revival of religion in many parts of this land, through an uncommon divine influence, after a long time of decay and deadness, and a sensible and very awful withdrawal of the Holy Spirit from his sanctuary among us.... The present work seems to be remarkable and extraordinary, on account of the numbers wrought upon. We never before saw so many brought under soul concern, and with great distress making the inquiry, 'What must we do to be saved?' And these persons were of all ages and character. With regard to the suddenness and quick progress of it, many persons and places were surprised with the gracious visit together, or near about the same time, and the heavenly influence diffused itself far and wide, like the light of the morning. Also [the work seems to be remarkable] in respect to the degree of operations, both in a way of terror, and in a way of consolation, attended in many with unusual bodily effects. Not that all who are accounted the subjects of the present work have had these extraordinary degrees of previous distress and subsequent joy. But many, and we suppose the greater number, have been wrought on in a more gentle and silent way, and without any other appearances than are common and usual at other times, when persons have been awakened to a solemn concern about salvation, and have been thought to have passed out of a state of nature into a state of grace. As to those whose inward concern has occasioned extraordinary outward distresses, the most of them, when we came to converse with them, were able to give what appeared to us a rational account of what so affected their minds.... The instances were very few in which we had reason to think these affections were produced by visionary or sensible representations, or by any other images than such as the Scripture itself presents to us. Of those who were judged hopefully converted, and made a public profession of religion, there have been fewer instances of scandal and apostasy than might be expected.... There appears to be more experimental godliness and lively Christianity than most of us can remember we have ever seen before.... And now we desire to bow the knee in thanksgiving to the God and Father of our Lord Jesus Christ, that our eyes have seen and our ears heard such things. And while these are our sentiments, we must necessarily be grieved at any accounts sent abroad representing this work as all enthusiasm, delusion, and disorder. Indeed, it is not to be denied, that in some places many irregularities and extravagances have been permitted to accompany it, which we would deeply bewail and lament before God, and look upon ourselves obliged, for the honor of the Holy Spirit, and of his operations on the souls of men, to bear a public and faithful testimony against; though at the same time it is to be acknowledged, with much thankfulness, that in other places where the work has greatly flourished, there have been few if any of those disorders and excesses. But who can wonder if, at such a time as this, Satan should intermingle himself to hinder and blemish a work so directly contrary to the interests of his own kingdom?... Finally, we exhort the children of God to continue instant in prayer, that He, with whom is the residue of the Spirit, would grant us fresh, more plentiful, and extensive effusions, that so this wilderness, in all the parts of it, may become a fruitful field; that the present appearances may be an earnest of the glorious things promised in the latter days, when she shall shine with the glory of the Lord arisen upon her, so as to dazzle the eyes of beholders, confound and put to shame all her enemies, rejoice the hearts of her solicitous and now saddened friends, and have a strong influence and resplendency throughout the earth. Amen. Even so, come, Lord Jesus; come quickly."

This paper was signed by eighteen ministers in the county of Suffolk, among whom were Colman, Sewall, Prince, Webb, Cooper, Foxcroft, Checkly, Gee, Eliot, and Moorhead of Boston; twelve in the county of Essex, nine in Middlesex, six in Worcester, ten in Plymouth, one in Barnstable, three in Bristol, three in York, five in New Hampshire, and one in Rhode Island. There were one hundred and fourteen in all who gave attestations, either by signing their names to the above document, or by sending written attestations. Ninety-six of the one hundred and fourteen took their first degree of Bachelor of Arts more than ten years previously; consequently before the revival commenced. Twenty-six took their first degrees above thirty years before. Attestations were received but from twelve ministers in Connecticut, as the proposal did not reach them in time.

We may add to this statement, as showing in some degree the extent of this revival, that while in 1729 the number of members in the Congregational and Presbyterian churches of this country may be estimated at thirty-three thousand, the number of communicants in 1745 could not be less than seventy-five thousand. "The *special* revivals of religion," says an able writer in the "American Quarterly Register," vol. 4, 1832, "were probably the means of adding from twenty thousand to thirty thousand members to the churches." The same writer adds, "The genuine fruits of holiness appeared, according to the acknowledgment of all parties, in multitudes of those who professed religion. They were Christians, who endured unto the end. This is the unanimous testimony of those men who were the best able to judge. Great numbers who were convinced of sin by Mr. Whitefield's preaching, gave ample evidence, living and dying, of sincere and fervent love to the commands of God. There is reason to believe that a *preparation* had been made for the descent of the Holy Spirit, many years before the revival commenced. The fasts and public reformations, the prayers and tears of good men, from 1700 to 1730, were not in vain."

One fact connected with the testimony against Whitefield, published by the faculty of Harvard college, we quote, as showing that then, as well as now, a difference of opinion existed as to written and extempore sermons. They thought his extempore manner of preaching "by no means proper," because extempore preachers are of necessity less instructive, the greater part of the sermon being commonly "the same kind of harangue which they have often used before, so that this is a most lazy manner" of preaching; and because it exposes the preacher to utter rash expressions, and even dangerous errors, as Whitefield, they thought, had done in several instances, probably from that cause. Assuredly he preferred extempore preaching to any other; yet he never pretended to preach without previous study. His sermons usually cost him as much previous labor as if they had been written; so that, in his case at least, it was not "a lazy way" of preaching. The errors which they said he had uttered, were a few hasty expressions, which he had retracted as soon as he had been reminded of them.

Itinerancy, which had also been objected against Whitefield as one of his crimes, he strenuously defended as scriptural and right; understanding an evangelist to be, what they said an itinerant was, "One that hath no particular charge of his own, but goes about from country to country, or from town to town in any country, and stands ready to preach to any congregation that shall call him to it." For the divine command, "Go ye into all the world, and preach the gospel to every creature," he argued, "authorizes the ministers of Christ, even to the end of the world, to preach the gospel in every town and country, though not 'of their own head,' yet whenever and wherever Providence should open a door, even though it should be in a place 'where officers are already settled, and the gospel is fully and faithfully preached.' This, I humbly apprehend, is every gospel minister's indisputable privilege." He further asked, "Was not the Reformation begun and carried on by itinerant preaching?" He then quoted from "Baxter's Reformed Pastor," a plan which had been adopted in some parts of England, for circular lectures by settled ministers selected for the purpose, and with the consent of the pastors.

In reference to Harvard college, Whitefield lived long enough to take a Christian's revenge. In 1764, he solicited from his friends donations of books for their library, which had recently been destroyed by fire, and four years afterwards, while his old opponent President Holyoke was yet in office, the following minute was entered on their records: "At a meeting of the President and Fellows of Harvard college, August 22, 1768, the Rev. G. Whitefield having, in addition to his former kindness to Harvard college, lately presented to the library a new edition of his Journals, and having procured large benefactions from several benevolent and respectable gentlemen; *voted*, that the thanks of the corporation be given to the Rev. Mr. Whitefield, for these instances of candor and generosity."

It will be readily supposed, that notwithstanding all the opposition which Whitefield met, there were yet many thousands always ready to attend on his ministry. It was now the close of 1744, but the cold of winter did not prevent vast crowds assembling at early services long before daylight. Speaking of the opposition he met, "so that," says he, "for a while my situation was rendered uncomfortable," he adds, "But amidst all this smoke a blessed fire broke out. The awakened souls were as eager as ever to hear the word. Having heard that I expounded early in Scotland, they begged that I would do the same in Boston. I complied, and opened a lecture at six in the morning. I seldom preached to less than two thousand. It was delightful to see so many of both sexes neatly dressed flocking to hear the word, and returning home to family prayer and breakfast before the opposers were out of their beds."

The late Rev. Dr. Archibald Alexander tells us, that when he was at Boston, in 1800, he found in the Old South church a lingering relic of Whitefield's times, in a convert of his day, a lady between eighty and ninety years of age, who belonged to a prayer-meeting founded then, which had been kept up weekly until within a few years. Of this, she was the only surviving member.

The "Evening Post," which seems to have been on the side of those who opposed Whitefield, in its issue of March 11, 1745, says, "Prince, Webb, Foxcroft, and Gee, are the directors of Mr. Whitefield's public conduct, as he himself has lately declared at Newbury." He had other powerful friends among the clergy, and still more among the laity, who invited him by vote into some pulpits where the pastors were "shy" of him.

On the 7th of February, we find him at Ipswich, where he spent several days. Mr. Pickering, of the Second church, declined admitting him into his pulpit, and assigned his reasons in a letter, which was published. It contains the usual objections set forth in the various "testimonies," and is remarkable only for one convenient metaphor. The Bishop of London had published on "Lukewarmness and Enthusiasm." Whitefield had said in reply, "All ought to be thankful to that pilot who will teach them to steer a safe and middle course;" and Pickering wittily asks, "But what if the pilot should take the vane for the compass?"

Early in March we find him making an excursion into the east, as we hear of him both at Berwick and Portland, in the then territory of Maine. In the latter place, he not only made a powerful impression on the people, but on their minister. In the outset a strong feeling existed against his preaching in the pulpit of the First church. Mr. Smith, the pastor, says in his "Journal," "The parish are like to be in a flame on account of Mr. Whitefield's coming; the leading men violently opposing." Under the date of May 19, after Whitefield's departure, we find in the "Journal" a remarkable passage: "For several Sabbaths, and the lecture, I have been all in a blaze; never in such a flame, and what I would attend to is, that it was not only involuntary, but actually determined against. I went to meeting resolving to be calm and moderate, lest people should think it was wildness and affectation to ape Mr. Whitefield; but God, I see, makes use of me as he pleases, and I am only a machine in his hand."

About the middle of March, we find our evangelist at Exeter, where he afterwards preached his last sermon. Here some of the more zealous members of the church had withdrawn, and formed a new church. Their conduct had been sanctioned by one council, and censured by another, two years before this time. Whitefield preached to them twice, though Mr. Odlin, the pastor of the church from which they had withdrawn, "solemnly warned and charged him against preaching in his parish." So says the "Evening Post," of March 25, which further calls the people to whom he preached, "Separatists."

In this spring of 1745, the first expedition for the capture from the French of the island of Cape Breton, near Nova Scotia, was set on foot. Colonel

Pepperell, a warm personal friend of Whitefield, and the only native of New England who was created a Baronet of Great Britain, was then at Boston, constantly attending Whitefield's lectures. On the day before he accepted a commission to be general in that expedition, he asked his opinion of the matter, and was told, with the preacher's usual frankness, that he did not indeed think that the scheme proposed for taking Louisburgh would be very promising; and that the eyes of all would be upon him. If he did not succeed, the widows and orphans of the slain soldiers would be like lions robbed of their whelps; but if it pleased God to give him success, envy would endeavor to eclipse his glory: he had need, therefore, if he went, to go with a single eye; and then there was no doubt, if Providence really called him, he would find his strength equal to the difficulties with which he would have to contend.

About the same time, Mr. Sherburne, another of Whitefield's friends, being appointed one of the commissioners, told him he must favor the expedition, otherwise the pious people would be discouraged from enlisting; not only did he say this, but he insisted that the evangelist should give him a motto for his flag, for the encouragement of his soldiers. Whitefield refused to do this, as it would not be consistent with his character as a minister of the gospel of peace. But as Sherburne would take no denial, he gave him, *Nil desperandum, Christo Duce*—[Nothing to be despaired of, Christ being leader.] In these circumstances a large number of men enlisted.

The soldiers and their officers now went farther, and before their embarkation requested him to give them a sermon. He preached to them from the text, "And every one that was in distress, and every one that was in debt, and every one that was discontented, gathered themselves unto him; and he became a captain over them." 1 Samuel 22:2. From this somewhat singular text, he discoursed on the manner in which distressed sinners came to Jesus Christ, the Son of David; and in his application, exhorted the soldiers to behave like the soldiers of David, and the officers to act like David's worthies; saying, that if they did so, there would be good news from Cape Breton. After this he preached to the general himself, who invited him to become one of his chaplains. Whitefield declined this, saying, that though he should esteem this an honor, yet, as he generally preached three times a day, to large congregations, he could do more service by stirring up the people to pray, thus strengthening the hearts and hands of the army. In this practice he persevered during the whole siege of Louisburgh. "I believe," said he, "if ever people went with a disinterested view, the New Englanders did then. Though many of them were raw and undisciplined, yet numbers were substantial persons, who left their farms and willingly ventured all for their country's good. An amazing series of providences appeared, and though some discouraging accounts were sent during the latter end of the siege, yet in about six weeks news came of the surrender of Louisburgh. Numbers flocked from all quarters to hear a thanksgiving sermon upon the occasion. And I trust the blessing bestowed upon the country through the thanksgivings of many, redounded to the glory of God."

Some time before this, the people of Boston had proposed to build for Whitefield "the largest place of worship ever seen in America," in which he should regularly preach; but, as usual, he feared this plan would abridge his liberty of itinerating: he thanked them for their offer, but decidedly declined to accept it. As his bodily strength increased, he began to move southward, and went through Rhode Island and Connecticut, preaching to thousands generally twice a day. He says, "Though there was much smoke, yet every day I had more and more convincing proof that a blessed gospel fire had been kindled in the hearts both of ministers and people."

About this time occurred a fact which delightfully shows how the enemies of this admirable man were often converted into friends. A colored trumpeter belonging to the English army resolved to interrupt him while delivering a sermon in the open air. For this purpose he went to the field, carrying his trumpet with him, intending to blow it with all his might about the middle of the sermon. He took his station in front of the minister, and at no great distance from him. The crowd became very great, and those who were towards the extremity pressed forward, that they might hear more distinctly, and caused such a pressure where the poor trumpeter stood, that he found it impossible at the time when he intended to blow his trumpet, to raise the arm which held it, by which means he was kept within the sound of the gospel as effectually as if he had been chained to the spot. In a short time his attention was powerfully arrested, and he became so deeply affected by the statements of the preacher, that he was seized with all the agonies of despair, and was carried to a house in the neighborhood. After the service, he was visited by Mr. Whitefield, who gave him suitable counsels, and from that time the trumpeter became a greatly altered man. So true is it in reference to the omnipotent and gracious Being,

> "Hearts base as hell he can control,
> And spread new powers throughout the whole."

While preaching at Boston, he was delighted to observe that the sheriff, who had heretofore been the leader of the persecution against him, now began to hear him preach; and his pleasure was vastly increased, when he saw the crowds come around him to inquire as to their highest interests.

Among these crowds was a somewhat remarkable gentleman of that city. He was a man of ready wit and racy humor, who delighted in preaching over a bottle to his ungodly companions. He went to hear Whitefield, that he might be furnished with matter for a "tavern harangue." When he had heard enough of the sermon for his purpose, he endeavored to quit the church for the inn, but "found his endeavors to get out fruitless, he was so pent up." While thus fixed, and waiting for "fresh matter of ridicule," the truth took possession of his heart. That night he went to Mr. Prince full of terror, and sought an introduction to ask pardon of the preacher. Whitefield says of him, "By the paleness, pensiveness, and horror of his countenance, I guessed he was the man of whom I had been apprized. 'Sir, can you forgive me?' he cried in a low, but plaintive voice. I smiled, and said, 'Yes, sir, very readily.' 'Indeed,' he said, 'you cannot when I tell you all.' I then asked him to sit down; and judging that he had sufficiently felt the lash of the law, I preached the gospel to him." This, with other remarkable conversions, gave increasing energy and influence to his preaching in Boston. "My bodily strength," he says, "is recovered, and my soul more than ever in love with a crucified Jesus."

Another illustration may also be here given of the meekness and gentleness which usually characterized our evangelist in his intercourse with his brethren. In his later visits to New England, it was Whitefield's usual practice to spend a few days with Dr. Hopkins. On one of these occasions, after preaching for the doctor on the Sabbath, the next day he proposed a ride into the country for exercise. During the ride, Whitefield spoke with regret of the views of their "good brother Edwards on the subject of the witness of the Holy Spirit." "Ah," asked Dr. Hopkins, "and what is the error?" Here Whitefield made a long pause; and Hopkins continued the conversation: "Do you believe, Mr. Whitefield, that the witness of the Spirit is a direct communication from God?" "I cannot say that I do," was the reply. "Well, do you believe that Christians have any other witness of the Spirit than that afforded by the testimony of their own holy affections?" "I cannot say that I do," Mr. Whitefield again replied. "Do you believe it to be any thing more or less," continued Hopkins, "than the Spirit producing in the heart the gracious exercises of repentance, faith, etc.?" "No, that is precisely my view of it," said Whitefield. "And that is precisely the view of good father Edwards," pleasantly returned Dr. Hopkins. Whitefield frankly acknowledged his error, and rejoiced that there was no disagreement on the subject.

CHAPTER X
FROM HIS LEAVING NEW ENGLAND TILL HIS ARRIVAL IN ENGLAND—LABORS IN THE MIDDLE AND SOUTHERN STATES—THE BERMUDAS. 1745-1748

Leaving New England, Whitefield proceeded first to New York, where he preached as he had formerly done, and found that the seed sown in past days had produced much fruit. Proceeding still southward, on his way towards Philadelphia, arriving in New Jersey, he says, "I had the pleasure of preaching by an interpreter to some converted Indians, and of seeing nearly fifty young ones in one school, near Freehold, learning the Assembly's Catechism." A blessed awakening had before this time been begun and carried on among the Delaware Indians, by the ministry of David Brainerd; no such work had been heard of since the days of the apostolic Eliot in New England.

Arriving in Philadelphia, Whitefield was rejoiced to find that his friend Gilbert Tennent was still blessed with success in his labors. Many, he says, were under "soul-sickness," and Tennent's health suffered much with walking from place to place to see them. The gentlemen connected with the new house in which Tennent preached, were, as well as Tennent himself, desirous of securing at least a portion of Whitefield's labors, and offered him eight hundred pounds a year, if he would become their pastor, and labor with them six months in the year, travelling the other six months wherever he thought proper. He thanked them, but declined.

Not unfrequently have we been told by frigid critics of the inferior character of Whitefield's printed sermons. But have they not looked too much for the beauties of style, and overlooked the simple energy of their scriptural truths? Even these printed sermons have, under God, accomplished wonders. In the year 1743, a young gentleman from Scotland, then residing at Hanover, in Virginia, had obtained a volume of Whitefield's sermons preached in Glasgow, and taken in shorthand, which, after a gentleman of Hanover, named Hunt, the father of a distinguished Presbyterian minister of that name, had studied with great personal benefit, he invited his neighbors to visit his house to hear read. By their plainness and fervor, attended with the power of God, not a few became convinced of their lost condition as sinners, and anxiously inquired the way of salvation. The feelings of many were powerfully excited, and they could not forbear bitter and violent weeping. The intelligence spread, curiosity prompted the desire of many others to attend such remarkable services; and one and another begged for admission, till the houses were crowded. Numbers were pricked to the heart; the word of God became quick and powerful; and, "What shall we do?" was the general cry. What to do or say the principal leaders knew not. They themselves had been led by a still small voice, they hardly knew how, to an acquaintance with the truth; but now the Lord was speaking as on mount Sinai, with a voice of thunder; and sinners, like that mountain itself, trembled. It was not long before Christians had the happiness to see a goodly number healed by the same word that had wounded them, and brought to rejoice in Christ, and his great salvation. "My dwelling-place," said Mr. Morris, one of their number, "was at length too small to contain the people, whereupon we determined to build a meeting-house merely for *reading*. And having never been used to social prayer, none of us durst attempt it." This *reading-house*, as it was called, was followed by others of like character, and the number of attendants and the power of divine influence were much increased. Mr. Morris, as the report spread, was invited to several places at a distance to read these sermons. The phrase, "Morris' reading-house," has come down by tradition to the present age, as well as important details of the opposition of the magistracy and other classes, who sought, but in vain, to stop the progress of the work.

Such was the origin of the Presbyterian church at Hanover, where, in after-days, William Robinson and President Davies accomplished such mighty triumphs, and where the sacred cause still flourishes.

Whitefield does not seem to have been made acquainted with these facts till he now arrived in the colony, and saw the happy effects which had been produced by the labors of the Rev. Messrs. Robinson, Tennent, Blair, and others. Of the visit of Whitefield among them, one of them writes, "Mr. Whitefield came and preached four or five days in these parts, which was the happy means of giving us further encouragement, and engaging others to the Lord, especially among the church people, who received his doctrine more readily than they would from ministers of the Presbyterian denomination." We may add here, that in 1747 there were four houses of worship in and around Hanover, which had sprung from the "mustard-seed" of the sermons taken in shorthand from Whitefield's lips at Glasgow.

Among the converts in the south who met Whitefield, was Isaac Oliver, who was both deaf and dumb, and had been so from his birth. Notwithstanding these great disadvantages, he could both feel and evince his strong feelings by the most significant and expressive signs. He could, for instance, so represent the crucifixion of the Lord Jesus Christ, as to be understood by every one; and among his own friends he could converse about the love of Christ in the language of signs, till he was transported in rapture and dissolved in tears. He was much beloved for his eminent piety.

Whitefield had not, during any portion of this time, forgotten Bethesda. The public had warmly sustained it, and he now went forward to see to its affairs, and to add to the orphan-house a Latin school, intending, indeed, before a long time to found a college.

The following account of the orphan-house in 1746, was written by Mr. Whitefield in the form of a letter to a friend, and published as a small pamphlet. We transcribe it from "White's Historical Collections of Georgia," published in 1854:

"Provide things honest in the sight of all men."—Rom. 12:17.

"Bethesda, in Georgia, March 21, 1745-6.

"Some have thought that the erecting such a building was only the produce of my own brain; but they are much mistaken; for it was first proposed to me by my dear friend the Rev. Mr. Charles Wesley, who, with his excellency General Oglethorpe, had concerted a scheme for carrying on such a design before I had any thoughts of going abroad myself. It was natural to think that, as the government intended this province for the refuge and support of many of our poor countrymen, numbers of such adventurers must necessarily be taken off, by being exposed to the hardships which unavoidably attend a new settlement. I thought it, therefore, a noble design in the general to erect a house for fatherless children; and believing that such a provision for orphans would be some inducement with many to come over, I fell in with the design, when mentioned to me by my friend, and was resolved, in the strength of God, to prosecute it with all my might. This was mentioned to the honorable trustees. They took it kindly at my hands, and wrote to the bishop of Bath and Wells for leave for me to preach a charity sermon on this occasion in the Abbey church. This was granted, and I accordingly began immediately to compose a suitable discourse. But knowing that my first stay in Georgia would necessarily be short, on account of my returning again to take priest's orders, I thought it most prudent first to go and see for myself, and defer prosecuting the scheme till I came home.... When I came to Georgia, I found many poor orphans, who, though taken notice of by the honorable trustees, yet, through the neglect of persons under them, were in miserable circumstances. For want of a house to bring them up in, the poor little ones were tabled out here and there; others were at hard services, and likely to have no education at all.

"Upon seeing this, and finding that his Majesty and Parliament had the interest of the colony much at heart, I thought I could not better show my regard to God and my country than by getting a house and land for these children, where they might learn to labor, read, and write, and at the same time be brought up in the nurture and admonition of the Lord. Accordingly, at my return to England, in the year 1738, to take priest's orders, I applied to the honorable society for a grant of five hundred acres of land, and laid myself under an obligation to build a house upon it, and to receive from time to time as many orphans as the land and stock would maintain. As I had always acted like a clergyman of the church of England, having preached in a good part of the London churches, and but a few months before collected near a thousand pounds sterling for the children belonging to the charity schools in London and Westminster, it was natural to think that I might now have the use at least of some of these churches to preach in for the orphans hereafter more immediately to be committed to my care. But by the time I had taken priest's orders, the spirit of the clergy began to be much imbittered. Churches were gradually denied me, and I must let this good design drop, and thousands, and I might add ten thousands, go without hearing the word of God, or preach in the fields. Indeed, two churches, one in London, namely, Spitalfields, and one in Bristol, namely, St. Philip's and Jacob, were lent me on this occasion, but those were all. I collected for the orphan-house in Moorfields two hundred and fifty pounds one Sabbath-day morning, twenty-two pounds of which were in copper. In the afternoon I collected again at Kennington Common, and continued to do so at most of the places where I preached. Besides this, two or three of the bishops, and several persons of distinction contributed, until at length, having gotten about a thousand and ten pounds, I gave over collecting, and went with what I had to Georgia. At that time multitudes offered to accompany me; but I chose to take over only a surgeon and a few more of both sexes, that I thought would be useful in carrying on my design. My dear fellow-traveller William Seward, Esq., also joined with them. Our first voyage was to Philadelphia, where I was willing to go for the sake of laying in provision. I laid out in London a good part of the thousand pounds for goods, and got as much by them in Philadelphia as nearly defrayed the families' expenses of coming over. Here God blessed my ministry daily....

"January following, 1739, I met my family at Georgia, and being unwilling to lose any time, I hired a large house, and took in all the orphans I could find in the colony. A great many also of the town's children came to school gratis, and many poor people that could not maintain their children, upon application, had leave given them to send their little ones for a month or two, or more as they could spare them, till at length my family consisted of between sixty and seventy. Most of the orphans were in poor case, and three or four almost eaten up with lice. I likewise erected an infirmary, in which many sick people were cured and taken care of gratis. I have now by me a list of upwards of a hundred and thirty patients, which were under the surgeon's hands, exclusive of my own private family. About March I began the great house, having only about one hundred and fifty pounds in cash. I called it *Bethesda*, because I hoped it would be a house of mercy to many souls. Many boys have been put out to trades, and many girls put out to service. I had the pleasure, the other day, to see three boys work at the house in which they were bred, one of them out of his time, a journeyman, and the others serving under their masters. One that I brought from New England is handsomely settled in Carolina; and another from Philadelphia is married, and lives very comfortably in Savannah. We have lately begun to use the plough, and next year I hope to have many acres of good oats and barley. We have nearly twenty sheep and lambs, fifty head of cattle, and seven horses. We hope to kill a thousand weight of pork this season. Our garden is very beautiful, furnishes us with all sorts of greens, etc., etc. We have plenty of milk, eggs, poultry, and make a good deal of butter weekly. A good quantity of wool and cotton have been given me, and we hope to have sufficient spun and wove for the next winter's clothing. The family now consists of twenty-six persons. Two of the orphan boys are blind, one is little better than an idiot. I have two women to take care of the household work, and two men and three boys employed about the plantation and cattle. A set of Dutch servants has been lately sent over. The magistrates were pleased to give me two; and I took in a poor widow, aged near seventy, whom nobody else cared to have. A valuable young man from New England is my schoolmaster, and in my absence performs duty in the family. On Sabbaths, the grown people attend on public worship at Savannah, or at White Bluff, a village near Bethesda, where a Dutch minister officiates. The house is a noble, commodious building, and every thing sweetly adapted for bringing up youth. Georgia is very healthy; not above one, and that a little child, has died out of our family since it removed to Bethesda."

A tabular statement follows this account, giving full particulars of the eighty-six children who to that period had been admitted into the establishment.

Old newspapers, as daguerreotyping the facts, and even the feelings of any particular period, are sometimes invaluable. In New York, as everywhere else, Whitefield had his enemies, and many charges were brought against him. But that there were those who took a strongly favorable view of his character and conduct, is very clear from an extract we give from "The New York Post-Boy," of April, 1746: "Mr. Whitefield's excellent parts, fine elocution, and masterly address; his admirable talent of opening the Scriptures, and enforcing the most weighty subjects upon the conscience; his polite and serious behavior, his unaffected and superior piety, his prudence, humility, and catholic spirit, are things which must silence and disarm prejudice itself. By these qualifications of the orator, the divine, and the Christian, he has not only fixed himself deeper in the affections of his former friends, but greatly increased the number wherever he has preached; and made his way into the hearts of several who, till this visit, had said all the severe things against him that enmity itself seemed capable of."

From this period, this paper especially noticed the various movements of this apostolic man; his arrivals in the city, his engagements in it, his departures from it, and the places of his destination, were all given with the minutiæ with which even the movements of monarchs are recorded.

It was not without its use that the organs of the public thus expressed their high sense of his character. In 1745, suspicions were whispered abroad as to the entire integrity of this excellent man in the appropriation of the funds collected for Bethesda. But happily for all parties, the magistrates of Savannah published in the Philadelphia Gazette an affidavit, that they had carefully examined Mr. Whitefield's receipts and disbursements, and found that what he had collected in behalf of the orphans, had been honestly applied, and that besides, he had given considerably to them of his own property.

Having done what he could at Bethesda, feeling his health failing him, needing resources for his orphans, and urged on by his love of preaching, Whitefield was soon again in the field, far away from his home. In the autumn of 1746, we find many passages in his journals and letters like these, while in Maryland: "I trust the time for favoring this and the neighboring southern provinces is come. Everywhere, almost, the door is opened for preaching, great numbers flock to hear, and the power of an ascended Saviour attends the word. For it is surprising how the Lord causes prejudices to subside, and makes my former most bitter enemies to be at peace with me.... Lately I have been in seven counties in Maryland, and preached with abundant success." At Charleston, South Carolina, he writes, January 1747, "The Lord Jesus is pleased to give me great access to multitudes of souls." A few weeks later, he writes from the same place, that Bethesda was never in a better condition; that he had opened a Latin school there during the winter, and that he hoped yet to see ministers furnished from Georgia.

In April, we again find him in Maryland, as he writes on the twenty-fifth of that month from Bohemia, in that province, and speaks of the success of Mr. Samuel, afterwards President Davies, in Virginia, but adds that a proclamation had been issued in that state against itinerants, so that he himself was shut out of it. In the middle of May he exults, "Maryland is yielding converts to the blessed Jesus. The gospel seems to be moving southward. The harvest is promising. The time of the singing birds is come;" and five days afterwards he says, "I have been now a three hundred miles' circuit in Maryland, and through one or two counties in Pennsylvania. Everywhere the people have a hearing ear, and I trust some have an obedient heart."

On the first of June we find him in Philadelphia, from whence he writes, "At present I have full work here. The congregations yesterday were large, and for this month past I have been preaching to thousands in different places." During the whole of this month his health was in a very critical state. Here we have a few sentences from his pen, as given on different days: "I am sick and well, as I used to be in England; but the Redeemer fills me with comfort. I am determined, in his strength, to die fighting.... I have almost a continual burning fever. With great regret I have omitted preaching *one* night to oblige my friends, and purpose to do so once more, that they may not charge me with murdering myself. But I hope yet to die in the pulpit, or soon after I come out of it.... Since my last, I have been several times on the verge of eternity. At present I am so weak that I cannot preach. It is hard work to be silent, but I must be tried every way."

Sickness did not interrupt Whitefield's labors, if he could move or preach at all. "I am determined," he says to Gilbert Tennent, "to die fighting, though it be on my *stumps*." He was soon after at New York, Newport, Portsmouth, and Boston. At New York he writes, "I am as willing to hunt for souls as ever. I am not weary of my work." On the next day he writes, "I have preached to a very large auditory, and do not find myself much worse for it." He did so again with success. He then says, "I shall go to Boston like an arrow out of a bow, if Jesus strengthen me. I am resolved to preach and work for Him until I can preach and work no more. I have been upon the water three or four days, and now eat like a sailor." He went on to Boston, where he heard of the sudden but joyful death of his venerable and excellent friend Dr. Colman. He adds, "My reception at Boston and elsewhere was like unto the first. Arrows of conviction fled and stuck fast. Congregations were larger than ever, and opposers' mouths were stopped."

After again making short visits to Philadelphia and Bohemia, Whitefield, according to previous arrangements, went to spend the winter in North Carolina. Before he left Bohemia, however, he wrote to his friends at New

York, who were intensely anxious about his health, but he could only say it was yet fluctuating. Even so was it when he arrived in North Carolina, yet he writes, "I am here, hunting in the woods, these *ungospelized* wilds, for sinners. It is pleasant work, though my body is weak and crazy. But after a short *fermentation* in the grave, it will be fashioned like unto Christ's glorious body. The thought of this rejoices my soul, and makes me long to *leap* my seventy years. I sometimes think all will go to heaven before me. Pray for me as a dying man; but Oh, pray that I may not go off as a *snuff*. I would fain die *blazing*—not with human glory, but with the love of Jesus."

Such was his weakness, that his journey to Bathtown, in North Carolina, was long and slow. Even a short ride was fatiguing and painful. Still, he preached with considerable power; cheered on from stage to stage by the hope that the conversion of "North Carolina sinners would be glad news in heaven." His letters indicated lively hopes of an extensive revival, but his expectations were not fully realized. His health was still exceedingly feeble, and his physicians ordered him to try a change of climate. He accordingly embarked for the Bermudas, where he landed, March 15, 1748.

The Bermudas are a group of four small islands lying about nine hundred miles east of Georgia. The largest of the islands is called St. George's, with a capital of the same name; the climate is remarkably fine, and well adapted for the temporary residence and recovery of invalids. Here Whitefield met with an exceedingly kind reception, and remained on the island with great benefit to his health, more than a month. We scarcely need to say that he was not idle during his residence here, but traversed the island from one end to the other, generally preaching twice a day. A few passages from his journal will best show the facts.

"The simplicity and plainness of the people, together with the pleasant situation of the island, much delighted me. The Rev. Mr. Holiday, minister of Spanish Point, received me in a most affectionate, Christian manner; and begged I would make his house my home. In the evening, I expounded at the house of Mr. Savage, at Port Royal, which was very commodious; and which also he would have me make my home. I went with Mr. Savage in a boat to the town of St. George, in order to pay our respects to the governor. All along we had a most pleasant prospect of the other part of the island; a more pleasant one I never saw. Mrs. Smith, of St. George, for whom I had a letter of recommendation from my dear old friend Mr. Smith, of Charlestown, received me into her house. About noon, with one of the council and Mr. Savage, I waited upon the governor. He received us courteously, and invited us to dine with him and the council. We accepted the invitation, and all behaved with great civility and respect. After the governor rose from the table, he desired, if I stayed in town on the Sunday, that I would dine with him at his own house.

"Sunday, March 20. Read prayers and preached twice this day, to what were esteemed here large auditories—in the morning at Spanish Point church, and in the evening at Brackish Pond church, about two miles distant from each other. In the afternoon I spoke with greater freedom than in the morning, and I trust not altogether in vain. All were attentive, some wept. I dined with Colonel Butterfield, one of the council; and received several invitations to other gentlemen's houses. May God bless and reward them, and incline them to open their hearts to receive the Lord Jesus.

"Wednesday, March 23. Dined with Captain Gibbs, and went from thence and expounded at the house of Captain F——le, at Hunbay, about two miles distant. The company here also was large, attentive, and affected. Our Lord gave me utterance. I expounded the first part of the eighth chapter of Jeremiah. After lecture, Mr. Riddle, a counsellor, invited me to his house; as did Mr. Paul, an aged Presbyterian minister, to his pulpit; which I complied with upon condition that the rumor was true, that the governor had served the ministers with an injunction that I should not preach in the churches.

"Sunday, March 27. Glory be to God! I hope this has been a profitable Sabbath to many souls; it has been a pleasant one to mine. Both morning and afternoon I preached to a large auditory, for the Bermudas, in Mr. Paul's meeting-house, which I suppose contains about four hundred. Abundance of negroes, and many others, were in the porch, and about the house. The word seemed to be clothed with a convincing power, and to make its way into the hearts of the hearers. Between sermons, I was entertained very civilly in a neighboring house. Judge Bascom, and three more of the council, came thither, and each gave me an invitation to his house. How does the Lord make way for a poor stranger in a strange land. After the second sermon I dined with Mr. Paul; and in the evening expounded to a very large company at Councillor Riddle's. My body was somewhat weak; but the Lord carried me through, and caused me to go to rest rejoicing. May I thus go to my grave, when my ceaseless and uninterrupted rest shall begin.

"Thursday, March 31. Dined on Tuesday at Colonel Corbusier's, and on Wednesday at Colonel Gilbert's, both of the council; and found, by what I could hear, that some good had been done, and many prejudices removed. Who shall hinder, if God will work? Went to an island this afternoon called Ireland, upon which live a few families; and to my surprise, found a great many gentlemen, and other people, with my friend Mr. Holiday, who came from different quarters to hear me. Before I began preaching, I went round to see a most remarkable cave, which very much displayed the exquisite workmanship of Him, who in 'his strength setteth fast the mountains, and is girded about with power.' While I was in the cave, quite unexpectedly I turned and saw Councillor Riddle, who, with his son, came to hear me; and while we were in the boat, told me that he had been with the governor, who declared he had no personal prejudice against me, and wondered I did not come to town and preach there, for it was the desire of the people; and that any house in the town, the court-house not excepted, should be at my service. Thanks be to God for so much favor. If his cause requires it, I shall have more. He knows my heart; I value the favor of man no farther than as it makes room for the gospel, and gives me a larger scope to promote the glory of God. There being no capacious house upon the island, I preached for the first time here in the open air. All heard very attentively; and it was very pleasant, after sermon, to see so many boats full of people returning from the worship of God. I talked seriously to some in our own boat, and sung a psalm, in which they readily joined.

"Sunday, April 3. Preached twice this day at Mr. Paul's meeting-house, as on the last Sabbath, but with greater freedom and power, especially in the morning; and I think to as great, if not greater auditories. Dined with Colonel Harvy, another of the council; visited a sick woman, where many came to hear; and expounded afterwards to a great company, at Captain John Dorrel's, Mrs. Dorrel's son, who with his wife courteously entertained me, and desired me to make his house my home. So true is that promise of our Lord, that 'whosoever leaves father or mother, houses or lands, shall have in this life a hundred-fold with persecution, and in the world to come, life everlasting.' Lord, I have experienced the one; in thy good time grant that I may experience the other also.

"Wednesday, April 6. Preached yesterday at the house of Mr. Anthony Smith, of Baylis Bay, with a considerable degree of warmth; and rode afterwards to St. George, the only town on the island. The gentlemen of the town had sent me an invitation by Judge Bascom; and he, with several others, came to visit me at my lodgings; and informed me that the governor desired to see me. About ten I waited upon his excellency, who received me with great civility, and told me he had no objection against my person or my principles, having never yet heard me; and he knew nothing with respect to my conduct in moral life, that might prejudice him against me; but his intentions were to let none preach in the island, unless he had a written license to preach somewhere in America, or the West Indies; at the same time he acknowledged that it was but a matter of mere form. I informed his excellency that I had been regularly inducted into the parish of Savannah; that I was ordained priest by letters dismissory from my lord of London, and was under no church censure from his lordship; and would always read the church prayers, if the clergy would give me the use of their churches. I added farther, that a minister's pulpit was always looked upon as his freehold; and that I knew one clergyman who had denied his own diocesan the use of his pulpit. But I told his excellency I was satisfied with the liberty he allowed me, and would not act contrary to his injunction. I then begged leave to be dismissed, as I was obliged to preach at eleven o'clock. His excellency said he intended to do himself the pleasure to hear me. At eleven, the church bell rung. The church Bible, prayer-book, and cushion, were sent to the town-house. The governor, several of the council, the minister of the parish, and assembly-men, with a great number of the town's people, assembled in great order. I was very sick, through a cold I caught last night; but read the church prayers. The first lesson was the fifteenth chapter of the first book of Samuel. I preached on those words, 'Righteousness exalteth a nation.' Being weak and faint, and afflicted much with the headache, I did not do that justice to my subject which I sometimes am enabled to do; but the Lord so helped me that, as I found afterwards, the governor and the other gentlemen expressed their approbation, and acknowledged they did not expect to be so well entertained. Not unto me, Lord, not unto me, but to thy free grace be all the glory!

"After sermon, Dr. F——bs, and Mr. P——t, the collector, came to me, and desired me to favor them and the gentlemen of the town with my company at dinner. I accepted the invitation. The governor, and the president, and Judge Bascom were there. All wondered at my speaking so freely and fluently without notes. The governor asked whether I used minutes. I answered, 'No.' He said it was a great gift. At table, his excellency introduced something of religion by asking me the meaning of the word Hades. Several other things were started about freewill, Adam's fall, predestination, etc., to all which God enabled me to answer so pertinently, and taught me to mix the *utile* and *dulce* [useful and pleasant] so together, that all at table seemed highly pleased, shook me by the hand, and invited me to their respective houses. The governor, in particular, asked me to dine with him on the morrow; and Dr. F——, one of his particular intimates, invited me to drink tea in the afternoon. I thanked all, returned proper respects, and went to my lodgings with some degree of thankfulness for the assistance vouchsafed me, and abased before God at the consideration of my unspeakable unworthiness. In the afternoon, about five o'clock, I expounded the parable of the prodigal son to many people at a private house; and in the evening had liberty to speak freely and closely to those who supped with me. O that this may be the beginning of good gospel times to the inhabitants of this town."

We might fill other pages from Whitefield's journal, but will only give two more passages. The first will show him in connection with the African race, in whose highest welfare he always took a special interest.

"Saturday, May 7. In my conversation these two days with some of my friends, I was diverted much in hearing several things that passed among the poor negroes, since I preached to them last Sunday. One of the women, it seems, said that 'if the book I preached out of was the best book that was ever bought at London, she was sure it had never all that in it which I spoke to the negroes,' The old man who spoke out loud last Sunday, and said 'yes' when I asked them whether all the negroes would not go to heaven, being questioned by somebody why he spoke out so, answered, that 'the gentleman put the question once or twice to them, and the other fools had not the manners to make any answer; till at last I seemed to point at him, and he was ashamed that nobody should answer me, and therefore he did.' Another, wondering why I said negroes had black hearts, was answered by his black brother, 'Ah, thou fool, dost not thou understand it? He means black with sin.' Two girls were overheard by their mistress talking about religion, and they said 'they knew, if they did not repent, they must be damned.' From all which I infer that these negroes on the Bermudas are more awake than I supposed; that their consciences are awake, and consequently prepared in a good measure for hearing the gospel preached to them."

Whitefield sums up the events which had occurred in connection with himself on the Bermudas, the praise of which islands has also been celebrated by the distinguished Bishop Berkeley, who resided there for some time, and by Waller the poet.

"Sunday, May 22. Blessed be God, the little leaven thrown into the three measures of meal begins to ferment and work almost every day for the week past. I have conversed with souls loaded with a sense of their sins, and as far as I can judge, really pricked to the heart. I preached only three times, but to almost three times larger auditories than usual. Indeed, the fields are white, ready to harvest. God has been pleased to bless private visits. Go where I will, upon the least notice, houses are crowded, and the poor souls that follow are soon drenched in tears. This day I took, as it were, another farewell. As the ship did not sail, I preached at Somerset in the morning to a large congregation in the fields; and expounded in the evening at Mr. Harvy's house, around which stood many hundreds of people. But in the morning and evening how did the poor souls weep. Abundance of prayers and blessings were put up for my safe passage to England, and speedy return to the Bermudas again. May they enter into the ears of the Lord of sabaoth. With all humility and thankfulness of heart will I here, O Lord, set up my *Ebenezer*, for hitherto surely hast thou helped me. Thanks be to the Lord for sending me hither. I have been received in a manner I dared not to expect, and have met with little, very little opposition indeed. The inhabitants seem to be plain and open-hearted. They have loaded me with provisions for my sea-store; and in the several parishes, by a private voluntary contribution, have raised me upwards of *one hundred pounds sterling*. This will pay a little of Bethesda's debt, and enable me to make such a remittance to my dear yoke-fellow, as may keep her from being embarrassed, or too much beholden in my absence. Blessed be God for bringing me out of my embarrassments by degrees. May the Lord reward all my benefactors a thousand-fold. I hear that what was given, was given heartily, and people only lamented that they could do no more."

Whitefield now transmitted to Georgia what had been collected for the orphan-house; but fearing a relapse, if he returned to the south during the hot season, which was near commencing, and pressed also again to visit England, he took his passage in a brig, and in twenty-eight days arrived at Deal.

On his voyage, he completed an abridgment, which he had previously begun, of "*Law's serious Call to a devout and holy Life*," which he endeavored to make more useful by excluding whatever is not truly evangelical, and illustrating the subject more fully, especially from the holy Scriptures. He also wrote letters to his friends, one of which strikingly illustrates his Christian humility. It bears date June 24, 1748. "Yesterday I made an end of revising all my journals. Alas, alas, in how many things I have judged and acted wrong. I have been too rash and hasty in giving characters both of places and persons. Being fond of Scripture language, I have used a style too apostolical, and at the same time I have been too bitter in my zeal. Wildfire has been mixed with it, and I find that I frequently wrote and spoke in my own spirit, when I thought I was writing and speaking by the assistance of the Spirit of God. I have, likewise, too much made inward impressions my rule of acting, and too soon and too explicitly published what had been better kept in longer, or told after my death. By these things I have hurt the blessed cause I would defend, and also stirred up a needless opposition. This has humbled me much, and made me think of a saying of Mr. Henry, 'Joseph had more honesty than he had policy, or he never would have told his dreams.' At the same time, I cannot but praise God, who fills me with so much of his holy fire, and carried me, a poor weak youth, through such a torrent, both of popularity and contempt, and set so many seals to my unworthy ministrations. I bless him for ripening my judgment a little more, for giving me to see and confess, and I hope in some degree to correct and amend some of my former mistakes."

In the early part of this year, 1748, the "Gentleman's Magazine" had announced Whitefield's death as having taken place in America. One of his first letters on his arrival at Deal in that year, says, "Words cannot express how joyful my friends were to see me once more in the land of the living, for I find the newspapers had buried me ever since April last. But it seems I am not to die, but live. O that it may be to declare the works of the Lord."

CHAPTER XI
LABORS IN ENGLAND AND SCOTLAND— CHAPLAIN TO LADY HUNTINGDON. 1748, 1749

On the evening of July 6, 1748, Whitefield again found himself in London, after an absence of nearly four years. Here he was welcomed with joy by many thousands. The large church of St. Bartholomew was at once thrown open to him, where multitudes flocked to hear, and where on the first Sabbath he had a thousand communicants. But in his own more immediate circle many things were in an unhappy condition. His congregation at the Tabernacle had been much scattered during his absence; Antinomianism had made sad havoc among the people; and one of this party threatened to rival him in Moorfields. Whitefield sent him word, "The fields are no doubt as free to you as to another. God send you a clear head and a *clean* heart. I intend preaching there on Sunday evening." He did so; and found "Moorfields as white to harvest as ever." Our evangelist was again called to mourn the evils of poverty. He found himself compelled to sell his household furniture, to pay, in part, the debts of his orphan-house, which were yet far from being cancelled; his aged mother, for whom he always retained the highest regard, also needed his aid. These and other trials pressed him sorely; but on the other hand, he felt happy in his work, and his congregation were soon reunited, and happy in his labors.

We have seen that as early as 1738, Lady Huntingdon, with his lordship her husband, as frequently as they could, heard Whitefield preach; since that period his lordship had died, leaving her ladyship a widow, in the thirty-ninth year of her age. At what period she became more openly and intimately Whitefield's friend does not appear; but when he landed at Deal from his third visit to America, she sent Howel Harris to bring him to her house at Chelsea, where he preached to large circles of the gay world, who thronged this then fashionable watering-place. For the benefit of this class of hearers, she soon after removed to London, at that time some three miles distant from Chelsea, appointed Whitefield her chaplain, and during the winter of 1748 and '49, opened her splendid mansion in Park-street for the preaching of the gospel. "Good Lady Huntingdon," he writes, "has come to town, and I am to preach twice a week at her house to the great and noble. O that some of them might be effectually called to taste the riches of redeeming love." On the first day appointed, Chesterfield and Bolingbroke, both of them well-known for their gayety and infidelity, and a circle of the nobility, attended; and having heard him once, they desired to come again. "Lord Chesterfield thanked me," he says. "Lord Bolingbroke was moved, and asked me to come and see him the next morning. My hands have been full of work, and I have been among great company. All accepted my sermons. Thus the world turns round. *'In all time of my wealth, good Lord, deliver me.'*"

The death-bed of Lord St. John Bolingbroke, whom we have already mentioned as one of his parlor-hearers, exhibited scenes unusual in the circle where he moved. The Bible was read to him, and his cry was, "God be merciful to me a sinner." "My Lord Bolingbroke," wrote Lady Huntingdon to Whitefield, "was much struck with his brother's language in his last moments. O that his eyes might be opened by the illuminating influence of divine truth. He is a singularly awful character; and I am fearfully alarmed, lest the gospel which he so heartily despises, yet affects to reverence, should prove the savor of death unto death to him. Some, I trust, are savingly awakened, while many are inquiring; thus the great Lord of the harvest hath put honor on your ministry, and hath given my heart an encouraging token of the utility of our feeble efforts."

It is related that the Rev. Mr. Church, a clergyman who died curate of Battersea, near London, one day called on Bolingbroke, who said to him, "You have caught me reading John Calvin; he was indeed a man of great parts, profound sense, and vast learning; he handles the doctrines of grace in a very masterly manner." "Doctrines of grace," replied the clergyman; "the doctrines of grace have set all mankind by the ears." "I am surprised to hear you say so," answered Lord Bolingbroke, "you who profess to believe and to preach Christianity. Those doctrines are certainly the doctrines of the Bible, and if I believe the Bible I must believe them. And let me seriously tell you, that the greatest miracle in the world is the subsistence of Christianity, and its continued preservation, as a religion, when the preaching of it is committed to the care of such unchristian men as you."

At this period Whitefield renewed his acquaintance with the Rev. James Hervey, who has not improperly been called the Melancthon of the second reformation in England. Among all the converts of our evangelist, no one was more distinguished for piety, or for his fascination as a writer, than this admirable clergyman. His writings, though too flowery in their style, were eminently suitable, as Whitefield himself says, "for the taste of the polite world." Hervey wrote to Whitefield, "Your journals and sermons, and especially that sweet sermon on 'What think ye of Christ?' were a means of bringing me to the knowledge of the truth." Whitefield felt the warmest attachment to Hervey in return, and when he introduced some of his works into America, wrote, "The author is my old friend; a most heavenly-minded creature; one of the first Methodists, who is contented with a small *cure*, and gives all he has to the poor. We correspond with, though we cannot see each other." Whitefield intimated in one of his journals his intention of sketching Hervey's character, but this was one of the many intended things which were never accomplished. Dr. Doddridge wrote a preface to one of his works, which Warburton, as might be expected, called "a weak rhapsody."

Under the auspices of Lady Huntingdon, a prayer-meeting was established for the women who, from the circles of rank and fashion, became the followers of the Lord. Among these were Lady Frances Gardiner, Lady Mary Hamilton, daughter of the Marquis of Lothian, who had attended the ministry of Whitefield in Scotland, Lady Gertrude Hotham and Countess Delitz, sisters of Lady Chesterfield, Lady Chesterfield herself, and Lady Fanny Shirley. "Religion," says Lady Huntingdon, when writing to Doddridge, "was never so much the subject of conversation as now. Some of the great ones hear with me the gospel patiently, and thus much seed is sown by Mr. Whitefield's preaching. O that it may fall on good ground, and bring forth abundantly."

Some one, we believe a bishop, complained to George II. of the popularity and success of Whitefield, and entreated his majesty in some way or other to silence him. The monarch, thinking, no doubt, of the class described by the martyr Latimer, as "unpreaching prelates," replied with jocose severity, "I believe the best way will be to make a bishop of him."

But if Whitefield was honored by some of the great, he received from others unmingled hostility. Horace Walpole, the gay man, and the corrupt courtier, thought it worth while to introduce the Methodist preacher into his "Private Correspondence." The statement he makes of professed facts is altogether incredible, but shows unmistakably the spirit of the writer. "The apostle Whitefield is come to some shame. He went to Lady Huntingdon lately, and asked for forty pounds for some distressed saint or other. She said she had not so much money in the house, but would give it him the first time she had. He was very pressing, but in vain. At last he said, 'There's your watch and trinkets, you don't want such vanities; I will have that.' She would have put him off; but he persisting, she said, 'Well, if you must have it, you must.' About a fortnight afterwards, going to his house, and being carried into his wife's chamber, among the paraphernalia of the latter the countess found her own offering. This has made a terrible schism; she tells the story herself. I had not it from Saint Frances, [Lady Fanny Shirley,] but I hope it is true." Every thing goes to prove the sincerity of his hope, though founded on falsehood.

It has generally happened that the most effective public speakers, whether secular or sacred, have been accused by a fastidious class with *vulgarisms*. So with Cicero, Burke, and Chatham; so with Patrick Henry and Daniel Webster; and to turn to eminent preachers, so with Luther, Latimer, and Whitefield. The reason was, that intent on the greatest good to the greatest number, they used what Dr. Johnson, after Daniel Burgess, called "market language." Dr. William Bates, an accomplished and courtly non-conformist minister, in the seventeenth century, once complained in the presence of his faithful but unpolished friend Daniel Burgess, that he found very little success in his work as a minister; when his aged brother smartly replied, "Thank your velvet mouth for that—too fine to speak market language." Whitefield, very happily for thousands, had no squeamishness of this sort.

Some ladies called one Saturday morning to pay a visit to Lady Huntingdon, and during the interview, her ladyship inquired of them if they had ever heard Mr. Whitefield preach. On being answered in the negative, she said, "I wish you would hear him; he is to preach to-morrow evening." They promised her ladyship they would certainly attend. They fulfilled their promise; and when they called on her ladyship the next Monday morning, she anxiously inquired if they had heard Mr. Whitefield on the previous evening, and how they liked him. The reply was, "Oh, my lady, of all the preachers we ever heard, he is the most strange and unaccountable! Among other preposterous things, would your ladyship believe it, he declared that Jesus Christ was so willing to receive sinners, that he did not object to receive even the devil's *castaways*! Now, my lady, did you ever hear of such a thing since you were born?" Her ladyship, in reply, said, "There is something, I acknowledge, a little singular in the invitation, and I do not recollect to have met with it before; but as Mr. Whitefield is below in the parlor, we will have him up, and let him answer for himself."

On Mr. Whitefield's entering the drawing-room, Lady Huntingdon said, "Sir, these ladies have been preferring a very heavy charge against you, and I thought it best that you should come up and defend yourself. They say, that in your sermon last evening, in speaking of the willingness of

Jesus Christ to receive sinners, you said, that 'so ready was Christ to receive sinners who came to him, that he was willing to receive even the devil's castaways.'" Mr. Whitefield immediately replied, "I certainly, my lady, must plead guilty to the charge; whether I did what was right, or otherwise, your ladyship shall judge when you have heard a fact. Did your ladyship notice, about half an hour ago, a very modest single rap at the door? It was given by a poor, miserable looking aged female, who requested to speak with me. I desired that she might be shown into the parlor, when she thus addressed me: 'I believe, sir, you preached last evening at such a chapel.' 'Yes, I did.' 'Ah, sir, I was accidentally passing the door of that chapel, and hearing the voice of some one preaching, I did what I have never been in the habit of doing—I went in; and one of the first things I heard you say, was, that Jesus Christ was so willing to receive sinners, that he did not object to receive the devil's castaways. Do you think, sir, that Jesus Christ would receive me?' I answered her that there was not a doubt of it, if she was but willing to go to him."

It is pleasant to add, that the impression conveyed in the singular language of Mr. Whitefield ended in the conversion of the poor woman to God. She gave satisfactory evidence that her great and numerous sins had been forgiven through the atonement of the Lord Jesus Christ. Was Mr. Whitefield to be censured for the use of this language?

In September, 1748, Mr. Whitefield made his third visit to Scotland, where he met with a cordial welcome, and where his labors became increasingly valued. Some of the clergy at Glasgow, Perth, and Edinburgh used their influence to exclude him from the pulpits, but the majority voted in his favor; and a full examination vindicated his character, and made his excellences more generally known. All the ministers who were disposed to invite him to preach, were at liberty to do so, except in the presbytery of Edinburgh; here, however, he was accommodated by the magistrates with a church to preach in whenever he visited the city. In Scotland he now warmly advocated the cause of the college in New Jersey: of the results of his labors we shall hear more hereafter.

On his return to London, Whitefield resumed his preaching at Lady Huntingdon's to "the great ones," as he calls them. Thirty, and sometimes even sixty persons of rank attended, although the newspapers gave false and degrading accounts of the reception he met with in Scotland. He now availed himself of the influence he possessed, to forward his intended college, in addition to his orphan-house, for which his plea was, "If some such thing be not done, I cannot see how the southern parts will be provided with ministers; for all are afraid to go over." On this ground he appealed to the trustees of Georgia; reminding them that he had expended five thousand pounds upon the orphan-house; begging them to relieve it, as a charitable institution, from all quit-rent and taxes; and especially to allow him the labor of blacks in cultivating the farm. "White hands," he said, "had left his tract of land uncultivated."

It will not be expected that Whitefield could stay long, even in the courtly circles of London, where he met with so much acceptance. We very soon find him among his old friends at Gloucester and Bristol. The bishop of the latter see, he says, behaved very respectfully to him; he visited also his old tutor, now become one of the prebendaries, and met with the old kindness received at Oxford. "I told him, that my judgment, as I trust, was a little more ripened than it was some years ago; and that as fast as I found out my faults, I should be glad to acknowledge them. He said the offence of the governors of the church would wear off as I grew *moderate*." The evangelist did not tell the doctor how little he cared for such moderation as the governors of the church in that day required; but he wrote to Lady Huntingdon, on the subject of their favor, "I am pretty easy about that. If I can but act an honest part, and be kept from *trimming*, I leave all consequences to Him who orders all things well." During this journey, many new converts were won. One of these was a counsellor, who was so much affected, that his zeal in inviting others to hear Whitefield led his wife to suspect him of madness.

An interesting fact connected with Gloucestershire, his native county, may be introduced in this place, though we are not sure that it occurred during this journey. John Skinner of Houndscroft was a strolling fiddler, going from fair to fair, supplying music to any party that would hire him. Having determined to interrupt Mr. Whitefield while preaching, he obtained a standing on a ladder raised to a window near the pulpit. Here he remained a quiet, if not an attentive hearer, till the text was read, when he intended to begin his annoying exercise on the violin. It pleased God, however, while he was putting his instrument in tune, to convey the word preached with irresistible power to his soul; his attention was diverted from his original purpose, he heard the whole sermon, and became a new man.

Happily Whitefield was blessed in bringing to Christ many who were made eminently useful. Among others we might mention the late Rev. Cornelius Winter, an eminent minister, who afterwards accompanied our evangelist in his last voyage to America, and who after his death conveyed his will to England, and sought ordination to return and labor in Georgia. Disappointed in this, he became an able and successful minister in England;

and also trained several young men for the Christian ministry, including the late celebrated William Jay of Bath. Whitefield had often been heard by Winter with great pleasure, for he admired his eloquence; but for some time no good effects were apparent. One night, while playing at cards, an amusement in which he much delighted, and though surrounded by a number of gay companions, the thought presented itself to Winter's mind that he might that evening hear his favorite preacher. He broke off from play in the midst of the game, which made his companions very angry, as they suspected where he was going. He tells us that it was a night much to be remembered. He had reason to hope the scales of ignorance were then removed from his eyes, he had a sense of his misery as a sinner, and was led to earnest inquiry after the way of salvation. It is scarcely necessary to say, that he never again played at cards.

From the exhilarating scenes of Gloucestershire and Bristol, we must accompany Whitefield into Cornwall, among the glens and dales of which, or on the seaside to a somewhat similar population and with almost equal success, he spoke "all the words of this life." The robust and determined miners of the west of England, whose very employment gives hardihood alike to their character and frame, at first received him in somewhat rough and unpolished style, but were soon after melted and transformed by the grace which had displayed its triumphs among their brethren at Kingswood. "I am just returned," he writes on one occasion, "from near the Land's End, where thousands and thousands heard the gospel gladly. Everywhere the word of God has run and been glorified. Every day I have been travelling and preaching; and could I stay a month, it might be spent to great advantage. At a place called Port Isaac, the Redeemer's stately steps were indeed seen. At Camelford I preached with great quietness in the streets. At St. Ann's we had a very powerful season; and yesterday at Redruth several thousands attended, and the word was quick and powerful." Again he writes, "Immediately after writing my last, I preached to many thousands at a place called Gwennap. The rain descended, but the grace of God seemed to fall like a gentle dew, sprinkling rain upon our souls. It was indeed a fine spring shower. In the evening I rode to St. Ives, and preached to many who gladly attended to hear the word; a great power seemed to accompany it. On the Lord's day I preached twice to great auditories. On Monday I preached again at Redruth, at ten in the morning, to nearly, as they were computed, ten thousand souls. Arrows of conviction seemed to fly fast." Again, in a communication to the Countess of Huntingdon, he says, "I have been very near the Land's End, and everywhere souls have fled to hear the word preached, 'like doves to their windows.' The harvest is great, yea, very great, but laborers are few. O that the Lord of the harvest would thrust out more laborers." And yet again he says, "Invitations are sent to me from Falmouth and several other places, but I cannot attend to them all at present. I want more tongues, more bodies, more souls, for the Lord Jesus. Had I ten thousand, he should have them all." Such was the noble spirit he displayed, and such were the manner and fruits of his "entering in among" the, at that time, benighted children of Cornwall. A great light shone upon them. They came from the caverns of the earth to welcome its rising, and to look upon its brightness. Thousands of them were indeed "brought out of darkness into marvellous light," and turned by it from sin to holiness, and from Satan to God; and thousands are still rejoicing in its beams.

On his return to London, Whitefield found his assemblies at the countess's "brilliant indeed," and Lord Bolingbroke still one among them. Of this talented nobleman our evangelist at this time indulged a happy hope, which, alas, seems never to have been realized.

In February, 1749, Whitefield made an excursion to Exeter and Plymouth, where he was agreeably surprised to find a great alteration had taken place since his preceding visit, five years before. He loved to "range," as he called it, "after precious souls," and happily for him and for others he found them. During this and subsequent visits to Plymouth, he resided with the Rev. Andrew Kinsman, an excellent Congregational minister, of whom we have already spoken. He was born in Devonshire in 1724, and was therefore ten years younger than Whitefield. While peculiarly amiable in his manners, and remarkable for his regard to his parents, he was unacquainted with the religion of the heart till his seventeenth year, when he met with a volume of Mr. Whitefield's sermons, and one of those on the new birth alarmed him. His pious friends were few, but his religious feelings were deeply moved, and God at length gave him "the oil of joy for mourning, and the garment of praise for the spirit of heaviness." Concerned for the highest interests of his relatives, he one night, as the family were retiring to rest, broke out, with intense emotion, "What, shall we go to bed without prayer? How do we know but some of us may awake in hell before morning?" This unexpected address struck the family with solemn awe; and while they looked at each other with conscious shame, for the neglect of so clear a duty, he fell upon his knees and prayed with so much readiness and fervor that it excited their astonishment.

As might be expected, his concern for others did not stop here; he was anxious that his neighbors might also find "the unsearchable riches of Christ." He began, therefore, to read Whitefield's sermons to as many as would attend, supposing, with Melancthon, that what had proved so great a blessing to himself, would not fail of similar effects on others, as soon as they were heard. After a short time, he began himself to expound and preach, and was encouraged by many conversions under his ministry, including those of his father, mother, and three sisters. Not long after these events, Whitefield, in entering on one of his voyages to America, had been compelled to stay at Plymouth, where Kinsman first saw and heard him. By a series of remarkable events, Mr. Kinsman was brought to settle as a minister at Plymouth, where the "Tabernacle" was erected on ground given by himself, and the congregation were served by him and other ministers with abundant success. In the whole neighborhood an extraordinary blessing attended his labors, and his usefulness and deliverances from danger were only second to those of Whitefield himself. Nor was he less respected, nor his ministry attended with less success, at Bristol and London—cities to which he was invited by Whitefield; who used to call Bristol *"Kinsman's America,"* alluding to his own reception and success in the western world.

On one occasion, when Whitefield was about to sail for America, he sent for Kinsman to London, and on his arrival dined with his distinguished friend at the Tabernacle house. After dinner there was a violent storm of thunder and lightning. As they stood at the window looking out on the raging elements, Mr. Kinsman, supposing a young clergyman who had dined with them, and who now stood by his side, to be a pious man, familiarly put his hand on his shoulder, and with great cheerfulness and energy repeated the lines of Dr. Watts:

> "The God who rules on high,
> And thunders when he please;
> Who rides upon the stormy sky,
> And manages the seas—
> *This awful God is ours,*
> Our Father, and our love!"

The words so appropriately introduced, and so emphatically spoken, made a deep impression on the mind of the young clergyman, and gave rise to a conversation which, by the blessing of God, led to his conversion.

At the Tabernacle in London, the ministry of Mr. Kinsman was greatly distinguished for its excellence and success, and he thought himself highly honored in preaching the first sermon delivered from the pulpit of the present Tabernacle. His musical voice, his lively and pathetic address, and the richness of the evangelical truths he proclaimed, brought numbers of all classes of society to hear him. Among them was Shuter, the comedian, to whom we shall again refer as a hearer of Whitefield, and who years afterwards, in an interview with Kinsman, drew a striking contrast between their professions, and bitterly lamented that he had not cordially embraced religion, when his conscience was impressed under the preaching of the great evangelist.

But we must not stay longer to speak of Kinsman; suffice it to say that he founded, in addition to Plymouth, a new church three miles from thence, at a place now called Devonport, and labored with energy and holy success till the sixty-ninth year of his age, when he died in triumph, February 28, 1793. Of such a man it was truly said, that for Whitefield "he retained the most filial affection to his dying day; and frequently travelled with, and consulted him as a father upon all his religious concerns."

In March Whitefield returned to London, where the feeble state of his health made him feel weary even in his success. He says, "I have seen enough of popularity to be sick of it, and did not the interest of my blessed Master require my appearing in public, the world should hear but little of me henceforward." Yet his zeal abated not. "I dread the thoughts of flagging in the latter stages of my road," is an expression often used in his letters to his friends. He thought that preaching and travelling contributed to his health. In a letter to Hervey, he says, "Fear not your weak body, we are immortal till our work is done. Christ's laborers must live by miracle; if not, I must not live at all, for God only knows what I daily endure. My continual vomitings almost kill me, and yet the pulpit is my cure; so that my friends begin to pity me less, and to leave off that ungrateful caution, 'Spare thyself.' I speak this to encourage you."

All this Whitefield meant. Hence in May we find him preaching at Portsmouth daily, for more than a week, to very large and attentive auditories; where was shown another remarkable instance of the power which attended his preaching, for many who a few days before were speaking all manner of evil against him, were very desirous of his longer stay to preach the gospel among them. From Bristol, June 24, he writes, "Yesterday God brought me here, after a circuit of about eight hundred miles, and enabled me to preach to, I suppose, upwards of a hundred thousand souls. I have been in eight Welsh counties, and I think we have not had one dry meeting. The work in Wales is much upon the advance, and likely to increase daily."

Whitefield returned to London to welcome his wife home from the Bermuda Islands. From her he learned that there his character had been aspersed by one of the clergy; but while he grieved over the fact, he said,

"I am content to wait till the day of judgment for the clearing up of my character; and after I am dead, I desire no other epitaph than this, 'Here lies George Whitefield. What sort of a man he was, the great day will discover.'"

In the midst of his sorrows, Whitefield was comforted by a visit from two German ministers, who had been laboring among the Jews with apparently happy results. He found also several of the peeresses, and others of "the great," cordially disposed to receive him; and shortly afterwards was visited by Mr. Grimshaw, a clergyman from Yorkshire, for whom in September he went to preach. Thousands in the village of Haworth attended his preaching, even ten thousand at a time, and a thousand communicants approached the table of the Lord. At Leeds also he preached, at the invitation of Mr. Wesley's people, to ten thousand persons, and Mr. Charles Wesley himself introduced him to the pulpit at Newcastle-upon-Tyne.

In the north of England the visits of Mr. Whitefield were always looked for with intense interest. In one of his letters, he thus describes the state of things there in August, 1756: "It is now a fortnight since I came to Leeds, in and about which I preached eight days successively, three times almost every day, to thronged and affected auditories. On Sunday last at Bradford, in the morning, the audience consisted of above ten thousand; at noon, and in the evening, at Birstal, of nearly double that number. Though hoarse, I was able to speak so that they all heard." These hallowed services were often spoken of by the late Rev. Dr. John Fawcett, for more than half a century an eminent Baptist minister of that neighborhood, to whose soul they proved a rich blessing. After having heard Whitefield at Bradford in the morning, he followed him to Birstal, where a platform was erected at the foot of a hill adjoining the town, whence Mr. Whitefield addressed an immense concourse of people, not fewer, it was believed, than twenty thousand, who were ranged before him on the declivity in the form of an amphitheatre. "I lay," says Fawcett, "under the scaffold, and it appeared as if all his words were addressed to me, and as if he had known my most secret thoughts from ten years of age. As long as life remains, I shall remember both the text and the sermon." Accustomed as he was to preach to large and promiscuous multitudes, when he looked on this vast assemblage, and was about to mount the temporary stage, he expressed to his surrounding friends a considerable feeling of timidity; but when he began to speak, an unusual solemnity pervaded the assembly, and thousands, in the course of the sermon, as was often the fact, gave vent to their emotions by tears and groans. Fools who came to mock, began to pray, and to cry out, "What must we do to be saved?"

Mr. Shirley, in giving an account of this same service, tells us that "not only the field, but the woodlands about it, were covered with crowds collected from different parts. An unusual solemnity pervaded this vast multitude, and at the close of the service the one hundredth psalm was sung, and concluded with Mr. Grimshaw's favorite doxology,

"'Praise God, from whom all blessings flow.'

The volume of sound produced by the united voices of thousands, while it reëchoed through the vale below, had such an effect as no language can describe."

Mr. Grimshaw was a very remarkable clergyman connected with the church of England, though found fault with on account of his irregularity. He studied at Cambridge for the ministry before he was acquainted with the reality of true religion. His conversion was very striking; after which he became a remarkably faithful and pungent preacher. He settled at Haworth, in Yorkshire, where Mr. Whitefield visited him.

In one of the services held by Mr. Whitefield in Yorkshire, a deep solemnity was created by providential circumstances. He had mounted the temporary scaffold to address the thousands before him. Casting a look over the multitude, he elevated his hands, and in an energetic manner implored the divine presence and blessing. With a solemnity peculiarly his own, he then announced his text, "It is appointed unto men once to die, but after this the judgment." Heb. 11:27. After a short pause, as he was about to proceed, a wild, terrifying shriek issued from the centre of the congregation. A momentary alarm and confusion ensued. Mr. Whitefield waited to ascertain the cause, and requested the people to remain still. Mr. Grimshaw hurried to the spot, and in a few minutes was seen pressing towards the place where Mr. Whitefield stood. "Brother Whitefield," said he, manifesting in the strongest manner the intensity of his feelings, and the ardor of his concern for the salvation of sinners, "you stand among the dead and the dying. An immortal soul has been called into eternity; the destroying angel is passing over the congregation; cry aloud, and spare not." The awful occurrence was speedily announced to the congregation. After the lapse of a few moments, Mr. Whitefield again announced his text. Again a loud and piercing shriek proceeded from the spot near where Lady Huntingdon and Lady Margaret Ingham were standing. A thrill of horror seemed to escape from the multitude when it was understood that a *second* person had fallen a victim to the king of terrors. When the consternation had somewhat subsided, Mr. Whitefield gave indications of proceeding with the service. The excited feelings of many were wound up to their highest point.

All was hushed; not a sound was to be heard; and a stillness like the awful silence of death spread over the assembly, as he proceeded in melting strains to warn the careless, Christless sinner to "flee from the wrath to come."

As winter was now approaching, Whitefield felt it important to return to the metropolis. During the tour he had made, he won to Christ not a few of those who afterwards laid the foundations of churches now flourishing in the counties of Lancaster, York, and Northumberland. He met, however, with so much "rude treatment here and there, as sent him home praying, 'Lord, give me a pilgrim heart for my pilgrim life.'" He was now in "winter quarters," but was neither idle nor useless. To use his own words, "The glory of the Lord filled the tabernacle, and the shout of a king was in the camp," and that from week to week. "Thousands, thousands crowded to hear." Every day also he heard of instances of conversion. One of these pleased him greatly. It was that of a boatswain, who, before hearing him, knew no more about divine truth "than the whistle he blew on board." He mentions also a boy eleven years of age, a woman of eighty, and a baker, who had been "a Jerusalem sinner," all of whom bowed before the cross, and placed their hopes of salvation on Him who died thereon.

CHAPTER XII
LABORS IN GREAT BRITAIN—FOURTH VISIT TO AMERICA—NEW TABERNACLE IN LONDON, AND TABERNACLE AT BRISTOL. 1750-1754

At the beginning of the year 1750, Whitefield was still in London. At this time his intended college at Bethesda occupied much of his attention. He wrote to his friends in every quarter for help. His usual appeal was, "We propose having an academy or college at the orphan-house. The house is large, and will hold a hundred. My *heart*, I trust, is larger, and will hold ten thousand." Though in London, his heart was in America. He says, "Ranging seems my province; and methinks I hear a voice behind me saying, 'This is the way, walk in it.' My heart echoes back, 'Lord, let thy presence go with me, and then send me where thou pleasest.' In the midst of all, America, *dear* America, is not forgotten. I begin to count the days, and to say to the months, 'Fly fast away, that I may spread the gospel-net once more in dear America.'"

Be it here mentioned, that amid the busy scenes of his life, and while surrounded with the flatteries of the great and noble, Whitefield did not forget the duties he owed to his mother. A person whom he had employed to obtain some comforts for her, had neglected the duty, so that the now aged matron might have felt a week's anxiety. He wrote to her, "I should never forgive myself, was I, by negligence or any wrong conduct, to give you a moment's needless pain. Alas, how little have I done for you. Christ's care for his mother excites me to wish I could do any thing for you. If you would have any thing more brought, pray write, honored mother. * * * Tomorrow it will be *thirty-five* years since you brought unworthy me into the world. O that my head were waters, and mine eyes fountains of tears, that I might bewail my barrenness and unfruitfulness in the church of God."

While he was now fully engaged in preaching, and was surrounded with flatteries, he did not forget his duty to conflict with sin. He writes, "I find a love of power sometimes intoxicates even God's dear children. It is much easier for me to obey than govern. This makes me fly from that which, at our first setting out, we are apt to court. I cannot well buy humility at too dear a rate."

Dr. Philip Doddridge, as every reader knows, was one of the most pious and accomplished preachers and writers of the Non-conformists of England in his day. Nor was his *missionary* zeal small in its degree. Though he died as early as 1751, he had said, "I am now intent on having something done among the dissenters, in a more public manner, for propagating the gospel abroad, which lies near my heart. I wish to live to see this design brought into execution, at least into some forwardness, and then I should die the more cheerfully." It was indeed the passion of his life to promote the interests of evangelical truth, and save the souls of men. And though, as his recent eulogist, the Rev. John Stoughton, has said, condemned by some, and suspected by others for so doing, he took a deep and sympathetic interest in the evangelical labors of Whitefield. It seems strange in our day to think of Whitefield being regarded as an enthusiast by orthodox dissenters. Yet there were those who did thus regard him. Bradbury poured on him streams of wit; Barker regarded his sermons as low and coarse; and another in writing calls him "honest, crazy, confident Mr. Whitefield." But Doddridge regarded him as far otherwise, and spoke of him as "a flaming servant of Christ." He prayed on one occasion at the Tabernacle, but Dr. Watts was much grieved by it; and when, on Whitefield's visiting Northampton, Doddridge gave him the use of his pulpit, the managers of the college of which he was president remonstrated with him for so doing.

The visit of Whitefield to Doddridge was in February, 1750, where he met with the Rev. Dr. Sir James Stonehouse, and the Rev. Messrs. Hartley and Hervey. The latter eminent clergyman thus writes: "I have lately seen that most excellent minister of the ever-blessed Jesus, Mr. Whitefield. I dined, supped, and spent the evening with him at Northampton, in company with Dr. Doddridge, and two pious, ingenious clergymen of the church of England, both of them known to the learned world by their valuable writings. And surely I never spent a more delightful evening, or saw one that seemed to make nearer approaches to the felicity of heaven. A gentleman of great worth and rank in the town invited us to his house, and gave us an elegant treat; but how mean was his provision, how coarse his delicacies, compared with the fruit of my friend's lips: they dropped as honey from the honey-comb, and were a well of life. Surely people do not know that amiable and exemplary man, or else, I cannot but think, instead of depreciating, they would applaud and love him. For my part, I never beheld so fair a copy of our Lord, such a living image of the Saviour, such exalted delight in God, such enlarged benevolence to man, such a steady faith in the divine promises, and such a fervent zeal for the divine glory; and all this without the least moroseness of humor, or extravagance of behavior, sweetened with the most engaging cheerfulness of temper, and regulated by all the sobriety of reason and wisdom of Scripture; insomuch that I cannot forbear applying the wise man's encomium of an illustrious woman to this eminent minister of the everlasting gospel: 'Many sons have done virtuously, but thou excellest them all.'"

In the month of March, 1750, a general alarm had been awakened by earthquakes in London, and fears were excited by pretended prophecies of still greater devastation. These signal judgments of Jehovah were preceded by great profligacy of manners, and its fruitful parent, licentiousness of principle. Dr. Horne, afterwards dean of Canterbury and bishop of Bristol, in a sermon preached at the time, says, "As to faith, is not the doctrine of the Trinity, and that of the divinity of our Lord and Saviour—without which our redemption is absolutely void, and we are yet in our sins, lying under the intolerable burden of the wrath of God—blasphemed and ridiculed openly in conversation and in print? And as to righteousness of life, are not the people of this land dead in trespasses and sins? Idleness, drunkenness, luxury, extravagance, and debauchery; for these things cometh the wrath of God, and disordered nature proclaims the impending distress and perplexity of nations. And Oh, may we of this nation never read a handwriting upon the wall of heaven, in illuminated capitals of the Almighty, Mene, Mene, Tekel, Upharsin—God hath numbered the kingdom, and finished it. Thou art weighed in the balances of heaven, and found wanting the merits of a rejected Redeemer, and therefore the kingdom is divided and given away."

The shocks felt in London in February and March of this year, were far more violent than any remembered for a long series of years. The earth moved throughout the whole cities of London and Westminster. It was a strong and jarring motion, attended with a rumbling noise like that of thunder. Multitudes of persons of every class fled from these cities with the utmost haste, and others repaired to the fields and open places in the neighborhood. Towerhill, Moorfields, and Hyde Park were crowded with men, women, and children, who remained a whole night under the most fearful apprehensions. Places of worship were filled with persons in the utmost state of alarm. Especially was this the case with those attached to Methodist congregations, where multitudes came all night, knocking at the doors, and for God's sake begging admittance. As convulsions of nature are usually regarded by enthusiasts and fanatics as the sure harbinger of its dissolution, a soldier "had a revelation," that a great part of London and Westminster would be destroyed by an earthquake on a certain night, between the hours of twelve and one o'clock. Believing his assertion, thousands fled from the city for fear of being suddenly overwhelmed, and repaired to the fields, where they continued all night, in momentary expectation of seeing the prophecy fulfilled; while thousands of others ran about the streets in the most wild and frantic state of consternation, apparently quite certain that the day of judgment was about to commence. The whole scene was truly awful.

Under these circumstances, the ministers of Christ preached almost incessantly, and many were awakened to a sense of their awful condition before God, and to rest their hopes of eternal salvation on the Rock of ages. Mr. Whitefield, animated with that burning charity which shone so conspicuously in him, ventured out at midnight to Hyde Park, where he proclaimed to the affrighted and astonished multitudes that there is a Saviour, Christ the Lord. The darkness of the night, and the awful apprehensions of an approaching earthquake, added much to the solemnity of the scene. The sermon was truly sublime, and to the ungodly sinner, the self-righteous pharisee, and the artful hypocrite, strikingly terrific. With a pathos which showed the fervor of his soul, and with a grand majestic voice that commanded attention, he took occasion from the circumstances of the assembly, to call their attention to that most important event in which every one will be interested, the final consummation of all things, the universal wreck of nature, the dissolution of earth, and the eternal sentence of every son and daughter of Adam. The whole scene was one of a most memorable character. Mr. Charles Wesley, Mr. Romaine, and others preached in a similar manner, and with like happy results.

At this period, Whitefield and his female friends especially, were the subjects of royal attention at the court of George the Second. It is said that on one occasion Lady Chesterfield appeared in a dress "with a brown ground and silver flowers," of foreign manufacture. The king, smiling significantly, said to her aloud, "I know who chose that gown for you—Mr. Whitefield; I hear you have attended on him for a year and a half." Her ladyship acknowledged she had done so, and professed her approbation of his character and ministry; and afterwards deeply regretted that she had not said more when she had so good an opportunity. Whitefield had occasion to wait on the secretary of state, in company with Dr. Gifford, a Baptist pastor in London, to ask relief for some persecuted Christians in Ireland, and was assured that "no hurt was designed by the state to the Methodists." He also renewed his friendship with the Messrs. Wesley, and several times exchanged pulpits with them. He writes, "I have now preached thrice in Mr. Wesley's chapel, and God was with us of a truth."

Again was our evangelist tired of London, and again had he grown sick for want of field-preaching. Accordingly he set out for Bristol and other parts of the west of England; and although rain and hail pelted him in his field-pulpits, he preached "about twenty times in eight or nine days." As soon as he found himself in his own element, he saw every thing in his old lights. He says, "Every thing I meet with seems to carry this voice with it: 'Go thou and preach the gospel; be a pilgrim on earth; have no party, or certain dwelling-place.' My heart echoes back, 'Lord Jesus, help me to do or suffer thy will. When thou seest me in danger of *nestling*, in pity, in tender pity put a thorn in my nest, to prevent me from it.'"

From Bristol, Whitefield went to Taunton, where he met with the Rev. Richard Pearsall, an eminent and excellent Presbyterian minister, of whom he speaks very highly; and from thence, on his way to Plymouth, he stayed at Wellington, to preach for the Rev. Risdon Darracott, who has ever since been distinguished as "the star in the west." Mr. Darracott was the son of a dissenting minister in Dorsetshire, where he was born in 1717, when Whitefield was three years old. He studied for the ministry under the Rev. Dr. Doddridge, at Northampton, and entered on his ministerial course in Cornwall in 1738, which situation he was most reluctantly compelled to leave two years afterwards from violent hemorrhage of the lungs. Under this alarming visitation he spent about six months with his friends in Devonshire, where his fervent-minded father had preached till his death at the age of forty. While here, he had a call to succeed a venerable minister at Wellington, who had recently deceased. He found the congregation small, and the number of communicants but twenty-eight. His ministry soon drew a large congregation, many of whom had never before made a profession of religion, and were first attracted into the town from the neighboring villages out of mere curiosity to hear him. The house of worship was soon insufficient to contain his hearers; and even when it was enlarged, many were frequently compelled to stand out of doors, unable to obtain an entrance. The Rev. Benjamin Fawcett, who preached his funeral sermon, said, "I never knew any congregation which appeared to have so many instances of abiding religious impressions;" and added, "I have good reason to believe that his ministry was owned to the effectual conversion of many hundreds of souls."

The night before the death of this excellent man, which took place in his forty-second year, he exclaimed, "Oh, what a good God have I, in and through Jesus Christ. I would praise him, but my lips cannot. Eternity will be too short to speak his praises." The physician coming in, he said to him, "Oh, what a mercy is it to be interested in the atoning blood of Jesus. I come to the Lord as a vile sinner, trusting in the merits and precious blood of my dear Redeemer. O grace, grace, free grace!" His last words were, "I am going from weeping friends to congratulating angels, and rejoicing saints in glory. He is coming. Oh, speed thy chariot wheels; why are they so long in coming? I long to be gone!" He left in his church more than two hundred communicants.

Whitefield and Darracott were congenial spirits, and Darracott, like his friend, had suffered much reproach in the cause of his Master; he was what Whitefield called him, "a flaming and successful preacher of the gospel." He had just at this time lost three lovely children. "Two of them," says Whitefield, "had died on the Saturday evening before the sacrament; but weeping did not prevent sowing. He preached the next day, and administered as usual. Our Lord strengthened him; and for his three natural, gave him above *thirty* spiritual children; and he is likely to have many more. He has ventured his little all for Christ; and last week a saint died who left him and his heirs two hundred pounds in land. Did ever any one trust in God, and was forsaken?" This interview with Darracott, and with good old Mr. Pearsall, who had been a preacher of righteousness before Whitefield was born, had an inspiring influence upon him. He says, "I *began* to take the field again at his dwelling for the spring! I begin to *begin* to spend and be spent for Him who shed his own dear heart's blood for me. He makes *ranging* exceedingly pleasant."

Soon after this, Whitefield went again into Yorkshire. At Rotherham he says, "Satan rallied his forces. The crier was employed to give notice of a bear-baiting. You may guess who was the bear! However, I preached twice. The drum was heard, and several watermen attended with great staves. The constable was struck, and two of the mobbers apprehended, but rescued afterwards." Sheffield and Leeds he found to be a new and warmer climate. Lancashire, however, was still but cold to him. All was quiet at Manchester, and he "humbly hoped some had enlisted," but no great impression was then made. At Bolton, a drunkard stood up behind him to preach; and the wife of the man who lent him the field, twice attempted to stab the workman who put up the stand for him. This roused him, and he bore down all opposition by a torrent of eloquence, which quite exhausted him. In the night, however, some rude fellows got into the barn and stables where his chaise and horses had been put, and cut them very shamefully. This conduct he called, "Satan showing his teeth."

To narrate the particulars of this journey would be little more than a repetition of scenes of insult and of success with which the reader has already become familiar. At Ulverston he says, "Satan made some small resistance. A clergyman, who looked more like a *butcher* than a minister, came with two others, and charged a constable with me; but I never saw a poor creature sent off with such disgrace."

One of the most remarkable conversions recorded in the history of the church occurred during this journey by the ministry of Mr. Whitefield. The full particulars are recorded in the Life of the Countess of Huntingdon, and can only be briefly mentioned here.

In the early period of Whitefield's ministry, many of the taverns became places where his doctrines and zeal were talked of and ridiculed. A Mr. Thorpe, and several other young men in Yorkshire, undertook at one of these parties to mimic the preaching of Mr. Whitefield. The proposition met with applause; one after another stood on a table to perform his part, and it devolved on Mr. Thorpe to close this irreverent scene. Much elated, and confident of success, he exclaimed, as he ascended the table, "I shall beat you all." Who would have supposed that the mercy of God was now about to be extended to this transgressor of his law? The Bible was handed to him; and by the guidance of unerring Providence, it opened at Luke 13:3: "Except ye repent, ye shall all likewise perish." The moment he read the text his mind was impressed in a most extraordinary manner; he saw clearly the nature and importance of the subject; and as he afterwards said, if he ever preached with the assistance of the Holy Spirit, it was at that time. His address produced a feeling of depression in his auditors; and when he had finished, he instantly retired to weep over his sins. He soon after became associated with the people of God, and died a successful minister of Christ, at Masborough, in Yorkshire, in 1776, about six years after the death of Mr. Whitefield. He was the father of the distinguished Rev. William Thorpe, of Bristol.

Passing on to Edinburgh, Whitefield was, as usual, received with the most unfeigned tenderness and joy, preaching to great multitudes of attentive and serious people, whose earnest desire to hear him made him exert himself beyond his strength. He says, "By preaching always twice, once thrice, and once four times in a day, I am quite weakened; but I hope to recruit again. Christ's presence makes me smile at pain." He returned to London, having preached about one hundred times, it was believed to not less than one hundred thousand people.

Among the occasional hearers of Whitefield when in Scotland, was the celebrated infidel historian, David Hume. An intimate friend having asked him what he thought of Mr. Whitefield's preaching, he replied, "He is, sir, the most ingenious preacher I ever heard; it is worth while to go twenty miles to hear him." He then repeated the following passage, which occurred towards the close of the discourse he had been hearing. "After a solemn pause, Mr. Whitefield thus addressed his numerous audience: 'The attendant angel is just about to leave the threshold, and ascend to heaven. And shall he ascend, and not bear with him the news of one sinner, among all this multitude, reclaimed from the error of his ways?' To give the greater effect to this exclamation, he stamped with his foot, lifted up his eyes and hands to heaven, and with gushing tears cried aloud, 'Stop, Gabriel! stop, Gabriel! stop, ere you enter the sacred portals, and yet carry with you the news of one sinner converted to God.' He then, in the most simple but energetic language, described what he called a Saviour's dying love to sinful man, so that almost the whole assembly melted into tears. This address was accompanied with such animated, yet natural action, that it surpassed any thing I ever saw or heard in any other preacher."

In the summer of 1751, Whitefield paid a second visit to Ireland, and was most hospitably received in Dublin by a respectable and opulent gentleman named Lunell, who had been brought to Christ by the first Methodist itinerant preacher in that city. During this excursion, Whitefield preached about eighty sermons, fourteen of them in Dublin, and seven in Limerick. His hearers in Dublin organized themselves into a public society, which does not seem to have met his approbation. He says, "This morning I have been talking with dear Mr. Adams, and can not help thinking that you have run before the Lord, in forming yourselves into a public society as you have done. I am sincere when I profess that I do not choose to set myself at the head of any party. When I came to Ireland, my intention was to preach the gospel to all; and if it should ever please the Lord of all lords to send me thither again, I purpose to pursue the same plan. For I am a debtor to all of every denomination, and have no design, if I know any thing of this desperately wicked and deceitful heart, but to promote the common salvation of mankind. The love of Christ constrains me to this."

During this visit, Whitefield a few times ventured out of the city to Oxmantown-green, then a large open place, situated near the royal barracks, where the Ormond and Liberty boys, two factions among the lowest class of the people, generally assembled on the Sabbath to fight with each other. The congregations at first were very numerous, and deeply affected, nor did any disturbance occur. Thus encouraged, the preacher ventured again, and gave notice of his intention to resume his labors. He went through the barracks, the door of which opened into the green, and pitched his tent near the barrack walls, not doubting of the protection, or at least of the interposition of the officers and soldiers, if there should be occasion for it. The multitude in attendance was indeed vast. After singing and prayer, Whitefield preached without molestation, except that now and then a few stones and clods of dirt were thrown at him. It being war-time, he took occasion to exhort his hearers, as was his usual practice, not only to fear God, but to honor the king; and prayed for the success of the king of Prussia. When the service was over, he thought to return home by the way he came, but, to his great surprise, a passage through the barracks was denied; and he was compelled to pass from one end of the green to the other, through thousands of Roman-catholics. He was unattended; for a soldier and four preachers who came with him had fled from the scene of danger, and he was seriously attacked by the mob. They threw vollies of stones upon him from all quarters, and he reeled backwards and forwards till he was almost breathless and covered with blood. At length, with great difficulty he staggered to the door of a minister's house near the green, which was kindly opened to him. For a while he continued speechless, and panting for breath; but his weeping friends having given him a cordial, and washed his wounds, a coach was procured, in which, amidst the oaths, imprecations, and threatenings of the rabble, he got safe home, and united in a hymn of thanksgiving with his friends. In a letter written to a friend soon after this event, he says, "I received many blows and wounds; one was particularly large, and near my temple: I thought of Stephen, and was in hopes, like him, to go off in this bloody triumph to the immediate presence of my Master."

Unpromising, however, as things were in Ireland, the labors of Whitefield, followed as they were by those of the Wesleys, became the foundation of a number of Christian societies that proved vast blessings to Ireland; and some of them grew into large churches, which continue to flourish till this day.

The society to which reference has been made, which assembled in Skinner's alley, secured ministerial aid from the late Rev. John Edwards, who was one of Whitefield's converts, and among the earliest preachers at the Tabernacle in London; and who also itinerated over nearly the whole of England, Scotland, and Ireland. The period was one of great persecution, and this good man had several remarkable preservations from death. At one time, while he resided in Dublin, he was returning from preaching at a village, when he was seized by a party of rude fellows, who declared they would throw him over the bridge into the Liffey. This was observed by an opposite political party, residing on the other side of the river, who encountered his assailants, and rescued him out of their hands, saying he lived on their side the river, and none should hurt him. At another time, having preached out of doors, a furious mob of the *White-boys*, a political party so called, beset the house in which he was, and threatened to burn it to the ground, unless he was driven out of it. His anxious friends could see but one way for his escape, which was through a window that opened into a garden belonging to a justice of the peace, who was himself a violent persecutor of the Methodists. Through this window Mr. Edwards was, like the apostle Paul, let down in a basket. Here he stood some time in great consternation, fearing the family might observe him, and charge him with breaking into the garden for improper purposes, and so both religion and himself would be injured. At length he ventured to knock at the door, and asked for the magistrate, to whom he ingenuously stated the facts, and who most generously protected and extended to him the hospitalities of his house for two days.

One fact more must be told of this excellent man. He resolved to visit a town to which had removed a number of soldiers who had received benefit from his ministry. He was met, however, by some of these pious men, who told him that the inhabitants were determined to take his life. Edwards was not to be dissuaded from his purpose; and on his arrival he immediately preached in the street, and several distinguished persons, including the mayor of the town, came to hear him, and by their influence prevented disturbance. After the service, the mayor invited him to breakfast with several of the principal inhabitants, and told him they were very glad he was come—that the people were extremely dissolute in their manners, and the clergy, both Protestants and Catholics, exceedingly remiss in their duty, and they hoped the Methodists would succeed in reforming the town. These gentlemen subscribed to the support of stated preaching, and extensive and lasting good was done.

Amid Whitefield's innumerable engagements and declining health, Bethesda and his beloved America could not be forgotten. While he was at Glasgow during this summer of 1751, he was greatly delighted to hear that Mr. Dinwiddie, brother-in-law to the Rev. Mr. M'Culloch, of Cambuslang, was appointed governor of Virginia. The gospel had been much opposed there, and he thought the appointment now made would greatly tend to check persecution.

Whitefield, as it appears to us, now very suddenly determined on another voyage to America. He arrived in London from Edinburgh in the early part of August, with improved health, the country air having healed his hemorrhage. He took a hasty leave of his friends, and set sail for Georgia, in the Antelope, Captain M'Lellan, taking several orphans with him. He arrived at Savannah Oct. 27, and had the happiness of finding the orphan-house in a prosperous condition. Here, however, he did not stay long; as in November we hear of him in his usual labors, and with his usual ardor engaged in his constant work of preaching. Having formerly suffered much from the climate of America in the summer, he determined again to embark for London, which he did in April. We can scarcely trace his object in this journey to and from America, except in some designs of the government to place Georgia on a new footing.

In June, 1752, Mr. Whitefield was found in the society of the Countess of Huntingdon at Bath, where he continued about three weeks, preaching every evening to great numbers of the nobility. Here he became acquainted with Mrs. Grinfield, a lady who attended on the person of Queen Caroline. "One of Cæsar's household," he writes, "hath been lately awakened, through her ladyship's instrumentality, and I hope others will meet with the like blessing." He afterwards visited her at the palace of St. James, and says, "The court, I believe, rings of her, and if she stands, I trust she will make a glorious martyr for her blessed Lord."

The Moravians, or United Brethren, were at one period on terms of very cordial friendship with the Messrs. Wesley and Whitefield. At the time of which we are writing, a series of strange absurdities, resembling the adoration of saints and other superstitions of popery, developed themselves among members of that body, at the head of which then stood Count Zinzendorf, to whom Whitefield wrote an urgent remonstrance on the subject. An open separation took place, and Mrs. Grinfield, the Rev. John Cennick, and some others, adhered to the count, while Whitefield and Lady Huntingdon endeavored to bring him back to what they believed the simplicity of the gospel. Lady Huntingdon, speaking of her final interview with him, says, "Our conference was long, and as the count honored me with his company for a few days, was resumed at intervals, always closing with a solemn scriptural prayer to our great and glorious Head, for the illuminating influences of his Spirit to guide us into all truth. We parted with the utmost cordiality."

"Dear Mr. Whitefield's letter," says Lady Huntingdon, "has much grieved the count. But his remonstrance is faithful, and the awful exposures he has reluctantly been forced to make, may be productive of the highest good in opening the eyes of many to the miserable delusions under which they lie."

A correspondence, indeed we may say friendship, had for years existed between Whitefield and the eminent philosopher Dr. Benjamin Franklin. The following, from a letter of Whitefield, August 17, 1752, shows his fidelity to the eminent citizen and statesman: "I find you grow more and more famous in the learned world. As you have made a pretty considerable progress in the mysteries of electricity, I would now humbly recommend to your diligent, unprejudiced pursuit and study, the mystery of the new birth. It is a most important, interesting study, and when mastered, will richly answer and repay you for all your pains. One, at whose bar we are shortly to appear, hath solemnly declared that, without it, we cannot enter into the kingdom of heaven. You will excuse this freedom. I must have *aliquid Christi*—something of Christ, in all my letters." This honest letter ought to have delighted the philosopher in his closet, even more than the eulogium he heard while standing behind the bar of the House of Lords, when Earl Chatham said of him, "Franklin is one whom Europe holds in high estimation for his knowledge and wisdom; one who is an honor, not to the English nation only, but to human nature."

In the course of the summer of 1752, and the following one, Whitefield visited Scotland twice, and preached much also throughout England and Wales. As usual, he greatly rejoiced in the presence and service of God, and never appears to have been more happy than in this period of his life. "Since I left Newcastle," he writes, "I have scarcely known sometimes whether I have been in heaven or on earth. Thousands and thousands flock twice or thrice a day to hear the word of life. God favors us with weather, and I would fain make hay while the sun shines. Oh that I had as many tongues as there are hairs in my head. The ever-loving, ever-lovely Jesus should have them all. Fain would I die preaching."

About this period also, Mr. Hervey and he were employed in revising each other's manuscripts; the former was then preparing his "Theron and Aspasio," a work which, though florid in its style, has been eminently useful in conducting many of its readers to a saving knowledge of the doctrines of the gospel. Of his friend's writings Mr. Whitefield says, "For me to play the critic on them, would be like holding up a candle to the sun. However, I will just mark a few places, as you desire. I foretell their fate; nothing but your scenery can screen you. Self will never bear to die, though slain in so genteel a manner, without showing some resentment against its artful murderer.... I thank you a thousand times for the trouble you have been at in revising my poor compositions, which I am afraid you have not treated with a becoming severity. How many pardons shall I ask for mangling, and, I fear, murdering your 'Theron and Aspasio?' If you think my two sermons will do for the public, pray return them immediately. I have nothing to comfort me but this, that the Lord chooses the weak things of this world to confound the strong, and things that are not, to bring to naught things that are. I write for the poor; you for the polite and noble. God will assuredly own and bless what you write."

Whitefield was now also very busy in erecting his second London Tabernacle, which he dedicated, June 10, 1753. We have, for the sake of completing the narrative of its first building, already given in our third chapter a statement of the second tabernacle, to which the reader is referred.

Both the judgment and inclination of Mr. Whitefield concurred to induce him to persevere in his itinerant course, correctly judging that in this way he best employed his peculiar talents. After preaching, therefore, with his usual fervor and success for a short time in his newly erected Tabernacle, he again set out towards Scotland, where he spent some days at Edinburgh and Glasgow, and preached generally twice, sometimes three times a day, and once five times. He says, "Attention sat upon all faces, and friends came round like bees, importuning me to stay another week." This he found too much for his strength, but still went forward, often expressing his desire to serve his divine Master to the utmost limit of his power, and his hopes to be with him soon in heaven. During this journey, including his return to London, where he arrived the latter end of September, he travelled about twelve hundred miles, and preached one hundred and eighty times, to many thousands of hearers.

As converts increased in Bristol and its neighborhood, Mr. Whitefield felt compelled to erect there also a "tabernacle." Lady Huntingdon was one of the earliest contributors to this important object, and through her influence Lord Chesterfield gave twenty pounds to it. He had no taste for religion, but he well understood oratory, and in his letter to Lady Huntingdon covering his remittance, he said, "Mr. Whitefield's eloquence is unrivalled, his zeal inexhaustible." The Earl of Bath sent fifty pounds, saying, "Mocked and reviled as Mr. Whitefield is by all ranks of society, still, I contend that the day will come when England will be just, and own his greatness as a reformer, and his goodness as a minister of the most high God."

The Tabernacle at Bristol was dedicated November 25, 1753, with a sermon from Whitefield. Its history is one of deep interest. Its early ministers were worthy of any age, but remarkably fitted for that in which their lot was cast; men of pith and power, undismayed at dangers, braving all kinds of difficulty and toil, and prepared equally for labor and sufferings in the cause of their great Master. Nor have later ministers dishonored their predecessors; the cause still flourishes, and the hallowed house has been the birthplace of many eminent Christians. What Whitefield then said of this house might often be said of it now: "It is large, but not half large enough; for if the place could contain them, nearly as many would attend as in London." He always delighted in his visits to this place, and laid here a foundation for vast benefits, even to the present day. On one of his visits to preach here, he began a series of sermons on the evening before the commencement of the fair. His text was, "Ho, every one that thirsteth, come ye to the waters; and he that hath no money, come ye, buy and eat; yea, come buy wine and milk without money, and without price." Isa. 55:1. The congregation was large, and thus he began: "My dear hearers, I fear that many of you are come to attend Bristol fair. So am I. You do not mean to show your goods until to-morrow; but I shall exhibit mine to-night. You are afraid purchasers will not come up to your price; but I am afraid my buyers will not come down to mine; for mine," striking his hand on the Bible, "are 'without money, and without price.'"

After the dedication of this Bristol Tabernacle, Whitefield preached in the open air in various parts of Somersetshire, at seven o'clock at night. "My hands and body," says he, "were pierced with cold; but what are outward things, when the soul is warmed with the love of God? The stars shone with exceeding brightness; by an eye of faith I saw Him who 'calleth them all by their names.' My soul was filled with a holy ambition, and I longed to be one of those who 'shall shine as the stars for ever and ever.'"

At this time he had a fine opportunity to show his Christian attachment to his old friends. Mr. John Wesley had, by a series of extraordinary labors, brought his life into great danger, and Whitefield, hearing of this while at Bristol, wrote a sympathizing letter to his brother Charles, in which he prays for the descending garment of Elijah to rest on the surviving Elisha, and encloses an ardent and solemn farewell to the invalid, who was supposed to be dying. He says, "The news and prospect of your approaching dissolution have quite weighed me down. I pity myself and the church, but not you. A radiant throne awaits you, and ere long you will enter into your Master's joy. Yonder he stands with a massy crown, ready to put it on your head, amidst an admiring throng of saints and angels. But I, poor I, that have been waiting for my dissolution these nineteen years, must be left behind to grovel here below. Well, this is my comfort, it cannot be long ere the chariots will be sent even for worthless me. If prayers can detain you, even you, reverend and very dear sir, shall not leave us yet. But if the decree is gone forth that you must now sleep in Jesus, may he kiss your soul away, and give you to die in the embraces of triumphant love. If in the land of the living, I hope to pay my best respects to you next week. If not, reverend and dear sir, farewell." He had soon the satisfaction of witnessing the recovery of his friend, who was to survive him more than twenty years.

We have already intimated that Whitefield used his influence in Scotland in favor of the New Jersey college, located at Princeton. In accordance with his advice, the friends of the college in this country sent over the Rev. Samuel Davies, afterwards president of the college, and the Rev. Gilbert Tennent, to promote its interests in the British islands. A few extracts from the manuscript diary of Davies, with the use of which we have been favored for this volume, will show the readiness of Whitefield to labor, or to "be nothing," so that the cause of Christ might be advanced. The deputation arrived in England in the closing month of 1753, and thus writes Davies:

"Wednesday, December 26. Mr. Whitefield having sent us an invitation last night to make his house our home during our stay here, we were perplexed what to do, lest we should blast the success of our mission among the dissenters, who are generally disaffected to him. We at length concluded, with the advice of our friends and his, that a public intercourse with him would be imprudent, in our present situation, and visited him privately this evening; and the kind reception he gave us revived dear Mr. Tennent. He spoke in the most encouraging manner as to the success of our mission. And in all his conversation discovered so much zeal and candor, that I could not but admire the man as the wonder of the age. When we returned, Mr. Tennent's heart was all on fire, and after we had gone to bed, he suggested that we should watch and pray; and we rose and prayed together till about three o'clock in the morning.

"Jan. 1. Went in the evening to hear Mr. Whitefield in the Tabernacle, a large, spacious building. The assembly was very numerous, though not equal to what is common. He preached on the parable of the barren fig-tree; and though the discourse was incoherent, yet it seemed to me better calculated to do good to mankind than all the accurate, languid discourses I ever heard. After sermon I enjoyed his pleasing conversation at his house."

It would seem that Messrs. Davies and Tennent had their trials, as well as their encouragements. Writing Jan. 14, Mr. Davies says, "Spent an hour with Mr. Whitefield. He thinks we have not taken the best method in endeavoring to keep in with all parties, but should 'come out boldly,' as he expressed it, which would secure the affections of the pious people, from whom we might expect the most generous contributions." On the evening after this, they dined with Whitefield at the house of a common friend, and he rejoiced in the abundant success they afterwards met with from nearly all parties.

"Jan. 25. Dined with Mr. Bradbury, who has been in the ministry about fifty-seven years. He read us some letters which passed between Mr. Whitefield and him, *anno* 1741; occasioned by Mr. Whitefield's reproving him in a letter for singing a song in a tavern, in a large company, in praise of old English beef. The old gentleman sung it to us, and we found it was partly composed by himself, in the high-flying days of Queen Anne. He is a man of a singular turn, which would be offensive to the greatest number of serious people; but for my part I could say,

'I knew 'twas his peculiar whim,
Nor took it ill, as't came from him.'"

In March, 1754, Whitefield, in company with twenty-two poor destitute children, sailed the fifth time for America.

CHAPTER XIII
FIFTH VISIT TO AMERICA—RENEWED LABORS IN GREAT BRITAIN—TOTTENHAM-COURT-ROAD CHAPEL. 1754-1763

On this voyage to America, Whitefield sailed for South Carolina by way of Lisbon. His health demanded repose; he thought that seeing Popery as it is when unrestrained by public opinion, might be of use to him in his future labors; and moreover, he had with him a number of orphans whom he wished comfortably to settle at Bethesda before he visited the northern provinces. It would be pleasant, if our limits would allow it, to furnish the letters he wrote from Lisbon during nearly four weeks, but a few sentences must suffice: "This leaves me an inhabitant of Lisbon. We have now been here almost a week, and I suppose shall stay a fortnight longer. A reputable merchant has received me into his house, and every day shows me the ecclesiastical curiosities of the country. O, my dear friend, bless the Lord of all lords, for causing your lot to be cast in such a fair ground as England, and giving you such a goodly heritage. It is impossible to be sufficiently thankful for civil and religious liberty, for simplicity of worship, and powerful preaching of the word of God. O for simplicity of manners, and a correspondent behavior. The air agrees with my poor constitution extremely well. Through divine assistance; I hope what I see will also improve my better part, and help to qualify me better for preaching the everlasting gospel."

In another letter he writes, "Never did civil and religious liberty appear to me in so amiable a light as now. What a spirit must Martin Luther and the first reformers be endued with, that dared to appear as they did for God. Lord, hasten that blessed time when others, excited by the same spirit, shall perform like wonders. Oh, happy England! Oh, happy Methodists, who are Methodists indeed! And all I account such, who, being dead to sects and parties, aim at nothing else but as holy a method of living to, and dying in the blessed Jesus."

He was heartily glad to get away from Popish processions and superstitious rites, and again to visit his "dear America."

Our evangelist arrived with his orphans at Beaufort, in South Carolina, May 27, 1754, greatly improved in health, with a heart burning with love and zeal for his Lord and Master. He says, with his usual energy, "Oh that I may at length learn to begin to live. I am ashamed of my sloth and lukewarmness, and long to be on the stretch for God." His family now consisted, "black and white," of one hundred and six members, all dependent on his personal efforts and influence. He regarded his charge as a stewardship for God, and collected accordingly, nothing doubting. It was now summer, and besides the oppressive heat, "great thunders, violent lightnings, and heavy rains" frequently beat upon him as he journeyed from place to place. His health improved, and his spirits rose as he advanced on his journey. At Charleston, and elsewhere, his labors were received with the same degree of acceptance as formerly, and he was much encouraged by the conversion of a clergyman, a faithful successor to Mr. Smith of the city just named, and the first student sent forth from Bethesda.

He arrived at New York, by water, July 27, and divided his labors between that city and Philadelphia almost entirely for nearly two months. In the latter city, he tells us, he was seized with violent *cholera morbus*, and brought to the gates of death. To use his own words, he "had all his cables out, ready to cast anchor within the port of eternity;" but he was soon "at sea again," although only able to preach once a day for some time. "Everywhere," he says, "a divine power accompanied the word, prejudices were removed, and a more effectual door opened than ever for preaching the gospel." When he looked at "the glorious range for hunting in the American woods," he was at a loss on which hand to turn.... "Affection, intense affection cries aloud, Away to New England, *dear* New England, immediately. Providence, and the circumstances of the southern provinces, point directly to Virginia."

While thus undecided, he visited his old friend Governor Belcher, then governor of New Jersey, and residing at Elizabeth town. He found the good old man ripening for heaven, willing to depart and to be with Christ. At this time the commencement of New Jersey college was held, and as a mark of their respect, the president and trustees conferred on him the honorary degree of master of arts. The meeting of the synod immediately followed, respecting which body he says, "I was much refreshed with the company of the whole synod; such a number of simple-hearted, united ministers I never saw before. I preached to them several times, and the great Master of assemblies was in the midst of us."

Influenced by what he saw and heard in New Jersey, Whitefield determined to go to New England, and to return from thence by Virginia to Georgia, and made his arrangements accordingly; it would comprise a circuit of more than two thousand miles, but he said, "The Redeemer's strength will be more than sufficient."

It has been thought that it was during this visit of Whitefield to New Jersey, and probably at the table of Governor Belcher, that he dined in company with a number of ministers, and held the often-reported conversation with "Father Tennent." After dinner, Mr. Whitefield adverted to the difficulties attending the Christian ministry; lamented that all their zeal availed but little; said that he was weary with the burden of the day; and declared his great comfort in the thought, that in a short time his work would be done, when he should depart and be with Christ. He then appealed to the ministers, if it was not their great comfort that they should soon go to rest. They generally assented, except Mr. Tennent, who sat next to Mr. Whitefield in silence, and by his countenance indicated but little pleasure in the conversation.

Seeing this, Mr. Whitefield, gently tapping him on the knee, said, "Well, brother Tennent, you are the oldest man among us; do you not rejoice to think that your time is so near at hand, when you will be called home?" Mr. Tennent bluntly answered, "I have no wish about it." Mr. Whitefield pressed him again. Mr. Tennent again answered, "No, sir, it is no pleasure to me at all; and if you knew your duty, it would be none to you. I have nothing to do with death; my business is to live as long as I can, as well as I can, until He shall think proper to call me home." Mr. Whitefield still urged for an explicit answer to his question, in case the time of death were left to his own choice. Mr. Tennent replied, "I have no choice about it; I am God's servant, and have engaged to do his business as long as he pleases to continue me therein. But now, brother, let me ask you a question. What do you think I should say, if I was to send my servant into the field to plough; and if at noon I should go to the field, and find him lounging under a tree, and complaining, 'Master, the sun is very hot, and the ploughing hard; I am weary of the work you have appointed me, and am overdone with the heat and burden of the day. Do, master, let me return home, and be discharged from this hard service?' What should I say? Why, that he was a lazy fellow, and that it was his business to do the work that I had appointed him, until I should think fit to call him home."

Accompanied by President Burr, Whitefield set out, October 1, for Boston, and arrived there on the 9th. Here he stayed a week, and saw there, morning after morning, three or four thousand people hanging in breathless silence on his lips, and weeping silent tears. Whitefield himself calls it "a lovely scene," and says he "never saw a more effectual door opened for the gospel. Sinners have been awakened, saints quickened, and enemies made at peace with me. Grace, grace! Surely my coming here was of God. Convictions *do* fasten, and many souls are comforted." Such were the crowds at the early sermons, that in order to reach the pulpit, he had to get in at the windows of the churches. In a letter to the Countess of Huntingdon, he wrote, "In Boston, the tide ran full as high as ever your ladyship knew it at Edinburgh, or in any part of Scotland."

While at Boston, Whitefield heard with much pleasure of the appointment of his friend Habersham as secretary to the new governor of Georgia, and wrote to him, "I wish you joy of your new honor. May the King of kings enable you to discharge your trust as becomes a good patriot, subject, and Christian. You have now a call, I think, to retire from business, and to give up your time to the public." Our evangelist travelled north as far as Portsmouth, in New Hampshire, generally preaching two or three times a day, till November 7, when he took his farewell at Boston, at four o'clock in the morning. Speaking of this journey, he says, "What have I seen? Dagon falling everywhere before the ark; enemies silenced, or made to own the finger of God; and the friends of Jesus triumphing in his glorious conquests. A hundredth part cannot be told. We had scarcely one dry meeting." When he arrived in the neighborhood of Portsmouth, the northern boundary of his journey, he was overwhelmed with humility as well as joy, by the large cavalcade which came out to meet and welcome him. He says of them, "They were too many;" and of this northern journey, "It seems to me the most important one I was ever engaged in."

Of no portion of Whitefield's life are we so ignorant as of the journey he now made from New England to the South. Journal, letters, historians, and newspapers alike fail us. Gillies tells us only that from Boston he "proceeded to Rhode Island, and went onward through Maryland and Virginia, with a prospect so pleasing, that he lamented he had not come sooner. The whole country seemed eager to hear the gospel, many coming forty or fifty miles, and a spirit of conviction and consolation appeared in every congregation. Prejudices seemed to have fled; churches were opened to him; high and low, rich and poor, now seemed to think favorably of his ministrations; and many acknowledged what God had done for their souls through his preaching, when he was there before." It scarcely appears probable that he went from Rhode Island to Maryland by water; but if he did not, he must have passed through New York, New Jersey, and Philadelphia, and we feel somewhat of surprise that no records of the journey appear to have been preserved.

Dr. Franklin relates a very characteristic anecdote of Mr. Whitefield, which probably occurred in Philadelphia or its neighborhood at a period not later than this. "The eloquent orator" was preaching in an open field, when a drummer was present, who was determined to interrupt the preacher, and rudely beat his drum in a violent manner, in order to drown his voice. Whitefield spoke very loud, but could not make so much noise as the instrument. He therefore called out to the drummer, "Friend, you and I serve the two greatest masters existing, but in different callings. You beat up for volunteers for King George, I for the Lord Jesus: in God's name, then, let us not interrupt each other; the world is wide enough for both, and we may get recruits in abundance." This speech had such an effect on the drummer, that he went away in great good-humor, and left the preacher in full possession of the field.

Virginia, alike from the success of his former labors there, and from the general characteristics of the people, must have presented a scene of intense interest to Whitefield at this time. Everywhere great preparations were made for his coming, and large congregations assembled to hear him. It is said, that on one occasion, as he was speaking on the banks of one of the rivers of this noble province, and spoke of the strength of human depravity, and the insufficiency of the means of grace to convert the sinner without the influence of the Holy Spirit: "Sinners," said he, "think not that I expect to convert a single soul of you by any thing that I can say, without the assistance of Him who is 'mighty to save.' Go and stand by that river, as it moves on its strong and deep current to the ocean, and bid it stop, and see if it will obey you. Just as soon should I expect to stop that river by a word, as by my preaching to stop that current of sin which is carrying you to perdition. Father in heaven, see! they are hurried on towards hell; save them, or they perish!" The impression which this address produced on his hearers was so strong, that they were ready to respond with trembling, "Save, Lord; we perish!"

Whitefield must have been highly gratified on reaching Charleston, in attending the ordination of the young minister there, his first student from Bethesda, of whom we have already spoken as succeeding Mr. Smith; and not less would he rejoice that one of the actors at the Charleston theatre had been "snatched as a brand from the burning."

Though we have not the exact date of his arrival at Savannah, we know that he remained there but a very short time. His health again declined, his former vomitings returned with violence, and his animal spirits failed with his strength. In February, 1755, we again find him at Charleston;

and in the latter end of March, he embarked for England, arriving, after a comparatively short voyage, at Newhaven, in Sussex, May the eighth.

Two strong impressions were made on the mind of Whitefield as he now looked on his native land. The first was that of grief on account of its condition. Nothing less than war with France was daily expected, for the French threatened to invade Britain, and were constantly making encroachments on her American colonies. "At this time," he says, "next to Jesus Christ, my king and my country were upon my heart, I hope I shall always think it my duty, next to inviting sinners to the blessed Jesus, to exhort my hearers to resist the first approaches of popish tyranny and arbitrary power. O that we may be enabled to watch and pray against all the opposition of antichrist in our own hearts; for, after all, there lies the most dangerous man of sin." His second feeling was one of holy joy; for during his absence the preaching of the gospel had been abundantly successful. He writes, "Glory be to the great Head of the church! The poor despised Methodists are as lively as ever; and in several churches the gospel is now preached with power. Many in Oxford are awakened to the knowledge of the truth; and I have heard almost every week of some fresh minister or another, who seems 'determined to know nothing but Jesus Christ, and him crucified.'"

At the Tabernacle in London, as might be expected, Whitefield enjoyed what he terms "golden seasons;" but by this time not a few of the London clergy had begun to preach Christ with holy fidelity; and as this was the principal thing he desired, he says his "call to go abroad was still more clear." Indeed, so little did he now esteem London as a sphere of labor, and so much did he regard places by the amount of their destitution, that he wished at once to return to America, without ranging through England or Scotland. Hence he says, "Methinks I could set out for America to-morrow, though I have not yet entered upon my country range."

But if he loved America most, England loved herself more, and he was drawn again into Gloucestershire and Bristol. He went also, at the request of Lady Huntingdon, to dedicate the new Tabernacle at Norwich, to which we have already referred. At this last place, he says, August 30, 1755, "Notwithstanding offences have come, there has been a glorious work begun, and is now carrying on. The polite and great seem to hear with much attention; and I scarcely ever preached a week together with greater freedom." For a long period the work of God abundantly prospered in connection with this "Tabernacle." Two years after its dedication, the Hon. and Rev. Walter Shirley preached some time in it, and had eight hundred communicants in fellowship, and he said of them, "Their experience, lives, and conversation are so excellent, that there is nothing like it in the whole kingdom."

On Whitefield's return to London, there were those who urgently entreated him to engage in a new controversy with the Messrs. Wesley, some of whose followers had been jealous of his success at Norwich. He declined, with his common remark, "I have no time for controversy," and reserved what he had to say till he could see them "face to face," simply writing to assure them that he had no party designs on foot.

Very soon after this, he set out for his northern circuit; and wonderfully indeed did the Lord grant him success. One thing, however, on this journey grieved him. His friends at Leeds, without his knowledge, had built a large church edifice. He saw at once, that this circumstance would create an "awful separation among the societies" formed by the Messrs. Wesley and his own friends; and lost no time in writing to those ministers, that they might endeavor to prevent a breach. Both the plan and the spirit of this undertaking so grieved him, that he exclaimed, "Oh this self-love, this self-will, is the *devil of devils*." This he wrote to Lady Huntingdon, a proof that party was not their object; and it is pleasant to add, that Whitefield's fears were groundless. Leeds, even then, contained population sufficient to fill both houses, and the whole movement "fell out rather to the furtherance of the gospel." During two months he preached twice, and some days three times, to greater numbers than ever before, inviting them to Christ, and "exhorting them to pray for King George, and the dear friends in America." He heard at this time, that the American ladies were making the soldiers' coats; and he immediately wrote to urge his own female friends in the new world to be "some of the most active in this labor of love."

Though Mr. Whitefield stood very high in the esteem of that class of ministers who embraced his views of evangelical truth, and who approved the plans he pursued for the evangelization of the world, they never considered him perfect, nor were some of them backward, when they deemed it needful, to reprove him. In a sermon he once preached in Haworth church, Yorkshire, of which his friend Grimshaw was the minister, having spoken severely of those professors of the gospel who, by their loose and evil conduct, caused the ways of truth to be evil spoken of, he intimated his hope, that it was not necessary to enlarge much on that topic to the congregation before him, who had so long enjoyed the labors of an able and faithful preacher; and he was willing to believe that their profiting appeared to all men. This latter expression roused Mr. Grimshaw's spirit, and notwithstanding his great regard for the preacher, he stood up and interrupted him, saying, with a loud voice, "O sir, for God's sake, do not speak so; I pray you, do not flatter. I fear the greater part of them are going to hell with their eyes open."

Notwithstanding the astonishing labors of Whitefield on this tour, he returned to London apparently in full flesh, and was congratulated by his friends on his improved appearance. Alas, all this, as he well knew, was disease, which indeed very soon became apparent. He was seized with inflammatory sore throat, that was followed by quinsy, assuming an almost fatal aspect. One physician prescribed silence and warmth, and the preacher "promised to be very obedient," but a few days afterwards, another recommended a perpetual blister: this proposal roused him, and he determined to try his own remedy—perpetual preaching. The remedy itself was painful, but he said, "When this grand catholicon fails, it is all over with me." At this time the sad news of the earthquake at Lisbon arrived in London; he was unable to preach on the subject, but when told of it he said, "Blessed be God, I am ready; I know that my Redeemer liveth. Oh that all in Portugal had known this! Then an earthquake would only be a *rumbling* chariot to carry the soul to God. Poor Lisbon, how soon are thy riches and superstitious pageantry swallowed up!"

In the winter of 1755-6, he was applied to to preach in the vicinity of the two great theatres, which he began to do in Long Acre chapel. Disturbances took place, and the Bishop of London interposed to stop him. In the end he erected Tottenham Court-road chapel, as already detailed in our third chapter.

Mr. Whitefield's ministry in London at this time was still successful. Thousands hung on his lips with delight, not a few of whom were won to the service of Christ. He tells us, among many similar facts, of the conversion of a Mr. Crane, who was afterwards appointed steward of the orphan-house in Georgia. This gentleman had one evening determined to visit the theatre, and set out for Drury-lane; that house being crowded, he resolved to go to Covent-garden; that also being so full that he could not obtain admittance, he changed his plan, and resolved on being entertained with one of Whitefield's sermons, and hastened to Tottenham Court-road chapel. It pleased God to impress the word on his heart, and he became an eminent Christian. So truly is the prediction verified, "I am found of them who sought me not."

During this year he published "A Short Address to Persons of all Denominations, occasioned by an Alarm of an intended Invasion." We have examined it, and not without pleasure. It is a faithful exposure of Popery and its bitter fruits.

It is a charge often preferred against the faithful ministers of Christ, by those whose consciences testify to their own guilt, that they are *personal* in their remarks, and mean to censure particular individuals. It is certain that this was often done by Mr. Whitefield, and sometimes with very happy effect. He once drew, from the conduct of his female servant, the picture of a Christian failing in his duty, which painfully distressed her, till he gave her an assurance of his entire forgiveness.

Nor was this the only time when his hearers were compelled to feel, "he means *me*." The celebrated comedian, Shuter, had a great personal regard for Mr. Whitefield, and not unfrequently attended his ministry. At one period of his popularity he was acting in a drama under the character of *Ramble*. During the run of the performance, he attended service at Tottenham Court chapel, and was seated in a pew exactly opposite the pulpit. Mr. Whitefield on that occasion gave full vent to his feelings, and in his own energetic manner invited sinners to the Saviour. While doing this, fixing his eye full on Shuter, he added, "And thou, poor *Ramble*, who hast long rambled from him, come also. Oh, end your rambling by coming to Jesus." Shuter was exceedingly struck, and going afterwards to Whitefield, he said, "I thought I should have fainted; how could you serve me so?"

In the early part of 1756, Whitefield was engaged in London, preaching and collecting for the poor not only at Bethesda, but also for the French Protestants. At the Tabernacle, a man came up to him in the pulpit, threatening his life, and handing him three anonymous letters denouncing sudden and certain death, unless he ceased to preach and to pursue the offenders by law. One of these letters Whitefield sent to the government, who at once offered a reward, and his majesty's pardon, to any one who would discover the writer. While this fact gratified, it also embarrassed him. He wrote to Lady Huntingdon, "My greatest distress is to act so as to avoid rashness on the one hand, and timidity on the other." For his own sake, he would not have cared about the matter; but looking at it as connected with the cause of civil and religious freedom, he wisely allowed the law to take its course at the hazard of his own life by assassination. Agreeably with the advice of the government, he carried the whole affair into the court of the King's Bench; this alarmed the offenders, and the annoyance ceased.

We next find him at Bristol, but not to rest, though the labors and anxieties of the winter and spring had nearly worn out his strength and spirits. Here he preached as usual, and then returned to London. During this journey he preached in several places in Gloucestershire, his native county, and in Bradford, Frome, Warminster, and Portsmouth, spending about three months in the tour.

In the county which gave Whitefield birth, is still to be seen a chair on which he often sat, and on which may be yet read the following lines:

> "If love of souls should e'er be wanting here,
> Remember me, for I am Whitefield's chair;
> I bore his weight, was witness to his fears,
> His earnest prayers, his interesting tears.
> His holy soul was fired with love divine:
> If thine be such, sit down and call me *thine*."

A very few weeks passed, and we find him in Kent. In a letter written July 27, after his visit to that county, he says, "The gospel flourishes in London. I am just returned from preaching at Sheerness, Chatham, and in the camp." On the next day he set off towards Scotland. On August 14, he writes from Sunderland, "How swiftly doth my precious time pass away! It is now a fortnight since I came to Leeds, in and about which I preached eight days, thrice almost every day, to thronged and affected auditories. On Sunday last at Bradford, in the morning, the auditory consisted of about ten thousand; at noon and in the evening, at Birstal, to nearly double the number. Though hoarse, I was helped to speak so that all heard. Next morning I took a sorrowful leave of Leeds, preached at Doncaster at noon, and at York the same night. On Wednesday, at Warstall, about fifty miles off; on Thursday, twice at Yarm; and last night and this morning, here." Wherever he labored, he heard of the good effects of his preaching in those places last year, and was constantly finding "many trophies of redeeming love." Such was the effect of the two sermons he preached at Birstal, that "several hundreds rode eight miles with him in the evening, singing and praising God."

In a day or two after this, we find him at Edinburgh and Glasgow, preaching, as usual, to vast crowds, and with his accustomed success. At the former places especially, even politicians gave him a cordial welcome, and thronged to hear him, while the newspapers applauded him for his spirit-stirring exposures of "Popish tyranny and arbitrary power." He preached twice every day in the Orphan-hospital park, and blended with almost every sermon rousing appeals to the Protestantism, courage, and loyalty of the Scotch. At the close of one of his sermons he pleaded the cause of the poor Highlanders, and collected at its close about three hundred dollars.

On his way back to London, Whitefield held a peculiarly solemn and refreshing meeting with his friends at Leeds; and after it, he braced his nerves by a tour of *mountain preaching* in company with his friend Grimshaw. But it was now late in October, and as he found "these cold countries bringing on his last year's disorder," and having, as he significantly says, "grown very prudent," he returned to London, and dedicated Tottenham Court-road church edifice. Another errand also had taken him to that city. The new governor of Georgia had sent for him, to consult with him before sailing to that colony. Whitefield met him, and was so much delighted with him, that he wrote off to Bethesda to prepare them for a *state* visit. He says, "Waited upon his excellency, and gave him, and all whom he pleases to bring, an invitation to Bethesda. Dear Mrs. C—— will make proper provision." He went even farther, and proposed that the governor, if possible, should be received at Bethesda with military honors.

The success of his new house of worship in Tottenham Court-road showed the necessity and propriety of its erection on that spot. Several persons of distinction came, and engaged permanent seats; and the place was often so crowded, that hundreds were unable to obtain admission. It was now usual with him to preach about fifteen times every week, which, with a weak appetite, want of rest, and much care upon his mind, greatly enfeebled him. He writes, "But the joy of the Lord is my strength; and my greatest grief is, that I can do no more for Him who hath done and suffered so much for me."

In the following year, 1757, Whitefield planned another journey to Scotland, at the time the general assembly of the church was held. Before leaving London, he had placed the affairs of his projected college in the hands of Lord Halifax, and he now seems to have hoped that this journey to Scotland would have promoted that object, as well as others. It is said, that about a hundred ministers at a time attended his sermons, thirty of whom invited him to a public entertainment. Lord Cathcart, his majesty's commissioner to the assembly, also invited him to his own table. Whitefield says that he preached "just fifty times" on this visit, which extended to about a month.

From Scotland he went, in June, as we have seen, to Ireland, and enjoyed, in the midst of no small persecution, much preaching, and much success. On his return to London, he found that the governor of Georgia had visited Bethesda, and promised to communicate his sentiments to Lord

Halifax, "concerning its being enlarged into a college;" but the pressure of public affairs hindered his application to the government. Bad news arrived from America, "about the fleet," and therefore Whitefield kept a fast-day at his houses of worship.

The health of our evangelist now sadly failed. He was brought to live on the "short allowance of preaching but once a day, and thrice on the Sunday;" very "short allowance" for *him*. Once, however, he broke through the restraint, and preached three times on the success of the king of Prussia; which, he says, "somewhat *recovered*" him, after he had been for a week at the gates of the grave. He was not able this winter to attempt what he considered great things; but Tottenham Court was his *Bethel*, as he called it. This house was then surrounded by a beautiful piece of ground, and he formed the plan of building on it an almshouse for "twelve godly widows," as a "standing monument that the Methodists were not against good works." This charity he soon carried into effect. His thoughts, however, were not confined to home. Although broken down in health and spirits, by weakness and want of rest, he watched the affairs of Prussia with intense interest, and assured the German Protestants, through Professor Francke, that "we looked on their distresses as our own."

In the spring of 1758, he laid the foundation-stone of his almshouse, and in June of the same year began to select its inmates. Pointing to these houses, some years afterwards, he said to a gentleman who was visiting him, "Those are my redoubts. The prayers of the poor women who reside in them, protect me in my house." Having arranged for the supply of his London pulpits, Whitefield went into the west of England, and proceeded from thence into Wales. But his health was so feeble, that he could not bear to drive, nor even ride in a one-horse chaise. The roads were rough, and riding shook him nearly to pieces. "Every thing," he says, "wearies this shattered bark now." A friend purchased for him a close chaise, advancing the money until he could conveniently repay it. He deeply felt this kindness, because by no other means could he have itinerated. "I would not," he says, "lay out a single farthing but for my blessed Master; but it is inconceivable what I have undergone these three weeks. *I never was so before.* O for a *hearse* to carry my weary carcass to the wished for grave." During all this tour he was unable to sit up in company even once; yet he often preached to ten or fifteen thousand people, and made their "tears flow like water from the rock." His views of himself at this time were more than usually humble. He said to Lady Huntingdon, "Oh, I am sick—sick in body, but infinitely more so in mind, to see so much dross in my soul. Blessed be God, there is One who will sit as a refiner's fire, to purify the sons of Levi. I write out of the burning bush. Christ is there; Christ is there!"

Among the many illustrations of Scripture which Whitefield often introduced into his sermons, one is truly worthy of record. Preaching from the words, "Wherefore, glorify ye the Lord in the fires," Isa. 24:15, he says, "When I was, some years ago, at Shields, I went into a glass-house, and standing very attentively, I saw several masses of burning glass of various forms. The workman took one piece of glass, and put it into one furnace, then he put it into a second, and then into a third. I asked him, 'Why do you put that into so many fires?' He answered me, 'Oh, sir, the first was not hot enough, nor the second, and therefore we put it into the third, and that will make it transparent.' 'Oh,' thought I, 'does this man put this glass into one furnace after another, that it may be rendered perfect? Oh, my God, put me into one furnace after another, that my soul may be transparent, that I may see God as he is.'"

In the month of July, Whitefield again set out for Scotland, preaching on his way in many pulpits, including "Bishop Bunyan's," as he used to call him, at Bedford, Berridge's at Everton, and Doddridge's at Northampton. Four Episcopal clergymen lent him their pulpits. His health received, for some time, little benefit, so that he sometimes feared he must return. But he adds, "Through divine strength, I hope to go forward; and shall strive, as much as in me lies, to die in this glorious work." He preached and collected in Scotland with his accustomed energy and success, and returned to London with his health somewhat renovated. This year he lost by death some of his earliest and warmest friends, including Hervey in England, and Presidents Burr and Edwards, and Governor Belcher, in America. Such removals gave him also "a desire to depart," but his work on earth was not yet done.

Three principal facts connected with our evangelist may be said to mark the year 1759. One was, that he had the satisfaction to clear off all his debts for the orphan-house. "Bethesda's God," he writes, "lives for ever, and is faithful and all-sufficient." He longed again to visit America, but several difficulties intervened for the present.

A second event which marked the year, was another journey to Scotland. He complains in his letters, that though his congregations at Edinburgh and Glasgow were never more numerous and attentive, yet, with respect to the power of religion, it was a dead time in Scotland, in comparison with London and several other parts of England. His presence in Scotland, however, at this time was very important, especially in collecting for his orphan-house and the Highland Society for the support of children. Many Scottish soldiers were now in America, which greatly increased the interest felt in every thing relating to it.

In this year, 1759, Mr. Whitefield also for the first time visited Brighthelmstone, now called Brighton, a very fashionable watering-place, where George IV. afterwards, while regent, built a tawdry tasteless palace. The preacher's first sermon was delivered under a tree in a field behind the White Lion inn. Among his congregation on that day was a young man named Tuppen, about eighteen years of age. He had been educated by a pious mother in the strict observance of the external parts of religion, but was entirely destitute of its power. He attended not so much from curiosity, as from the intention to insult and interrupt the preacher. He tells us, "I had therefore provided myself with stones in my pocket, if opportunity offered, to pelt the preacher; but I had not heard long, before the stone was taken out of my heart of flesh; and then the other stones, with shame and weeping, were dropped one by one out upon the ground." The words, "Turn ye, turn ye," became the means of turning him from sin to God. Mr. Tuppen became an excellent Christian minister, and labored as a pastor for some years in Portsmouth. He then removed to the city of Bath, where he originated a congregation, and built a house for public worship. He was succeeded in this important sphere by the late distinguished William Jay, who labored there for about sixty-four years.

Such was the prosperity attendant on the efforts of Messrs. Whitefield, Madan, Romaine, Berridge, Venn, and Fletcher, at Brighton, that Lady Huntingdon felt it her duty to erect a church edifice there, and being unable to do it in any other way, sold her jewels to the amount of nearly three thousand five hundred dollars. The cause still flourishes there, and very many have been turned to righteousness.

While Whitefield's ministry at the Tabernacle was at its height of popularity, Foote, a comedian of eminent talent for mimicry, who was frequently in difficulties on account of his love of ridicule, by which indeed his life was shortened, employed his wit to bring the distinguished preacher into contempt. One of his biographers says, that "very pressing embarrassments in his affairs compelled him to bring out his comedy of '*The Minor*,' in 1760, to ridicule Methodism, which, though successful, gave great offence, and was at last suppressed." Of this miserable piece of buffoonery, it may be enough to say, that Foote, and the agents employed at the Tabernacle and Tottenham Court-road chapel to collect materials from

Whitefield for the accomplishment of their object, were so disgracefully ignorant of the inspired writings, as not to know that what they took for Mr. Whitefield's peculiar language was that of the word of God.

Lady Huntingdon interposed in the matter, first with the Lord Chamberlain, by whose license alone any play could then be performed in London, and then with Mr. Garrick, the latter of whom assured her that he would use his influence to exclude it, and added, that had he been aware of the offence it was adapted to give, it should never have appeared with his concurrence. The representation of this piece of mummery, as might have been expected, considerably increased Whitefield's popularity, and brought thousands of new persons to hear the gospel: thus Providence gave him the victory over his opposers.

To report the sicknesses, the labors, and the successes of Whitefield from this time to that of his sixth embarkation for America, would be little more than a repetition of the past. Suffice it to say, that in England, and in Scotland, he labored amid much ill-health, and surrounded with many dangers; but at length, having found an Episcopal clergyman, the Rev. John Berridge, a man of somewhat eccentric manners, but of great learning, of eminent piety, and of burning zeal, who was willing to labor for a time in London, Whitefield set sail in the ship Fanny, Captain Archibald Galbraith, bound from Greenock to Virginia, June 1, 1763, and arrived at Rappahannock, after a tedious, but otherwise pleasant voyage of about twelve weeks, in the last week of August.

CHAPTER XIV
SIXTH VISIT AND LABORS IN AMERICA—RENEWED LABORS IN GREAT BRITAIN. 1763-1767

Whitefield was now for the sixth time in America. He was twelve weeks on the voyage; but though tedious, it had done him good. "I enjoyed," he says, "that quietness which I have in vain sought after for some years on shore." Owing to the violence of his asthma, he had set sail "with but little hopes of farther public usefulness;" but after being six weeks at sea, he wrote to a friend, "Who knows but our latter end may *yet* increase? If not in public usefulness, Lord Jesus, let it be in heart-holiness. I know who says Amen. I add, Amen and amen."

On his arrival in Virginia, Whitefield was surrounded by many Christian friends, the fruits of his former labors in that colony, but whom he had not hitherto known. It was with great difficulty, however, that he preached to them; for though his general health was better, his breathing was very bad. The months of September, October, and November, he spent in Philadelphia. He says, "Here are some young bright witnesses rising up in the church. Perhaps I have already conversed with forty *new creature* ministers of various denominations. Sixteen popular students, I am credibly informed, were converted in New Jersey college last year. What an open door if I had strength! Last Tuesday we had a remarkable season among the Lutherans; children and grown people were much impressed." Ill as he was, he preached twice a week, and with his usual success.

He intensely desired at this time to visit Georgia, but was absolutely prohibited by his physicians, till he had recovered his strength. In the end of November, therefore, he passed over into New Jersey, visiting the college, and Elizabethtown. He tells us that at the college he had "four sweet seasons." His spirits rose at the sight of the young soldiers who were to fight when he had fallen. It was now winter, and "cold weather and a warm heart" put him in good spirits, so that he was able to preach three times a week.

A young man, a member of the college, hearing that Whitefield was to preach in the neighborhood, and being more than a little anxious to ascertain whether he really deserved all the celebrity he enjoyed, went to hear him. The day was very rainy, and the audience was small; the preacher, accustomed to address thousands, did not feel his powers called forth as at other times. After having heard about one-third part of the sermon, the young man said to himself, "The man is not so great a wonder after all—quite commonplace and superficial—nothing but show, and not a great deal of that;" and looking round upon the audience, he saw that they appeared about as uninterested as usual, and that old father ——, who sat directly in front of the pulpit, and who always went to sleep after hearing the text and plan of the sermon, was enjoying his accustomed nap. About this time, Whitefield stopped. His face went rapidly through many changes, till it looked more like a rising thunder-cloud than any thing else; and beginning very deliberately, he said, "If I had come to speak to you in my own name, you might rest your elbows upon your knees, and your heads upon your hands, and sleep; and once in a while look up and say, 'What does the babbler talk of?' But I have not come to you in my own name. No; I have come to you in the name of the Lord God of hosts, and"—here he brought down his hand and foot at once, so as to make the whole house ring—"and I must, and will be heard." Every one in the house started, and old father —— among the rest. "Aye, aye," continued the preacher, looking at him, "I have waked you up, have I? I meant to do it. I am not come here to preach to stocks and stones; I have come to you in the name of the Lord God of hosts, and I must, and I will have an audience." The congregation was fully aroused, and the remaining part of the sermon produced a considerable effect.

From New Jersey, Whitefield passed on to New York, where he says, "Such a flocking of all ranks I never saw before at New York.... Prejudices have most strangely subsided. The better sort flock as eagerly as the common people, and are fond of coming for private gospel conversation. Congregations continue very large, and I trust saving impressions are made upon many." Such also was his influence as a philanthropist, that though prejudices ran high against the Indians, on account of a threatened insurrection in the south, he collected about six hundred dollars for Dr. Wheelock's Indian school at Lebanon, Conn., which he soon after visited with much pleasure.

An extract of a letter from New York, dated Jan. 23, 1754, which appeared in the Boston Gazette, may show the esteem in which he was held: "The Rev.

George Whitefield has spent seven weeks with us, preaching twice a week, with more general approbation than ever; and has been treated with great respect by many of the gentlemen and merchants of this place. During his stay he preached two charity sermons, the one on the occasion of the annual collection for the poor, in which double the sum was collected that ever was upon the like occasion; the other was for the benefit of Mr. Wheelock's Indian school at Lebanon, for which he collected, notwithstanding the present prejudices of many people against the Indians, the sum of one hundred and twenty pounds. In his last sermon, he took a very affectionate leave of the people of this city, who expressed great concern at his departure. May God restore this great and good man, in whom the gentleman, the Christian, and accomplished orator shine forth with such peculiar lustre, to a perfect state of health, and continue him long a blessing to the world and the church of Christ."

Leaving New York, he visited and preached, as far as his strength would allow, at Easthampton Bridge, Hampton, and Southhold, on Long Island; at Shelter Island, and at New London, Norwich, and Providence.

Whitefield arrived at Boston in the end of February, 1764, and was welcomed by multitudes with cordial affection; and again he saw "the Redeemer's stately steps in the great congregation." Boston at that time was visited with small-pox, and Whitefield therefore devoted much of his labor to the adjacent towns. Writing from Concord, he says, "How would you have been delighted to have seen Mr. Wheelock's Indians. Such a promising nursery of future missionaries, I believe, was never seen in New England before. Pray encourage it with all your might." About two months after his arrival in Boston, his illness returned, but did not long prevent him from preaching, and the people still flocked in crowds to hear him. He left Boston for the south; but messengers were sent to entreat his return, and especially urged him to renew his six o'clock morning lecture. He did return, but was now unable to preach at the early hour they desired; he appeared, however, in the pulpit for some time on three occasions in the week, and such was the number of converts discovered, that after he had left it was proposed to send him a book filled with their names, as desiring his return.

We ought to have said, that according to the Boston Gazette, about the time of the arrival of Whitefield, "at a meeting of the freeholders and other inhabitants of the town of Boston, it was unanimously voted that the thanks of the town be given to the Rev. George Whitefield, for his charitable care and pains in collecting a considerable sum of money in Great Britain for the distressed sufferers by the great fire in Boston, 1760. A respectable committee was appointed to wait on Mr. Whitefield, to inform him of the vote, and present him with a copy thereof."

Notwithstanding the earnest entreaties of his friends, he left Boston in the early part of June. On the first of that month he wrote, "Friends have even constrained me to stay here, for fear of running into the summer's heat. Hitherto I find the benefit of it. Whatever it is owing to, through mercy, I am much better in health than I was this time twelve months, and can preach thrice a week to very large auditories without hurt; and every day I hear of some brought under concern. This is all of grace."

Sorrowfully parting from his friends at Boston, Whitefield left them for New York by way of New Haven. Here he preached to the students, and had taken his leave of them; but such was the impression he had made on their minds, that they requested the president to go after him, to entreat for another "quarter of an hour's exhortation." He complied with the request, and the effect was what he called "the *crown* of the expedition." He continued at New York till the end of August. While there he writes, "At present my health is better than usual, and as yet I have felt no inconvenience from the summer's heat. I have preached twice lately in the fields, and we sat under the blessed Redeemer's shadow with great delight. My late excursions upon Long Island, I trust, have been blessed. It would surprise you to see above one hundred carriages at every sermon in the new world."

On his way to Philadelphia, in September, Whitefield preached at the New Jersey college commencement; for which, and for the influence he had exerted in favor of the institution, the trustees sent him a vote of thanks. His reception at the college was all he could desire. The governor and the ex-governor of the state, with many other gentlemen, attended, and every other mark of respect was shown him. At Philadelphia, he describes the effect of his labors as "great indeed," and as usual, he was compelled to exclaim, "Grace, grace!"

Leaving Pennsylvania, he went on through Virginia; here he tells us, in places as "unlikely as *Rome* itself," he found societies of Christians, formed and led on by a wealthy planter of that colony; they met him in a body, wishing publicly to identify themselves with him. "Surely the *Londoners*," he writes, "who are fed to the full, will not envy the poor souls in these parts. I almost determine to come back in the spring" from Georgia to them.

On one occasion, while he was preaching in this colony, a Mr. Allen, afterwards a member of the eminent Mr. Davies' church at Hanover, and who, with his family, "addicted himself to the ministry of the saints," fell on the ground at full length, suddenly, as if shot through the heart, and lay for the remainder of the evening as one who was dead. His descendants are now very numerous, and many of them are among the most zealous Christians in that state.

From Virginia, Whitefield proceeded to South Carolina, and, Nov. 22, wrote, "At Newbern, last Sunday, good impressions were made. I have met with what they call 'New Lights' in almost every place, and have the names of several of their preachers." Having preached at Charleston, he passed on to Bethesda, and had the happiness to find the whole colony in a prosperous condition. Here he spent the winter, and writes, "Peace and plenty reign at Bethesda. All things go on successfully. God hath given me great favor in the sight of the governor, council, and assembly. A memorial was presented for an additional grant of lands, consisting of two thousand acres. It was immediately complied with. Both houses addressed the governor on behalf of the intended college. A warm answer was given; and I am now putting every thing in repair, and getting every thing ready for that purpose. Every heart seems to leap for joy at the prospect of its future usefulness to this and the neighboring colonies. He who holdeth the stars in his right hand will direct, in due time, whether I shall directly embark for England, or take one tour more to the northward. I am in delightful winter quarters for once. His excellency dined with me yesterday, and expressed his satisfaction in the warmest terms. Who knows how many youths may be trained up for the service of the ever-loving and altogether lovely Jesus. Thus far, however, we may set up our Ebenezer. Hitherto the bush hath been burning, but is not consumed." To this statement he adds, "Mr. Wright hath done much in a little time; but he hath worked night and day, and not stirred a mile for many weeks. Thanks be to God, all outward things are settled on this side the water. The auditing the accounts, and laying the foundation for a college, hath silenced enemies and comforted friends. The finishing of this affair confirms my call to England at this time."

But the intense anxiety of multitudes to hear his preaching, prevented Whitefield from leaving America for several months longer. He had, indeed, as early as the middle of February, determined not to visit New England till his return from Europe; but arriving at Charleston, he was compelled to devote to labors there the whole month of March, and then set out for Philadelphia, preaching at many places on his way. He says, "All the way from Charleston to this place the cry is, 'For Christ's sake, stay and preach to us.' Oh for a thousand lives to spend for Jesus."

The heat of the weather made it indispensable for his health that he should go to sea, and July 5th he once more arrived in England, on his last return voyage from America. He says, "We have had but a twenty-eight days' passage. The transition has been so sudden, that I can scarcely believe that I am in England. I hope, ere long, to have a more sudden transition into a better country." When he arrived in his native land, he was ill of a nervous fever, which left him extremely weak in body, and unable to exert himself as formerly. Yet, still intent on his work, he did what he could, in expectation of soon entering into his eternal rest. "Oh, to end life well!" he writes; "methinks I have now but one river to pass over. And we know of One who can carry us over without being ankle deep."

On Whitefield's arrival in England, he found that his excellent friend the Countess of Huntingdon was erecting a large and beautiful church edifice in the fashionable city of Bath, and to that place he at once repaired. There he found several of his clerical brethren preaching in the private chapel at Bretby Hall, belonging to the Earl of Chesterfield, who had placed it for the time being at the disposal of Lady Huntingdon. On Whitefield's arrival, this place was of necessity exchanged for the Park, where the concourse of people was as vast as ever.

October 6, he preached the dedicatory sermon of Lady Huntingdon's church at Bath, to an immense crowd. To his friend Robert Keen, Esq., one of the managers of his London houses, he wrote, "Could you have come, and have been present at the opening of the chapel, you would have been much pleased. The building is extremely plain, and yet equally grand. A most beautiful original! All was conducted with great solemnity. Though a wet day, the place was very full, and assuredly the great Shepherd and Bishop of souls consecrated and made it holy ground by his presence."

He made but a short stay at Bath, and returned to London, still feeble and tottering, but still compelled to labor. He had an interview with his old friend John Wesley, who says of him, "He seemed to be an old man, being fairly worn out in his Master's service, though he has hardly seen fifty years; and yet it pleases God that I, who am now in my sixty-third year, find no disorder, no weakness, no decay, no difference from what I was at five and twenty, only that I have fewer teeth, and more gray hairs." Writing to a friend at Sheerness, in Kent, Jan. 18, 1766, Whitefield says, "I am sorry to acquaint you that it is not in my power to comply with your request, for want of more assistance. I am confined in town with the care of two important posts, when I am only fit to be put into some garrison among invalids." By some means, however, he obtained a release, for in March we find him at Bath and Bristol. Writing, March 17, he says, "The uncertainty of my motions has made me slow in writing; and a desire to be a while free from London cares, has made me indifferent about frequent hearing from thence. Last Friday evening, and twice yesterday, I preached at Bath, to very thronged and brilliant auditories."

Whitefield's interest in America was not lessened by his absence from it. He ardently loved it, and wished for the return of its peace and prosperity. He hoped, with many others, that the repeal of the Stamp Act would lead to this result; hence, we find in his Letter-book this entry: "March 16, 1766, Stamp Act repealed. *Gloria Deo.*"

Among the remarkable men of his day was Samson Occam. He was descended, on his mother's side, from Uncas, chief of the Mohegans. He was born in 1723, of parents who led a wandering life, depending on hunting and fishing for subsistence. None cultivated their lands, all dwelt in wigwams, and Samson was one of the very first of the tribe who learned to read. About the year 1740, at the age of seventeen, he was converted by the labors of Whitefield, Gilbert Tennent, and their companions. In a year or two he had learned to read his Bible with ease, and to his great advantage. He was a pupil at the school originally founded by Dr. Wheelock, at Lebanon, Conn., for the benefit exclusively of Indians, four years, and was then a teacher for eleven years. In 1759, he was ordained by the Suffolk Presbytery, and became an eminently zealous preacher to the scattered Mohegans. In 1766, in company with the Rev. Mr. Whitaker of Norwich, he went to England to advocate the cause of Dr. Wheelock's Indian school, which school was afterwards merged in Dartmouth college, of which Mr. Wheelock was also founder and first president. Occum preached in the churches of Whitefield and Lady Huntingdon, as well as in some others of different denominations. We remember half a century ago hearing an old lady at Kidderminster, the town of Richard Baxter, describe a scene which occurred in Fawcett's church in that town. Occum had preached, and a handsome collection had been taken for his object; with tears of gratitude and joy the good man thanked them, and in tones which neither the weeping nor the mimetic talent of the old lady would allow her fully to imitate, assured them that the blessing of many ready to perish would come upon them. The place was a Bochim, and nothing could prevent the people from having the plates again carried round, that they might add to the liberal contributions they had already made.

Occum preached in Great Britain from three to four hundred sermons; and as no North American Indian had ever preached in England before, public curiosity was great, and his pecuniary success considerable. He brought to this country, with his companion, as the produce of their labors, more than forty-five thousand dollars. In 1772 he published an interesting sermon which he preached to an Indian at his execution. An excellent portrait of him was published in England.

Dr. Timothy Dwight writes, "I heard Mr. Occum twice. His discourses, though not proofs of superior talents, were decent; and his utterance in some degree eloquent. His character at one time labored under some imputations; yet there is good reason to believe that most, if not all of them were unfounded; and there is satisfactory evidence that he was a man of piety." An account of the Montauk Indians, written by Occum, is preserved in the "Historical Collections." He died at New Stockbridge, N. Y., July, 1792. It has been said that the first Sunday-school in these United States was founded in the house of his sister, a few months after his death.

Occum was somewhat of a wit, and could well apply his talent in his conflict with the enemies of divine truth. He once ended a long controversial conversation with a Universalist, by saying, "Well, well, remember, if you are correct, I am safe; if you are not correct, I am safe. I have two strings to my bow; you have but one."

In June, 1766, we again find Whitefield in the neighborhood of Bristol, whence he writes, "As my feverish heat continues, and the weather is too wet to travel, I have complied with the advice of friends, and have commenced a Hot-wells water drinker twice a day. However, twice this week, at six o'clock in the morning, I have been enabled to call thirsty souls to come and 'drink of the water of life freely.' Tomorrow evening, God willing, the call is to be repeated, and again on Sunday." On his return to London, he writes, under date of September 25, "Many in this metropolis seem to be on the wing for God; the shout of a king is yet heard in the Methodist camp. Had I wings, I would gladly fly from pole to pole; but they are clipped by thirty years' feeble labors. Twice or thrice a week I am permitted to ascend my gospel throne. The love of Christ, I am persuaded, will constrain you to pray that the last glimmering of an expiring taper may be blessed to the guiding of many, wandering souls to the Lamb of God."

The good providence of God now gave Whitefield a colleague in the ministry at the Tabernacle and Tottenham Court-road chapel, the Rev. Torial Joss. This gentleman had spent many years as captain at sea; converted by divine grace, and filled with holy zeal, he devoted his popular talents to the welfare of his fellow-men, preaching both on sea and land. In a remarkable manner, Mr. Whitefield became acquainted with him, and, without his knowledge, published that he would preach in his houses of worship, which, though with extreme reluctance, Joss did. These services were often renewed, and Whitefield gave him no rest till he abandoned the sea, and devoted himself to the ministry. Everywhere he was popular, and everywhere useful. He continued minister of the two places in London—spending four or five months in each year travelling and preaching—for twenty-seven years after the death of his friend, and then departed from earth, in 1797, in holy triumph, in the 66th year of his age.

One of the most extraordinary men in modern times was the late Rev. Rowland Hill, who erected Surrey chapel, London, and continued to preach in it till his death, in his eighty-ninth year, in 1833. He was eminently dignified in person, possessed extraordinary zeal, and was honored by his great Master with probably more success in the direct work of saving souls than any other minister of his day. He was a man of considerable rank, his father being a gentleman of title, one of his brothers a member of Parliament for many years, representing his native county, and the late eminent statesman and soldier Lord Hill was his nephew. Mr. Hill himself in early life became a Christian, and was educated for the ministry in the established church, but violated its rules, and preached wherever he could; for many years he was greatly persecuted by his own family, some of whom, however, in the end sustained the yoke of Christ. When Rowland began his somewhat erratic career, the opposition from his father was so great, that he was reduced sometimes to extreme poverty; and he was exactly the man to be encouraged by such men as Whitefield and Berridge. We give a few extracts from letters addressed to him by Whitefield, which certainly show no small degree of ardor, though we cannot see in them what Hill's clerical biographer, Mr. Sidney, professed to find, "an aspiration after the honors, when he had no prospect of the sufferings of martyrdom." The fact was, that Mr. Sidney was offended with Whitefield, as he was with his venerable uncle, Mr. Hill, for having deviated from the rigid laws of the establishment. It is only needful to introduce the first letter by saying that it was dated, London, December 27, 1766, and was sent in answer to one in which Mr. Hill had asked his counsel.

"About thirty-four years ago, the master of Pembroke college, where I was educated, took me to task for visiting the sick and going to the prisons. In my haste I said, 'Sir, if it displeaseth you I will go no more.' My heart smote me immediately; I repented, and went again; he heard of it—threatened—but for fear he should be looked on as a persecutor, let me alone. The hearts of all are in the Redeemer's hands. I would not have you give way; no, not for a moment. The storm is too great to hold long. Visiting the sick and imprisoned, and instructing the ignorant, are the very vitals of true and undefiled religion. If threatened, denied degree, or expelled *for this*, it will be the best degree you can take—a glorious preparative for, and a blessed presage of future usefulness. I have seen the dreadful consequences of giving way and looking back. How many by this wretched cowardice, and fear of the cross, have been turned into pillars, not of useful, but of useless salt. Now is your time to prove the strength of Jesus yours. If opposition did not so much abound, your consolations would not so abound. Blind as he is, Satan sees some great good coming on. We never prospered so much at Oxford as when we were hissed at and reproached as we walked along the streets, as being counted the dung and offscouring of all things. That is a poor building which a little stinking breath of Satan's vassals can throw down. Your house, I trust, is better founded. Is it not built upon a rock? Is not that rock the blessed Jesus? The gates of hell, therefore, shall not be able to prevail against it. Go on, therefore, my dear man, go on. Old Berridge, I believe, would give you the same advice; you are honored in sharing his reproach and name. God be praised that you are enabled to bless when others blaspheme. God bless and direct and support you. He will, he will. Good Lady Huntingdon is in town; she will rejoice to hear that you are under the cross. You will not want her prayers, or the poor prayers of, my dear honest young friend, yours, in an all-conquering Jesus."

The opposition Mr. Hill met with from his parents increased, and the threat of his degree being withheld, was, on the part of the university authorities, more determined; still, however, he persevered in his preaching and his visits, in violation of the laws of discipline. In June, 1767, Mr. Whitefield wrote him: "I wish you joy of the late high dignity conferred upon you—higher than if you were made the greatest professor in the university of Cambridge. The honorable degrees you intend giving to your promising candidates, [allowing some of his fellow-students to preach in the various places which he had visited,] I trust will excite a holy ambition, and a holy emulation; let me know who is first honored. As I have been admitted to the degree of doctor for near these thirty years, I assure you I like my field preferment, my airy pluralities, exceedingly well. For these three weeks last past I have been beating up for fresh recruits in Gloucestershire and South Wales. Thousands and thousands attended, and good Lady Huntingdon was present at one of our reviews. Her ladyship's aid-de-camp preached in Brecknock-street, and Captain Scott, that glorious field-officer, lately fixed up his standard upon dear Mr. Fletcher's horseblock at Madeley. Being invited thither, I have a great inclination to lift up the Redeemer's ensign next week in the same place; with what success, you and your dearly beloved candidates for good old methodistical contempt shall know hereafter. God willing, I intend fighting my way up to town. Soon after my arrival there, I hope thousands and thousands of volleys of prayers, energetic, effectual, fervent, heaven-besieging, heaven-opening, heaven-taking prayers, shall be poured forth for you all. Oh, my dearly beloved and longed-for in the Lord, my bowels yearn towards you. Fear not to go without the camp; keep open the correspondence between the two universities. Remember the praying legions—they were never known to yield. God bless those that are gone to their respective *cures*—I say not *livings*, a term of too modern date. Christ is our life; Christ is the Levite's inheritance, and Christ will be the true disinterested Levite's lot and portion and all. Greet your dear young companions whom I saw; they are welcome to write when they please. God be your physician under your bodily malady. A thorn, a thorn! but Christ's grace will be sufficient for you. To his tender, never-failing mercy I commit you."

A few weeks after this, Mr. Hill was much depressed in spirits, partly from bodily illness, partly because he was about to leave Cambridge and its surrounding villages, where he had latterly so frequently preached, but chiefly from the fact that he was going home, where he would again meet the frowns of his honored parents, for what they deemed his overrighteousness. In the midst of all this, however, he knew that he would meet at Hawkstone, his father's residence, the cordial welcome of his sister and elder brother, Richard Hill, afterwards a baronet. This gentleman had lately become a village preacher and a visitor of prisons, like his brother. Under these circumstances he was addressed by Whitefield, in his own peculiar and energetic style: "What said our Lord to Martha? 'Did I not say unto thee, If thou wouldest believe, thou shouldst see the glory of God?' Blessed, for ever blessed be the God and Father of our Lord Jesus Christ, for what he hath done for your dear brother. A preaching, prison-preaching, field-preaching *esquire*, strikes more than all the black gowns and lawn sleeves in the world. And if I am not mistaken, the great Shepherd and Bishop of souls will let the world, and his own children too, know that he will not be prescribed to in respect to men, or garbs, or places; much less will he be confined to any order or set of men under heaven. I wish you both much, very much prosperity. You will have it—*you will have it*. This is the way, walk ye in it. Both Tabernacle and [Tottenham Court-road] chapel pulpits shall be open to a captain or an esquire sent of God. The good news from Oxford is encouraging. Say what they will, preaching should be one part of the education of a student in divinity. I pray for you night and day."

On the arrival of Mr. Hill at his father's beautiful seat, it was his happiness to find that his brother Brian, afterwards useful as a clergyman, was added to the number of believers in Christ; he learned also, that one of his college friends had been threatened to have an exhibition, or yearly gift towards his university expenses, withdrawn, unless he renounced his evangelical doctrines and practices. The reader will now understand Mr. Whitefield's letter: "I have been sadly hindered from answering your last letter, delivered to me by your brother. I gave it him to read, and we had, I trust, a profitable conference. God be praised if another of your brothers is gained. What grace is this! Four or five out of one family—it is scarcely to be paralleled. Who knows but the root, as well as the branches, may be taken by and by? Abba, Father, all things are possible with thee! Steadiness and perseverance in the children will be one of the best means, under God, of convincing the parents. This present opposition I think cannot last very long; if it does, to obey God rather than man, when forbidden to do what is undoubted duty, is the invariable rule. Our dear Penty [afterwards the Rev. Thomas Pentycross] is under the cross at Cambridge. But

"'Satan thwarts, and men object,
Yet the thing they thwart effect.'

I should be glad if any one's exhibition was taken from him for visiting the sick, etc. It would vastly tend to the furtherance of the gospel; but Satan sees too far, I imagine, to play such a game now. Let him do his work; he is only a mastiff chained. Continue to inform me how he barks, and how far he is permitted to go in your parts; and God's people shall be more stirred up to pray for you all."

The close of Mr. Hill's life was truly interesting and instructive. As has been intimated, he preached with scarcely diminished power until within a few weeks of his death. During the last two or three years of his life he very frequently repeated the following lines of an old poet:

"And when I'm to die,
Receive me, I'll cry,
For Jesus has loved me, I cannot tell why;
But this I can find,
We two are so joined,
That he'll not be in glory, and leave me behind."

"The last time he occupied my pulpit," writes his neighbor, the Rev. George Clayton, "when he preached excellently for an hour, in behalf of a charitable institution, he retired to the vestry after service under feelings of great and manifest exhaustion. Here he remained until every individual except the pew-openers, his servant, and myself had left the place. At length he seemed with some reluctance to summon energy enough to take his departure, intimating that it was in all probability the last time he should preach in Walworth. His servant went before to open the carriage-door, the pew-openers remaining in the vestry. I offered my arm, which he declined, and then followed him as he passed down the aisle of the chapel. The lights were nearly extinguished, the silence was profound, nothing indeed was heard but the slow majestic tread of his own footsteps, when, in an undertone, he thus soliloquized:

"'And when I'm to die,' etc.

To my heart this was a scene of unequalled solemnity, nor can I ever recur to it without a revival of that hallowed, sacred, shuddering sympathy which it originally awakened."

When the good old saint lay literally dying, and when apparently unconscious, a friend put his mouth close to his ear, and repeated slowly his favorite lines:

"And when I'm to die," etc.

The light came back to his fast-fading eye, a smile overspread his face, and his lips moved in the ineffectual attempt to articulate the words. This was the last sign of consciousness which he gave.

We could almost wish that every disciple of Christ would commit these lines, quaint as they are, to memory, and weave them into the web of his Christian experience. Confidence in Christ, and undeviating adherence to him, can alone enable us to triumph in life and death.

In November, 1766, Whitefield again visited Bath and Bristol, and then passed on to Gloucestershire and Oxford. Never did so many of the nobility attend his ministry as he now saw at Bath, and the results of his whole journey were such as to fill him with the most devout gratitude. He saw too the number of his clerical friends largely increasing, and especially rejoiced in the fact that the excellent Fletcher, of Madeley, preached in his pulpits in London. He writes of this event, "Dear Mr. Fletcher has become a *scandalous* Tottenham Court preacher.... Were we more scandalous, more good would be done.... Still, 'the shout of a king is yet heard' in the Methodist camp."

In January, 1767, Whitefield wrote a recommendatory preface to the works of John Bunyan, whom he pleasantly designated, "Bishop Bunyan;" and as soon as the weather would permit, we find him at Norwich, and then at Rodborough, Woodstock, Gloucester, and Haverfordwest, from which last place he wrote, "Thousands and thousands attend by eight in the morning. Life and light seem to fly all around." On a second visit to Gloucester on this tour, he wrote, "Blessed be God, I have got on this side the Welsh mountains. Blessed be God, I have been on the other side. What a scene last Sunday! What a cry for more of the bread of life! But I was quite worn down."

In September following, he again visited the north of England, writing from day to day in high spirits. September 28, he says, "My body feels much fatigued in travelling; comforts in the soul overbalance;" and from Leeds, October 3, he writes, "Field and street preaching have rather bettered than hurt my bodily health."

Whitefield now returned to London, to sustain a heavy disappointment. The negotiations relative to the college at Bethesda were this winter brought to an issue. A memorial addressed to his Majesty was put into the hands of the clerk of the Privy Council, setting forth the great utility of a college in that place to the southern provinces; and praying that a charter might be granted upon the plan of the college in New Jersey. This memorial was transmitted by the clerk of the Privy Council to the lord president, and by his lordship referred to the Archbishop of Canterbury, to whom also a draft of an intended charter was presented by the Earl of Dartmouth. A correspondence followed all this between the archbishop and Whitefield; the consequence of which was, that his grace gave the draft of the college to the lord president, who promised he would consider of it; and gave it as his opinion that "the head of the college ought to be a member of the church of England; that this was a qualification not to be dispensed with; and also, that the public prayers should not be extempore ones, but the liturgy of the church, or some other settled and established form." Whitefield replied that these restrictions he could by no means agree to, because the greatest part of the contributions for the orphan-house came from Protestant dissenters; and because he had constantly declared that the intended college should be founded upon a broad foundation, and no other.

"This," said he, "I judged I was sufficiently warranted to do, from the known, long-established, mild, and uncoercive genius of the British government; also from your grace's moderation towards Protestant dissenters; from the unconquerable attachment of the Americans to toleration principles, as well as from the avowed habitual feelings of my own heart. This being the case, and as your grace, by your silence, seems to be like-minded with the lord president; and as your grace's and his lordship's influence will undoubtedly extend itself to others, I would beg leave, after returning all due acknowledgments, to inform your grace that I intend troubling your grace and his lordship no more about this so long depending concern. As it hath pleased the great Head of the church in some degree to renew my bodily strength, I propose now to renew my feeble efforts, and to turn the charity into a more generous, and consequently into a more useful channel. I have no ambition to be looked upon as the founder of a college; but I would fain act the part of an honest man, a disinterested minister of Jesus Christ, and a true, catholic, moderate presbyter of the church of England."

Thus ended Whitefield's labors to establish a college at Bethesda. Berridge, and not a few others of his friends rather rejoiced in his disappointment, as they thought there was some fear, uncontrolled as the institution might hereafter be by men of established principles of piety, that an unconverted ministry might be increased by its means.

CHAPTER XV
HIS LAST LABORS IN GREAT BRITAIN—COLLEGE AT TREVECCA—EARL OF BUCHAN—TUNBRIDGE WELLS. 1767-1769

Whitefield had abandoned the idea of a charter for a college at present, but he was yet ardently desirous of a public academy being added to his orphan-house, similar to what existed at Philadelphia before a college charter was granted. He thought that if this could be done, a better day might arrive, when a charter on broad principles might be obtained. He developed his whole plan in a letter to Governor Wright. Feeling too the uncertainty of life, he wrote to his friend Mr. Keen, "None but God knows what a concern is upon me now, in respect of Bethesda. As another voyage, perhaps, may be the issue and the result of all at last, I would beg you and my dear Mr. H—— to let me have all my papers and letters, that I may revise and dispose of them in a proper manner. This can do no hurt, come life or come death."

October 28th, 1767, Whitefield preached at the London Tabernacle before the society for promoting religious knowledge among the poor, usually called, The Book Society. This society had been organized seventeen years before this period, and included in it such men as Watts, Doddridge, and Gifford. He gave way to all the zeal of his heart while he discussed the petition, "Thy kingdom come." Luke 11:2. The congregation was immense, many had to go away unable to obtain admittance. It was believed that a larger number of dissenting ministers were present than ever before heard a sermon from an Episcopal minister, and the collection reached more than five hundred dollars, or above four times the usual amount, besides eighty new annual subscribers. After the service, he dined with a very large party, including the ministers, where harmony reigned, and much respect was shown him.

It may be readily supposed, that with advancing years and increasing experience, some changes might have taken place both in the style and manner of Whitefield's preaching. The Rev. Cornelius Winter, who had become somewhat closely associated with him, says, "He dealt more in the explanatory and doctrinal mode on the Sabbath morning than at any other time, and sometimes made a little, but by no means an improper show of learning. His afternoon sermon was more general and exhortatory. In the evening, he drew his bow at a venture; vindicated the doctrines of grace, fenced them with articles and homilies, referred to the martyr's seal, and exemplified the power of divine grace by quotations from the venerable Foxe. Sinners were then closely plied, numbers of whom, from curiosity, coming to hear for a minute or two, were often compelled to hear the whole sermon. How many in the judgment-day will rise to prove that they heard to the salvation of the soul. Upon the members of society, the practice of Christianity was then usually inculcated, not without some pertinent anecdote of a character worthy to be held up for an example, and in whose conduct the hints recommended were exemplified. On Mondays, Tuesdays, Wednesdays, and Thursdays, he preached at six in the morning; and never, perhaps, did he preach greater sermons than at this hour." This, with the frequent administration of the Lord's supper to hundreds of communicants, was his usual plan for several years; but now he became more colloquial in his style, with but little action; he gave pertinent expositions of the Scriptures, with striking remarks, all comprehended within an hour. Winter adds, "The peculiar talents he possessed, subservient to great usefulness, can be but faintly conceived from his sermons in print; though, as formerly, God has made the reading of them useful, and I have no doubt that in future they will have their use."

But even yet our evangelist had to engage in war. The opposition of the universities in Oxford and Cambridge to the principles and practices introduced by Whitefield, Wesley, and their companions, grew and strengthened, till an event occurred at Oxford singularly remarkable in its history for opposition to evangelical religion, which for many years continued to excite very extraordinary interest. The London "St. James' Chronicle," of Thursday, March 17, 1763, contained the following "extract of a letter from Oxford:" "On Friday last, six students, belonging to Edmund Hall, were expelled the university, after a hearing of several hours before Mr. Vice-Chancellor and some of the heads of houses, for holding methodistical tenets, and taking upon them to pray, read, and expound the Scriptures, and singing hymns in a private house. The —— of the —— [The Principal of the Edmund Hall, Rev. Dr. Dixon] defended their doctrines from the Thirty-nine Articles of the established church, and spoke in the highest terms of the piety and exemplariness of their lives; but his motion was overruled, and sentence pronounced against them. Dr. ——, [Dixon,] one of the heads of houses present, observed, that as these six gentlemen were expelled for having too much religion, it would be very proper to inquire into the conduct of some who had too little; and Mr. —— [Dr. Nowell] was heard to tell their chief accuser, that the university was much obliged to him for his good work."

To detail the events which followed this extraordinary act, and to describe the excitement thus created, form no part of the design of our volume. We have referred to the fact because Mr. Whitefield and his friend Sir Richard Hill took part in the controversy. Referring to Dr. Nowell's assertion to Mr. Higson, their "chief accuser," and who was also their tutor, that the university was obliged to him, Whitefield says to the Vice-Chancellor, "What thanks, reverend sir, he may meet with from the whole university I know not; but one thing I know, namely, that he will receive no thanks for that day's work from the innumerable company of angels, the general assembly of the first-born which are written in heaven, or from God the Judge of all, in that day when Jesus the Mediator of the new covenant shall come in his own glory, in the glory of the Father and his holy angels, and gather his elect from all the four corners of the world.

"It is true, indeed, one article of impeachment was, that 'some of them were of *trades* before they entered into the university.' But what evil or crime worthy of expulsion can there be in that? To be called from any, though the meanest mechanical employment, to the study of the liberal arts, where a natural genius hath been given, was never yet looked upon as a reproach to, or diminution of any great and public character whatsoever. Profane history affords us a variety of examples of the greatest heroes, who have been fetched even from the plough to command armies, and who performed the greatest exploits for their country's good. And if we examine *sacred* history, we shall find that even David, after he was anointed king, looked back with sweet complacency to the rock from whence he was hewn, and is not ashamed to leave it upon record, that God took him away from the sheepfolds, as he was following the ewes great with young; and, as though he loved to repeat it, he took him, he says, 'that he might feed Jacob his people, and Israel his inheritance.'

"But why speak I of David, when Jesus of Nazareth, David's Lord and David's King, had for his reputed father a carpenter? and in all probability, as it was a common proverb among the Jews, that 'he who did not teach his son a trade, taught him to be a thief,' he worked at the trade of a carpenter himself. For this, indeed, he was reproached and maligned: 'Is not this,' said they, 'the carpenter's son?' Nay, 'Is not this the carpenter?' But who were these maligners? The greatest enemies to the power of godliness which the world ever saw, the scribes and Pharisees, that 'generation of vipers,' as John the Baptist calls them, who, upon every occasion, were spitting out their venom, and shooting their arrows, even bitter words, against that Son of man, even that Son of God who, to display his sovereignty, and confound the wisdom of the worldly wise, chose poor fishermen to be his apostles; and whose chief of the apostles, though brought up at the feet of Gamaliel, both before and after his call to the apostleship, labored with his own hands, and worked at the trade of a tent-maker."

It is pleasant to know that the young men thus expelled became useful in the church of Christ. One of them, indeed, Erasmus Middleton, who had been sustained at Oxford by Mr. Fuller, a dissenter and banker in London, was ordained in Ireland by the bishop of Down, and having married a lady of the ducal family of Gordon, in Scotland, was curate successively to the Rev. Messrs. Romaine and Cadogan in London, and finally rector of Turvey, in Bedfordshire, where he was the immediate predecessor of the sainted Legh Richmond.

Many delightful evidences yet exist that as Whitefield drew nearer the end of his career on earth, his holy zeal increased, rather than lessened. We have lying before us three of his letters, not included either in the collection of his printed correspondence, or in the lives which have been published. The first was addressed to a gentleman at Wisbeach, and appears to have been written from London. It is dated Sept. 25, 1766.

"Dear Sir—As your letter breathes the spirit of a sincere follower of the Lamb of God, I am sorry that it hath lain by so long unanswered; but bodily weakness, and a multiplicity of correspondents, both from abroad and at home, must be pleaded as excuses. 'Blessed be God, our salvation is nearer than when we believed.' It should seem that you have now served three apprenticeships in Christ's school, and yet I suppose the language of your heart is, 'I love my Master, and will not go from him;' and Oh, what a mercy, that whom Jesus loves, he loves to the end! Do you not begin to long to see him more than ever? Do you not groan in this tabernacle, being burdened? Courage, courage; he that cometh will come, and will not tarry. Oh that patience may have its perfect work! Many in this metropolis seem to be on the wing for God; the shout of a king is yet heard in the Methodist camp. Had I wings, I would gladly fly from pole to pole; but they are clipped by thirty years' feeble labors. Twice or thrice a week I am permitted to ascend my gospel throne. The love of Christ, I am persuaded, will constrain you to pray that the last glimmering of an expiring taper may be blessed to the guiding of many wandering souls to the Lamb of God."

The second letter was written from the same city, February 12, in the following year, and was addressed to Captain Scott, a military officer then "quartered at Leicester." This gentleman, in early life, had been much devoted to the gayeties of fashionable society; long after he had entered the army, he was converted to God, under the ministry of the Rev. W. Romaine; and a few weeks before Mr. Whitefield addressed to him this letter, he had begun to preach the grand message of reconciliation. He afterwards left the army, was ordained as a Congregational minister, and labored for many years in almost innumerable places in city and country, with abundant success.

"What, not answer so modest a request, namely, to snatch a few moments to send dear Captain Scott a few lines? God forbid. I must again welcome him into the field of battle. I must again entreat him to keep his rank as captain, and not suffer any persuasions to influence him to descend to the low degree of a common soldier. If God will choose a red-coat preacher, who shall say unto him, 'What doest thou?'

"Prevent thy foes, nor wait their charge;
But call the lingering battle on;
But strongly grasp thy seven-fold targe,
And bear the world and Satan down.

"Strong in the Lord's almighty power,
And armed in panoply divine,
Firm mayest thou stand in danger's hour,
And prove the strength of Jesus thine.

"The helmet of salvation take,
The Lord the Spirit's conquering sword;
Speak from the word, in lightning speak;
Cry out, and thunder from the Lord.

"Through friends and foes pursue thy way,
Be mindful of a dying God;
Finish thy course, and win the day,
Though called to seal the truth with blood.

"Gladly would I come, and in my poor way endeavor to strengthen your hands; but alas, I am fit for nothing, but, as an invalid, to be put into some garrison, and now and then put my hand to some old gun. Blessed be the Captain of our salvation for drafting out some young champions to reconnoitre and attack the enemy. You will beat the march in every letter, and bid the common soldiers not halt, but go forwards. Good Lady Huntingdon wishes you much prosperity. Pray write to her at Brighthelmstone, [now Brighton,] Sussex. She will most gladly answer you; and I assure you, her Ladyship's letters are always weighty. Hoping one day or another to see your face in the flesh, and more than hoping to see you crowned with glory in the kingdom of heaven, I must hasten to subscribe myself, my dear captain, yours in our all-glorious Captain-general,

"G. WHITEFIELD."

The last letter we shall introduce in this connection was addressed by Whitefield to the Honorable and Rev. Walter Shirley, of Ireland, a near relative of the Countess of Huntingdon, who breathed, as a minister of Christ, much of the spirit of his great Master. It was dated, Bath, Dec. 8, 1767:

"Rev. and very dear Sir—How glad was I to hear by the London Shunamite, [Mrs. Herritage,] that you and your lady were well; that God had given you a son; that you reflected on your preaching at Tottenham Court chapel with pleasure; that you had gotten a curate; and, to complete all, that you intended to visit England next spring. This news rejoiced me before I left town, and was most grateful to our good Lady Huntingdon, whom I have the honor of waiting upon at this time in Bath. She hath been sick, nigh unto death, but through mercy is now somewhat recovered, though as yet unable to write much. This her ladyship much regrets on your account; and therefore enjoins me to inform you, that your letter did not reach her hands till many weeks after the proper time; that ever since she has been visited with lingering sickness, but begs you will not linger in coming over to our Macedonia to help us. The thought of it seems to refresh her heaven-born soul. Blessed be God, her ladyship still takes the lead.

"She is now doing honor to the remains of the Earl of Buchan, who sweetly slept in Jesus last week. All hath been awful, and more than awful. On Saturday evening, before the corpse was taken from Buchan house, a word of exhortation was given, and a hymn sung in the room where the corpse lay. The young Earl stood with his hands on the head of the coffin, the Countess Dowager of Buchan on his right hand, Lady Ann Agnes, and Lady Isabella Erskine on his left, and their brother the Hon. Thomas Erskine next to their mother, with Miss O——, Miss W——, Miss G——; on one side all the domestics, with a few friends on the other. The word of exhortation was received with great solemnity, and most wept under the parting prayer. At ten, the corpse was removed to good Lady Huntingdon's chapel, where it was deposited within a place railed in for that purpose, covered with black baize, and the usual funeral concomitants, except escutcheons.

"On Sunday morning, all attended in mourning at early sacrament. They were seated by themselves, at the feet of the corpse, and with their head servants, received first, and a particular address was made to them. Immediately after receiving, these verses were sung for them:

"'Our lives, our blood, we here present,
If for thy truth they may be spent:
Fulfil thy glorious counsel, Lord;
Thy will be done, thy name adored.

"'Give them thy strength, O God of power,
Then let men rave or devils roar,
Thy faithful witnesses they'll be;
'Tis fixed, they can do all through thee!'

"Then they received this blessing: 'The Lord bless you, and keep you; the Lord lift up the light of his countenance upon you; the Lord cause his face to shine upon you, and give you peace;' and so returned to their places.

"Sacrament ended, and a blessed sacrament it was, the noble mourners returned to the good Countess of Huntingdon's house, which was lent them for the day. At eleven, public worship began. The bereaved relatives sat in order within, and the domestics round the outside of the rail. The chapel was more than crowded. Near three hundred tickets, signed by the present earl, were given out to the nobility and gentry, to be admitted. All was hushed and solemn. Proper hymns were sung, and I preached on the words, 'Blessed are the dead that die in the Lord.' Attention sat on every countenance, and deep and almost universal impressions were made. The like scene, and if possible more solemn, was exhibited in the evening, and I was enabled to preach a second time, and a like power attended the word as in the morning. Ever since, there hath been public service and preaching twice a day. This is to be continued till Friday morning, then all is to be removed to Bristol, in order to be shipped off to Scotland. The inscription on the coffin runs thus: 'His life was honorable—his death blessed—he sought earnestly peace with God—he found it, with unspeakable joy, alone in the merits of Jesus Christ, witnessed by the Holy Spirit to his soul—he yet speaketh. Go and do likewise.'

"I have often wished for you here. Congregations are very large, attentive, and deeply impressed. Great numbers of all ranks crowd to see and hear; and I trust many will also feel. Surely the death of this noble earl, thus improved, will prove the life of many. He behaved like the patriarch Jacob, when by faith, leaning upon his staff, he blessed his children. The earl added, 'Yea, and they shall be blessed.' He laid his hands on, and blessed his children, assuring them of his personal interest in Jesus. He had great foretastes of heaven. 'Had I strength of body,' cried he, 'I would not be ashamed, before men and angels, to tell what the Lord Jesus hath done for my soul. Come, Holy Ghost—come, Holy Ghost; happy, happy, happy!' and then sweetly slept in Jesus. All surviving relatives still feel the influence. They sit round the corpse, attended by their domestics and supporters, twice a day. Good Lady S—— gets fresh spirits. The present noble earl, I believe, hath got the blessing indeed, and seems, upon the best evidence, to determine to know nothing but Jesus Christ, and him crucified. He hath behaved in the most delicate manner to the Countess, and other noble survivors."

The summer of 1768 brought to Whitefield a series of changes. For the last time he now visited Edinburgh, where he found his congregations as large, and his Christian friends as affectionate as ever. Soon after his return to London, Mrs. Whitefield was seized with inflammatory fever, and died, as we have already seen, on the 9th of August. His own health too was more than declining. He writes, "I have been in hopes of my own departure. Through hard writing, and frequent preaching, I have burst a vein. The flux is in a great measure stopped; but rest and quietness are strictly enjoined."

"Rest and quietness!" With Whitefield such things were impossible as long as he could move or speak. His fire must burn till its whole material was expended; his heart overflowed, and he must labor till his body sank under exhaustion. No persecution could appall him, no sickness could long keep him from his beloved engagements. He would preach till he died, being fully assured that his "labor was not in vain in the Lord."

Neither Whitefield nor any of his friends could ever be the advocates of an unlearned ministry. Many of the men engaged under his direction, and preaching in what was already called "Lady Huntingdon's connection," needed, as they well knew, a better education than they possessed. Hence her ladyship obtained a lease of an old structure, supposed to have been part of an ancient castle erected in the reign of Henry the Second. The date over the entrance, now almost effaced, is 1176. It was called Trevecca House, was situated in the parish of Talgarth, in South Wales, and was for some time the residence of Howel Harris. This building was opened as a college for religious and literary instruction, and the chapel dedicated to the preaching of the everlasting gospel, Aug. 24, 1768, the anniversary of the Bartholomew act, and of the birth of her ladyship. Mr. Whitefield preached from Exod. 24:24: "In all places where I record my name, I will come unto thee and bless thee;" and on the following Sabbath he addressed a congregation of some thousands, who assembled in the court before the college. His text on that occasion was, "Other foundation can no man lay than that is laid, which is Jesus Christ." When speaking of the dedication of the college, Mr. Whitefield says, "What we have seen and felt at the college is unspeakable."

After her ladyship's death the institution was removed to Cheshunt, about thirteen miles north of London, where it still flourishes under the presidency of the Rev. Dr. W. H. Stowell.

In the early part of 1769, Mr. Whitefield was for some weeks seriously ill, but towards the close of March, he was able to write, "Through infinite mercy I have been able to preach four days successively." During his illness he received many offers of assistance from his brethren in the ministry, but from none more cordially than from the Honorable and Rev. Mr. Shirley. Writing to him, April 1, Whitefield says:

"How much am I obliged to you for your two kind letters, and more especially for the repeated offers of your ministerial assistance. They will be most gratefully accepted, and, I humbly hope, be remarkably succeeded by Him who hath promised to be with us always, even unto the end of the world. Blessed be His name, we have been favored with most delightful passover feasts. The shout of the King of kings is still heard in the midst of our Methodist camps; and the shout of, Grace, grace! resounds from many quarters. Our almighty Jesus knows how to build his temple in troublous times. His work prospers in the hands of the elect countess, who is gone to Bath, much recovered from her late indisposition. Worthy Lady Fanny Shirley proposes soon to follow, in order to reside there. Some more coronets, I hear, are likely to be laid at the Redeemer's feet. They glitter gloriously when set in and surrounded by a *crown of thorns*.

"'Subjects of the Lord, be bold;
Jesus will his kingdom hold;
Wheels encircling wheels must run,
Each in course to bring it on.'"

That the friendship of Dr. Franklin towards Mr. Whitefield was sincere, cannot be doubted; there is, however, somewhat painful in the thought, that even in this connection Franklin could not conceal his scepticism. In 1769 both these eminent men were in London, and every one knows that the state of our country was very trying. Franklin thus wrote to Whitefield: "I am under continued apprehensions that we may have bad news from America. The sending soldiers to Boston always appeared to me a dangerous step; they could do no good, they might occasion mischief. When I consider the warm resentment of a people who think themselves injured and oppressed, and the common insolence of the soldiery, who are taught to consider that people as in rebellion, I cannot but fear the consequences of bringing them together. It seems like setting up a smith's forge in a magazine of gunpowder. I *see* with you that our affairs are not well managed by our rulers here below; I wish I could *believe* with you, that they are well attended to by those above: I rather suspect, from certain circumstances, that though the general government of the universe is well administered, our particular little affairs are perhaps below notice, and left to take the chance of human prudence or imprudence, as either may happen to be uppermost. It is, however, an uncomfortable thought, and I leave it."

It would have been strange indeed if Whitefield had allowed a letter closing in this manner to pass without a remark; hence we are prepared to find that, in his own handwriting, at the foot of the autograph letter, he wrote, "*Uncomfortable* indeed! and, blessed be God, *unscriptural*; for we are fully assured that 'the Lord reigneth,' and are directed to cast *all* our own care on him, because he careth for us." Could Dr. Franklin have seen the splendid results of that management which he thought indicated the absence of a particular providence—could he have beheld the vast Republic, the abode of liberty, commerce, literature, and religion, which in less than a century has grown out of the insurgent colonies—he would surely have exclaimed, in the language of the prophet, "Verily there is a God in the earth!"

In July, Whitefield was called by Lady Huntingdon to visit Tunbridge Wells, a popular watering place in Kent, some twenty or thirty miles from London, to dedicate a new and beautiful house to the service of God. The congregation was far too large to be accommodated within the walls; he therefore preached out of doors from a mount in the court before the house. His text was, "This is none other but the house of God, and this is the gate of heaven." Gen. 28:17. This sermon is said to have been one of his most eloquent and thrilling efforts; the lofty energy of his tones, the utter forgetfulness of himself in the all-absorbing interest of his subject, the very impersonation of the truths which he uttered as he stretched forth his hand, "Look yonder; what is that I see? It is my agonizing Lord! Hark, hark! do you not hear? O earth, earth, earth, hear the word of the Lord!" thrilled the vast congregation, riveting the eye, piercing the conscience, and holding strong men breathless before the resistless might of his inspired eloquence. After the service he delivered an exhortation, and on the next day again preached and administered the Lord's supper.

He now began to prepare for his *seventh*, and as it proved, his *last* voyage to America, especially to visit his beloved orphans and friends in Georgia. The only thing which seems to have grieved him, was the pain of parting for a time from his London friends. This was nothing new, but his feelings were even less reconciled to the event than formerly. "Oh," he says, "these partings! without a divine support they would be intolerable. Talk not of taking *personal* leave; you know my *make*. Paul could stand a whipping, but not a weeping farewell."

The text of his last sermon was John 10:27, 28: "My sheep hear my voice, and I know them, and they follow me: and I give unto them eternal life; and they shall never perish, neither shall any man pluck them out of my hand." The sermon was printed, and that very incorrectly; but a few sentences will show that it was strikingly characteristic: "These words, it will be recollected, were uttered by Christ at the feast of dedication. This festival was of bare human invention, and yet I do not find that our Lord preached against it. And I believe that when we see things as we ought, we shall not entertain our auditories about rites and ceremonies, but about the grand thing. It is the glory of Methodists, that while they have been preaching forty years, there has not been, that I know of, one single pamphlet published by them about the non-essentials of religion.... The Lord divides the world into sheep and goats. O sinners, you are come to hear a poor creature take his last farewell; but I want you to forget the creature and his preaching. I want to lead you further than the Tabernacle—even to mount Calvary, to see with what expense of blood Jesus Christ purchased 'his own.' Now, before I go any further, will you be so good, before the world gets into your hearts, to inquire whether you belong to Christ or not. Surely the world did not get into your hearts before you rose from your beds. Many of you were up sooner than usual. [The sermon was preached at seven o'clock in the morning.] I hope the world does not get into your hearts before nine. Man, woman, sinner, put thy hand upon thy heart, and say, Didst thou ever hear Christ's voice so as to follow him?... I once heard Dr. Marryatt, who was not ashamed of 'market language,' say at Pinner's Hall, 'God has a great dog to fetch his sheep back when they wander.' He sends the devil after them, to bark at them; but instead of barking them further off, he barks them back to the fold.... 'None shall pluck them out of my hand.' This implies that there is always somebody plucking at Christ's sheep. The lust of the flesh is plucking; the pride of life is plucking; and the devil is continually plucking at them; 'but nothing shall pluck them out of my hand;' I have bought them, and am gone to heaven to 'prepare a place for them.'"

Of this sermon, as taken in shorthand and printed, Whitefield received a copy while at Deal, and was much dissatisfied with it. He says, "This morning I received a surreptitious copy of my Tabernacle farewell sermon, taken, as the shorthand writer professes, verbatim as I spoke it. But surely he is mistaken. The whole is so injudiciously paragraphed, and so wretchedly unconnected, that I owe no thanks to the misguided, though it may be well-meant zeal of the writer and publisher, be they who they will." Had Whitefield known that the lad of seventeen who had thus taken down his sermon, would hereafter become a devoted and useful minister of Christ, the secretary of the London Missionary Society, the originator of the London Religious Tract Society, and for many years the editor of the London Evangelical Magazine, and the author of "Village Sermons," which have circulated by hundreds of thousands of volumes in both hemispheres, how would his heart have warmed towards him. Let us copy from the journal of George Burder, as given in his life by his son, the Rev. Dr. H. F. Burder, a short passage:

"August, 1769. About this time I heard Mr. Whitefield preach several sermons, particularly his two last in London; that at Tottenham Court chapel on Sabbath morning, and that at the Tabernacle on Wednesday morning at seven o'clock. I remember a thought which passed my mind, I think, as I was going to hear his last sermon—'Which would I rather be, Garrick or Whitefield?' I thought each, in point of oratory, admirable in his way. I doubt not conscience told me which was best. I wrote Mr. Whitefield's sermons in shorthand, though standing in a crowd. The latter I copied out, and by the request of a friend it was printed in about a week. I remember sitting up part of a night to write it out, and at the same time I observed the comet which then appeared. The sermon was very incorrect, and Mr. Whitefield being detained at Deal before he left England, saw it, and complained of it."

Before we entirely separate from the Tabernacle, we wish to record some other interesting facts associated with it, especially relating to Thomas Wilson, Esq., for many years the treasurer of Hoxton, afterwards Highbury, college, who gave the ground on which the latter building stands, devoted his fortune to the extension of the cause of Christ, and in addition to many other noble acts, erected five large houses of worship in the British metropolis, capable of seating eight thousand persons. The father of this gentleman was for many years a devoted deacon of a Congregational church, but entered into full sympathy with the labors of Whitefield, attending the Tabernacle on Lord's-day evenings. "To this circumstance, perhaps, may be traced much of his own zeal for the glory of God, and no inconsiderable portion of that public spirit which afterwards distinguished his son Thomas, who well remembered being carried in his nurse's arms, in company with his parents, to the scene of Whitefield's ministry, and listening with such interest as one so young was likely to feel, to a preacher of surpassing eloquence and power." The Rev. Dr. Morison, one of his biographers, adds: "Thus did he imbibe in early life a strong prepossession for animated public address, which he never lost in after-years, and which he never failed to urge upon all youthful candidates for the sacred office. As might have been expected, the Tabernacle became his Sabbath home, where he was wont to listen to men of fervent eloquence, and of purely evangelical sentiment. He entered, while very young, into communion with the church in that place, and afforded a pleasing example of early and consistent dedication to the service of Christ."

Having finished the service of the Tabernacle which we just now described, Whitefield went immediately to Gravesend, twenty miles from London, to set sail, embarking in the Friendship, Captain Ball, for Charleston. His companions on the voyage were Messrs. Winter and Smith, both of them young ministers of lively zeal; and the former especially, was distinguished in after-life by great success in his labors for Christ and his church. Whitefield wrote, "I am comfortable on every side—a civil captain and passengers; all willing to attend on divine worship, and to hear of religious things."

But delay was the lot of our evangelist and his friends. They arrived in the Downs, and had to stay there about a month waiting for a fair wind. While here, he was delighted with a most unexpected visit from Dr. Gibbons of London, and the Rev. Mr. Bradbury of Ramsgate, who had met at Deal to ordain a young minister. He says, "Wednesday, Sept. 13, I went on shore, and attended an ordination solemnity at the dissenting meeting. Several ministers officiated. Several important questions were asked and answered before, and a solemn charge given after imposition of hands. But the prayer put up in the very act of laying on of hands, by Dr. Gibbons, was so affecting, and the looks and behavior of those that joined so serious and solemn, that I hardly know when I was more struck under any one's ministration. The ordination being over, at the desire of the ministers and other gentlemen, I went and dined with them: our conversation was edifying; and being informed that many were desirous to hear me preach, I willingly complied; and I trust some seed was sown the same evening at Deal, which, by God's heavenly blessing, will spring up to life eternal. The people of Deal seemed very civil, and some came to me who had not forgotten my preaching to them, and their deceased friends and parents, thirty-two years ago."

Whitefield tells a somewhat amusing anecdote of Dr. Gibbons, on one of his visits on board. The worthy doctor was unused to the sea, and became sea-sick, so that he was obliged to lie down for some time in the state-cabin. "There," says our evangelist, "he learned more experimentally to pray for those who do business in the great waters." While yet in the Downs, Whitefield preached not only on board, but at Ramsgate and elsewhere. On September 25, in company with many other ships, they sailed, but soon were again compelled to cast anchor over against New Romney and Dungenness. At length, however, they cleared the channel, and after a long and dangerous voyage arrived safe at Charleston, S. C. Happily, Whitefield's health had become greatly renovated, so that he felt better than after any voyage he had made for many years. In his memorandum he wrote:

"November, 1769. For the last week we were beating about our port, within sight of it, and continued for two days in Five-fathom hole, just over the bar. A dangerous situation, as the wind blew hard, and our ship, like a young Christian, for want of more ballast, would not obey the helm. But through infinite mercy, on November 30, a pilot-boat came and took us safe ashore to Charleston, having been on board almost thirteen weeks. Friends received me most cordially. Praise the Lord, O my soul, and forget not all his mercies. Oh, to begin to be a Christian and minister of Jesus!" On the very day of his landing, Whitefield preached at Charleston, and learned from his friend Mr. Wright that all was well at Bethesda.

CHAPTER XVI
SEVENTH VISIT AND LABORS IN AMERICA--DEATH. 1769, 1770

Whitefield now lost no time in proceeding to his beloved Bethesda, which at present wore a very inviting aspect. Writing, January 11, 1770, he says, "Every thing exceeds my most sanguine expectations. I am almost tempted to say, 'It is good for me to be here;' but all must give way to gospel ranging—divine employ!

"'For this, let men revile my name,
I'll shun no cross, I'll fear no shame;
All hail, reproach!'"

In another letter he says, "The increase of this colony is almost incredible. Two wings are added to the orphan-house, for the accommodation of students; of which Governor Wright laid the foundation, March 25, 1769."

An official paper of the Georgia legislature will show the esteem in which Whitefield was held by that body.

"Commons House of Assembly, Monday, Jan. 29, 1770. Mr. Speaker reported, that he, with the house, having waited on the Rev. Mr. Whitefield, in consequence of his invitation, at the orphan-house academy, heard him preach a very suitable and pious sermon on the occasion; and with great pleasure observed the promising appearance of improvement towards the good purposes intended, and the decency and propriety of behavior of the several residents there; and were sensibly affected, when they saw the happy success which has attended Whitefield's indefatigable zeal for promoting the welfare of the province in general, and the orphan-house in particular. Ordered, that this report be printed in the Gazette.

"JOHN SIMPSON, Clerk."

In pursuance of this vote, we find in the Georgia Gazette as follows: "Savannah, January 31, 1770. Last Sunday, his Excellency the Governor, Council, and Assembly, having been invited by the Rev. Mr. Whitefield, attended divine service in the chapel of the orphan-house academy, where prayers were read by the Rev. Mr. Ellington, and a very suitable sermon was preached by the Rev. Mr. Whitefield, from Zechariah 4:10, 'For who hath despised the day of small things?' to the great satisfaction of the auditory; in which he took occasion to mention the many discouragements he met with, well known to many there, in carrying on the institution for upwards of thirty years past, and the present promising prospect of its future and more extensive usefulness. After divine service, the company were very politely entertained with a handsome and plentiful dinner; and were greatly pleased to see the useful improvements made in the house, the two additional wings of apartments for students, one hundred and fifty feet each in length, and other lesser buildings, in so much forwardness; and the whole executed with taste, and in so masterly a manner; and being sensible of the truly generous and disinterested benefactions derived to the province through his means, they expressed their gratitude in the most respectful terms."

On February 10, we find a letter written at Charleston by Whitefield to his friend Mr. Robert Keen of London:

"Through infinite mercy, this leaves me enjoying a greater share of bodily health than I have known for many years. I am now enabled to preach almost every day, and my poor feeble labors seem not to be in vain in the Lord. Blessed be God, all things are in great forwardness at Bethesda. I have conversed with the governor in the most explicit manner, more than once, concerning an act of Assembly for the establishment of the intended orphan-house college. He most readily consents. I have shown him a draft, which he much approves of, and all will be finished at my return from the northward; in the meanwhile the building will be carried on. As two ministers from New Jersey and Rhode Island have been soliciting benefactions for their respective colleges, no application of that nature can be made here; but the Lord will provide.... Since my being in Charleston, I have shown the draft to some persons of great eminence and influence. They highly approve of it, and willingly consent to be some of the wardens. Nearly twenty are to be of Georgia, and about six of this place; one of Philadelphia, one of New York, one of Boston, three of Edinburgh, two of Glasgow, and six of London. Those of Georgia and South Carolina are to be qualified; the others to be only honorary corresponding wardens."

Two days afterwards he again writes to the same friend, "In a few months, I hope all will be completed. But what may these few months produce? Lord Jesus, prepare us for whatsoever thou hast prepared for us, and give peace in our time, for thine infinite mercy's sake. You must expect another draft soon. God be praised for that saying, 'It is more blessed to give than to receive.' You would be pleased to see with what attention the people hear the word preached. I have been in Charleston near a fortnight—am to preach at a neighboring country parish church next Sunday, and hope to see Georgia the week following. Perhaps I may sail from thence to the northward, and perhaps embark from thence. Lord Jesus, direct my goings in thy way. I am blessed with bodily health, and am enabled to go on my way rejoicing. Grace, grace!"

On returning to Bethesda, his heart seems to have been full of the orphan-house and the college. For the direction of the latter, he prepared a series of rules, and especially provided for the reading of the old Puritan and Non-conformist writers of the seventeenth and eighteenth centuries. Every letter he wrote contained references to the improved state of his health, and the increased number of preaching engagements which he was now able to fulfil. His spirits seem to have been better, and his exultations in the divine kindness more ardent than ever, while his correspondence indicates much heavenly-mindedness, and lively desires for the highest happiness of his friends.

As Whitefield had now been in the south more than five months, we are not surprised to find that applications poured in from every part of the north, entreating him to revisit the scenes of other years. He left Bethesda and its affairs in the hands of persons worthy of his confidence, of whom he said, "Such a set of helpers I never met with."

After some hesitation as to where he should first go, he set out for Philadelphia, where he arrived on the 6th of May. Writing three days afterwards, he says, "The evening following, I was enabled to preach to a large auditory, and have to repeat the delightful task this evening. Pulpits, hearts, and affections, seem to be as open and enlarged to me as ever." On the 24th he again wrote, "A wide and effectual door, I trust, has been opened in this city. People of all ranks flock as much as ever. Impressions are made on many, and I trust they will abide. To all the Episcopal churches, as well as most of the other places of worship, I have free access. Notwithstanding I preach twice on the Lord's day, and three or four times a week besides, yet I am rather better than I have been for many years. This is the Lord's doing." On June 14, he says, "This leaves me just returned from a one hundred and fifty miles' circuit, in which, blessed be God, I have been enabled to preach every day. So many new as well as old doors are open, and so many invitations sent from various quarters, that I know not which way to turn myself."

Of his last visit to New Jersey, Bishop White of Philadelphia, then a young man of twenty-three, says, "When he was on his way from Philadelphia to Boston, late in the summer, he had been prevailed on to promise to cross from Bristol to Burlington, and to preach there. I happened to be in the latter place, and staying in the house of a relative, when it was announced that Mr. Whitefield was at a tavern on the other side of the river. He was expected to be escorted by my relative. I went with him; and we returned in a boat with Mr. Whitefield and his company. He preached to the assembled citizens in front of the court-house, and afterwards dined at the house of my relative. During dinner, he was almost the only speaker, as was said to be common; all present being disposed to listen."

A few days after this visit, we find him at New York, writing, June 30, "I have been here just a week. Have been enabled to preach four times; and am to repeat the delightful task this evening. Congregations are larger than ever. Blessed be God, I have been strengthened to itinerate and preach daily for some time. Next week I purpose to go to Albany; from thence, perhaps to the Oneida Indians. There is to be a very large Indian congress; Mr. Kirkland accompanies me. He is a truly Christian minister and missionary. Every thing possible should be done to strengthen his hands and his heart. Perhaps I may not see Georgia till Christmas. As yet, I keep to my intended plan, in respect to my returning. Lord Jesus, direct my goings in thy way. The heat begins now to be a little intense; but through mercy I am enabled to bear up bravely. What a God do we serve!"

On the twenty-ninth of July, he again writes from the same city, and it is the *last entry* in his memorandum: "Since my last, and during this month, I have been above a five hundred miles' circuit; and have been enabled to preach and travel through the heat every day. The congregations have been very large, attentive, and affected; particularly at Albany, Schenectady, Great Barrington, Norfolk, Salisbury, Sharon, Smithfield, Poughkeepsie, Fishkill, New Rumbart, New Windsor, and Peck's Hill. Last night I returned hither, and hope to set out for Boston in two or three days. O what a new scene of usefulness is opening in various parts of this world! All fresh work where I have been. The divine influence has been as at first. Invitations crowd upon me both from ministers and people, from many, many quarters. A very peculiar providence led me very lately to a place where a horse-stealer was executed. Thousands attended. The poor criminal had sent me several letters, hearing I was in the country. The sheriff allowed him to come and hear a sermon under an adjacent tree. Solemn, solemn! After being by himself about an hour, I walked half a mile with him to the gallows. His heart had been softened before my first visit. He seemed full of solid, divine consolation. An instructive walk! I went up with him into the cart. He gave a short exhortation. I then stood upon the coffin—added, I trust, a word in season—prayed—gave the blessing, and took my leave. Effectual good, I hope, was done to the hearers and spectators. Grace, grace!"

Our local histories seem to delight to honor Whitefield by the introduction of his name whenever they have an opportunity. In a notice of Sharon, in "Barber's Historical Collections of Connecticut," the writer says, "In the latter part of July, 1770, the Rev. George Whitefield passed through this town on a preaching tour. There was considerable opposition to his being admitted into the meeting-house, and arrangements had been made to hold the service in an orchard still standing near the meeting-house, in case he should be refused. Mr. Smith, [the Rev. Cotton Mather Smith, a descendant of Cotton Mather,] invited him into the pulpit, though strongly opposed by a considerable number of influential men. An immense congregation from this and the neighboring towns filled the meeting-house to overflowing. His text was, 'Marvel not that I said unto you, Ye must be born again.' He proceeded to discourse on the doctrine of the new birth with astonishing power and eloquence, and the congregation were much moved by the power of the truth and Spirit of God. The concluding words of his discourse were a quotation, with a little variation, from the close of the fourth chapter of Solomon's Song. 'Awake, O north wind, and come, thou south; blow upon *this* garden, that the spices thereof may flow out. Let my Beloved come into *this* garden, and eat his pleasant fruits.' Many of the inhabitants of Sharon followed him for several successive days, to hear the word of life from this devoted minister of the cross."

We think it must have been in this journey that Whitefield's ministry was blessed to the conversion of a young man who has left his mark on the age. Benjamin Randall was born in New Castle, New Hampshire, in 1749. In his twenty-second year he was brought under the ministry of Whitefield, by which means he became deeply convinced of sin, and was soon after converted to God. In 1776, he united with a Calvinistic Baptist church; but before long began to preach what he accounted more correct doctrines in his native town, and was honored of God to effect a very powerful and extensive revival. He is considered the founder of the denomination of Freewill Baptists, which now comprises from eleven to twelve hundred churches, more than a thousand pastors and licentiates, and upwards of fifty thousand communicants. Mr. Randall was a man of strong mental powers, and though he had not a classical education, he was a good English scholar, aspired after general and religious knowledge, had fine discriminating talent, and was remarkable for the perseverance with which he pursued whatever he undertook. Above all, like his spiritual father, he possessed what a living preacher has well called, "a passion for souls."

From New York Whitefield proceeded to Boston, and short extracts from two of his letters, and those *the last* he wrote, will show his position and his feelings:

September 17, he says to Mr. Wright, at Bethesda, "Fain would I come by Captain Souder, from Philadelphia; but people are so importunate for my stay in these parts, that I fear it will be impracticable. 'My God will supply all my need according to the riches of his grace in Christ Jesus.' Two or three evenings ago, I was taken in the night with a violent flux, attended with retching and shivering, so that I was obliged to return from Newbury; but through infinite mercy I am restored, and to-morrow morning hope to begin again. Never was the word received with greater eagerness than now. All opposition seems, as it were, for a while to cease. I find God's time is the best. The season is critical as to outward circumstances; but when forts are given up, the Lord Jesus can appoint salvation for walls and for bulwarks; he has promised to be a wall of fire round about his people. This comforts me concerning Bethesda, though we should have a Spanish war. You will be pleased to hear, I never was carried through the summer's heat so well."

And finally, to his dear friend Mr. Keen of London, he wrote from Portsmouth, New Hampshire, September 23, just one week before his death, "By this time I thought to be moving southward. But never was greater importunity used to detain me longer in these northern parts. Poor New England is much to be pitied; Boston people most of all. How grossly misrepresented! What a mercy that our Christian charter cannot be dissolved! Blessed be God for an unchangeable Jesus! You will see, by the many invitations, what a door is opened for preaching the everlasting gospel. I was so ill on Friday that I could not preach, though thousands were waiting to hear. Well, the day of release will shortly come, but it does not seem yet; for by riding sixty miles I am better, and hope to preach here to-morrow. I trust my blessed Master will accept these poor efforts to serve him. O for a warm heart! O to stand fast in the faith, to acquit ourselves like men, and be strong! May this be the happy experience of you and yours. I suppose your letters are gone for me in the Anderson to Georgia. If spared so long, I expect to see them about Christmas. Still pray and praise. I am so poorly, and so engaged when able to preach, that this must apologize for not writing to more friends: it is quite impracticable."

Whitefield's hope to "preach here to-morrow" was fully realized. In the "Pennsylvania Journal and Weekly Advertiser," we find a letter from Portsmouth, dated Sept. 28, 1770, which says, "Last Sunday morning came to town from Boston, the Rev. George Whitefield, and in the afternoon he preached at the Rev. Dr. Haven's meeting-house; Monday morning he preached again at the same place, to a very large and crowded audience. Tuesday morning a most numerous assembly met at the Rev. Dr. Langdon's meeting-house, which it is said will hold nearly six thousand people, and was well filled, even the aisles. Evening he preached at the Rev. Mr. John Rodgers' meeting-house in Kittery, and yesterday at the Rev. Mr. Lyman's in York, to which place a number of ladies and gentlemen from town accompanied him. This morning [Friday] he will preach at the Rev. Dr. Langdon's meeting-house in this town."

We are now approaching the closing scene, and are invited to hear Whitefield's last sermon. On his way to Newburyport, where he had engaged to preach on Sunday morning, September 30, he was entreated to preach at Exeter. This had been the scene of some of his former triumphs. He was once preaching here, when a man was present who had loaded his pocket with stones to throw at the preacher. He heard his prayer with patience, but as soon as he had read his text, the man took a stone out of his pocket and held it in his hand, waiting for an opportunity to throw it. But God sent a word to his heart, and the stone dropped from his hand. After the sermon, the poor fellow went to Mr. Whitefield, and said, "Sir, I came here to-day with the intention of breaking your head, but God has given me a broken heart." This man was converted to God, and lived an ornament to the gospel.

As though it had been felt by the public that this might be our preacher's last sermon, inconvenient as Saturday noon must be for the assembling of a congregation for worship, such a multitude was collected that no house could contain them, and Whitefield, for nearly two hours, discoursed to an attentive crowd in the open air. Of this last sermon at Exeter, a gentleman who was present has given a deeply interesting and affecting account. The relator was then in his eighty-sixth year, but he retained a strong remembrance of the most trivial incidents connected with that extraordinary man. He says:

"It was usual for Mr. Whitefield to be attended by Mr. Smith, who preached when he was unable on account of sudden attacks of asthma. At the time referred to, after Mr. Smith had delivered a short discourse, Mr. Whitefield seemed desirous of speaking; but from the weak state in which he then was, it was thought almost impossible. He rose from the seat in the pulpit, and stood erect, and his appearance alone was a powerful sermon. The thinness of his visage, the paleness of his countenance, the evident struggling of the heavenly spark in a decayed body for utterance, were all deeply interesting; the spirit was willing, but the flesh was dying. In this situation he remained several minutes, unable to speak; he then said, 'I will wait for the gracious assistance of God, for he will, I am certain, assist me once more to speak in his name.' He then delivered perhaps one of his best sermons, for the light generally burns most splendidly when about to expire. The subject was a contrast of the present with the future; a part of this sermon I read to a popular and learned clergyman in New York, who could not refrain from weeping when I repeated the following: 'I go, I go to rest prepared; my sun has arisen, and by aid from heaven, given light to many; 't is now about to set for—no, it cannot be! 't is to rise to the zenith of immortal glory; I have outlived many on earth, but they cannot outlive me in heaven. Many shall live when this body is no more, but then—Oh, thought divine!—I shall be in a world where time, age, pain, and sorrow are unknown. My body fails, my spirit expands; how willingly would I live for ever to preach Christ! but I die to be with him. How brief, comparatively brief, has been my life, compared with the vast labors I see before me yet to be accomplished; but if I leave now, while so few care about heavenly things, the God of peace will surely visit you.' These, and many other things he said, which, though simple, were rendered important by circumstances; for death had let fly his arrow, and the shaft was deeply enfixed when utterance was given to them: his countenance, his tremulous voice, his debilitated frame, all gave convincing evidence that the eye which saw him should shortly see him no more for ever. When I visited the place where he is entombed, Newburyport, I could not help saying, 'The memory of the just is blessed,' Few are there like George Whitefield; however zealous, they do not possess the masterly power, and those who do, too often turn it to a purpose that does not glorify God."

We have already spoken of the Rev. Daniel Rodgers, a descendant of the martyr of that name, and pastor of the second congregational church at Exeter. It was this old friend of Whitefield who had importuned him to preach at Exeter. The "*Almanack Journal*" of this excellent man contains the following items of the activity of our "eloquent orator" in his closing days: "September 10, 1770, dear Mr. Whitefield preached here, A. M., ten o'clock. 11th, Mr. Whitefield preached again in Mr. Parsons' meeting-house. 12th, I rode over to Rowley, Mr. Whitefield preached there. 14th, a storm of rain. 15th, the rain continues. Mr. Whitefield went to Boston, not well. 25th, I heard dear Mr. Whitefield preach. 26th, he went to Kittery, and preached for brother John; P. M. I rode to York. 27th, Mr. Whitefield preached at York; P. M. we returned to Portsmouth. 28th, Mr. Whitefield preached his farewell sermon; I returned home. 29th, dear Mr. Whitefield preached for me the last sermon he ever preached."

Mr. Smith's account of the closing scene will not be considered too minute in its details. "Before he commenced his journey of fifteen miles from Portsmouth to Exeter, Mr. Clarkson, senior, observing him more uneasy than usual, said to him, 'Sir, you are more fit to go to bed than to preach.' Whitefield's reply was, 'True, sir;' but turning aside, he clasped his hands together, and looking up, said, 'Lord Jesus, I am weary *in* thy work, but not *of* thy work. If I have not yet finished my course, let me go and speak for thee once more in the fields, seal thy truth, and come home and die.' His last sermon was from 2 Cor. 13:5, 'Examine yourselves, whether ye be in the faith. Know ye not your own selves, how that Jesus Christ is in you, except ye be reprobates?' He dined at Captain Gillman's. After dinner, Mr. Whitefield and Mr. Parsons rode to Newbury. I did not get there till two hours after them. I found them at supper. I asked Mr. Whitefield how he felt after his journey. He said he was tired, therefore he supped early, and went to bed. He ate a very little supper, talked but little, asked Mr. Parsons to discharge the table, and perform family duty, and then retired up stairs."

The Rev. Dr. Hallock tells us, that, in 1822, he visited Newburyport and the tomb of Whitefield. He was then told by persons whom he considered reliable, that when Whitefield was retiring to his chamber on this last evening of his life, many were so desirous to see and hear him, that he stood on the stairs with a lamp in his hand, and there gave them a tender spiritual address.

We resume Mr. Smith's account: "He said he would sit and read till I came to him, which I did as soon as possible; and found him reading the Bible, with Dr. Watts' Psalms lying open before him. He asked me for some water-gruel, and took about half his usual quantity; and kneeling down by his bedside, closed the evening with prayer. After a little conversation, he went to rest, and slept till two in the morning, when he awoke, and asked for a little cider; he drank about a wine-glass full. I asked him how he felt, for he seemed to pant for breath. He said to me, 'My asthma is coming on again; I must have two or three days' rest. Two or three days' riding, without preaching, would set me up again.' Soon afterwards, he asked me to put the window up a little higher, though it was half up all night. 'For,' said he, 'I cannot breathe; but I hope I shall be better by and by: a good pulpit sweat to-day may give me relief; I shall be better after preaching.' I said to him, 'I wish you would not preach so often.' He replied, 'I had rather wear out than rust out.' I then told him, I was afraid he took cold in preaching yesterday. He said he believed he had; and then sat up in bed, and prayed that God would be pleased to bless his preaching where he had been, and also bless his preaching that day, that more souls might be brought to Christ. He prayed for direction whether he should winter in Boston, or hasten to the southward; and he prayed for a blessing on his Bethesda college, and his dear family there, for the Tabernacle and Chapel congregations, and all connections on the other side of the water; and then he laid himself down to sleep again.

"This was near three o'clock. At a quarter past four he awoke, and said, 'My asthma, my asthma is coming on; I wish I had not given out word to preach at Haverhill on Monday; I don't think I shall be able; but I shall see what to-day will bring forth. If I am no better to-morrow, I will take two or three days' ride!' He then desired me to warm him a little gruel; and in breaking the fire-wood, I waked Mr. Parsons, who thinking I knocked for him, rose and came in. He went to Mr. Whitefield's bedside, and asked him how he felt. He answered, 'I am almost suffocated. I can scarcely breathe, my asthma quite chokes me.' I was then not a little surprised to hear how quickly, and with what difficulty he drew his breath. He got out of bed, and went to the open window for air. This was exactly at five o'clock. I went to him, and for about the space of five minutes saw no danger, only that he had a great difficulty in breathing, as I had often seen before. Soon afterwards, he turned himself to me, and said, '*I am dying.*' I said, 'I hope not, sir.' He ran to the other window, panting for breath, but could get no relief. It was agreed that I should go for Dr. Sawyer; and on my coming back, I saw death on his face; and he again said, '*I am dying.*' His eyes were fixed, his underlip drawing inward every time he drew breath. I persuaded him to sit down in the chair, and have his cloak on; he consented by a sign, but could not speak. I then offered him a glass of warm wine; he took half of it, but it seemed as if it would have stopped his breath entirely. He went towards the window, and we offered him some warm wine, with lavender drops, which he refused.

"In a little time he brought up a considerable quantity of phlegm. I then began to have some small hopes. Mr. Parsons said he thought Mr. Whitefield breathed more freely than he did, and would recover. I said, 'No, sir, he is certainly dying.' I was continually employed in taking the phlegm out of his mouth with a handkerchief, and bathing his temples with drops, rubbing his wrists, etc., to give him relief, if possible, but all in vain; his hands and feet were as cold as clay. When the doctor came in, and saw him in the chair leaning upon my breast, he felt his pulse, and said, 'He is a dead man.' Mr. Parsons said, 'I do not believe it; you must do something, doctor.' He said, 'I cannot; he is now near his last breath.' And so indeed it was; for he fetched but one gasp, and stretched out his feet, and breathed no more. This was exactly at six o'clock. We continued rubbing his legs, hands, and feet, with warm cloths, and bathed him with spirits for some time, but all in vain. I then put him into a warm bed, the doctor standing by, and often raised him upright, continued rubbing him and putting spirits to his nose for an hour, till all hopes were gone. The people came in crowds to see him."

Whitefield seems to have had somewhat of a presentiment that his death would be unattended with any remarkable expression of spiritual enjoyment. In his last preceding visit to this country, he had spent a day or two under the roof of the Rev. Dr. Finley, then president of the college at Princeton, New Jersey. One day Dr. Finley said at the dinner-table, "Mr. Whitefield, I hope it will be very long before you will be called home; but when that event shall arrive, I shall be glad to hear the noble testimony you will bear for God." Whitefield replied, "You would be disappointed, doctor; I shall die silent. It has pleased God to enable me to bear so many testimonies for him during my life, that he will require none from me when I die. No, no. It is your dumb Christians, who have walked in fear and darkness, and thereby been unable to bear a testimony for God during their lives, that he compels to speak out for him on their death-beds."

We resume Mr. Smith's narrative: "The Rev. Mr. Parsons, at whose house my dear master died, sent for Captain Fetcomb, and Mr. Boadman, and others of his elders and deacons, and they took the whole of the burial upon themselves, prepared the vault, and sent and invited the bearers. Many ministers of all persuasions came to the house of the Rev. Mr. Parsons, where several of them gave a very particular account of their first awakenings under his ministry several years ago, and also of many in their congregations that, to their knowledge, under God, owed their conversion to his coming among them, often referring to the blessed seasons they had enjoyed under his preaching; and all said, that this last visit was attended with more power than any other, and that all opposition fell before him. Then one and another would pity and pray for his dear Tabernacle and Chapel congregations, and it was truly affecting to hear them bemoan America and England's loss. Thus they continued for two hours, conversing about his great usefulness, and praying that God would scatter his gifts, and drop his mantle among them."

Dr. Gillies says, "Early next morning, Mr. Sherburn of Portsmouth sent Mr. Clarkson and Dr. Haven with a message to Mr. Parsons, desiring that Mr. Whitefield's remains might be buried in his own new tomb, at his own expense; and in the evening several gentlemen from Boston came to Mr. Parsons, desiring the body might be carried there. But as Mr. Whitefield had repeatedly desired to be buried before Mr. Parsons' pulpit, if he died at Newburyport, Mr. Parsons thought himself obliged to deny both these requests."

Mr. Parsons, in a note to his funeral sermon, says, "At one o'clock all the bells in the town were tolled for half an hour, and all the vessels in the harbor gave their proper signals of mourning. At two o'clock the bells tolled a second time. At three the bells called to attend the funeral. The Rev. Dr. Haven of Portsmouth, and the Rev. Messrs. Rodgers of Exeter, Jewet and Chandler of Rowley, Moses Parsons of Newbury, and Bass of Newburyport, were pall-bearers. Mr. Parsons and his family, with many other respectable persons, followed the corpse in mourning."

"The procession," says Mr. Smith, "was only one mile, and then the corpse was carried into the Presbyterian church, and placed at the foot of the pulpit, close to the vault; the Rev. Daniel Rodgers made a very affecting prayer, and openly declared, that, under God, he owed his conversion to that dear man of God whose precious remains now lay before them. Then he cried out, 'O my father, my father!' then stopped and wept as though his heart would break; the people weeping all through the place. Then he recovered, and finished his prayer, and sat down and wept. Then one of the deacons gave out the hymn,

"'Why do we mourn departing friends?'

some of the people weeping, some singing, and so on alternately. The Rev. Mr. Jewet preached a funeral discourse; and made an affectionate address to his brethren, to lay to heart the death of that useful man of God, begging that he and they might be upon their watchtower, and endeavor to follow his blessed example. The corpse was then put into the vault, and all concluded with a short prayer, and dismission of the people, who went weeping through the streets to their respective places of abode."

The Rev. Mr. Rodgers, from whose "Almanack Journal" we have quoted, records that the vast assembly at the funeral consisted of "four, since thought five thousand people," and adds, Oct. 7, "I preached from those words in the first Philippians, 'Having a desire to depart and be with Christ,' etc. I spoke extempore, somewhat largely, of dear Mr. Whitefield's character."

The late venerable Mr. Bartlet of Newburyport, some years ago, erected a monument to the memory of Whitefield in the church beneath which his remains are interred. The cenotaph was executed by Mr. Struthers of Philadelphia, after a design of Strickland, and the inscription which follows was written by the late Rev. Dr. Ebenezer Porter, of the Theological seminary at Andover.

THIS CENOTAPH

is ERECTED, WITH AFFECTIONATE VENERATION,

To the Memory

OF

THE REV. GEORGE WHITEFIELD,

BORN AT GLOUCESTER, ENGLAND, DECEMBER 16, 1714;
EDUCATED AT OXFORD UNIVERSITY; ORDAINED 1736.
IN A MINISTRY OF THIRTY-FOUR YEARS,
HE CROSSED THE ATLANTIC THIRTEEN TIMES,
AND PREACHED MORE THAN EIGHTEEN THOUSAND SERMONS.
AS A SOLDIER OF THE CROSS, HUMBLE, DEVOUT, ARDENT,
HE PUT ON THE WHOLE ARMOR OF GOD:
PREFERRING THE HONOR OF CHRIST TO HIS OWN INTEREST, REPOSE,
REPUTATION, AND LIFE.
AS A CHRISTIAN ORATOR, HIS DEEP PIETY, DISINTERESTED ZEAL, AND VIVID IMAGINATION,
GAVE UNEXAMPLED ENERGY TO HIS LOOK, UTTERANCE, AND ACTION.
BOLD, FERVENT, PUNGENT, AND POPULAR IN HIS ELOQUENCE,
NO OTHER UNINSPIRED MAN EVER PREACHED TO SO LARGE ASSEMBLIES,
OR ENFORCED THE SIMPLE TRUTHS OF THE GOSPEL BY MOTIVES SO PERSUASIVE AND AWFUL, AND WITH AN INFLUENCE SO POWERFUL,
ON THE HEARTS OF HIS HEARERS.
HE DIED OF ASTHMA, SEPTEMBER 30, 1770.
SUDDENLY EXCHANGING HIS LIFE OF UNPARALLELED LABORS
FOR HIS ETERNAL REST.

OLD SOUTH CHURCH, BOSTON.

MONUMENT

OLD SOUTH, AT NEWBURYPORT

CHAPTER XVII
TESTIMONIES AND FACTS ILLUSTRATIVE OF WHITEFIELD'S CHARACTER

"Last evening," says a letter from Boston, October 1, 1770, to the "Pennsylvania Journal," "we were informed by a melancholy messenger from Newburyport, that yesterday morning about six o'clock, at that place, the renowned and Rev. George Whitefield, chaplain to the Right Hon. the Countess of Huntingdon, etc., was, by a sudden mandate, summoned to the bosom of his Saviour. He had been preaching in divers parts of this province since his arrival from the southward, with his usual diligence and energy; was now from a tour to the province of New Hampshire on his return to this town, but being seized with a violent fit of the asthma, was in a short space translated from the labors of this life to the enjoyment of a better.

"Of this truly pious and very extraordinary personage, little can be said but what every friend to vital Christianity who has sat under his ministry will readily attest. In his public performances throughout Europe and British America, he has, for a long course of years, astonished the world as a prodigy of eloquence and devotion. With what frequency and cheerfulness did he ascend the desk, the language of his actions being ever, 'Wist ye not that I must be about my Master's business?' With what divine pathos did he plead with, and persuade by the most engaging incitements, the impenitent sinner to the practice of piety and virtue. Filled with the spirit of grace, he spoke from the heart; and with a fervency of zeal perhaps unequalled since the apostles, ornamented the celestial annunciations of the preacher with the graceful and most enticing charms of rhetoric and oratory. From the pulpit he was unrivalled in the command of an ever-crowded and admiring auditory; nor was he less entertaining and instructive in his private conversation and deportment. Happy in a remarkable ease of address, willing to communicate, studious to edify, and formed to amuse—such, in more retired life, was he whom we lament. And while a peculiar pleasantry enlivened and rendered his company agreeable, his conversation was ever marked with the greatest objects of his pursuit—virtue and religion. It were to be wished that the good impressions of his ministry may be long retained;

and that the rising generation, like their pious ancestors, may catch a spark of that ethereal flame which burnt with such lustre in the sentiments and practice of this faithful servant of the most high God."

Another contemporaneous article says, "Dr. Cooper of Brattle-street, called an enthusiast by none, won early to serious religion by his [Whitefield's] instrumentality, delivered a sermon upon his death, in which he pronounced a strong eulogy in favor of his holy and successful activity in the cause of vital and practical religion through the English dominions. Pews, aisles, and seats were so crowded, and heads and shoulders were in such close phalanx, that it looked as though a man might walk everywhere upon the upper surface of the assembly, without finding an opening for descending to the floor."

When the news of Mr. Whitefield's death reached Georgia, its inhabitants vied with each other in showing him the highest respect. All the black cloth in the stores was bought up; the pulpit and desk of the church, the branches, the organ-loft, and the pews of the governor and council were covered with black. The governor and council in deep mourning convened at the state-house, and went in procession to church, where they were received by the organ playing a funeral dirge. Two funeral sermons were there listened to by the authorities. In the Legislature high eulogiums were pronounced on the admirable preacher, and a sum of money was unanimously appropriated for removing his remains to Georgia, to be interred at his orphan-house; but the inhabitants of Newburyport strongly objected, and the design was relinquished. Forty-five years later when a new county was formed in Georgia, it received the name of Whitefield in commemoration of his worth and useful services.

In a letter from Dr. Franklin to a gentleman in Georgia, he says, "I cannot forbear expressing the pleasure it gives me to see an account of the respect paid to his memory by your assembly. I knew him intimately upwards of thirty years; his integrity, disinterestedness, and indefatigable zeal in prosecuting every good work, I have never seen equalled, I shall never see excelled."

Of course it would be expected that the sermons at Savannah would be of great interest. Such a discourse was delivered by the Rev. Mr. Ellington, who very truly said, "Whitefield's longing desires for the salvation of immortal souls would not admit of his being confined within the limits of any walls. How he has preached, with showers of stones, and many other instruments of malice and revenge about his ears, many of his surviving friends can witness. But having the salvation of sinners at heart, and a great desire to rescue them from the power of an eternal death, he resolved to spend and be spent for the service of precious and immortal souls; and spared no pains and refused no labor, so that he might administer to their real and eternal good. He died like a hero on the field of battle. Thousands in England, Scotland, and America have great reason to bless God for his ministrations."

Who shall attempt to describe the feelings of the congregations at the Tabernacle and Tottenham Court chapels, when the news of their pastor's death first reached them? All were indeed clothed in mourning. By Whitefield's own previous appointment, the Rev. John Wesley preached the funeral sermon at Tottenham Court-road chapel. The preacher bore this testimony: "In his public labors he has for many years astonished the world with his eloquence and devotion. With what divine pathos did he persuade the impenitent sinner to embrace the practice of early piety and virtue. Filled with the spirit of grace, he spoke from the heart with a fervency of zeal perhaps unequalled since the days of the apostles; and adorned the truths he delivered with the most graceful charms of rhetoric and oratory. From the pulpit he was unrivalled in the command of an ever-crowded auditory. It was the love of God shed abroad in his heart by the Holy Ghost which filled his soul with tender, disinterested love to every child of man.... Mention has been already made of his unparalleled zeal, his indefatigable activity, his tender-heartedness to the afflicted, and charitableness towards the poor. But should we not likewise mention his deep gratitude to all whom God had used as instruments of good to him? of whom he did not cease to speak in the most respectful manner, even to his dying day. Should we not mention that he had a heart susceptible of the most generous and the most tender friendship? I have frequently thought that this, of all others, was the distinguishing part of his character. How few have we known of so kind a temper, of such large and flowing affections! Was it not principally by this that the hearts of others were so strongly drawn and knit to him? Can any thing but love beget love? This shone in his very countenance, and continually breathed in all his words, whether in public or private. Was it not this which, quick and penetrating as lightning, flew from heart to heart; which gave that life to his sermons, his conversation, his letters? Ye are witnesses."

The Rev. John Newton preached a funeral sermon at Olney, where he was then settled, from the highly appropriate text, "He was a burning and a shining light," John 5:35, in which he thus speaks of Whitefield: "Some ministers are burning and shining lights in a peculiar and eminent degree. Such a one, I doubt not, was the servant of God whose death we now lament. I have had some opportunities of looking over the history of the church in past ages; I am not backward to say, that I have not read or heard of any person, since the apostles' days, of whom it may be more emphatically said, 'He was a burning and a shining light,' than the late Mr. Whitefield; whether we consider the warmth of his zeal, the greatness of his ministerial talents, or the extensive usefulness with which the Lord honored him. I do not mean to praise the man, but the Lord who furnished him, and made him what he was. He was raised up to shine in a dark place. The state of religion when he first appeared in public, was very low in our established church. I speak the truth, though to some it may be an offensive truth. The doctrines of grace were seldom heard from the pulpit, and the life and power of godliness were little known. Many of the most spiritual among the dissenters, were mourning under a sense of a great spreading declension on their side. What a change has taken place throughout the land within a little more than thirty years; that is, since the time when the first set of despised ministers came to Oxford! And how much of this change has been owing to God's blessing on Mr. Whitefield's labors, is well known to many who have lived through this period, and can hardly be denied by those who are least willing to allow it.... His zeal was not like wildfire, but directed by sound principles, and a sound judgment.... The Lord gave him a manner of preaching which was peculiarly his own. He copied from none, and I never met with any one who could imitate him with success."

With regret we tear ourselves away from Romaine and Toplady, from Pemberton and Parsons, and from a multitude of others who bore testimonies like those we have given, but which would exceed the limits of our narrative.

Mr. Newton, after his removal to London, once breakfasting with a company of noblemen and gentlemen, was asked if he knew Mr. Whitefield. He answered in the affirmative, and remarked, that as a preacher Mr. Whitefield far exceeded every other man of his time. Mr. Newton added, "I bless God that I lived in his time: many were the winter mornings I rose at four o'clock to attend his Tabernacle discourses at five; and I have seen Moorfields as full of lanterns at these times, as I suppose the Hay market is full of flambeaux on an opera night." As a proof of the power of Mr. Whitefield's preaching, Mr. Newton said, that a military officer at Glasgow, who had heard him preach, laid a wager with another, that at a certain charity sermon, though he went with prejudice, he would be compelled to give something. The other, to make sure that he would not, laid aside all the money out of his pockets; but before he left the church, he was glad to borrow some, and lose his bet. Mr. Newton mentioned as another striking illustration of Mr. Whitefield's persuasive oratory, his collecting after one sermon £600, or about $3,000, for the inhabitants of an obscure village in

Germany, that had been burned down. After this sermon, Whitefield said, "We shall sing a hymn, during which those who do not choose to give their mite on this awful occasion, may sneak off." Not one moved; he came down from the pulpit, ordered all the doors to be shut but one, at which he held the plate himself, and collected the large sum we have named. Mr. Newton farther stated what he knew to be a fact, that at the time of Whitefield's greatest persecution, when obliged to speak in the streets, in one week he received not fewer than a thousand letters from persons distressed in their consciences by the energy of his preaching.

A gentleman of title in England was one day examining some works of the distinguished sculptor, John Bacon. Among them he observed a bust of Mr. Whitefield, which led him to remark, "After all that has been said, this was truly a great man; he was the founder of a new religion." Mr. Bacon replied, "A new religion, sir?" "Yes," said the baronet; "what do you call it?" "Nothing," was the reply, "but the old religion revived with new energy, and treated as though the preacher meant what he said."

Several interesting narratives have been given of visits to the tomb of Whitefield, which show the preciousness of his memory.

In 1834, the Rev. Andrew Reed, D. D., of London, and the late Rev. James Matheson, D. D., of Durham, visited this country as a deputation to its churches from the Congregational Union of England and Wales. In describing their visit to Newburyport, Dr. Reed says, "We had a conference with the pastors here, and afterwards went to the church which is enriched with the remains of Whitefield. The elders of the church were present in the porch to receive us. We descended to the vault. There were three coffins before us. Two pastors of the church lay on either side, and the remains of Whitefield in the centre. The cover was slipt aside, and they lay beneath my eye. I had before stood in his pulpits; seen his books, his rings, and chairs; but never before had I looked on part of his very self. The skull, which is perfect, clean, and fair, I received, as is the custom, into my hand. I could say nothing; but thought and feeling were busy. On returning to the church, I proposed an exercise of worship. We collected over the grave of the eloquent, the devoted, and seraphic man, and gave expression to the sentiments that possessed us, by solemn psalmody and fervent prayer. It was not an ordinary service to any of us."

In the year 1835, a similar deputation visited this country from the Baptist Union of Great Britain and Ireland. It consisted of the late Rev. F. A. Cox, D. D., of London, and the Rev. James Hoby, D. D., then of Birmingham. They also visited the tomb of our never-to-be-forgotten evangelist. We give a few sentences from their report: "We made an excursion to Newburyport, thirty-nine miles from Boston, to see the tomb of Whitefield. On our arrival, we hastened to the depository of the precious remains of that eminent servant of God.... We descended with some difficulty into the subterraneous vault, which is immediately behind the pulpit, in a small chamber like a vestry, external to the body of the church. Deep expectant emotions thrilled through our bosoms, while a kind of trap-door was opened, and we descended beneath the floor to another door, which stood perpendicularly, by which we entered, or rather crept, into the awful and silent sepulchre. There were three coffins placed in parallel lines; two of them containing the mortal part of Mr. Parsons and Mr. Prince, pastors of the church. We instinctively took our seats, the one on the one coffin, the other on the other, with the coffin of Whitefield between, over which, when the upper part of the lid was removed, to reveal the skeleton secrets of the narrow prison-house, we bent in solemn stillness and awe. We gazed on the fragments—we contemplated and handled the skull of that great preacher of righteousness—we thought of his devoted life, his blessed death, his high and happy destiny; and whispered our adorations of the grace that formed him both for earth and heaven."

The following lines were written by the departed and amiable William B. Tappan, on visiting this spot in September, 1837.

"And this was Whitefield!—this, the dust now blending
With kindred dust, that wrapt his soul of fire—
Which, from the mantle freed, is still ascending
Through regions of far glory, holier, higher.

Oh, as I gaze here with a solemn joy
And awful reverence, in which shares Decay,
Who, this fair frame reluctant to destroy,
Yields it not yet to doom which all obey—
How follows thought his flight, at Love's command,
From hemisphere in sin, to hemisphere,
Warning uncounted multitudes with tears—
Preaching the risen Christ on sea and land—
And now those angel journeyings above!
Souls, his companions, saved by such unwearied love!"

In December, 1845, one of the London daily papers, "The Sun," contained a somewhat extended account of Whitefield in New England, and especially his death, funeral, and tomb, from which we borrow mementos that in both hemispheres may be interesting "for generations to come."

"I was spending Sunday at Old Ipswich, in the latter part of last September, when by accident I fell in with an old inhabitant of the town who had heard Whitefield preach there. He was a sort of patriarch of the place, and as he sat on one of the stones which surrounded the ancient orthodox meeting-house, his grey locks streaming from beneath his queerly shaped hat, and attired in his primly cut old fashioned coat, he appeared no bad representative of the departed Puritans who, in former days, had soberly and decently obeyed the call of the Sabbath bell, and worshipped in the same temple whose steeple now casts its shadow athwart the green sward beneath.... As the bell of Old Ipswich church swung out that bright Sabbath morning, it was a pretty sight to see the village people coming from different points to the decaying old church, which was situated, as most country churches in New England are, on a hill-top. While I was enjoying the scene, the old man to whom I have alluded, and who was sitting on a stone, accosted me, and asked me if I was not a stranger 'in these parts.' On my informing him that I was, he pointed out to me the 'lions' of the neighborhood, and wound up by asking, 'I suppose, sir, you've heard of Whitefield?'

"'Of Whitefield? to be sure I have.'

"'Well, I've seen Whitefield, George Whitefield stood on this very stone,' (dropping his stick feebly from his shaking hands,) 'and I heard him preach here.'

"'And do you remember any thing about him?' I asked.

"'Well, I guess I do. I was but a bit of a boy then; but here he stood on this stone, looking like a flying angel, and we call this Whitefield's pulpit to this day.... There was folks here from all parts to hear him; so he was obliged to preach outside, for the church wasn't half big enough for 'em, and no two ways about it. I've heard many parsons sin' that time, but none on 'em could come nigh him, any how they could fix it.'

"'Do you remember any thing of his sermons?' I inquired.

"'Oh, I was too young to notice aught, sir, but the preacher hisself and the crowds of people, but I know he had a very sweet voice; and as I said, when he spread his arms out, with a little Bible in his hand, he looked like a flying angel. There never were so many people, afore nor since, in Old Ipswich. I suppose, sir, you'll be going to see his bones? He was buried at Newburyport, and you can see 'em if you like.'

"I made up my mind that I would see them, if possible. On the following day, I went over to Newburyport by railroad, and proceeded first to the house in which Whitefield died. It was at the time the residence of the Rev.

Jonathan Parsons, the first regular pastor of the Presbyterian Society in the town. It is a plain unpretending structure, possessing no other claims to attention than its being the spot where the last scene of Whitefield's career was enacted. I knocked, and asked of a lady who answered my summons, if I might be allowed to see the room in which Mr. Whitefield died. She very courteously showed me up a flight of stairs into a chamber, which, she said, Mr. Whitefield used to sleep in. 'Here is the place he died in,' said the lady, as she showed me a little entry just outside the door of the chamber, directly over the entrance to the house. 'He lay the night before he died,' said the lady, 'in that bed-chamber; and when he was struck with death, he ran out to this entry window for breath, and died while sitting in a chair opposite to it.'

"The Federal-street church, where Whitefield was buried, was but a short distance from the house in which he died, and on my way to it I called on the sexton.... He preceded me through the aisle of the church, and opening a little narrow door by the side of the pulpit, we passed into a dim gloomy room behind it, and from thence descending four or five steps, found ourselves in a brick vault which lay directly under the pulpit. It was two or three minutes before my eyes got accustomed to the gloom; but soon objects became discernible, and I saw three old coffins, two of them serving as supporters to the third, which lay across them.... The sexton trimmed his lamp, then lifted the lid of an old coffin, and holding the flame close to it, said, 'Here, look in, ... THAT'S THE MAN.'

"Yes, there lay the man, or at least, all that remains of the once mighty preacher. A strange awe came over me at his words, '*That's the man.*' I took the skull in my hands, and examined it carefully. The forehead was rather narrow than broad, and by no means high. I soon put it back again to the coffin."

Among the more prominent traits in the character of Whitefield, we may designate his *indifference to his own honor and ease*, of which his narrative contains almost innumerable illustrations. In the preparation of the deed of trust for his intended college, he entirely omitted his own name, that the proposed trustees might accept the office without suffering contempt for being connected with him. It was not pretence which led him often to say, "Let the name of George Whitefield perish, if God be glorified." On the same principle of almost self-annihilation he acted in reference to the accumulation of money. He secured nothing for himself. It does not seem that what he left to his friends by his will was or could be paid; what had been left him as legacies had been nearly all expended, and would have been entirely, had he lived to return to his beloved Bethesda. By his will he placed the institution in the hands of Lady Huntingdon, who sent out ministers and other persons to conduct it. But soon after this, the buildings were burnt down. After the fire, came the Revolutionary war, which tended to unsettle the tenure of property, and at the time of its close, the whole plans, alike of the orphan-house and the college, were nearly unknown. The authorities of Savannah, in accordance with the high regard which they still entertained for Whitefield's memory, secured whatever they could of the wreck, the proceeds of which they invested in a school for the young, which yet flourishes.

Perhaps no man was ever more thoroughly *fond of labor*. From a memorandum in which Mr. Whitefield recorded the times and places of his ministerial labors, it appears that from the period of his ordination to that of his death, which was thirty-four years, he preached upwards of *eighteen thousand sermons*. It would be difficult to imagine how many thousand miles he travelled. When he ascertained that his physical powers began to fail, putting himself on what he called "short allowance," he preached *only once on every week-day, and three times on the Sabbath*. In view of his various journeyings in the slow and inconvenient modes of travelling then in use, his thirteen voyages across the Atlantic, and all that he accomplished, it appears that few men ever performed so much labor within the same period.

Nearly every one who has attempted a description of Whitefield has said much of his *extraordinary voice*. It is known that Garrick was heard to say that he would give a hundred guineas if he could say "Oh!" as Whitefield did. The late Rev. Dr. Haweis, speaking of his "wonderful voice," and of its sweetness and variety of tone, said he believed on a serene evening it might be distinctly heard for nearly a mile. Others have given similar evidence.

The late Sir George Beaumont, no mean authority on such a subject, thus familiarly speaks: "Oh yes; I heard that young gentleman this morning allude to 'roaring Whitefield,' and was amused at his mistake. It is a common one. Whitefield did not roar. I have been his auditor more than once, and was delighted with him. Whitefield's voice could be heard at an immense distance; but that was owing to its fulness, roundness, and clearness. It was a perfectly sound voice. It is an odd description, but I can hit upon no better; there was neither crack nor flaw. To describe him as a bellowing, roaring field preacher, is to describe a mountebank, not Whitefield. He had powers of pathos of the highest order. The tender, soft, persuasive tones of his voice were melodious in the extreme. And when he desired to win, or persuade, or plead, or soothe, the gush of feeling which his voice conveyed at once surprised and overpowered you."

Speaking on the authority of his tutor, the Rev. Cornelius Winter, the late excellent Mr. Jay says that Whitefield's voice was incomparable: not only distinct and loud, but abounding with every kind of inflection, and perfectly under his power; so that he could render every thing he expressed, however common or insignificant in itself, striking and affecting.

This distinguished man had a peculiar talent for making the *narration of facts tell in the pulpit*. Nothing occurred among even his own family connections, but he would make it contribute to the edification of his auditors. One Lord's day morning, with his usual fervor he exhorted his hearers to give up the use of means for the spiritual good of their relatives and friends only with their lives. He told them he had a brother, for whose spiritual welfare he had very long used every possible means. He had warned him, and prayed for him, but all apparently to no purpose, till a few weeks previous; when that brother, to his astonishment and joy, came to his house, and with many tears declared that he had come up from the country to testify to him the great change which divine grace had wrought in his heart, and to acknowledge with gratitude his obligation to the man by whom God had wrought. Mr. Whitefield added, that he had that morning received information, that on his brother's return to Gloucestershire, where he resided, he dropped down dead as he was getting out of a stagecoach. "Let us pray always," said he, "for ourselves, and for those who are dear to us, and never faint."

This habit of making every occurrence bear on his ministry, Mr. Winter, who knew him more intimately, and has told us more of his private life and conduct than any other man, tells us was "perfectly in character with Mr. Whitefield. He turned every thing into gold; he improved every thing for good. Passing occurrences determined the matter of his sermons, and, in some degree, the manner of his address. Thus, if he had read on astronomy in the course of the week, you would be sure to discover it. He knew how to convert the centripetal motion of the planets to the disposition of the Christian towards Christ; and the fatal attraction of the world was very properly represented by a reference to the centrifugal. If he attended any extraordinary trial, he would avail himself of the formality of the judge in pronouncing sentence. It would only be by hearing him, and by beholding his attitude and tears, that a person could well conceive the effect; for it was impossible but that solemnity must surround him who, under God, became the means of making all solemn."

He sometimes made use of an incident of history in the reign of Henry VIII. The apprentices of London appeared before that monarch, pleading his pardon for their insurrections, manifesting intense feeling on the matter, and praying for "mercy, mercy." "Take them away, take them away," was the monarch's request, moved by the sight and the cries of these youths, "I cannot bear it." The application, as will be readily supposed, was, that if an earthly monarch of Henry's character could be so moved, how prevalent must be the plea of the sinner in the ears of infinite Love.

The case of two Scotchmen in the convulsion of the state at the time of Charles II. served him on more than one occasion. These men, having to pass some of the troops, were thinking of their danger, and meditating the best way of escape, when one of them proposed wearing a skullcap; but the other, thinking that would imply distrust of the providence of God, determined to proceed bareheaded. The last was the first laid hold of, and being asked, "Are you for the covenant?" replied, "Yes;" and being further asked, "What covenant?" answered, "The covenant of grace;" by which reply, eluding farther inquiry, he was allowed to pass; but the other, not answering satisfactorily, received a blow from the sabre, which penetrating through the cap, struck him dead. In the application, Mr. Whitefield, warning against vain confidence, exclaimed, "Beware of your skullcaps."

An American clergyman has told us that he once related to Whitefield an affecting occurrence, but did it with the ordinary brevity and feeling of common conversation. Afterwards he heard Mr. Whitefield preach, and tell this same story with such nature, pathos, and power, that the clergyman found himself weeping like a child. It has been well said, that he spoke with the tones of the soul; and that his gestures were impelled by the same spontaneous magical influence which made them, as well as his words, seem part of his soul. Indeed, he threw his soul into every thing he did and said.

It is said that Whitefield would sometimes rise in the sacred desk, and for a minute or two looking in silence around his vast audience, as if salvation or perdition teemed in every cast of his eye, would burst into tears, while the swift contagion, before he uttered a word, had reached every heart that could feel, and dimmed every eye that could weep.[2]

While his path to the sinner's heart was thus met with tears, he was never without strength or aim. He struck everywhere. He swung his glittering weapon, "the sword of the Spirit," in every direction, the same whether he preached in the cushioned and carpeted pulpit to lords, ladies, and gentlemen, or encountered a mob of stage-players and merry-andrews in the open field. He insisted on instant, visible, decisive action in his hearers. All was commotion where he moved. The very earth would seem to be shaken with the thunder of his eloquence; the heavens seemed, in the bold metaphor of Isaiah, to "drop down from above, and the skies to pour down righteousness," when he set the trumpet of the gospel to his lips, and made the notes of salvation or perdition ring in the ears of dying men. Such unwonted sounds startled the multitude into life, rousing energies that were forthwith enlisted either for or against the mighty cause which he advocated, with the boldness and fervor of one who had received immediate commission from heaven. His sacred ambition was content with nothing short of the conquest of thousands.

It has been well said by a living American writer, that "Whitefield was, in sacred eloquence, what Handel was in sacred music. There was an air, a soul, and a *movement* in his oratory, which created indescribable emotion in his vast assemblies, and if Handel, with a thousand auxiliary voices and instruments, astonished the multitude in Westminster Abbey, even to raising them on their feet, by the performance of his Messiah, Whitefield did greater wonders in his single person by *preaching* the Messiah to the immense crowds in Tottenham Court-road and Moorfields."

The same writer has said elsewhere, "The influence of Whitefield and Edwards on theology and pulpit eloquence were immense. There was in those two men indeed 'a diversity of gifts, but the same spirit,' The intellect prevailed in Edwards, the impassioned in Whitefield. Pure truth came forth from the mind of the one as nakedly demonstrated as it ever was on the pages of Newton and Locke; for Edwards, when but a child, read Locke with enthusiasm. From the soul of Whitefield it came forth arrayed in the gorgeous robes of his own many-colored imagination, baptized in the tenderness of his own sympathetic spirit. At times, indeed, the thunders of Sinai seemed to shake the sacred desk, but the softer music of the harp of Zion was more congenial with his compassionate spirit, though he was always bold for God, and braved danger in every form for the salvation of sinners. It is not strange that American preachers venerate, even to enthusiasm, the memory of such a man, and visit his dust, enshrined as it is in the bosom of New England, with feelings of indescribable interest. His labors were for us; his rest is with us; his example is before us. The first were indefatigable; the second is peaceful; the last is glorious."

The Rev. Mr. Winter says, "I hardly ever knew him to go through a sermon without weeping more or less;" and again, "It was only by beholding his attitude and tears, that one could well conceive of the effect." No doubt there was a connection between the tears of Whitefield and his piety; but it must not be supposed that he was always "the weeping prophet;" he could smile as well as weep. A venerable lady in New York, known to some yet living, speaking of the influence which first won her heart to God, said that "Mr. Whitefield was so cheerful that it *tempted her to be a Christian*."

Every thing about this distinguished man excited attention. His voice, accompanied by his look from crossed eyes, and proceeding from a man of his robust frame, produced wonderful effects. It is said that when once preaching in a graveyard, two young men conducted themselves improperly, when he fixed his eyes upon them, and with a voice resembling thunder, said, "Come down, ye rebels." They instantly fell, neither of them being inclined again to come into contact with such a look, or to hear such a voice.

He was once preaching to a vast crowd of people in southern Pennsylvania, which was at that time ignorant and uncivilized. He was incessantly disturbed by their noise, and twice reproved them with great severity. At length he was so overcome by their noisy and irreverent conduct, that he stopped short, dropped his head into his hands, burst into a flood of tears, and exclaimed, "Oh, Lord God, I am ashamed that these people are provoking thy wrath, and I dare not reprove them a third time." Such was the effect of his conduct and feeling, that his audience became perfectly quiet, and remained so till the end of his discourse.

We have before us two narratives of his preaching during very heavy storms. Dr. Campbell, a successor of Whitefield in the *Tabernacle* in London, and whose ministry has been marked by much of the power and success of his great predecessor, has given to the first of these narratives the title of "*Thunder and Eloquence*." Before he commenced his sermon on this occasion, long darkening columns crowded the bright sunny sky of the morning, and swept their dull shadows over the building, in fearful augury of the storm.

His text was, "Strive to enter in at the strait gate; for many, I say unto you, shall seek to enter in, and shall not be able." "See," said he, pointing to a shadow that was flitting across the floor—"see that emblem of human life. It passed for a moment, and concealed the brightness of heaven from our view; but it is gone. And where will ye be, my hearers, when your lives have passed away like that dark cloud? Oh, my dear friends, I see thousands sitting attentively, with their eyes fixed on the poor unworthy preacher. In a few days, we shall all meet at the judgment-seat of Christ. We shall form a part of that vast assembly that will gather before the throne; and every eye will behold the Judge. With a voice whose call you must abide and answer, he will inquire whether on earth you strove to enter in at the strait gate; whether you were supremely devoted to God; whether your hearts were absorbed in him. My blood runs cold when I think how many of you will then seek to enter in, and shall not be able. Oh, what plea can you make before the Judge of the whole earth? Can you say it has been your whole endeavor to mortify the flesh, with its affections and lusts—that your life has been one long effort to do the will of God? No; you must answer, 'I made myself easy in the world by flattering myself that all would end well; but I have deceived my own soul, and am lost.'

"You, O false, and hollow Christian, of what avail will it be that you have done many things—that you have read much in the sacred word—that you have made long prayers—that you have attended religious duties, and that you have appeared holy in the eyes of men? What will all this be, if, instead of loving Him supremely, you have been supposing you should exalt yourself in heaven by acts really polluted and unholy?

"And you, rich men, wherefore do you hoard your silver? Wherefore count the price you have received for Him whom you every day crucify in your love of gain? Why—that when you are too poor to buy a drop of cold water, your beloved son may be rolled to hell in his chariot, pillowed and cushioned around him."

The eye of the preacher gradually lighted up as he proceeded, till towards the close it seemed to sparkle with celestial fire. With his whole energy he exclaimed, "O sinners, by all your hopes of happiness, I beseech you to repent. Let not the wrath of God be awakened. Let not the fires of eternity be kindled against you. See there!" pointing to the lightning, which played on the corner of the pulpit, "it is a glance from the angry eye of Jehovah!" Raising his finger in a listening attitude, as the distant thunder grew louder and louder, and broke in one tremendous crash over the building, he continued, "Hark! It was the voice of the Almighty as he passed by in his anger!" As the sound died away, he covered his face with his hands, and knelt beside his pulpit, apparently lost in inward and intense prayer. The storm passed rapidly away, and the sun, beaming forth in his might, threw across the heavens a magnificent arch of peace. Rising, and pointing to the beautiful object, he exclaimed, "Look upon the rainbow, and praise Him who made it. Very beautiful it is in the brightness thereof. It compasseth the heavens about with glory; and the hands of the Most High have bended it!"

On another occasion, as Mr. Whitefield was preaching in Boston, on the wonders of creation, providence, and redemption, a violent storm of thunder and lightning came on. In the midst of the sermon it attained to so alarming a height that the congregation sat in almost breathless awe. The preacher closed his note-book, and stepping into one of the wings of the desk, fell on his knees, and with much feeling and fine taste repeated:

"Hark, the Eternal rends the sky!
A mighty voice before him goes—
A voice of music to his friends,
But threatening thunder to his foes:
'Come, children, to your Father's arms;
Hide in the chambers of my grace,
Till the fierce storm be overblown,
And my revenging fury cease—'

"Let us devoutly sing to the praise and glory of God this hymn, Old Hundred."

The whole congregation instantly rose, and poured forth the sacred song, in which they were accompanied by the organ, in a style of simple grandeur and heartfelt devotion that was probably never surpassed. By the time the hymn was finished the storm was hushed. The remainder of the services were well adapted to sustain the elevated feeling which had been produced; and the benediction with which the good man dismissed the flock was universally received with streaming eyes, and hearts overflowing with tenderness and gratitude.

Another writer has thus described his appearance in the pulpit. There was nothing in the appearance of this extraordinary man which would lead you to suppose that a Felix would tremble before him. He was something above the middle stature, well proportioned, and remarkable for a native gracefulness of manner. His complexion was very fair, his features regular, and his dark blue eyes small and lively. In recovering from the measles he had contracted a squint with one of them; but this peculiarity rather rendered the expression of his countenance more remarkable, than in any degree lessened the effect of its uncommon sweetness. His voice excelled both in melody and compass; and its fine modulations were happily accompanied by that grace of action which he possessed in an eminent degree, and which has been said to be the chief requisite in an orator. To see him when he first commenced, one would have thought him any thing but enthusiastic and glowing; but as he proceeded, his heart warmed with his subject, and his manner became impetuous and animated; till, forgetful of every thing around him, he seemed to kneel at the throne of Jehovah, and to beseech in agony for his fellow-beings.

After he had finished his prayer, he knelt for a long time in profound silence, and so powerful was the effect on the most heartless of his audience, that a stillness like that of the tomb pervaded the whole house.

Mr. Tracy, in his narrative of "the Great Awakening" about 1740, has admirably remarked, "It is often said that Whitefield cannot have been a very great man, because his printed sermons contain only plain, common thoughts, such as men of ordinary minds habitually use. But what made those thoughts so common? They were not common when he began to utter them. In England especially, and to a considerable extent here also, they astonished his hearers by their strangeness. What is more common than a voyage across the Atlantic? But was Columbus, therefore, only an ordinary man? The case of Copernicus is more nearly parallel. He reasserted a truth which had been uttered, repudiated, and forgotten. That truth is now common, even among school-boys. But was he, therefore, only a child in intellect?"

There are yet extant about eighty of the sermons by which Whitefield agitated nations, and the more remote influence of which is still distinctly to be traced, in the popular divinity and national character of Great Britain and of the United States. Of these compositions, Sir James Stephen, an evangelical Episcopalian of London, wrote at some length in the "Edinburgh Review," 1838, and we shall make no apology for borrowing a portion of his remarks, combining them with some of our own.

It is true, that these sermons have fallen into very general neglect; for to win permanent acceptance for a book, into which the principles of life were not infused by its author, is a miracle which not even the zeal of religious proselytes can accomplish. Yet, inferior as were his inventive to his mimetic powers, Whitefield is entitled, among theological writers, to a place which, if it cannot challenge admiration, may at least excite and reward curiosity. Many, and those by far the worst of his discourses, bear the marks of careful preparation. Take at hazard a sermon of one of the preachers usually distinguished as evangelical, add a little to its length, and subtract a great deal from its point and polish, and you have one of his more elaborate common topics discussed in a commonplace way; a respectable mediocrity of thought and style; endless variations on one or two cardinal truths—in short, the task of a clerical Saturday evening, executed with piety, good sense, and exceeding sedateness. But open one of that series of Whitefield's sermons which bears the stamp of having been conceived and uttered at the same moment, and imagine it recited to myriads of eager listeners with every charm of voice and gesture, and the secret of his unrivalled fascination is at least partially disclosed. He places himself on terms of intimacy and unreserved confidence with you, and makes it almost as difficult to decline the invitation to his familiar talk as if Montaigne himself had issued it. The egotism is amusing, affectionate, and warm-hearted, with just that slight infusion of self-importance without which it would pass for affectation. In his art of rhetoric, personification holds the first place; and the prosopopœia is so managed as to quicken abstractions into life, and to give them individuality and distinctness without the exhibition of any of those spasmodic and distorted images which obey the incantations of vulgar exorcists. Every trace of study and contrivance is obliterated by the hearty earnestness which pervades each successive period, and by the vernacular and homely idioms in which his meaning is conveyed.

It is in the grandeur and singleness of purpose that the charm of Whitefield's preaching seems to have consisted. You feel that you have to do with a man who lived and spoke, and who would gladly have died, to deter his hearers from the path of destruction, and to guide them to holiness and peace. His gossipping stories, and dramatic forms of speech, are never employed to hide the awful realities on which he is intent. Conscience is not permitted to find an intoxicating draught in even spiritual excitement, or an anodyne in glowing imagery. Guilt and its punishment, pardon and spotless purity, death and an eternal existence, stand out in bold relief on every page. From these the eye of the teacher is never withdrawn, and to these the attention of the hearer is riveted. All that is poetic, grotesque, or rapturous is employed to deepen these impressions, and is dismissed as soon as that purpose is answered. Deficient in learning, meagre in thought, and redundant in language as are these discourses, they yet fulfil the one great condition of genuine eloquence. They propagate their own kindly warmth, and leave their stings behind them.

The enumeration of the sources of Whitefield's power is still essentially defective. Neither energy, nor eloquence, nor histrionic talents, nor any artifices of style, nor the most genuine sincerity and self-devotedness, nor all these united, would have enabled him to mould the religious character of millions in his own and future generations. The secret lies deeper. It consisted in the theology he taught—in its perfect simplicity and universal application. "Would ministers," says he, "preach for eternity, they would then act the part of true Christian orators; and not only calmly and coolly inform the understanding, but by pathetic and persuasive address, endeavor to move the affections and to warm the heart. To act otherwise, betrays a sad ignorance of human nature, and such an inexcusable ignorance and indifference in a preacher, as must constrain the hearers to suspect, whether they will or not, that the preacher, let him be whom he will, only deals in the false commerce of unfelt truth." His eighteen thousand sermons were but so many variations on two key-notes: man is guilty, but may obtain forgiveness; he is immortal, and must ripen here for endless weal or woe hereafter. Expanded into innumerable forms, and diversified by infinite varieties of illustration, these two cardinal principles were ever in his heart and on his tongue. Let who would invoke poetry to embellish the Christian system, or philosophy to explore its esoteric depths, from his lips it was delivered as an awful and urgent summons to repent, to believe, and to obey. To set to music the orders issued to seamen in a storm, or to address them in the language of Aristotle or Descartes, would have seemed to him not a whit more preposterous than to divert his hearers from their danger and their refuge, their duties and their hopes, to any topics more trivial or more abstruse. In fine, he was thoroughly and continually in earnest, and therefore possessed that tension of the soul which admitted neither of lassitude nor relaxation, few and familiar as were the topics to which he was confined. His was, therefore, precisely that state of mind in which alone eloquence, properly so called, can be engendered, and a moral and intellectual sovereignty won.

Nor less important is it to remark, though we need not illustrate it at length, that much was effected by every one seeing that he always forgot himself in his subject, and rested only on heaven for success. He felt himself called to serve Christ, and gave himself to his task, to save sinners, and he cared for nothing else. No one ever doubted his sincerity when he prayed, "Help me, Friend of sinners, to be nothing, to say nothing, that thou mayest say and do every thing, and be my all in all." If the same feelings were fully shown by the ministry at present, our messages would tell more on the hearts of our hearers.

We need hardly remind the reader that Whitefield was remarkable for *a devotional spirit*. Probably no man ever lived nearer to God. Had he been less prayerful, he would have been less powerful. It has been said that during a few of the last years of his life he read the voluminous exposition of Matthew Henry, comprising six quarto volumes, in a kneeling posture, pausing and praying that God would engraft upon his mind the instructions of that extraordinary man. When he came before his auditors, he looked like one who had been with God. This it was which won for him the title of *seraphic*—he was a human *seraph*, and burnt out in the blaze of his own fire. Usually for an hour or two before he went into the pulpit, he claimed retirement. In this claim he was imperative, and would not be interrupted in his seasons of hallowed intercourse with God.

Engaged almost incessantly in preaching, or in preparation for it, it was impossible, however much he desired it, to pay many private visits of a religious nature. We are told, however, that on one occasion, when a young minister, afterwards exceedingly popular and useful, was once visiting him, he was sent for to visit a poor woman who had been so dreadfully burnt that she could not survive many hours. He went immediately, and prayed with her. He had no sooner returned, than she called out, "Oh, where is Mr. Whitefield?" Urged by her entreaty, her friends requested him to visit her a second time. He complied, and again prayed with her. The poor afflicted woman continued still to desire his presence. When her friends came for him a third time, "I begged of him," said the young clergyman, "not to go; for he could scarcely expect to do any good. 'Your nerves are too weak, your feelings are too acute to endure such scenes.' I shall never forget his mild reproof: 'Leave me; my Master can save to the uttermost, to the *very uttermost*.'"

In conversation with his friends, Whitefield was as far removed as possible from duplicity and mere compliment. He invited from his friends whatever of instruction and of reproof they considered him to need. And while he was always ready to receive reproof, he was, when called to the duty, ready to give it, and often in a way which his friends did not expect. A censorious professor of religion, knowing the doctrinal differences between the two men, asked Whitefield if he thought they would see Mr. John Wesley in heaven. His answer was truly admirable: "No, sir, I fear not; for he will be so near the throne, and we shall be at such a distance, we shall hardly get sight of him."

It is said, that when he was once travelling in company with a Christian man, they had occasion to stay for a night at a road-side tavern. After they had retired, they were greatly annoyed by a company of gamblers, who were in an adjoining room. Whitefield could not rest, and told his friend that he would go into the room and reprove them for their conduct. The other remonstrated against his doing so, but in vain. He went; and unhappily, his words fell apparently powerless upon them. Returning, he laid down to sleep. "What," asked his companion, "did you gain by your trouble?" Whitefield characteristically answered, "A soft pillow."

In his intercourse with general society, Mr. Whitefield never forgot his dignity as a servant of Jesus Christ. When he was in the zenith of his popularity, Lord Clare, who knew that his influence was considerable, applied to him by letter, requesting his influence at Bristol at the ensuing general election. To this request Mr. Whitefield replied, that in general elections he never interfered; but he would earnestly exhort his lordship to use great diligence to make his own particular "calling and election sure."

Mr. Whitefield was greatly distinguished, even from early life, for neatness in his person, order in his apartments, and regular method in the management of all his affairs. He was accustomed to say that a minister should be "without a spot;" and on one occasion remarked, that he could not feel comfortable if he knew that his *gloves* were out of their proper place. The advantages of such habits are numerous. They save time, give a degree of comfort which can only be known by experience, and add not a little to the dignity of the Christian minister.

The device upon Whitefield's seal, of which probably few impressions are now to be found, was truly characteristic. It was a winged heart soaring above the globe, and its motto was, "*Astra petamus*"—Let us seek heaven.

CHAPTER XVIII
CHARACTER OF WHITEFIELD AS A PREACHER—CENTENNIAL COMMEMORATIONS

In suggesting a few of the characteristics of Whitefield's preaching, we are very greatly indebted to an excellent anonymous writer in the London Evangelical Magazine for 1853. We consider as among the reasons of his success, and as worthy of our imitation,

First, *the prominence given to the leading truths of salvation, and the constant exaltation of Christ in them*. There needs no minute inquiry, or great analytical care, to ascertain what was the pervading theme of this popular minister: it was "Christ, and him crucified," and the glorious truths that hover around the cross, and derive from it their being and lustre. There was no other subject, in Whitefield's estimation, that was worthy of preëminence, and to unfold, elucidate, and apply it, was the great design of his labors. He saw in it such a wonderful adaptation to the necessities and condition of fallen humanity, that he stood in the midst of its wants and woes with all the confidence of a good physician who had a sovereign and sufficient remedy to propose. He knew that there was no case which it could not meet, no moral disease from which it would not recover, no spiritual need which it would not supply; and therefore, however far gone men might be from original righteousness, however hardened in sin, sunk in iniquity, or however elevated by the delusions of a false morality and fancied self-righteousness, he propounded this as the only and all-sufficient antidote, at once to destroy and heal, to kill and to make alive. As to the spurious production of a rationalistic theory on the one hand, or the prescriptions of ceremonial virtue and sacramental grace on the other, he knew them not. He saw at once their hollowness and insufficiency, and would not mock the necessities of our fallen nature, or aggravate the wounds which sin had made by a proposal of them. His acquaintance with the human heart was deep, and his knowledge of the different modifications of the original disease was so great, that he despaired of relief from any expedients save that which infinite Wisdom had devised, and which "the gospel of the grace of God" revealed. Philosophy with all its discoveries, and reason with all its powers, the law with all its authority, and virtue with all its rewards, he knew could only, like the priests and the Levites, have passed the patient by, and left him to despair, till a greater than they should arrive, and say, "I will come and heal you." On that adorable Personage, therefore, and the wonders of his skill and love, he delighted to dwell. Every sermon was full of Christ; every discourse was odorous of him. From whatever part of revealed truth he derived his text, and with whatever peculiar development of man's moral physiology he had to do, there was something to suggest, to demonstrate the need, or the suitableness, or the all-sufficiency of the Saviour of the world. To set him forth, in the glories of his wonderful person, the variety of his offices, the perfection of his righteousness, the completeness of his atonement, and the plenitude of his grace, was his perpetual aim. To these he gave continual prominence, at all times, and in every place. There was no reserve, no equivocation, no partial statement on such themes. It was a full, clear, consistent gospel. From his lips the gospel gave no "uncertain sound." This made him a welcome messenger of glad tidings to all. This gave him a key to the hearts of many, who, as they stood around him, and wondered at him, like those five thousand whom the Redeemer fed with "five loaves and two small fishes," found all their appetites suited, and all their necessities supplied. It was the magic power which arrested them; the centre of gravitation which attracted them; the bread of life which fed them. "As Moses lifted up the serpent in the wilderness," so now was the Son of man lifted up by the ministry of this his devoted herald; and far as the camp extended, and wide as the circumference of poison and death was spread, the wounded looked thereon and lived. A restorative virtue issued from it. The hardest heart was softened. The most obstinate in rebellion was overcome. The blindest saw. The moral lepers were cleansed. The broken in heart were made whole, and the spiritually dead were raised to life. "This was the Lord's doing, and it was marvellous in their eyes." They beheld the man. They heard him preach. They felt the power. It was because He was exalted among them who had said, "I, if I be lifted up from the earth, will draw all men unto me."

Secondly, *the glow of feeling, the melting compassion, which pervaded his own soul*. Oh, it is supremely delightful and deeply affecting to observe the tender affection and melting pathos with which Whitefield propounded and proclaimed the precious truths and everlasting verities of the gospel to his fellow-men. He stood among them as one of their race, one of their number, conscious of the common misery into which all had fallen, and weeping over the miseries and ruin in which by nature they were alike involved. As he opened up the treasures of infinite mercy, and the riches of redeeming love to their view, he wept to think how long they had been unknown or despised by many, and with what base ingratitude thousands would probably still turn away from them. As one who saw their immortal being in jeopardy, and their souls standing on the verge of irretrievable ruin, he hastened, with joy in his countenance and tenderness in his heart, to tell them of One who was "mighty to save," and that "now was the accepted time, and now the day of salvation." Not as one who had a cold lecture on ethics to deliver, or a dissertation on philosophy to expound, or a problem in mathematics to solve, did he proceed to such a work; but as one who felt the weight of his great commission, and knew the worth of never-dying souls. The evil of sin, the danger of impenitence, the powers of the world to come, the glories of heaven, and the unutterable miseries of the regions of woe, were visibly present to his own mind; and of these, "out of the abundance of his heart," he spoke to others. He could not be calm, he could not be apathetic on such themes as these.

"Passion was reason, transport temper, here."

And with much of the melting tenderness of Him who wept over Jerusalem, he spoke of these things to all that resorted to him. What moving words did he utter on Blackheath hill, in the Tabernacle pulpit, and on Kingswood mount! His vivid eye beamed with the glow of tenderness, and his tears, as he spoke, oft-times moistened his little Bible or bedewed the ground. In his printed sermons, which doubtless are but feeble specimens of his free and fervent manner, there are strains of tender pathos and impassioned oratory, which it is almost impossible to read even now without being moved to share in his feelings and in the emotions which they must have enkindled around; and in the perusal of which we wonder not that, in all the circumstances, the place in which he stood was a Bochim—a place of weeping. Oh, the melting power, the exquisite pathos, the tender expostulation of this preëminent man, and unrivalled preacher of the gospel of our salvation! We wish we could catch them now—that all preachers possessed them; that the rising ministry especially would emulate him in these things. Whitefield showed his intense feeling, not from the mere power of ratiocination, or from the poetic memento, or for the sake of producing effect by the tears that were unfelt, or which only flowed from the surface; but from the meltings of a tender heart, influenced by a Saviour's love, and overflowing with the commiseration of a benign compassion for dying multitudes around. Doddridge's beautiful hymn,

"Arise, my tenderest thoughts, arise,"

one might almost think was written at Whitefield's side. The tenderness of John, and the "weeping" of Paul, were blended in him with the boldness of Peter. The love that agonized in the garden of Gethsemane, and bled on the cross of Calvary, was largely diffused through all his powers.

Thirdly, *the direct address of his ministry*. The characteristic mode of his preaching, and the style of his public ministrations, was, to direct his appeal to the hearts and consciences of his hearers, and to "preach *to* the people all the words of this life." It was not an harangue *before* them. It was not an oration beautifully prepared, read, or delivered in their hearing, and presented simply for their acceptance and admiration; but a direct address, an affectionate appeal, a solemn and earnest communication of the message he had received from God to them. Oh, we have sometimes thought, what a marked difference there ought to be between the ministrations of a servant of Christ to his fellow-immortals, on things of eternal importance in which they are personally and deeply concerned, and the delivery of a lecture from the philosopher's desk, or even of a dissertation on theology from the professorial chair. So thought the apostles. So thought the prophets and public teachers of sacred mysteries of old. They had the "burden of the Lord" to deliver, and it was *unto* the people. They had an embassy to execute, and it was by negotiating directly with, and in the consciences of their hearers. Whitefield caught their spirit, proceeded in their way, and did such mighty execution, not by the mere symmetrical illustration of divine truth, but by the direct presentation of it to their minds. They had not to ask, "For whom is all this intended?" and, "Is it designed for us?" They felt that it was. It came home to their consciences, and to their very hearts. They could not transfer it to others, nor avoid the application of it to themselves. Had the preacher called them by name, which in his skilful delineation of character, he sometimes virtually did, they could not have been more certain that he intended it for them, and that it was at their peril to neglect or pass it by. "I have a message from God unto thee," he substantially said in every discourse he uttered, and the people were compelled to believe it. "Go, and tell this people," said the divine voice to Isaiah, "Ye hear indeed, but do not understand; ye see indeed, but do not perceive." "Therefore," said Peter, "let all the house of Israel know assuredly that God hath made that same Jesus, *whom ye have crucified*, both Lord and Christ." "Now then," said Paul, "we are ambassadors for Christ; as though God did beseech *you* by us, we pray *you*, in Christ's stead, *be ye* reconciled to God." Such was the tenor of the apostolic ministry. Such the secret of its mighty power and success. And such also was the characteristic of the faithful and seraphic Whitefield, by which he knocked at the door of many hearts, and those hearts were opened to him, to his message, and to his Lord. His plan was that of heavenly wisdom; his appeal was the same. "Unto you, O men, I call, and my voice is to the sons of men." In him were verified the poet's graphic lines:

"There stands the messenger of truth; there stands
The legate of the skies: his theme divine,
His office sacred, his credentials clear.
By him the violated law speaks out
Its thunders; and by him, in strains as sweet
As angels use, the gospel whispers peace.
He stablishes the strong, restores the weak,
Reclaims the wanderer, binds the broken heart,
And sues the sinner to return to God."

Fourthly, *his habitual dependence on the Spirit of God, and his earnest aspirations for the manifestation of his power*. That he was conscious of his own superior talents as an orator, and knew how to employ them on sacred themes; that he skilfully wielded all the weapons of a well-studied eloquence to gain access to the human mind, and knew both how to alarm and how to persuade, and could attempt both with as much success probably as any speaker, either of ancient or modern times; that he had a large and minute acquaintance with the powers and passions of the human soul, and knew well when and how to touch the hidden springs of its energies and actions; that he had a good amount of common and sacred learning at his command, and like that Apollos whom among the early teachers of Christianity he most resembled, was "mighty in the Scriptures;" and that he delighted to expatiate on the wonders and glories of redemption as a restorative scheme preëminently adapted to interest and attract, to impress and rule our common nature—are facts open to all who inspect his writings and accompany him in his labors, and will be denied by none. But with all these, and amid all, in every sermon he composed and delivered, and in his most impassioned addresses to his hearers, there is manifested an underlying and all-pervading dependence on the power and grace of the Spirit of God, which was in character, if not in degree, meek, humble, genuine, entire, like that of the most eminent apostle or adoring saint at the foot of the divine throne. With him it was not merely a sentiment, but a feeling; and that feeling constant and habitual, as it was in him who in the review of his labors said, "I have planted, Apollos watered, but God gave the increase." He knew that none but the almighty Spirit could gain effectual access to the spirit of man; and that not even a Melancthon, a Luther, or a Whitefield, could make old Adam yield, unless constrained by a superior power. He seemed to stand in the valley of vision among the dry bones, as the prophet did, and while he addressed them with something like a prophet's power, he had no expectation or hope of success until the wind of heaven came down and blew upon them. Therefore he prophesied to it as well as to them. "Come from the four winds, O breath, and breathe upon the slain, that they may live," was often the mighty cry of his soul, before preaching, while preaching, and after preaching. It seemed to be his joy, his only, his all-sustaining confidence, that he lived under "the dispensation of the Spirit," and wrought in a day, and preached upon a theme, in connection with which "the ministration of the Spirit" was to be "glorious," by his wonderful works of conviction, conversion, and sanctification, among the children of men. To that Spirit, as the glorifier of Christ, he often devoutly and earnestly appealed. Sometimes, in the midst of an unusual flow of tender and eloquent address to his hearers on his favorite theme of the glories and grace of his divine Master, he would pause in solemn silence, and lifting up his hands and his voice to heaven, and carrying the hearts of his audience with him, invoke aloud the descending and all-consuming fire. The present God was acknowledged and felt. The word came "in demonstration of the Spirit and of power." And while the habitual aim of his preaching was to exalt "Christ Jesus the Lord," and while he reasoned, and opened the Scriptures, and taught and alarmed or invited his hearers, in the most touching strains of urgent remonstrance and tender entreaty, to accept now "the great salvation," the inward state of his soul was that of entire reliance on the presence and coöperation of the Holy Spirit of God. To him were sent up his most intense aspirations. In all the records of his success, to that Spirit the honor is always ascribed. "Not I, but the grace of God which was with me," is the grateful acknowledgment he makes in the review of every field occupied and every triumph won. And thus it was that the fabric of his ministry, and of all his ministrations, in the multitudinous labors which he directed against the kingdom of darkness and of Satan in his day, was like the mystic vision which Ezekiel saw, *instinct with life*. The spirit of the living creatures was in the wheels. "When this went, those went; when this stood, those stood; when this was lifted up from the earth, those were lifted up." It was all life. A living preacher; a living theme; a living power, giving life, and spreading it all around. Therefore it was that life followed in the region of death, and at his coming the desert rejoiced, and the wilderness blossomed as the rose.

> "Dry bones were raised, and clothed afresh,
> And hearts of stone were turned to flesh."

By preaching such as we have now attempted to describe, thousands and tens of thousands were gathered to Christ. "An exceeding great army" stood up. Slumbering churches were awakened, religion was revived, and "righteousness and praise" were caused to "spring forth before all the nations." And as this apostolic man surveyed the amazing scene, and glanced at the wide circumference of his labors, in the British Isles and in the New World, he might have exclaimed, as one before him had done,

"Now thanks be unto God, who always causeth us to triumph in Christ, and maketh manifest the savor of his name by us in every place." "Through mighty signs and wonders, *by the power of the Spirit of God,* from Jerusalem round about to Illyricum, I have fully preached the gospel of Christ." "For I am not ashamed of the gospel of Christ: for it is the power of God to salvation; to the Jew first, and also to the Greek." Who, in the remembrance of Whitefield and his times, will not long for their return, and exclaim, "Awake, awake; put on strength, O arm of the Lord; awake, as in the ancient days." "O that thou wouldest rend the heavens, that thou wouldest come down, that the mountains might flow down at thy presence, as when the melting fire burneth, the fire causeth the waters to boil, to make thy name known to thine adversaries, that the nations may tremble at thy presence!" Spirit of the living God, descend and replenish with thy power all our souls, our ministry, our temples, our land.

In estimating the character of Whitefield, it should be observed that *he dealt with his hearers, individually and collectively, as immortal beings.* To use the language of Isaac Taylor, "he held MAN as if in the abstract, or as if whatever is not common to all men were forgotten. The most extreme diversities, intellectual and moral, differences of rank, culture, national modes of thought, all gave way and ceased to be thought of; distinctions were swept from the ground where he took his position. At the first opening of his lips, and as the rich harmony of his voice spread its undulations over the expanse of human faces, and at the instant when the sparkle of his bright eye caught every other eye, human nature, in a manner, dropped its individuality, and presented itself in its very elements to be moulded anew. Whitefield, although singularly gifted with a perception of the varieties of character, yet spoke as if he could know nothing of the thousands before him but their immortality and their misery; and so it was that these thousands listened to him.

"No preacher whose history is on record, has trod so wide a field as did Whitefield, or has retrod it so often, or has repeated himself so much, or has carried so far the experiment of exhausting himself, and of spending his popularity, if it could have been spent, but it never was spent. Within the compass of a few weeks he might have been heard addressing the negroes of the Bermuda islands, adapting himself to their infantile understandings, and to their debauched hearts; and then at Chelsea, with the aristocracy of rank and wit before him, approving himself to listeners such as the lords Bolingbroke and Chesterfield. Whitefield might as easily have produced a Hamlet or a Paradise Lost, as have excogitated a sermon which, as a composition, a product of thought, would have tempted men like these to hear him a second time; and as to his faculty and graces as a speaker, his elocution and action, a second performance would have contented them. But in fact Bolingbroke, and many of his class, thought not the hour long, time after time, while, with much sameness of *material* and of language, he spoke of eternity and of salvation in Christ.... Floods of tears moistened cheeks rough and smooth; and sighs, suppressed or loudly uttered, gave evidence that human nature is one and the same when it comes in presence of truths which bear upon the guilty and the immortal without distinction."

The Rev. Dr. James Hamilton of London has admirably delineated Whitefield, in a passage which must be admired by all who read it: "Whitefield was the prince of English preachers. Many have surpassed him as sermon-makers, but none have approached him as a pulpit orator. Many have outshone him in the clearness of their logic, the grandeur of their conceptions, and the sparkling beauty of single sentences; but in the power of darting the gospel direct into the conscience, he eclipsed them all. With a full and beaming countenance, and the frank and easy port which the English people love—for it is the symbol of honest purpose and friendly assurance—he combined a voice of rich compass, which could easily thrill over Moorfields in musical thunder, or whisper its terrible secret in every private ear; and to this gainly aspect and tuneful voice he added a most expressive and eloquent action. Improved by conscientious practice, and instinct with his earnest nature, this elocution was the acted sermon, and by its pantomimic portrait enabled the eye to anticipate each rapid utterance, and helped the memory to treasure up the palatable ideas. None ever used so boldly, nor with more success, the highest styles of impersonation: as when he described to his sailor-auditors a storm at sea, and compelled them to shout, 'Take to the longboat, sir!' His 'hark, hark!' could conjure up Gethsemane with its faltering moon, and awake again the cry of horror-stricken innocence; and an apostrophe to Peter on the holy mount would light up another Tabor, and drown it in glory from the opening heaven. His thoughts were possessions, and his feelings were transformations; and he spoke because he felt, his hearers understood because they saw. They were not only enthusiastic amateurs, like Garrick, who ran to weep and tremble at his bursts of passion, but even the colder critics of the Walpole school were surprised into momentary sympathy and reluctant wonder. Lord Chesterfield was listening in Lady Huntingdon's pew when Whitefield was comparing the benighted sinner to a blind beggar on a dangerous road. His little dog gets away from him when skirting the edge of a precipice, and he is left to explore the path with his iron-shod staff. On the very verge of the cliff this blind guide slips through his fingers and skims away down the abyss. All unconscious, the owner stoops down to regain it, and stumbling forward—'Good God, he is gone!' shouted Chesterfield, who had been watching with breathless alarm the blind man's movements, and who jumped from his feet to save the catastrophe.

"But the glory of Whitefield's preaching was his heart-kindled and heart-melting gospel. But for this, all his bold strokes and brilliant surprises might have been no better than the rhetorical triumphs of Kirwan and other pulpit dramatists. He was an orator, but he only sought to be an evangelist. Like a volcano where gold and gems may be darted forth as well as common things, but where gold and molten granite flow all alike in fiery fusion, bright thoughts and splendid images might be projected from his pulpit, but all were merged in the stream which bore along the gospel and himself in blended fervor. Indeed, so simple was his nature, that glory to God and good will to man had filled it; there was room for little more. Having no church to found, no family to enrich, and no memory to immortalize, he was simply the ambassador of God; and inspired with its genial piteous spirit—so full of heaven reconciled and humanity restored—he soon himself became a living gospel. Radiant with its benignity, and trembling with its tenderness, by a sort of spiritual induction a vast audience would speedily be brought into a frame of mind—the transfusing of his own; and the white furrows on their sooty faces told that Kingswood colliers were weeping, or the quivering of an ostrich plume bespoke its elegant wearer's deep emotion. And coming to his pulpit direct from communion with his Master, and in the strength of accepted prayer, there was an elevation in his mien which often paralyzed hostility, and a self-possession which made him amid uproar and confusion the more sublime. With an electric bolt he would bring the jester in his fool's cap from his perch on the tree, or galvanize the brickbat from the skulking miscreant's grasp, or sweep down in crouching submission and shamefaced silence the whole of Bartholomew fair; while a revealing flash of sententious doctrine, of vivified Scripture, would disclose to awe-struck hundreds the forgotten verities of another world, or the unsuspected arcana of their inner man. 'I came to break your head, but, through you, God has broken my heart,' was a sort of confession with which he was familiar; and to see the deaf old gentlewoman who used to mutter imprecations at him as he passed along the streets, clambering up the pulpit stairs to catch his angelic words, was a sort of spectacle which the triumphant gospel often witnessed in his day. And when it is known that his voice could be heard by twenty thousand, and that ranging all the empire, as well as America, he would often preach thrice on a working-day, and that he has received in one week as many as a thousand letters from persons awakened by his sermons, if no estimate can be formed of the results of his ministry, some idea may be suggested of its vast extent and singular effectiveness."

Very admirably has a writer in the North British Review compared and contrasted Whitefield and Wesley. He says, "Few characters could be more completely the converse, and in the church's exigencies, more happily the supplement of one another, than were those of George Whitefield and John Wesley; and had their views been identical, and their labors all along coincident, their large services to the gospel might have repeated Paul and Barnabas. Whitefield was soul, and Wesley was system. Whitefield was a summer cloud which burst at morning or noon a fragrant exhalation over an ample track, and took the rest of the day to gather again; Wesley was the polished conduit in the midst of the garden, through which the living water glided in pearly brightness and perennial music, the same vivid stream from day to day. After a preaching paroxysm, Whitefield lay panting on his couch, spent, breathless, and deathlike; after his morning sermon in the foundry, Wesley would mount his pony, and trot and chat, and gather simples, till he reached some country hamlet, where he would bait his charger, and talk through a little sermon with the villagers, and remount his pony and trot away again. In his aërial poise, Whitefield's eagle eye drank lustre from the source of light, and loved to look down on men in assembled myriads; Wesley's falcon glance did not sweep so far, but it searched more keenly and marked more minutely where it pierced. A master of assemblies, Whitefield was no match for the isolated man. Seldom coping with the multitude, but strong in astute sagacity and personal ascendency, Wesley could conquer any number one by one. All force and impetus, Whitefield was the powder-blast in the quarry, and by one explosive sermon would shake a district, and detach materials for other men's long work—deft, neat, and painstaking, Wesley loved to split and trim each fragment into uniform plinths and polished stones. Or, taken otherwise, Whitefield was the bargeman or the wagoner who brought the timber of the house, and Wesley was the architect who set it up. Whitefield had no patience for ecclesiastical polity, no aptitude for pastoral details—with a beaver-like propensity for building, Wesley was always constructing societies, and with a king-like craft of ruling, was most at home when presiding over a class or a conference. It was their infelicity that they did not always work together—it was the happiness of the age, and the furtherance of the gospel, that they lived alongside of one another."

CENTENNIAL COMMEMORATIONS.

When a century had elapsed from the commencement of Whitefield's public labors, it was deemed desirable by many in England to hold public services of a devotional and practical character, in celebration of the event. Especially was it designed that such celebrations should have a reference, as far as possible, to advance open-air preaching. The first services of this character were very properly held in the Tabernacle, London, on May 21, 1839, and well do we remember with what intense interest, in common with thousands, we attended them. Ministers and laymen of at least four religious denominations assisted in them, and eloquently discoursed on subjects illustrating the grace of God in connection with Whitefield, but still more intent were they on benefiting the present and future generations of men. Dr. Campbell delivered a sermon on the character and labors of Apollos, illustrated by those of Whitefield; the late Dr. Cox discoursed on the genius and labors of Whitefield; the late Rev. John Blackburn described the past and present state of religion in England; and the Rev. John Young, LL. D., urged the propriety, duty, and necessity of open-air preaching. In addition to these sermons, several admirable speeches were made, and every thing was marked by a spirit of earnest devotion. A small volume, containing the sermons and speeches, was printed, and put into extensive circulation.

About the same time, a number of ministers of the Congregational order met in a central town of Gloucestershire, when one of them suggested, that "as the present year was the centenary of the Rev. George Whitefield's labors in reviving the apostolic practice of open-air preaching, it might be desirable to commemorate them by a special religious open-air celebration. It was further remarked, that Whitefield was a native of Gloucester; that as many ministers present presided over churches instituted by his ministry; that as Stinchcombe hill, in the very centre of the county, presented a most beautiful and eligible spot for a public meeting; and as upon its summit, a century ago, Whitefield himself had preached and showed the glad tidings of the kingdom of God, it seemed a duty to improve the opportunity it offered of addressing, on the gracious persuasives of the cross, a large concourse of persons, many of whom might never hear the gospel, and of promoting in the county the revival of evangelical religion, which God so highly honored his devoted servant in commencing in our land."

The suggestion was most cordially received, arrangements were made, and, July 30, 1839, though the weather was unfavorable, the meeting was attended by at least seven thousand persons. A large preaching stand was erected for the ministers, nearly one hundred of whom were present. Sermons were preached by the Rev. Drs. Matheson and Ross, and by the Rev. Messrs. T. East, J. H. Hinton, and J. Sibree; and addresses were given, and the devotional exercises led by many others. The services were solemnly impressive. The late Josiah Conder, Esq., wrote two hymns especially for the occasion, which are well worthy of preservation; we therefore transfer them to our pages.

I

How sweet from crowded throngs,
Zion, ascend thy songs,
With choral swells through echoing aisles!
Where brethren, brethren meet,
These songs rise doubly sweet,
From humbler rooms or loftier piles.

But here, not made with hands,
A nobler temple stands;
Here, 'mid thy works, O God, we bow,
Where all around, above,
Proclaims thy power and love;
Oh, tune our hearts to praise thee now.

We bless thy gracious care,
For many a house of prayer,
Where saints may meet with conscience free,
To keep thy simple rites,
In which thy church delights,
And unforbidden, wait on thee.

But now, beneath the sky,
We raise our songs on high,
To Him who gave all nature birth;
While the free air wafts round
To distant vales the sound—
Praise to the Lord of heaven and earth.

So to the mountain air
The Saviour breathed his prayer;
So 'mid green hills or deserts rude,
The poor he meekly taught,
And gracious wonders wrought,
Or fed the famished multitude.

So did apostles teach;
So did our Whitefield preach;
These hills have heard his fervent prayer:
Oh, let the saving word
Throughout our land be heard,
Free as the light, and open as the air.

II

Where is the voice of Whitefield now?
Where does his mantle rest?
Oh, for Elisha's from the plough,
With kindred zeal possessed!
Apostles of heroic mould,
With love seraphic fired,
Divinely called, like those of old
At Pentecost inspired!

Oh Thou, our Head, enthroned on high,
By whom thy members live,
Wilt thou not hear our fervent cry,
The holy unction give?
In all the plenitude of grace
Thy gifts of might bestow;
And by us, Lord, in every place,
Thy saving virtue show.

This Christian land with error teems,
The blind by blinder led;
The sophist weaves his Atheist schemes;
Wide has the poison spread.
Arise, O Lord, send forth thy word;
Thy faithful heralds call;
And while the gospel trump is heard,
Let Satan's bulwarks fall.

Free, pure, and vital as the light,
God's message to our race;
Like genial gales the Spirit's might,
Sovereign, mysterious grace.
Breathe forth, O wind, and to new birth
Quicken the bones of death;
Regenerate this withered earth;
Give to the dying breath.

It is pleasant to add to this account, that satisfactory evidences were given that some, during these services, were brought to the saving knowledge of "the truth as in Jesus." And it may be mentioned as a singular circumstance, that an old man one hundred and three years of age attended on this occasion, who had been carried in his mother's arms to this same spot to hear Whitefield preach just a century before.

The last centenary service to which we shall make reference, is the one held at the *Bristol* Tabernacle, November 25, 1853. The sermon on *The Character of Whitefield*, by the Rev. John Angell James, was from the text, "This one thing I do." Phil. 3:13. In it he said:

"We hear much in our days about the adaptation of the gospel to the age. There is no word I more hate or love, dread or desire, according to the sense in, or the purpose for which it is used, than this word *adaptation* as applied to preaching. Now, if by adaptation be meant, more philosophy, and less Christianity; more of cold abstract intellectualism, and less of popular, simple, earnest statement of gospel truth; more profound discussion and artificial elaboration addressed to the learned few, and less of warm-hearted appeal to the multitude, may God preserve us from such adaptation, for it is high-treason against truth and the salvation of souls. But if by this be meant a stronger intelligence, a chaster composition, a sterner logic, a more powerful rhetoric, a more correct criticism, and a more varied illustration, but all employed to set forth the gospel as comprehending those two great words, *redemption and regeneration*, let us have it; we need it; and come in ever such abundance, it will be a blessing.

"Adaptation! the gospel is adaptation, from beginning to end, to every age of time, and to all conditions of humanity. It is God's own adaptation. It is he who knows every ward of the lock of man's nature, who has constructed this admirable key; and all the miserable tinkering of a vain and deceitful philosophy can make no better key, nor can all the attempts of a philosophizing theology make this key better fit the wards of the lock.

"Adaptation! was not the gospel in all its purity and simplicity adapted to human nature as it existed in commercial, scholastic, philosophical Corinth? And did not Paul think so when he determined to know nothing there, but 'Christ, and him crucified?' Was it not by this very gospel, which many are "beginning to imagine is not suited to an intellectual and philosophical age, that Christianity fought its first battles, and achieved its victories over the hosts of darkness? Against the axe, the stake, the sword of the gladiator, and the lions of the amphitheatre; against the ridicule of wits, the reasoning of sages, the interests, influence, and craft of the priesthood; against the prowess of armies, and the brute passions of the mob, Christianity, strong in its weakness, sublime in its simplicity, potent in its isolation, asking and receiving no protection from the sceptre of the monarch or the sword of the warrior, went forth to do battle with the wisdom of Greece and the mythology of Rome. Everywhere it prevailed, and gathered its laurels from the snows of Scythia, the sands of Africa, the plains of India, and the green fields of Europe. With the gospel alone she overturned the altars of impiety in her march. Power felt his arm wither at her glance. She silenced the lying oracles by the majesty of her voice, and extinguished the deceptive light of philosophy in the schools, till at length she who went forth forlorn and weeping from Calvary to the tomb of Joseph of Arimathea, ascended, upon the ruins of the temples, the idols, and the altars she had demolished, to the throne of the Cæsars, and with the diadem on her brow, and the purple on her shoulders, gave laws to the world from that very tribunal where she had been dragged as a criminal and condemned as a malefactor.[3]

"Adaptation! is not justification by faith the very substance of the gospel, and was it not by this doctrine that Luther effected the enfranchisement of the human intellect, from the chains of slavery which had been forged in the Vatican; achieved the liberation of half Europe from the yoke of Rome, and gave an impulse to human thought and vital Christianity which has not yet spent itself, and never will, till it issues in the jubilee of the nations and the glories of the millennium?

"Adaptation! did not Whitefield move this kingdom almost to its centre, and equally so our then great transatlantic colony to its extremities, fascinating alike the colliers of Kingswood and the citizens of the metropolis; and by this mighty theme enable myriads to burst the chains of sin and Satan, and to walk abroad disenthralled by the mighty power of redeeming grace?

"Adaptation! is not this gospel now proving its power in heathen countries to raise the savage into civilized man, the civilized man into the saint, and in this ascending scale of progression, the saint into the seraph?

"And yet, with these proofs of the power of the gospel to adapt itself to every age of the world, and to every condition of humanity, there are those who want something else to effect the regeneration of mankind. 'And I, if I be lifted up, will draw all men unto me.' So said the Saviour of men. The cross is the great moral magnet for all ages and all countries, to draw men from barbarism to civilization, from sin to holiness, from misery to happiness, and from earth to heaven; and it were as rational to say the loadstone had lost its original power of polar attraction, and the mariner's compass is an old, stale invention, and must now be replaced with some new device, better adapted to the modern light of science, as to suppose that the doctrine of the cross had become effete, and must give way to some new phase of theological truth.

"I now consider the *manner* in which Whitefield carried out his own purpose into action. '*One thing I do*:' and *how* did he accomplish it?

"Never was the joyful sound sent over the world by a more magnificent *voice*. All his biographers labor, as do the historians of Greece in describing the power of Demosthenes, to make us understand his wondrous oratory.

Perhaps, after all, that which gives us the most vivid idea of it is, not the *crowds* it attracted, moved, and melted, but that it warmed the cold and calculating Franklin, and fascinated the philosophical and sceptical Hume. Heaven rarely ever gave, or gives to man the faculty of speech in such perfection. But what is particularly worthy of notice is, that he trusted not to its native power, but increased that power by assiduous cultivation. His matchless elocution was not only an endowment, but an acquirement. If he preached a sermon twenty times, he went on to the last improving his method of delivering it, both as to tones and action; not for theatrical display—no man was ever more free from this—but to carry out his 'one thing'—*the salvation of souls*. He knew, and deeply and philosophically entered into the meaning of that text, 'Faith cometh by hearing;' and he also knew that attentive hearing comes by the power of speaking. With such a theme as the gospel, with such an object as salvation, with such an aim as eternity, and such a Master to serve as Christ, he would not give utterance to such subjects, and for such purposes, in careless and slovenly speech. He studied to be the orator, that he might thus pluck souls as brands from the burning. In this let us imitate him. Of all our faculties, that of speech is perhaps least cultivated, yet is most susceptible of cultivation, and pays best for the pains bestowed upon it. My brethren, speech is the great instrument of our ministerial labor. Our assault upon the rebel town of Mansoul is to be carried on, and our entrance to be effected, to use the language of Bunyan, at ear-gate. The tongue, rather than the pen, is the weapon of most of us. For the love of souls, let us endeavor to be good speakers. With the loftiest themes in the universe for our subjects, do, do let us endeavor to speak of them in some measure worthily. It is an instructive and astounding, and to us humiliating and disgraceful fact, that the stage-player, whether in comedy or in tragedy, takes ten times more pains to give effective utterance to his follies, vices, and passions, for the amusement of his audience, than we do to eternal and momentous truths for the salvation of ours. The stage seems the only arena where the power of oratory is much studied. Should this be?

"A few characteristics of Whitefield's manner deserve emphatic mention and particular attention, as connected with the execution of his one great purpose. The first I notice is *solemnity*. He never, as did some of his followers, degraded the pulpit by making it the arena of low humor and wit; abounding in anecdote, and even in action, he was uniformly solemn. His deep devotional spirit contributed largely to this, for his piety was the inward fire which supplied the ardor of his manner. He was eminently a man of prayer; and had he been less prayerful, he would also have been less powerful. He came into the pulpit from the closet, where he had been communing with God, and could no more trifle with merry humor at such a time than could Moses when he came down from the mount to the people; or than the high-priest when he came out from the blazing symbols of the divine presence between the cherubim in the holy of holies; or Isaiah when he saw the Lord of hosts, high and lifted up, with his train filling the temple. Happily the age and taste for pulpit buffoonery is gone, I hope never to return.

''Tis pitiful to count a gain when you should woo a soul.'

It was the stamp and impress of eternity upon his preaching, that gave Whitefield such power. He spoke like a man that stood upon the borders of the unseen world, alternately rapt in ecstasy as he gazed upon the felicities of heaven, and convulsed with terror as he seemed to hear the howlings of the damned, and saw the smoke of their torment ascending from the pit for ever and ever. His maxim was to preach, as Apelles painted, for eternity, and he said, if ministers preached for eternity, they would then act the part of true Christian orators. And tell me, my brethren, what are all the prettinesses, the beauties, or even sublimities of human eloquence—what the similes, metaphors, and other garniture of rhetoric—what the philosophy and intellectualities which many in this day are aiming at, to move and bow and conquer the human soul, compared with 'the powers of the world to come?'

"But there was another characteristic of Whitefield's manner, and that was its *tenderness*. Our Lord, as to his humanity, was a man of sorrows, and therefore of tears; so was Paul, so was Whitefield. Perhaps the latter somewhat too much so, at any rate far too much so for any preacher but himself, and with him the fountain of his tears was somewhat too full and flowing. But Oh, what an apology for this, and what a stroke of pathetic eloquence was that appeal when on one occasion he said, 'You blame me for weeping, but how can I help it, when you will not weep for yourselves, although your immortal souls are on the verge of destruction, and for aught I know you are hearing your last sermon, and may never more have an opportunity to have Christ offered to you.' Man is an emotional as well as an intellectual creature, and sympathy is one of the powers of our physical and mental economy. The passions are of an infectious nature, and men feel more in a crowd than in solitude. The adage of the ancient elocutionist is still true, 'If you wish me to weep, weep yourself.' Whitefield's tears drew forth those of his audience, and his pathos softened their hearts for the impressions of the truth. It is forgotten by many preachers that they may do much by the heart, as well as by the head. We are not the teachers of logic, mathematics, metaphysics, or natural philosophy, which have nothing to do with the heart, but of religion, the very seat of which is there; and *we* address ourselves not only to the logical, but to the æsthetical part of man's complex nature. By argument, I know we must convince, but we must not stop in the judgment, but go on to reach the heart, and we ourselves must feel as well as reason. *Clear, but cold,* is too descriptive of much modern preaching. It is the frosty moonlight of a winter's night, not the warm sunshine of a summer's day. A cold preacher is likely to have cold hearers. Cold! What, when the love of God, the death of Christ, the salvation of souls, the felicities of heaven, and the torments of hell are the theme? Enthusiasm here is venial, compared with lukewarmness.

"Need I say that *earnestness* was characteristic of Whitefield's preaching? Yes, that one word, perhaps, more than any other in our language, is its epitome. An intense earnestness marked its whole career, and was carried to such a pitch as to subject him, as did that of Paul, to the imputation of madness. The salvation of souls was so entirely the one thing that engrossed his soul, his time, his labors, that not a step deviated from it. Every moment, every day, was an approximation to it. His devotions, his recreations, if any such he had, his journeys, his voyages, his sermons, his correspondence, were all referred to this one end. His exertions never relaxed for a moment, and he, with his great compeer Wesley, made the trial so seldom made, what is the utmost effect which, in the way of saving souls, may be granted to any one preacher of the gospel in any age or country.

"What may not be done, and is not done by earnestness? It gives *some* success to any error, however absurd or enormous, and to any scheme of wickedness, however flagrant and atrocious. What is it that has given such success to popery, to infidelity, to Mormonism? *Earnestness.* And shall the apostles and advocates of error be more in earnest than the friends of truth? Whitefield often quoted Betterton the player, who affirmed that the stage would soon be deserted if the actors spoke like the preachers. And what *would* empty the play-house, that is, dulness and coldness, *does* often empty the meeting-house. 'Mr. Betterton's answer to a worthy prelate,' says Whitefield, 'is worthy of lasting regard.' When asked how it is that the clergy, who speak of things *real,* affected the people so little, and the players, who speak only of things imaginary, affected them so much, replied 'My lord, I can assign but one reason—we players speak of things imaginary as though they were real, and too many of the clergy speak of things real as though they were imaginary.' It is not always so. Many a preacher, even in our own day, by the unaffected earnestness of his manner, carries away his audience upon the tide of his own feeling. They hear what he says, they see what he feels, his eye helps his tongue, the workings of his countenance disclose the feelings of his heart; his manner is a lucid comment upon his matter, breaks down the limits which words impose upon the communication of ideas, and gives them not only an apprehension of the meaning, but a sense of the importance of his subject, which unimpassioned language and manner could not have done.

"I name but one thing more as characteristic of this great man, and which it would be well for us to imitate, and that is, his *dauntless courage*. See him not only facing mobs, defying threats, and even lifting up his pulpit amid the wild uproar of a London fair, the boldest achievement that a speaker ever accomplished, but holding on his noble career unterrified, and working amid the storm of obloquy that came upon him from so many quarters. Who that has ever read, can ever forget Cowper's exquisite description of him?

"'Leuconomus—beneath well-sounding Greek
I show a name a poet must not speak—
Stood pilloried on infamy's high stage,
And bore the pelting storm of half an age,
The very butt of slander, and the blot
For every dart that malice ever shot.
The man that mentioned him at once dismissed
All mercy from his lips, and sneered and hissed.
His crimes were such as Sodom never knew,
And perjury stood up to swear all true;
His aim was mischief, and his zeal pretence,
His speech rebellion against common-sense:
A knave when tried on honesty's plain rule,
And when by that of reason, a mere fool.
The world's best comfort was, his doom was passed,
Die when he might, he must be damned at last.
Now truth, perform thine office, waft aside
The curtain drawn by prejudice and pride,
Reveal—the man is dead—to wondering eyes,
This more than monster, in his proper guise.
He loved the world that hated him; the tear
That dropped upon his Bible was sincere:
Assailed by scandal and the tongue of strife,
His only answer was—a blameless life;
And he that forged, and he that threw the dart,
Had each a brother's interest in his heart.
Paul's love of Christ, and steadiness unbribed,
Were copied close in him, and well transcribed.
He followed Paul—his zeal a kindred flame,
His apostolic charity the same.

Like him, crossed cheerfully tempestuous seas,
Forsaking country, kindred, friends, and ease.
Like him he labored, and like him, content
To bear it, suffered shame where'er he went.
Blush, calumny! and write upon his tomb,
If honest eulogy can spare the room,
Thy deep repentance of thy thousand lies,
Which, aimed at him, have pierced the offended skies;
And say, Blot out my sin, confessed, deplored,
Against thine image, in thy saint, O Lord.'

"What but a guilty cowardice is it, a false and pusillanimous shame, that keeps us in these days from some novel and bolder method of aggression upon the domain of darkness? Are we not wanting here in that moral courage which would make us, when conscious of doing right, indifferent to the stare of the ignorant, and the wonder of the timid; to the shaft of ridicule, and the malignant censure of the cynic? How enslaved are we by the fetters of custom, or restrained by the trammels of conventiality! How little are we disposed to go out of the usual track, even in saving souls! Very few are disposed to imitate the boldness, ingenuity, and novelty of that noble-hearted brother,[4] who hired a disengaged theatre in the city where he dwelt, and for four months preached there to listening and well-behaved crowds, the gospel of salvation; and for his reward had very many given to him, who are his joy now, and will be his crown of rejoicing in the presence of Christ at his coming. Who can see Paul on Mars-Hill, addressing himself to the sages and their followers of all sects, and preaching to them a doctrine so repugnant to the mythology of the temple and the philosophy of the schools, as Christ, the last judgment, and the resurrection of the body, without being impressed with the moral courage of such an act? It is this spiritual heroism that is wanted in our modern preaching, and indeed, which was no less needful when the Methodistic company commenced their preaching.

"Nor is it only in this unwillingness to go off from our own ground for saving souls that our guilty cowardice is seen, but in the disposition to shirk the more solemn and searching truths of revelation. Are we not giving way too much to the fastidiousness of modern taste and refinement, which is craving after smooth things; which desires the sentimental, the picturesque, the imaginative, but turns with disgust from the solemn, the alarming, the awakening? Are we not too gentle and courteous to mention such a word as 'hell' to modern ears polite? Are we not too fearful to break in with the thunders of a violated law upon those who are at ease in Zion? I do not ask for a gross, revolting method of describing the punishment of the wicked, as if the preacher delighted in harrowing up the feelings of his audience. This is as disgusting as if, in order to keep men from crime, our judges and magistrates were ever and anon giving a minute detail of the process of an execution, and the convulsive pangs of an expiring wretch suspended to the beam of the gibbet. We ask not for a harsh, scolding, and denunciating style of preaching; but we do want more of the unflinching boldness, and the dauntless courage, which, are necessary to fidelity, and absolutely essential to him who would win souls to Christ. It is too generally forgotten, that our Lord Jesus, who was incarnate love, was the most solemn and awful of all preachers. He whose gentle spirit so often breathed out itself in invitation, and whose compassion melted into tears, at other times robed himself in terror, and uttered the most alarming peals of divine indignation. What we need for our ministry is this mixture of tenderness and solemnity, which entered so deeply into the ministry of Christ, and was so characteristic of his servant, whose labors we this day commemorate and commend."

Hear also the Rev. John Glanville, the present successor of Whitefield in the Tabernacle at Bristol: "And such preaching *must continue*, if the world is to be saved. Nothing but this is suited to man's necessities; nothing else can meet man's miseries. The battle must be fought with the old, well-tried, but not worn-out weapons. God has provided them, and we must use them. We require nothing else; the world has not outgrown the old gospel, so as to need something new to soothe its sorrows and satisfy its wants.

"Not that ministers can now produce the effect Whitefield did. He was a man standing alone. The charm and power of his preaching have never been explained. It was all fire and flame, shooting out red-hot thunderbolts against the citadels of sin. It was an undivided soul, solemnly consecrated to one object—an entire life, zealously employed in one thing. As he preached, every feature spoke, the whole man became vocal, and the truth of God stood out in its full proportions and beauty, in the bright and broad daylight of heaven. So unreserved was his self-consecration, that every thing was deemed impertinent which obtruded upon, or interfered with the one great end of his existence. He lived in communion with God—more in heaven than on earth. He was much at the foot of the throne, and got his strength there; he prevailed with men, because he had prevailed with God. His whole soul was filled with life, and fired with love, from being in habitual contact with the cross.

"And *we* must pursue the same course, and try to do the same thing. We have the power, and we must bring it forth and use it. God has given the machinery, and it is for us to set it in motion. The world is perishing, and we must save it; it is dying, and we must give it life. God from his eternal throne calls us—Christ from his bleeding cross speaks to us—voices from the abodes of sin, and the regions of despair, sound in our ears. And we all, as ministers and as members, must rise up in the vigor of piety and the fervor of prayer. We must rise up from the slumbers of selfishness, and tear off the fetters of the world, and act as those who believe in the existence of an eternal heaven and an eternal hell, and that all souls will be found in the one or in the other—as those who have a great work to do, and but a short and uncertain time to do it in. Awake, awake, put on strength, O arm of the Lord; awake, as in the ancient days, in the generations of old."

FOOTNOTES:

[1] Dr. Prince, in a note, here says, "Though people were *then*," in the time of the earthquake, "generally frightened, and many awakened to such a sense of their duty as to offer themselves to our communion, yet very few came to me *then* under deep convictions of their unconverted and lost condition, in comparison of what came *now*. Nor did those who came to me *then*, come so much with the inquiry, 'What shall we do to be saved?' as to signify they had such a sense of their duty to come to the Lord's table that they dare not stay away any longer."

[2] The New York Evangelist, in 1830, made the remark, that "Whitefield would have lost much of his oratorical influence on his hearers, had his speaking eyes been covered with a pair of modern spectacles."

[3] See Dr. John M. Mason's Funeral Sermon for Mrs. Graham.

[4] The Rev. Richard Knill of Chester, formerly a missionary in India, and afterwards in Russia, since deceased.—B.